Love Believes All Things

Love Believes All Things
TRUST GOD'S WILL

KYLE EDWARD HESTER

LitPrime Solutions
21250 Hawthorne Blvd
Suite 500, Torrance, CA 90503
www.litprime.com
Phone: 1-800-981-9893

© 2025 Kyle Edward Hester. All rights reserved.

No part of this book may be reproduced, stored in a retrieval system, or transmitted by any means without the written permission of the author.

Published by LitPrime Solutions: 06/13/2025

ISBN: 979-8-88703-325-9(sc)
ISBN: 979-8-88703-326-6(e)

Library of Congress Control Number: 2025912957

Any people depicted in stock imagery provided by iStock are models, and such images are being used for illustrative purposes only.

Certain stock imagery © iStock.

Because of the dynamic nature of the Internet, any web addresses or links contained in this book may have changed since publication and may no longer be valid. The views expressed in this work are solely those of the author and do not necessarily reflect the views of the publisher, and the publisher hereby disclaims any responsibility for them.

CONTENTS

Introduction vii

Chapter 1.	The Sower and His Seed. .1
Chapter 2.	God's Will. 36
Chapter 3.	Appointed to Wrath 57
Chapter 4.	Increased Faith 88
	Our Prerogative 119
Chapter 5.	The Approach of Christ 120
Chapter 6.	Choosing or Rejecting. .151
Chapter 7.	Love vs. Lust. 181
	The Impasse 217
Chapter 8.	Opposite-Phobia 218
Chapter 9.	Marriage 248
	Wisdom 278
Chapter 10.	Faith 279
	The Whole Picture. 310
Chapter 11.	Love One Another 311
Chapter 12.	Love Everyone. 348

Afterthought. 383
Appendix: Scripture Passages. 385

INTRODUCTION

Beareth all things, believeth all things, hopeth all things, endureth all things.

1 Corinthians 13:7

I was telling my adult Sunday school class about how I met Jesus shortly before Christmas 1971 at a Christian halfway house in Victoria, Texas. Months prior to that, during Labor Day weekend at a rock festival in Satsop, Washington, I saw a terribly violent scene that really shook me up. As I spoke, Grandma Schoonmaker's eyes began tearing up. She said she was living in Aberdeen at the time, just up the road from Satsop. She and her church were praying for all of us young lost souls at the festival. We both instantly felt like their prayers were answered. Her prayers helped save my soul.

A hundred thousand people or more were crowded at Satsop. I was tripped out on LSD for a couple days and nights with no sleep, watching the rock and roll. A Jesus rock band opened the day with songs and preaching onstage Sunday morning at ten o'clock. It didn't matter to me, but some rude crude dudes down front jeered so loudly that the microphones picked up their profanity. One band member spoke about Jesus and got drowned out, so another band member tried. I thought the Christians had a right to be heard. I understood nothing of what they said except that they were for Jesus, and I was good with this—not that I was listening. By the time the mob booed them off the stage, I was disenchanted with my crowd.

Just after twelve noon, a folk singer came on. Someone drove an old flatbed truck carelessly in front of the stage while the folk singer was playing. When the announcer went up, he said the truck, which contained watermelons to sell from local fields, had just disrupted the music. It had. Simply impromptu, he suggested we boycott the truck. The next thing we knew, a gang rushed the truck and began stealing the watermelons. Two farm boys punched and threw the thieves off as fast as they could. A whole watermelon broke over the head of a guy climbing up the side, and he fell off. I sat back down where I was. I didn't want to see it.

A great yell arose from the crowd. I stood back up to see. The truck was being driven straight into the crowded field and was headed our way. There was no doubt that these guys had panicked. One guy was driving toward the gate as fast as he could, while the other guy hung on to the back of the cab for dear life. I was shocked, and I was afraid some people had been run over. Angry guys were throwing rocks at them, breaking out the glass. One young man got on the running board and punched the driver in the face. The old truck was ugly enough too. The crowd parted, and the truck went right past us.

After that, it turned into a bad trip for me. Nobody around was fit to talk to. No one could handle it. The whole bunch of us were totally stoned and freaked out. That was the last time I took psychedelic drugs. But you know what else? You and I may not know who has been praying for us and how well God has answered their prayers.

A couple years later, I worked at a gas station for a scary, tough boss named Jesse. The guy was big, hard-looking, and it seemed like he hated me—probably because I had bumper stickers for Jesus glued on all sides of my car. For months, he let me know in certain ways that he wanted me out of there. For instance, he was hosing down the driveway once when I asked him for the hose to cool a boiling radiator; he just dropped it on the pavement in front of my feet. I picked it up and kept working.

He would chew me out for little things and then say that if I didn't like it, he would get my last pay from the cash register. As if it didn't matter to me, I told him, "No thanks. I need the job." I'm not exaggerating—he would have killed me.

One morning when I got there, his car was parked, but he was not in the station office. Dark and early, the place was empty. He was asleep in the front seat of his car, drunk. I woke him up, but he was very hungover. He said he had driven around all night with his loaded revolver, looking to kill a man if he found him.

Prayer pays. I was shopping and saw some big fat loaves of golden bread sliced an inch thick. When I spotted the bread, I thought of all the meat and fixings I could pile on to do it right. I was just thinking of my appetite, nothing else.

The next day, when business was slow, the boss and I were sitting on the stools in the office saying absolutely nothing, looking out the front windows. We often said nothing for a long time. I pulled out this big, gorgeous, mouthwatering sandwich with the thick bread. Jesse's eyes locked onto it. He had to ask, "Where's mine?"

I hadn't thought about it. Since I didn't live far from work, I suggested I run home and get him one. He liked that idea.

The way to a man's heart is through his stomach. We were buddies after that. More sandwiches were passed in the days following. Amazing how that works. Soon after, he made me the night manager.

Some months later when I went to quit, it wasn't easy. I gave my notice. Jesse hired someone else and was training him, but one evening, he talked me into staying. That meant that in order to keep me, he had to fire the other man.

Eventually, I did move on. When I returned the following year on vacation, I found Jesse still there. He was excited to tell me that he had a new baby at home, his marriage was better, and his diet, drinking, and health had all improved. He had lost a lot of weight. He was glad to see me because my friendship had touched his life. I don't know, but maybe Jesse became a Christian too. All I've got is a photograph.

Let God's love be our focus. The harsh warnings in the Bible are good and true. We know the dangers in life; they are sometimes small and sometimes big. The aftereffects of sin are devastating. In other words, we get in trouble. Human nature denies the obvious. Every bit weightier than the question is the answer. We have it in Jesus Christ: faith.

A couple young women sat down with me once and let me explain my faith. It isn't every day you get to let your line out while two listeners allow you to finish your presentation. People were more open in those days. I said it as best as I could. Then one of the ladies, smiling on her way out, said, "I hope you find what you are looking for."

It was a cliché back then. That's right. She couldn't begin to allow that I had seen the light and I was happy in Jesus. She wasn't able to see the way God had accepted my faith. I have even talked to believers who are this oblivious to the message of God's grace.

We were all young and struggling bit by bit to catch the good life. Hearts searching for truth and who are new in the faith fumble with complex ideas. Jesus said we will see a lot of senseless contradictions from beginning to end. That hurts His Church. Capable theologians wrestle with honest problems of interpretation, doctrines, and denominational rivalries. Christianity is many times patchy. We all get things wrong sometimes in different ways.

Outsiders come in to disrupt the effort. They subvert and misuse words to their own advantage. Cults grow with claims that are only a semblance of biblical truth. Christians take the blast of too much resistance. Repentant believers coming from a life of sin and ungodly habits will learn the truth in stages.

Christ gives us the Bible for guidance. With all the buzzwords and preferred verses, it's too bad that Christians live in stubborn disobedience. Where are we going? We ought to study the Scriptures to see how to act.

We stress and strain to hold our heads up. Losing sight leads to doubt. Do you know how good life gets? Be sure in your heart and see the Holy Spirit's power in your hands. We can't hold on to God by our own strength. Isn't it obvious? We aren't saved by what we do, nor do we deserve to be. Our hearts must be *"knit together in love"*

(Colossians 2:2) to gain more assurance of faith. How can we grow unless it's by faith? Don't lean on circumstantial evidence, but lean fully on God. It has to be God proving himself in and through you.

The victory is in the totality of our Savior's sacrifice. Your acceptance of Jesus and His acceptance of you testifies of His truth. This protects you from dark forces and other influences. You get the aptitude for gratitude and begin to serve Jesus.

Be the responsible help that someone else needs. Christians fail in fellowship if they are still trying to get their own needs met. If we all are weak and ineffective, from where will the growth come? Take the meat of God's Word and put it alongside a dependence on Jesus Himself. If one member suffers, we all suffer. If we all stay weak, the one member continues to suffer. Life changes when disciples of the Lord join together for the better and give support.

Too often, Christians see needy people and think, *Get them out of here!* Imagine if everyone joined in. Wouldn't it go over better if we had more help? People help in their own way, but perfect love has come in the name of Jesus Christ.

We remain here for one another and to reach the unbelievers. God doesn't just take us home in a heartbeat, but He leaves us here to serve. Eternal life in Jesus Christ is true. Death will come and we will go to Heaven, but until then we have work to do. Yes, Christians should love one another fervently, if for no other reason than that our love wins the lost. We should all be bubbling over with this idea. How few of us who are saved pass through such a breaking point as to be changed and converted from old desires? We should get to work. Jesus' love is compelling. Delayed adolescent believers do less and don't take their responsibility seriously. Our job is to spread the Word.

Suppose you and your friends were going on vacation together; you'd get excited as the trip approaches. You'd boost each other's excitement.

In the Old Testament, twelve men—Joshua, Caleb, and ten others—went into Canaan as spies. The ten said it was too dangerous to try to defeat the Canaanites. Because they doubted God, the people of Israel wandered in the desert forty years, then they took the Promised Land most victoriously. Joshua and Caleb were the only two men alive from the original population. The chances of that happening were next to nothing—zero odds or nil. Not even Moses crossed over the Jordan.

Jesus healed ten lepers, but only one went back to thank Him. Is one out of ten average? You get an A for being in the top 10 percent of the class, for missing one in ten questions; you get a B when you are at 80 percent. This isn't going to help the others. Anything less is not best.

Jesus said to go the extra mile. Suppose we open a hamburger stand. We put it on a busy street with lots of cars racing by, but the business doesn't go. I say to put a sign out front that says, "Two for the price of one this week." Think it's a bad idea? We're already losing money. My thought is that if customers come in for our hamburger once, just one time, they're more apt to return. We have a burger they want, and they don't know it yet. Do you agree? If you've come in just once, you are more likely to stop again. This is why Jesus taught generosity. Hunger makes them aware of what they're missing. We fill an unknown need.

For example, our witness, a generous attitude toward others, wins souls more often than shunning people. We operate in weakness, at a loss, and go broke. We urgently pray to win souls, save sinners from sin, and keep them from going to Hell. I would die to reach one more. They simply haven't reached this decision or figured out how to turn around. Holding the line on sin doesn't always mean you push people away.

Let me tell it another way. We run a place that sells fast food, but the customers are slow. We are losing money. Should we raise the prices just to pay the bills? I've eaten in joints where I thought they did just that. I don't go back. A bit of business sense and insight lowers prices to drive up the profit. But of course, you have to start with quality you believe in. Value is what they want to pay for.

I may run souls off by expecting my stern corrections to bring repentance. It's good to tolerate an unbeliever to allow adequate time for patience, (1 Corinthians 5:9–10). Do I attack or attract? It's a judgment call.

We had a new man in church for a while who was a little rough. The first time he and I met was in my adult Sunday school class. He was starved. I was teaching about how faith, love, hope, and patience all work together. I remember. He was very enthusiastic about it.

He had been in serious sin, and he regretted it.

My new friend was soon baptized. He was painting the church with us one day when he and another friend clashed. It was nearly a fistfight. My old friend told me on Sunday to forget this new guy. I asked, "How can I have enough time to disciple and help him if you run him off?"

That had just happened. He never came back.

Don't lower your standards, but raise them and lower your expectations. A fake put-on does show. Be willing. A heartfelt concern shows. We can do better.

Salvation is not conditional on purity, but is very much the other way around. Jesus gives righteousness to us. Young little David slew the giant Goliath. Grasp God's grace first to conquer sin and let bad habits go. Give the victory to God.

Christians can move ahead with hope. Good things happen. Things turn out right. So look out. It's up to each of us to watch and profit from how Jesus operated. If we approach life like this, we begin to live with people honestly and generously. Your prayers are being heard. First, cling to love alone. Love believes all things.

> *To them who by patient continuance in well doing seek for glory and honor and immortality, eternal life.*
> Romans 2:7

Email address: kylehester@gmail.com

CHAPTER 1

The Sower and His Seed

A sower went out to sow his seed: and as he sowed, some fell by the way side; and it was trodden down, and the fowls of the air devoured it. And some fell upon a rock; and as soon as it was sprung up, it withered away, because it lacked moisture. And some fell among thorns; and the thorns sprang up with it, and choked it. And other fell on good ground, and sprang up, and bore fruit an hundredfold. And when he had said these things, he cried, He that hath ears to hear, let him hear.

Luke 8:5–8

We all have ears, but Jesus speaks to our hearts in this parable. Don't we all have hearts? People fall by the wayside, and in their predicament, they cry out to us. If we speak to them in the name of Jesus, do they hear us? God knows that even as Christians, there are people to whom we choose to talk and others whom we choose to pass by. The downtrodden get picked off by the devil, and do we care? The hardhearted listen a bit and believe our message, yet we cannot be sure they actually get saved because far too often, trouble hits and they fall away. Pity them if their faith caves.

The value of what we give is bigger than what we ask people to give up. Does our love stand, or are we disturbed and destroyed with anxiety? Isn't it the right time now for us, you and me, to hear Jesus and seek the poor lost? *"To day if ye will hear his voice, harden not your hearts"* Hebrews 4:7. Listen! The ones who get saved are the ones who hear; they believe and bear good fruit.

Soon after my salvation, I rode my bicycle over to a little Bible bookstore and bought my first pocket red-letter New Testament with Psalms. Nobody told me to do this. It was a nice day, so I just did it. I don't remember why. I rode to the park where my friend Charlie was working in the refreshment stand. She was the one who had led me to receive Jesus. I showed her what I had. I could not have been more proud of my little Bible if it had been a brand-new car. I read it everywhere I went after that.

I came to the parable of the Sower and the seed. It stunned me. Nothing jarred me quite like this. It was not that I understood everything I was reading, but a dreadful panic struck me. It froze me and made me doubt my soul. I asked myself, *Which kind of seed am I? Is my Christianity another phase of mine? Could my interest in Jesus pass and move on like other fads in my life?* The words of Jesus rang true. When this parable cropped up, it was positively frightening to me. It was an immense blow to me.

After reading the parable, I wondered if my willpower could prove dependable. This was two months after I had entered the Omni House drug-abuse program in Texas, where I had personally met Jesus. I was shaking off the harsh effects of several years in the psychedelic drug craze. I was shocked by the obvious seriousness of Jesus' parable. If I was a bad seed, I would wind up in Hell! Was Christianity just another trend? It was all new to me.

The hippie drug years had caught me just as I finished high school in 1969. It seemed like LSD was a great discovery, a solution to all things. But I can tell you exactly where I was when I came to this page in my Bible. After receiving Jesus in December of 1971, I returned to Seattle in May to win my friends to Jesus. Instead of me drawing them out of sin, they talked me into smoking marijuana the first evening back. I got stoned the next twelve days. I ran for my life and left Seattle. After that, I quit dope for good.

My dog, Roo, and I hitchhiked on I-90 and headed east as far as New York. Can you guess how shook I was in mid-Montana when I read the parable of the Sower? Could the spiritual life I had found have faded that fast? Jesus' Holy Spirit whispered to me. He said the way this parable hit me so hard indicated that I got the point and truly felt its weight. My qualms were with myself and not with the Bible. Anyone who receives the Word of the Lord is like fertile ground that bears good fruit, and this is a true Christian. Any person who fails to hear is lost. I had reacted strongly to this charge for the one reason that I was born again. Would an unsaved person be this affected? The Spirit of Jesus reassured me that I was His.

This parable gave me tremendous encouragement. The Word of God blessed me right from the time I received Jesus. All Christians will have the anointing of God: *"and ye need not that any man teach you"* 1 John 2:27. We can be sure now you know what's right when God's love is the rule. *"But as touching brotherly love ye need not that I write unto you: for ye yourselves are taught of God to love one another"* 1 Thessalonians 4:9. God was first. He then surrounded me with good supportive fellowship.

Christianity is said to be narrow. We believe that the Bible is uniquely true. Current world culture allows every whim as long as people aren't dogmatic. Worldly wisdom tells us that it doesn't matter if the rules change as long as everybody goes along. Modern social conventions are capricious, subject simply to the consent of those who use them. Since rules and rulers have frequently failed, we should question authority. Indeed, societal breakdown helps to establish new assumptions. Truth and error then continue to be shaped. Such passing logic assumes reality is fluid.

Unsolved arguments rotate within the bumpy history of Christianity, regrettably. Today's Christians must once again advance the premise that God has revealed the only reliable record in our cherished Scriptures. Be ready to defend the inerrancy of the Bible. God's Word has the truth of our origin, and we must keep faith in the future. God wants us to reach higher with a greater understanding and more freedom to see his truth. God expects us to be civil with others. The roughness in life should smooth us.

Jesus commands us to give witness of His salvation everywhere. Do you know a few Christians who have become disgruntled and impatient? They want to quit and throw in the towel. What philosophy is that? We all form an approach to our beliefs. Do you tell people you meet that you are a Christian? If I believe in Jesus, then should I start down the street going to every door until I find one person who will be saved. I may have to go a long way before a poor soul allows me into their home to lead them in the sinner's prayer. Some believers have printed their own account on paper to hand out. I don't go to every door or stand and preach.

> *And they were astonished at His doctrine; for His Word was with power.*
> Luke 4:32

I think I'm following the plan God has set for my life. You may be focusing on those who are lost or only the ones you think are most ready to believe so as not to waste time. Are you of the old opinion that some people should not be handed the gospel? The Lord allows thorny hard to convince people in our lives and some are admittedly impossible. To advance God's mission in the best way, we must desperately pray for the faith to love them, all.

Mysteries of the Kingdom

> *And he said, Unto you it is given to know the mysteries of the kingdom of God: but to others in parables; that seeing they might not see, and hearing they might not understand.*
> Luke 8:10

You might get a better handle on the entire Bible if you master this verse. Mysteries are secrets that were formerly unknown or unheard of and that no one could guess. With the revelation of Jesus Christ in the New Testament, there is now this clarification. We can learn. You have to be a believer in the Holy Spirit of God to understand. Nice and concise, good seed fell on bad ground.

Jesus taught the meaning of His parables to His disciples. He said He wouldn't teach the crowds as plainly. What did He mean by that? Jesus purposely said He would not tell the explanation clearly so that the people "might not see, and…not understand." And we would have thought He wanted everybody to know.

When I was a kid in school, the teachers said that if we couldn't spell a word, we should look it up in the dictionary. I didn't do the best in school, but how, I still ask, am I going to find a word in the dictionary if I don't know how to spell it? The teachers often repeated the axiom, "Learn to use your dictionary!" Honestly, I always wondered what they meant. Where do I go to learn the dictionary? I must've missed that day.

After I got out of school, I noticed that all the signs said, "Help wanted. Experience required." How was I ever going to get my first job? Everyone had it figured out but me.

Jesus explained the parables to His inner circle. Do you think God only speaks to those He chooses and keeps the rest in the dark? When Jesus declared the dichotomy that some would receive His teaching and some would not, He recognized the way this split already existed.

I came to faith by the eager kindness of wonderful Christians. I was there with all the appearance of my rebellious generation. Generous friends and strangers had the liberty to share their faith with me. Was I saved by faith or by fate? One of the things we believe as Christians is to share the conviction of our hearts. It's a pattern. I was saved by someone else's faith to simply believe in me. They prayed for me and inspired me. This is God's plan. I was given *faith* by their *love*!

Disciples get the Word of God and teach others. Here is the story of the Sower: *"Faith cometh by hearing, and hearing by the word of God"* (Romans 10:17). After I met Jesus, I learned how to see the needs of others and be quick. I hoped they heard me and I prayed they would respond. It was like the old expression, "Tomorrow may be too late!"

Jesus proclaimed the kingdom of God to everyone, but not everyone got it. Directly before this parable, Luke wrote, *"He went throughout every city and village, preaching and shewing the glad tidings of the kingdom of God"* Luke 8:1. God is holding some things back still. Maybe it's because His plan is unfolding. We get it all with graduating wisdom.

The ways of the Lord are much higher than our ways. Why did Jesus preach parables that people didn't understand? He revealed truth at the proper time. I'm not going against God, but I pray that the Holy Spirit would definitely make Jesus better known, and I want Him to enlighten all believers especially.

The people were aware that there was a prophet in Israel. When Jesus walked the land, the people went out to hear Him. Many believed. Jesus loved all, but He was afraid that His teaching made them more accountable and His presence made them more responsible than before. He knew when He told things to them they would be judged extra severely for refusing Him. Jesus said, *"For unto whomsoever much is given, of him shall be much required: to whom men have committed much, of him they will ask the more."* Luke 12:48. Would Jesus be doing them a favor to say less? It was a mercy not to clue people in. Jesus always left room for faith, so He never eliminated all doubt. Scripture has enough.

When we are given more, we are required to act on it. Jesus kept the full truth back because His time to die had not yet come. Then when His suffering and resurrection were accomplished, everybody in the world could be informed.

Jesus was Jewish. Up to this point in time, God had given His testimony primarily to Israel. *"He came unto his own, and his own received him not"* John 1:11. In the two millennia since, the whole world is obligated to hear and believe. God *"now commandeth all men everywhere to repent"* Acts 17:30. The revelation of God's plan did not come by prophets only, but it also came by Jesus Christ Himself.

Nowhere in the expanse of our universe has there ever been a change like the difference Jesus made. He opens human hearts; nothing again will compare anywhere else in eternity.

God looks for real faith. Israel was *"uncircumcised in heart and ears"* (Acts 7:51). They didn't see or hear God. *"Behold their ear is uncircumcised, and they cannot hearken; behold, the word of the Lord is unto them a reproach; they have no delight in it"* (Jeremiah 6:10).

Jesus brought a *new* covenant, showing the glad tidings of the kingdom of God. Salvation doesn't come to us because of the good we do. Israel missed their call entirely: *"He cried, He that has ears to hear, let him hear"* (Luke 8:8). If they had no ears, Jesus would've healed them. The Apostle Paul said that faith is "inward" and that *"circumcision is that of the heart, in the spirit, and not in the letter; whose praise is not of men, but of God"* (Romans 2:29). He then said, *"For they are not all Israel, which are of Israel"* (Romans 9:6). Paul learned it all over again like he had never heard it before. Let's emphasize the *new* thought, not of the old law but the new.

> *But when the fullness of the time was come, God sent forth his Son, made of a woman, made under the law.*
> Galatians 4:4

If one does not get the proper sense of this and related passages, it can lead to much misinterpretation. It is very important to note that Jesus came under the Old Law. To understand the Bible, keep in mind what blessings God let slip away from Israel that then went to the rest of us. You and I must catch the importance. It's not typical to say it today. Israel had the written Word of God before anyone else (Romans 3:1–2). They had Jesus first (Acts 3:26). The Word went out from there.

Since the time of Jesus Christ, people everywhere in the world have encountered the truth and are without excuse. You and I know that God considers every person on earth accountable for their sin, and every nation is judged. We can no longer hide from such compelling thoughts. This tells the correct attitude for a serious

Christian to live by. There's a good reason to witness. We take a big, solemn responsibility to ourselves for lost sinners. I want to see the greater work of the Church. God has deemed the redeemed to be this light in the darkness. Bible-believing Christians hold faith dear, so we want our love clear; people will be brought near.

The Mystery of Faith

Now the parable is this: The seed is the word of God.
Luke 8:11

The Word is out. God gives His love to the whole world. Whosoever believes will not die, but will receive eternal life. Who misses this call? God doesn't miss anyone who calls on Him. We must sow the word of *faith* with the *love* of God.

Like I said, the first time I read this parable, I was stunned. Some people get it and some don't. I had to learn what it meant. Which one was I? Faith comes by hearing the Word of God. The seed is planted. This is the *mystery of faith*. How will it grow? Nobody really wants to pass up Heaven.

This passage is initially a salvation parable, but it carries a lesson on maturity. Consequently, another question fits in the mix also. Why do some Christians get it while others, it seems, don't? Some of us fall while other Christians grow. Let me answer this question with a question. Why does God call some to be Bible teachers if it is not for these teachers to make an impact? You and I must not be stagnant in our lives. Have we no sympathy? A teacher, by definition, cannot be quiet.

The Word is out. Nothing has been more published than the Bible. The good news of Jesus Christ is no longer a mystery, but a ministry. It's no longer the Law of Moses, but the Law of Christ. His way is love. Why fail to make that point stick? Keep moving.

We have a long way to go. On one hand, the population is growing faster than we can keep up with; on the other hand, high-tech communication, information, and mass media offer the brightest time ever in history. We instantly reach every place. Whatever stripe or schooling, each passing day, we are closer to the last day.

People are coming to Jesus in record numbers many places. On our watch, the demand for good pastors and teachers is being outstripped. Out in the open to worldly elements and without the best guidance, new Christians and false believers become tangled in a big snarl of danger. We constantly fight our old carnal nature. Satan fights us too. Those who follow righteousness will flee the temptations and shun the pleasures of this old world to gain for themselves and for others all the riches of God's glorious Heaven. Life has a lot to offer. Our grounding must be in the Bible, the absolute *Word of God*.

Jesus is the cornerstone (Ephesians 2:20), so you and I are not free to go just any way we want. A cornerstone in a building is the first piece of the foundation upon which all else rests; it is a reference point where every measure starts. The city of Seattle has a cornerstone in an old building downtown, at First and Yesler. It is the cornerstone for that building and in plans for the entire city. Two other points in the city core, higher up on Yesler Street and over on Denny Way, make a triangulation for the engineering department to assess and draw the grid with altitudes, angles, and distances. We who set our sights on Jesus must in turn give a true reading for others to follow. We aren't free to believe whatever we think!

The house my wife and I live in has a plat, a plot, filed with the city. Archives show dimensions of this property with the exact measurements of the house, where it sits on the land, distance from each edge of the property line to the foundation, and the elevation of the house in relation to the street. All this is recorded for a reference in building plans, for future additions, and for hooking up the water, sewer, phone, and electricity running from the alley and street. Every street in the area is mapped with plans that show the relation of roads and homes. The city notes slopes on every hill and counts manholes and light poles all the way back to the cornerstone at First Avenue and Yesler Way.

City records detail what is below ground, especially with

downtown skyscrapers, where hundreds of heavy anchor cables run deep into the ground and each one threads among endless underground wiring, pipes, and tunnels—all crowded between tall buildings. City engineers can accurately trace the history of every lot back to the time the department began. Hazards must be predicted in any future development. Jesus is our cornerstone. The Bible is our sure foundation on which the Church sits secure.

Spreading the Word of God has taken centuries of constant effort and countless servants to bring us to where we are today. Our understanding has to relate back to the beginning. It also has to apply to the goal of our future. We must apply the truth to our lives or God will apply it to us. If you judge yourself, God will not have to condemn you.

What is *the mystery of the faith*? Do you know? This phrase is so packed. *"Holding the mystery of the faith in a pure conscience."* 1 Timothy 3:9. Partly told before, the mystery is now open; it's the plan of salvation. How does the seed sprout? It has to do with us and our consciences. More so, it's New Testament love.

Jesus Christ went to Calvary to gain us salvation. Foolish questions should be avoided such as, "Where did God come from?" He sits on the throne above all, the revelation of which has gone out to the world. Which came first—the chicken or the egg? Someone cared enough to tell you, and you believed.

We are holding the mystery of faith like a vase holds brightly colored flowers. Are we holding its brilliance, or are we hiding it where none can see it? The truth has a power of its own. It is no longer a mystery. We have a living hope. Does our attitude reflect that we care to give the love of Jesus? We would not want to live in a way that darkens our consciences or weakens this work.

The conception of a baby is a fantastic mystery. We cannot explain how so much is encoded and loaded in the very first instant of a human being's life. A zygote contains the characteristics, propensities, and personality that will be seen throughout its days. The genetic code even determines longevity if by "chance" he or she is able to escape the dangers and make it that far. Somehow, the little fertilized egg knows how to get from the ovary to the womb.

This simplest set of cells, an "organism" by definition, has become a new individual, separate, self-sustaining life.

One of the smallest babies on record weighed less than two-thirds of a pound at birth, yet survived and developed normally. She entered high school on time. She was an honor student and a musician, and she loved to rollerblade. It is amazing that from the moment her life began, before her mom and dad were told, the different facets of her physical, intellectual, and emotional being were already in her.

What a strange thing it is that so many intelligent, educated people think life's origin is best explained from an evolutionary scientific point of view. How generic! How does the process work unless an intelligent Creator put design into every single element? I like the Bible's version. Darwinism is an utter leap of faith. I don't want to revert to such theory. Someone has said, "None of us is related to a zucchini plant."

The beginning of life is a mystery. Do you remember being born? Somehow, we just wake up and here we are. Do you remember the second you woke up this morning? Nor did this planet record the origin of our species; it did not have a clue. Ancient history and consciousness didn't just begin with accidental awareness. God kept it secret. And you won't remember falling asleep tonight either. Death and the end of life are mysterious. What happens next after death appears empty, but it's not so with *the mystery of the faith*. And it's not hard to figure people pay for their sins when this is all over.

While two of us were standing at a hamburger stand one afternoon waiting for our order, I was talking to the teenage girl behind the counter. She happened to be the daughter of a friend. I asked her if she knew the high school girl who had just been killed the week before in a car accident. She said she did.

The other girl behind the counter told me she had two friends who were killed in another car accident. I asked her if it made her think. She said it had been a big shock to her. I talked to this second girl about death, asking her what she thought. How many young people fail to make it to adulthood? I brought up various recent news stories reporting the deaths of young people and other tragic accounts. I told her that we all need to think and be careful and use common sense.

Then I asked her this question: "If you die tonight, do you know where you will be tomorrow morning?"

"I would be in Heaven," she said.

I asked her, "How would you get there?"

Here comes the interesting part. Without hesitating, she kind of shrugged her shoulders and said, "They'd come and take me."

"Who would come and take you?" I asked.

"I don't know." She didn't have an answer.

"Would it be angels?"

"Yeah, it'd be angels." She seemed a little relieved with that suggestion.

"Angels would take you up?" I asked. "How do you know about this?"

Her answer was a fabulous clincher: "Oh, something my grandmother said—and *Star Trek*."

Honest—that is exactly what she said.

Then I told her that my friend and I were Christians. I explained briefly that Jesus was our Savior, and I told her what we believe about the way to Heaven.

People around Seattle don't seem to know the Bible. While waiting at the airport for my daughter to return from Hawaii on an overdue flight, I was sitting with a stranger who was waiting for his wife coming from the east. We talked mostly about our children and how well they were doing. He was proud of his. Most of them were grown-up. We agreed on the importance of parenting and of the future ambitions of the coming generation.

Then I asked him what hopes his children had for eternity. He didn't know what I meant. I said, "If one of your kids died tonight, where would they be in the morning?"

"I don't know," he said.

"You have done all you can to see that they have the best upbringing and you are concerned for their lives, but have you prepared them for life after death?"

I told him a few stories about the deaths of young people in the news, dear lives cut short.

"Well, I don't like to think about that," he said.

"You buy insurance, don't you?" I suggested. "You insure your car, your health, your house, and your life. You had to think about doing that."

I wasn't just asking him if he was afraid to die, like we so often do when we buttonhole people. The question I posed pointed to his children. I asked him again, "What if you suddenly lost one of your loved ones and then had to face this question?"

I asked this man if he had any church in his background. He had no familiarity with matters of faith. I suggested that he consider Jesus and the claims of Christianity. He received it very well, and I trust God's Spirit to water the seed sown.

One day while at work, I was talking on the phone to a businessman, someone I have known for years. We were catching up on news about family and current times. Next we were discussing new technologies. It led us to the subject of passenger-jet crashes, which is when my friend blurted out, "It doesn't matter. We are all going sometime."

"It's true," I agreed. "Everybody who goes up in a jet comes down one way or another." So I asked him the loaded question: "If your plane crashed into the ground, where would you be then?"

"Well, I wouldn't be anywhere."

"No," I crassly said. "I mean if your plane crashed with you on board, where would you go next?"

"Oh," he said. "I would go to another planet."

That's really what he said! So I asked him, "And how would you get there?"

"I don't believe in all that religious stuff, they're all the same. Christianity, whatever. If Heaven was real, people would be lining up to go there."

He already knew that I was a Christian.

"They are lining up at my church," I told him.

He said he's going to another planet. Can you beat that? He doesn't even know how he's getting there. If there was a way to get to another planet, wouldn't everyone want to go? Actually, he was quick to recognize the seed I was trying to plant.

A little gal named Marty from the county water department regularly comes by where I work. We always chat and kid each other because she is cute and fun and, if I may say so, a bit of a ding-a-ling. She knows it. It's her ruse.

Marty grew up in California. She was a true product of the sixties' hippie days. She probably attended too many parties. She has sort of outgrown that now, lives a natural lifestyle, and has a grown daughter like I do. I love to talk with Marty.

One day, she was there chatting, so I asked her about the dry season we were having and how the water supply was doing. I thought she might have an inside story from the water department. Instead, she began to eagerly tell me all about our endangered planet and the pending destruction of the environment. Then she went on about the afterlife and how she will be coming back in another body to see it all when it is better. She's serious. It was just like her—an environmentalist quasi-Buddhist or Hindu.

"What happens," I asked, "if the earth is scorched over time and you have no life-sustaining place to come back to in your next incarnation?"

Her eyes got wide, and she looked straight back at me in empty surprise.

"I don't know," she said.

I said, "I suppose you will have to wait longer in limbo."

"That's it! That's right!" she blurted out. "You wait."

"Well," I repeated, "if the earth becomes uninhabitable and there are fewer people on earth in the future, there won't be enough bodies for all the people who are coming back to life."

"Yeah—you will have to wait."

I continued. "Makes me wonder, with all the constant population growth we have—there are billions today, seven billion maybe—

where did all the souls come from that are here now? There didn't used to be so many people, ever, and now they are all put here together at one time. Where did they all come from?"

"I don't know."

Marty's mind was swimming now. It was easy to see the panic all at once on her face. She was getting real, real worried—weird, really.

"What do people say where you go? What do you call it? Where do you gather?"

"Oh! I don't go to any of those organized things, there is no place I go for it."

So I asked, "Where do you get all these ideas to think what you do?"

I tried to come across as sympathetic, but I was chuckling at the same time. She and I always enjoy each other. I was getting a real big kick out of her this time.

"I just think this all up," she said. "It's just in me."

Then I threw her another pitch. "Maybe it used to be that there were more animals and fewer people, so now more of us have advanced to become people."

"That's it!"

She was very relieved to have a plausible explanation. It was all done in fun and she is sweet, but Marty seems very lost. I mentioned that I was a Christian and said Jesus gives us the hope of a direct resurrection to Heaven. Honest, she asked me no questions.

You and I also were sinful at one time, yet we received salvation. Do we want to do something for the lost? You can see they want help, but they've been tricked. Unbelief is ingrained in all of us. Can they be saved? Pray for Jesus to stop all sin.

I believe that love can be strong enough to defeat the long-held myths that delude troubled souls. The devil cheats those by the wayside. Can people run so far that the Lord God can never again find them? I believe our faith can grow stronger—strong enough to give faith to other people. Jesus certainly wins difficult hearts and saves their souls from Hell.

Lest They Should Believe

> *Those by the way side are they that hear; then cometh the devil, and taketh away the word out of their hearts, lest they should believe and be saved.*
>
> Luke 8:12

People often see there is a devil before they admit there's a Savior. That's how it went for me. We shouldn't underestimate the evil in the devil. He jumps wayward souls to take the Word right out of their hearts. He prevents their faith from growing. We should appreciate our fellow human beings and not write them off too fast. God's Word never returns to Him void. There's a purpose in life.

They play hardball in the big leagues, yet the better athletes win by keeping cool. Allow your friends and relatives more time to see how counterproductive and costly their behavior is. Believers can be patient with disagreements. When you are convinced in your faith and confident of it, you'll stay fair in love.

We win many with gentleness, some with firmness, and even a few by harshness. Do we dare say how plainly trapped and troubled everybody is? Yes, I love to spring them from the trap of Satan. Count on the hope you have; our love can get to be powerful.

> *Those who oppose him he must gently instruct, in the hope that God will grant them repentance leading them to a knowledge of the truth, and that they will come to their senses and escape from the trap of the devil, who has taken them captive to do his will.*
>
> 2 Timothy 2:25–26 NIV

Grab hold of the truth of the Bible; it will take over your life. Randy California was the lead guitarist in the sixties' San Francisco acid-rock band Spirit. He later met a tragic end in Hawaii. His son was caught in the riptide, and the boy had to be rescued. As a dad would, Randy jumped into the ocean to save his child. He pushed his son to safety, but the strong current took the life of this heroic father. That is how real our hearts must be and how quick our reactions should be in going after desperately lost people.

You know people who are lost. Some carry a lot of animosity. Do we confront them openly? Many people blame Christians for everything that's wrong, like it's God's fault. Where did they jump over the fence? I've pointed out to a few unbelieving friends that their resentment is unwarranted. Ecology and the environment is a big hot-button sticking point. This is their issue. As offhanded right and wrong they may be, we need to be honest to make ourselves heard. We were all lost at one time; we are all sinners still.

It had always appeared to me that adults looked too serious, and now I see why. Have you known people in their forties who have died of natural causes? As my life lengthened to middle age, I sadly lost dear family and friends. I knew some who died in their twenties and thirties. That caught my attention. People in their prime die in car accidents or of major health problems like diabetes, heart attacks, and strokes. This has been very sobering. Young people have been sheltered. They have not yet met grief and sadness.

When you are young, life should be fun, not devastating. Responsibility and caution are also wanted in good order to make us prepare for a secure future. The odd thing is that more people make a decision for Jesus earlier in life, while the hearts of many others grow harder with age.

Jesus told another parable about a man who planted a vineyard (Luke 20:9–18). The man fixed it up and leased it, so he could go away to a far country. When the season was over, he sent a servant back to his vineyard, expecting to collect a profit. The wicked tenants caught the servant, beat him, and ran him off. The owner sent another. They stoned him, wounded him in the head, and he was shamefully treated. They ran him off. If that wasn't enough, the landlord sent yet another servant to collect rent. They killed him too (Matthew 21:38–39). Many more were sent, and they were all beaten or killed as well.

The owner then sent his own son, whom he loved. He thought

the tenants had to respect him, but they killed the one who was the heir, thinking they could keep the land. Jesus said the lord of the vineyard would kill these murderers and *"give the vineyard to others,"* a prophetic foretelling of the time of the Christian church age, the age of grace, which was about to come upon the whole world.

The Pharisees must've known what Jesus was saying, and they saw Him as a threat. Jesus knew exactly what He was saying. He furnished them with this old quote: *"The stone which the builders rejected is become the head of the corner"* (Mark 12:10; Psalm 118:22). The leaders of Israel had beaten and killed prophets for centuries, and they were now going to kill Jesus, even though Jesus was revealing this new covenant from God.

Jesus knew this was not a pretty world. Can you see how difficult it must have been for Him to travel around and preach to cold hearts? He knew the eager crowds who came to hear and receive Him would turn and reject Him. Jesus said in Luke 8:12, *"Then cometh the devil, and taketh away the word out of their hearts, lest they should believe."* Our Savior came to defeat Satan, so you and I can never be taken captive again.

Jesus visited His hometown of Nazareth to speak, and they tried to kill Him there. What did He say that infuriated them? These were people who knew Him as He was growing up. He wanted to bless and help them because He loved them. Jesus was disappointed, able to do only a few miracles for them.

Imagine the townspeople. Their hardness was like kryptonite on Superman. *"And he marveled because of their unbelief."* What did He do next? *"He went round about the villages, teaching"* (Mark 6:6). Jesus continued to teach the Word. In the passage after this, Jesus sent His disciples out two by two. Jesus began to double His effort. Let's not get set back in our efforts, but let's pick up our feet and move forward.

Many people around us today see Christians as just a bunch of dirty hypocrites who brag one day and sin the next. To them, we are a lot of dependent personalities and spineless ninnies. They view Christianity as just a religious rubber crutch. Suppose only one such naysayer is right; would that make us all wrong? If we start down that road and entertain such notions, we will have the heart of salvation stolen from us.

Be optimistic. If our faith is make-believe and we all are liars, what does that make God? It makes Him right, because He does say we *are* sinners. The earth is full of sinners. Does that make God less righteous? We know He is right. Stop arguing, stay true.

We are too often up and down. God would say we shouldn't get so dispirited as to ask, "What's the use?" Not all Christians experience steady upward spiritual growth. Some real Christians sprout up and fade away, yet come back again later to maturity. The unbelievers give up. Your concerns are genuine. Do not let the downfall of others shake your faith. Keep praying.

Jesus came to save us. It was a struggle for Him. In the parable of the Sower and the seed, is He the Sower? Jesus spoke here from His heart, telling us of His personal distress. Jesus has described His own life here. He described His ministry and, unfortunately, the face of denial with anything whatsoever about an ideal kingdom of God.

The Fear of Punishment

> *They on the rock are they, which, when they hear, receive the word with joy; and these have no root, which for a while believe, and in time of temptation fall away.*
> Luke 8:13

There are many weak souls living life in crisis, and aren't living life in Christ. People work themselves up about Jesus for a while, getting all excited about renewal, *"and in time of temptation fall away."* A lot of unsuspecting people are left only assuming they are Christians. They take God for granted. Sadly, they fail the test of time. Your future, your life could change suddenly, crash down.

My friend Marty was truly stunned to visualize herself in

limbo after death, unable to return to earth if it becomes a lifeless, uninhabitable, environmental bio-wasteland. The first time I read through this parable of the Sower, especially Luke 8:13, I was rocked. It was scary to feel so lost. Those who "have no root" try hard for a while, but then they fall away as they get tempted. They certainly do leave, "*for if they had been of us, they would no doubt have continued with us*" (1 John 2:19). That is sad! Life gets traumatic.

Our desire for a good life will ward off the challenging temptations. A good conscience resists sin. The fear of punishment alone never saves us from sin. Fear can only warn us. We might know the difference between right and wrong, but faith acts wisely.

Here is what fear does. Envision a tightrope stretched over a height in a circus tent. You are up there walking out on that rope. To look down is suicide because the pull of gravity will come up from the floor and all at once grab your feet. You must look directly forward, keeping your chin up and your eyes focused on the goal. It is much easier to walk a straight line in the safety of your living room where there is no height, but it is much harder to accomplish this while suspended in the air with a crowd in suspense below. As real as it gets, fear is not going to keep us from falling, but it will cause us to stumble (Romans 7:8–11). We are vexed with sin. We are strained in temptation and overwhelmed by instruction. "*For rulers are not a terror to good works, but to the evil*" (Romans 13:3). The Christian life is not governed by the fear of God as much as by His love. Getting this victory in Jesus is our true faith.

Keep your eyes fixed to the end because the Lord does not want us to look back unless it is to see how much He has done for us. Can we thank God enough? Pursue a full blessing, knowing that God will not deny devotion. How can so many hearts be as hard as rock? God tests the cold soul who has refused His Spirit. Jesus will lift up those who follow Him. Strive for the prize and encourage the fainthearted. Counsel them to fight through their irrational limitations. We must ignore all distraction. In anything you name, there are the hang-on type and the truly dedicated.

The student is not the teacher, but a few students truly are lifelong learners, and they continue in life as teachers. Worst of all are the boring, burned-out teachers, as you know if you've been in a classroom with one. Exceptional students are recognized by teachers and identified for their fantastic examples.

God's promise of greater blessings and rewards brings us toward conformity. People need good examples a lot more than they need to be pounded on. How do we instill faith in the heart of the unfaithful or penetrate the impenitent? This gnawing question has haunted me. If people want to give their hearts to God, how do we show them the way? Everyone has opposing forces outside pushing the other way. We each have confusion and temptation within. Can we predict or control what's holding others back? Your honest compassion is the best answer for them.

Be strong in faith, swift to forgive, and adept at endearing yourself to the lost. It is human nature to want others to suffer for their sins. The grudge we hold against them is a taut knot in our hearts. Too many times, we can turn our anger toward God. Where, then, is our lasting hope? *"Be ye kind"* Ephesians 4:31–32. Your new nature speaks volumes.

Nearly everyone believes in their own righteousness. It is a regrettable thing, but if people have any notion at all about religion, they suppose self-effort and good life win reward. Fewer people have heard the simplicity of the gospel. We have a long way to go in this world—further than we think—to tell the good news of Jesus Christ. A lot of people assume what they've heard the most, a poor effort and a bad life is paid back. Kindness pays. Ask a few people around you and see what they know of God's grace and hope.

More than once people have answered "Yes" after I have asked them if they were going to Heaven, but then when I asked them how they knew that, they said something like "I'm a nice guy." It is good to be nice. Niceness is a virtue. But perhaps it's an American idea that just by being nice, everyone gets into Heaven. Where did we get that from? I want everybody to be nice, but it doesn't buy time in eternity. Pleasant people can be like nice rocks and *"receive the word with joy; and these have no root"* Luke 8:13. That's hard.

Unbelieving people can have principled thinking and ugly attitudes. Let's not be naïve. The disgust and violence are all around. Each of us has an indebted responsibility to society. We pass ourselves off as good or bad. People shovel blame and add less than is their duty. Are you hurting or helping? These powerfully destructive forces run rampant in humanity. It's impossible to escape, but God's love is totally possible and available every day. Our goal is to instill Christian love in whomever we can so their faith simply won't fail. *"For with God nothing shall be impossible"* (Luke 1:37).

The truth of Jesus Christ is being preached to the lost. It's painfully frustrating to think that some people fake conversion. Their rejection hurts. It hurts to think we are bringing someone to salvation when their actions are really a sham. You cannot tell about people, though; maybe they will make a commitment later.

A few people give Christianity a look, seeking answers and going through the motions, only to go with the flow back to sin. The love of money, the pleasures of entertainment, and even the security of family are all powerfully appealing. In today's convoluted world, it takes the faith of a martyr to love righteousness.

I remember walking through downtown Seattle with a friend before I was saved. An enthusiastic young man was standing on a corner passing out gospel tracts. I was open, but my friend was scornful. She knew this guy. She said he was big on Jesus half the time, but would revert back to his old ways the other half of the time. For that reason, she was unimpressed by his witness. He interested me though. I wasn't thinking *if* I became a Christian, but *when* I became a Christian, I would not be so on and off. This guy didn't have his act together, but I always remember him for the way he was able to get back on the street for Jesus. I pray about where we are today. You worry for the future, and we know what's needed now! Like the classic song goes, "What we need now is love."

That Which Fell

And that which fell among thorns are they, which, when they have heard, go forth, and are choked with cares and riches and pleasures of this life, and bring no fruit to perfection.

Luke 8:14

If anything, people take only a little of the truth in God's Scripture. Jesus told of the Sower and the seed, *"which fell among thorns."* The thorns, He said, represent the *"cares and riches and pleasures of this life."* So many people *"draw back unto perdition"* (Hebrews 10:39) and surrender to *"the pleasures of sin"* (Hebrews 11:25). Christians don't belong in that group, but we do slip.

My thoughts begin to spin as I recount stories of friends over the years. In my first months at Omni House recovering from the drugs, I saw people quit their past and then go directly back to it, worse than before. It scared me. What worried me more was my own roaming spirit—and I still feel it today.

True Christians can be influenced by old friends. We hang on to bad habits. New converts keep on finding pleasures in old places. One of the best guys to me at Omni House was Larry. He was one of several staff members who stuck close to me as I went through my first critical months of recovery.

Somebody asked me one day if the effects of the drugs ever resurfaced, if I'd ever had a flashback. Before I could answer, Larry said, "He's on one big flashback all the time!"

It was a very mixed-up time for me.

Larry and others stayed on my case day after day. I'll always remember it. They saved my life. Larry pushed me to get serious and asked me to pledge to stay off drugs.

"I can't promise you," I told him. "I don't want to go back to drugs, but promises are made to be broken."

"You don't have to promise us," Larry said. "We will promise you that you won't go back."

That was some tall Texan Christian talk, and I took him at his word.

Our staff would speak at community meetings. One time I was asked if I had ever had a bad trip on LSD. When I got finished telling about my one horrendous huge bad trip, my friends escorted me away. I was shaking and weak in the knees.

In over fifty long years since, I have never again seen the total group effort made to surround me, support me, and single me out. That is what it took for me. I suppose God knew ahead of time to put me in a super situation with a whole lot of new loving friends. Something very special happened with them.

After I had been at Omni House for several months, Larry moved out to take a job in another town. I soon heard that he had drifted away from his faith and no longer believed at all. He had renounced his faith. By that time, my faith was growing marvelously.

About a year later, I saw Larry at a wedding. At the reception, I got a chance to talk to him about what I had heard.

"Is it true?" I asked. "Have you given up on Jesus?"

"It's true," he said.

"Then you don't consider yourself a Christian anymore?" I was asking him that in front of other people at the table.

He admitted it. "No, I'm not a Christian anymore."

"Larry, one time you told me, 'once saved, always saved.' Do you remember telling me that?"

"Yes."

"What do you think about it now?" I asked.

"I don't believe it anymore."

I said to him, "I just wanted to hear it from you—because I have heard what other people have said about you."

We spent the evening talking. Larry appreciated my approaching him on that. He even prayed with me. I visited him later in Corpus Christi where he lived. He wasn't quick to get back to where he should have been spiritually. Unfortunately, he and I did not keep up the communication, and it has been decades since we've talked. Larry meant a lot to me since he was one of the people who saved my life.

Seeing other young people come and go in those days made me think about what kind of Christian I wanted to be. How could you worship Jesus and then turn on Him? Backsliding and sinning Christians have remained an issue with me.

I expect Christians to land on their feet running while sinners self-destruct, but often, it's the other way around; sinners repent for their health's sake, and too many truly saved souls fall.

People claim to believe in themselves. They have a stronger desire for their own success. They think about what they can gain and all they can keep. They don't care much for the things of the Lord.

Few of the so-called strong Christians stick around, be sure, if they're going to fall away; it isn't that they have no faith, but their problem is that they have dead faith. Remember, "*faith, if it hath not works, is dead, being alone*" (James 2:17). There are also those so-called doubting Christians who do stick around like tares or weeds among the wheat, and we should be careful. They are only looking out for themselves.

There are many who see and "*when they have heard, go forth, and are choked with cares*" (Luke 8:14), and these are not the cares of others. These are people who compete in this world, envious and angry. The luxuries people chase have grown into big industries.

Some people decide they don't want to be Christians. What happens to a person who knowingly understands the truth of Jesus and refuses to receive His Holy Spirit? You might expect that something terrible happens to people who are conscious of the truth just long enough to taste the hope of Heaven and they know what Jesus gained for them on the cross, and yet they continue to rebel. They have the "*knowledge of the truth*" (Hebrews 10:26–31), but haven't taken the truth to heart. There is a difference.

Anyone who understands the gospel well enough but refuses God's gift of eternal life as described in the New Testament has denied all things. They face the furious vengeance of the judgment (Hebrews 12:25–29). Their punishment is going to be worse. Jesus told a story of a man who found a great treasure in a field (Matthew 13:44). That man hurriedly sold everything he had to buy the field.

Jesus desires the believer's heart to be such that he spends a full life with the most fantastic hope of coming into God's kingdom. If not, you get nothing. Jesus said, as a matter of fact, to flat give up every other ambition. It is great gain to seek the Lord and His love.

> *Return to thine own house, and shew how great things God hath done unto thee. And he went his way, and published throughout the whole city how great things Jesus had done unto him.*
>
> Luke 8:39

    Jesus took a big departure from the religious order of the day when he put God's ministry in the hands of ordinary people, like the man out of whom He cast demons, as seen in the verse above. Not only did Jesus call working-class men to be His Apostles, He called all His followers to give their hearts to spread the news.

    Jesus didn't come in the order of the Levitical priesthood nor was He brought up as a Pharisee. He was not royalty, other than He was in the family line of King David. His kingdom is not of this world. Jesus was a carpenter's son. Those religious leaders didn't recognize His ministry, but showed disapproval so they failed to see He was the expected One. Jesus trusted His work to the ordinary folks.

    Jesus was born a common man. The Pharisees judged people. Here came Jesus—the Lord, God, and Judge. The parable of the Sower surely drew a good pattern and set a new standard by which people would be rated. Jesus taught more reliably than could be allowed by their religious order—He had so much more than what would be tolerated.

    In essence, the authorities failed with their never-ending requirements. Their regulations paled in contrast to the accuracy of Jesus' allegorical depictions of behavior. The conduct of these rulers in their contemporary and temporary theocracy put up a dark backdrop to Jesus' righteous wisdom.

    Our Lord offered His life even before Christianity was formed. He opened a total change. He gave His all in advance of our time.

We can't trust in our own ways. We don't rest on our laurels. We rest squarely on the finished work of Christ.

In their rule, the Pharisees held themselves in dominion over the people, condemning them instead of interceding for them. It became that way all over again centuries later in the Middle Ages when the Roman Catholic Church thought to determine a person's relationship to God. The clergy claimed to be the sole keepers of Holy Writ. The Bible was kept in Latin for the exclusive benefit of consecrated, educated superiors, and it was "protected" from lesser, or lower, quizzical readers.

Class distinction was accepted for centuries for practical reasons. The tortured interpretations of church doctrine held precedence over the Holy Scriptures. Official Church doctrine went beyond the true meaning of the Bible.

Over the centuries, there's been clergy who doubted the Bible's inerrancy. They kept it so they could use it for themselves, bending it to their own advantage. The Reformation began when men like John Wycliffe arrived. Wycliffe was born in about 1330. He later attended Oxford. He identified the great notion that every Christian being filled with the Holy Spirit of God is able to grapple with the truths of the Bible. He said we have as much right to speak as do church cardinals and popes. By John Wycliffe's time, many in the hierarchy had come under criticism and disrepute.

Wycliffe didn't tolerate at all the corrupting of the truth of Jesus Christ. He felt that the practice of faith, virtue, and a good conscience gave anyone the ability to interpret Scripture. Sinners, heretics, and infidels may study theology, he said, but they do not gain in any way the wisdom of it. The institution of the church not only ruled over its citizenry, but wanted to judge their eternal souls. Meanwhile, John Wycliffe worked to bring the Bible into the world of ordinary folk. He worked for all believers to live in love.

We have the sacred Scriptures in our hands today because of so many believers, changed lives and good efforts. Faithful Christians have kept the account right. We can assess a correct response to God with stories like the demon-possessed man whom Jesus freed. This man told everyone his story. God, the almighty Sovereign, places a big responsibility on one and all. See how faith and gratitude work. It's a lot to understand. A crisis of the soul brings this clarity. Time tests the truth. Wisdom requires higher learning, but not necessarily higher education. The good news is that the New Testament clearly gives us more to see in Jesus.

The Good Ground

> *But that on the good ground are they, which in an honest and good heart, having heard the word, keep it, and bring forth fruit with patience.*
>
> Luke 8:15

God brings fruit from an honest and good heart that keeps patience. Jesus throws a hard-to-hit curveball right over home plate with just this one word—patience. Unless you have it, you will not bear fruit. Is a person a Christian if the fruit of the Spirit does not come right away? Life takes time. Every one of us must yield an increase of the fruit, giving true proof with a good heart. How? Right now? Jesus brings fruit. Patience means perseverance over time. It is everything to triumph in life.

The first time someone witnessed to me was in November 1969. He was a young man like me, and we were working together in the steel mill here in West Seattle. He started talking while we worked, telling me about the gospel and warning me about Hell to come. I invited him to come home with me after work so we could talk some more. He was at my apartment on Delridge Way for an hour or two. I had not been the least bit interested in anything spiritual and had never considered an afterlife or invisible spiritual dimension, but only the physical and tangible, the here and now. We simply agreed a lot on decency and morality. I never worked with this guy again and never even saw him again. He would not know that I found Jesus two years later, in part because of his zeal to share his faith.

This little seed began to grow below the surface in the following months. For instance, there was the evening I was walking up the street from my apartment. It was a party apartment my friend Vern and I had. My brother was back from Vietnam and was out of the army. We partied continually for a couple months. We stayed high on dope and drugs all over the city. I got in really bad shape.

I stepped out the door one evening by myself. I hadn't gone far up the sidewalk when I looked up and saw a cross overhead on the roof above the doorway of an old church. I had never noticed it before, even though this was only half a block away from my apartment. Churches and crosses never grabbed my attention, so I don't know why it stood out that night. I didn't even know there was a church on my block. Suddenly, it was there. Why is that? I certainly understood it better two years later after Jesus moved into my heart. These were necessary parts of my story and how I came to be saved.

For decades after that, I drove by that old church building without stopping to tell them how their cross affected me that night. Forty eight and a half years later, I drove by on a Saturday about noon. Balloons and a sign that said "Free Barbeque" stood in front of the church. My friend Leta and I were on our way to take care of some business. After that, we were looking for lunch. The free barbeque sounded cheaper than what we had in mind, so we went back over there. I had hardly closed my car door when I saw Leta out on the walkway hugging a big smiling guy who had his arms around her. I was thinking that they got acquainted pretty fast, but they actually already knew each other. This was really special to her. She was a new Christian, baptized in our church last year, and he was right there now reinforcing her faith. Out of this whole city, the Lord landed us here at this time, and Leta knew this man.

Leo is a leader in that church. I had a chance to tell him about the night I saw that old cross. He was nine years old back then, and he is still with it, inviting everyone to stop by for a barbeque. They have a barbeque at the church every other week. Leo and others were glad to hear my story, and I wanted to thank them and see if they were still holding out the gospel. You and I just might not know everything that is going on around us.

One day toward the end of 1973, I became friends with Ron and Jean, who were having a garage sale in San Antonio. We had a great discussion about prophecies in the Bible because it was just after the Yom Kippur War in Israel. I went back to the garage sale the next day. Having just moved into town, I bought more stuff and invited Ron and Jean to church. They came.

Ron was just out of the army with a new career. After Ron and Jean had attended church for a few months, the pastor's message got to Jean. Ron and Jean were talking in the car on the way home when Jean realized she was not a Christian, so they prayed for salvation. They were faithful in church, always bringing their little boy too. They were a real nice family.

After a few years in youth ministries, they gave themselves to full-time service. Ron saw how he needed to give up his worldly values. He let go to live for Jesus. I was happy to see their faith before, but now I rejoiced even more to think about the blessing they would be to others. They both surrendered their hearts to God and dedicated their lives for His service and glory. This story is about the things God is looking for in our hearts and lives.

The faith of believers can win doubtful souls. Rather than think of the many worrisome thoughts spreading around today, we can ignore the discouragement of a cynical world. We can have confidence and patience to believe that the Lord's work is growing bigger and better than ever.

A few years ago at work, out of the blue, I had a smiley face pop up on my computer screen with a little blurb that asked, "Is this the Kyle Hester who knows Ron and Jean?"

Over thirty years had passed since we had talked. Last I heard, they were moving back to Oklahoma to attend Bible school. Now they have more kids than I knew, and they are all grown up. Ron says that after working with youth and summer camps, he then successfully pastored a church for decades. Ron and Jean are very happy. Ron said something to me about our friendship that was very neat and was in reference to his ministry. He said, "Kyle, when you get to Heaven, you will see how much fruit you have in your life—more than you know." God has blessed them over and over with multiplied years of ministry for the kingdom of God.

With patience, we run through life to the finish. It's somehow easy to complain and to find fault and make excuses rather than watch good things happen. Complaining gets us down. The truth endures. Entire Christian churches taxi around the runway to see which way the wind is blowing without ever actually taking off. We're not going to stop all the bad days and all the wrong ways. We try to avoid anything that may be upsetting. Really, let's get on with life and never mind the drawbacks.

Temptations are not always the old familiar sins. You may be moral but have too many material possessions or might be living without them. When others get more things than you or when they have more success or go more places, don't be disheartened. Don't be distracted when the bargains and sales pull you. Why stress if desires tempt you? You may have bad health or bad luck. Apply patience. Don't watch too much TV. Relax another way. Wait on the Lord.

In another place in the Bible, Jesus told a parable about an unclean spirit that was cast out (Matthew 12:43–45). When the spirit returned, the "house" was still empty, so he went and brought seven other spirits, each one more wicked, and made the state of that man far worse than at first. It should be clear to the defenders of the faith that the mere absence of sin does not indicate the presence of righteousness. Nor is one's goodness representative of God's will. Each of us needs to have God's call from above.

Coveting riches breeds impatience and leads to downfall. We could be sinning just by wishing. Are you thinking about stealing? Make-believe fantasies are misleading and pretending is dishonest as well. We are wrong to compare ourselves with others, wanting to have what they have, expecting that more could be enough. Try to redirect the tendencies other people have and turn them away from sin. Renew hearts in faith along with love.

I asked a young Middle Eastern woman who was working as a

cashier if she knew where she would be after this life is over. She said that if her good works outweighed her bad works, she would go to Heaven, but if her bad deeds outweighed her good, she would go to Hell. (That must be a nervous way to live.) I explained to her how the way of Jesus Christ can get her into Heaven for free, and I asked if she had heard this before. She said she had heard this through her Christian friends. See, she has heard it. Be patient and know that God is at work. He is doing better than we might guess. Don't leave yourself out.

It will take a great deal of patience and persistence in some churches to effectively motivate the members to venture beyond their safe haven of the sanctuary. The attendance is stable, the leadership is solid, and the pastor is preaching. Don't change the formula. Sinners are not apt to come through those doors. Yes, God wants us in church, but He also wants to take us out of church and into the world. People are hopeless without Jesus.

The story of the Sower and the seed is personal. It glimpses the grief of Jesus. His mother and brothers were there every time the parable is told in the three Synoptic Gospels. The secret of Jesus' heart is bared. His words fell on deaf ears. Did He teach them to sow on good ground only? Jesus called out to everyone all over.

Righteousness and sin are incompatible and irreconcilable. Man's free will and God's sovereignty are two parallel lines that don't intersect. We point in opposite directions. God doesn't bend, and neither can we. In all eternity, there is just this one exception, with the greatest love: God gave us His Son. The lines were bent. The rules were changed.

The item left in the balance is our unbelief. The Sower scattered seed over good ground and bad. Unlike what Jesus described, wouldn't a good farmer be careful with his precious seed? The first thing a farmer does is prepare the field. He clears the other vegetation and the rocks. Then he plows long straight rows in the soil. He doesn't throw any of his seed in the road. What was Jesus talking about here and who was He thinking of? Was He speaking of Israel or possibly of the Gentile church coming shortly? Jesus was referring to Himself and His ministry.

Given a finite time, Jesus felt urgent about reaching people. He was keenly aware that most people would be lost in the end. Some of His seed fell on the listening ears of Gentiles who had the right response, and Jesus was surprised at this. He is reaching out to unlikely people in this parable, to us—the unlucky and the unlikable. We are now expected to reach those who haven't yet believed. They have no root, and we who have repented must *love* with our *faith* even those who bear no fruit.

> *And he said, So is the kingdom of God, as if a man should cast seed into the ground; and should sleep, and rise night and day, and the seed should spring and grow up, he knoweth not how.*
>
> Mark 4:26–27

Our faith does not have to have the know-how, but must only have patience with God. Who can know what God is accomplishing over time? Real Christians who believe in the Supreme Being believe just as much in the "Supreme doing."

A tree broadcasts seed far and wide, but few seeds take root and grow. Of these few little trees, few grow to be big. True to life, nature illustrates Jesus' approach.

One reason to love trees is to imagine the odds. They stand in place. They come from a little seed, in a variety of ways, and from who knows how far. They find a fertile spot to grow and weather the elements and outlive humans by centuries.

I marvel at trees in town left standing in the city's industrial areas. A few trees hold on next to a gravel parking lot or behind an old warehouse and escape attention. A few seedlings will bed beside old sooty factories. Give them credit for finding a home along the streets and fences. Admire them for enduring the neglect. They bravely stand out, as they have not yet been spotted and thinned out. They ignore the threat of progress when the ax of new construction will fell them someday.

It would be a bigger fluke yet if one of these stray city trees would cast a seed far away somewhere, someplace where the little one roots and lasts. Even a planted tree on the parking strip of a residential area has a slim chance of yielding just one new seedling with a future.

There is going to be a future. With forest trees, most saplings do not usually survive to grow into tall long-living trees due to birds, squirrels, unfavorable microclimates, and hostile terrain. Trees are designed by God to produce innumerable seeds in order to overcome every natural hazard and to loyally maintain their species. If Jesus thought it right to spread His message far and wide, then we must see His example. Stay rooted in His cause, and please don't give up; see what sprouts. A remarkable thought, love people.

Jesus lifted up those who were weak in faith. He encouraged the timid and helped some sinners. Jesus sought these odd people and those most overlooked. How do we bear fruit? It takes faith to believe all things.

It's not like we believe everything people tell us. Don't be gullible. There are millions of crazy ideas out there and plenty of dangerous deals. We, however, want to believe everything God says and take it the way He means it.

We want God to give us everything we can think of. Is He going to solve all problems? That might not be good for you and me. God loves us. Why doesn't He give us all we ask, take away what is undesirable, and remove people we don't like? He sees it the other way around. God wants us to do as He says.

We are not getting it. What did He make us for? Never underestimate what God is doing in Jesus, our Creator and Savior. Maybe you are still asking yourself if such a real change has happened. Consider what love we've received from Him. He calls us His children. We are nothing less. We are His. What does this mean? In His infinite love, our inheritance in Heaven is more awesome than anyone on earth imagines; it is an enormous surprise. This big thought ought to do something for us right away.

If we can help get this hope fully established in the Christian mind and make it stick now, we will see more amazing things. It takes so long to surrender. God wants to show His favor. Friends can be aware of this and yet rebuff His kindness. Hell is terribly uninviting. We have enough warning—and life is too short.

God's will for us is to be dedicated to *love* in *faith*. Take the Word of Jesus Christ to the ends of the world (Luke 24:45–47); this is the New Testament. A couple years before I became a Christian, a young long-haired guy was witnessing on the street. He told me about a man who had left his job to serve Jesus and who had given away his money. I told him it would have been better to have kept the job and money and to live to help God in the long run.

Sinners shun the way of Jesus. They feel little guilt or remorse. See how low in spirit all of us are. Be tolerant. Any poor soul can pray. Shame and tension are put aside in Christ. The Holy Spirit gives believers reassurance, and love rests on faith.

One day, a bird got into our church. It frantically flew around in the rafters for a long time, darting about trying to find a way out. The tiny bird got tired and rested on a pew. It looked up, saw an open window, and flew out. We don't want to reach for everything we see. Learn what God has. Our changes will lead toward better chances. Leave the bad troubles behind you. Believers remain rooted in *faith* and bear fruit in *love*, and this only comes by patience.

> *No man, when he hath lighted a candle, covereth it with a vessel, or putteth it under a bed, but setteth it on a candlestick, that they which enter in may see the light.*
> Luke 8:16

Parable of the Fig Tree

> *Then he told this parable: "A man had a fig tree, planted in his vineyard, and he went to look for fruit on it, but did not find any. So he said to the man who took care of the vineyard, 'For three years now I've been coming to look for fruit on this tree and haven't found any. Cut it down! Why should it use up the soil?' 'Sir,' the man replied, 'leave it alone for one more year, and I'll dig around it and fertilize it. If it bears fruit next year, fine! If not, then cut it down.'"*
> Luke 13:6–9 NIV

CHAPTER 2

Thomas saith unto him, Lord, we know not whither thou goest; and how can we know the way? John 14:5

By the quality of his question, we see that Thomas had the nature of a leader. Jesus told the disciples that He was leaving to prepare a home for them in Heaven. He said that they could not come yet. The fact that Thomas stepped up to ask about this reveals he was a thinking man. He wanted more direction. He asked Jesus two modest details: "We don't know where you are going, so how can we find the way?" The first question was "Where are you going?" The second question was "How do we get there?" The following week, Jesus put Thomas on the path pointing the way.

At my job, customers phone to ask our address and how to find us. We get two kinds of callers. Some want to know the specific location of our shop, others want me to spell out the route to take. My job is to be diplomatic.

I start by giving detailed directions, say what streets to take and where to turn. That's when some callers interrupt, saying, "Just tell me where you are. I will find you."

I don't usually think like that, so I tell them where we are and leave it to them. They are good with that and hang up. I can't help wondering how they'll find us.

Someone might say, "Just tell me what you are near. Give me a landmark."

Fine, I think; that only gets them close. For them, it is good enough; it starts them on their way. I'm not convinced they ever arrive. There's more than one way to lose a customer.

If on a phone call I start to tell people where we are and they stop me and say, "Just tell me how to get there," I certainly want to give our location, streets, stoplights, corners, etc. A person should have at least an idea of where they should end up. *C'est la vie!*

Customers ask odd questions. One day, a caller asked, "Do you have a location?" That's exactly what he said. Yeah, we are driving in a van with a cell phone, and I'm hanging out the side door. Think about it—are we a shop with no location? The next day, a caller asked, "Do you know what time you close?" Like I haven't figured it out.

Thomas' question was not foolish. First, to get him there, Jesus solved his sin problem. From then on, Thomas led others in the way. It was the same then as it is now—difficult to know just what the will of God is. How do we get eternal life? Let's rephrase the question: "Lord, we don't know where *we* are going, so how do we get there?" We have the answer now, but it was not easy in that day for Thomas and the other founders of the faith. Did people know? Explain it.

> *And the world passeth away, and the lust thereof: but he that doeth the will of God abideth forever.*
> 1 John 2:17

We all differ in our personalities and in our values. To a degree, we are all greedy. Our values are "Do unto others as you would have them do unto you" (Matthew 7:12). All people understand this. Part of us lacks the mind to see the needs of others. Basically, the human nature is selfish. We naturally want the sympathy of those around us. Even with that, though, we know it is right to love others. Something is holding us back.

We each express ourselves in our own way. I stay quiet sometimes, but other times, I talk. From one time to another, people vary in the way they take us: *"And of some have compassion, making a difference; and others save with fear"* Jude 22–23. What works for one person may not work for another.

Jesus was readying these pitiable friends for what was to come. The Last Supper was the last-minute preparation. Jesus told them, *"Let not your heart be troubled…I go to prepare a place for you"* John 14:1. The idea of the will of God was not new, but the only map they had for the road ahead was the Old Testament.

Don't expect they understood what they didn't know. The Bible they were raised with didn't prepare them for what was about to happen. Thomas was going to learn the answer to his first question. Jesus was going to Heaven. How were Thomas and his friends going to get there? Let's think about it. Thomas was not in the courtyard with Peter when Jesus was on trial. He was not in the courtroom with Jesus. He was not noted to be with John on the hill of Golgotha beneath the cross. We don't know where he was on the third day, Easter morning, when Jesus Christ was resurrected from the grave. Thomas was absent that evening, the first day of the week.

A week later, again on Sunday, the first day of the week, Jesus appeared and Thomas was there. He saw the way to Heaven indeed. He could honestly say, "Now I have seen." Thomas believed in God, and so he believed in Jesus also.

There is a traceable tradition that says Thomas was faithful. He traveled around telling the story of Jesus and His love. Our Savior paid the price for us to come. This is the message. Follow Jesus through the cross to the resurrection. "Doubting Thomas" no longer, he evangelized extensively east of Israel to what is now Iraq, Iran, and on to India. There are numerous accounts saying he went to these places. Archaeological evidence substantiates his ministry. There are also fanciful stories about Thomas.

Jews migrated along trade routes in those days. The early Christians also moved into many of these regions. Thomas spread the good news of Jesus far and wide for years. The toll of centuries and invading hordes have erased much of his work, but pockets of remnant descendants in these areas claim the Apostle Thomas as their missionary. He was one of the firsthand witnesses to the biggest event of all time, the crucifixion, and he was one of the first to spread the gospel to the world.

Except for the one who handed Jesus to the priests because of his greed for money, the Apostles remained faithful. Thomas had been bound in sin too and lost like the rest of everybody. The Apostles of Christ were chosen, but they were all born sinners because of original sin. They were not sinless like Jesus. Everyone must give an account. This is orthodoxy. The cross made Thomas go.

The Two Gunmen

For whosoever shall do the will of God, the same is my brother, and my sister, and mother.
Mark 3:35

There are more people who have never heard about Jesus. Have you ever lived in darkness or know what that's like? Many around here think Christianity is old hat. Lots of people live saintly lives. They are good as can be. Does that make them Christian? No. Goodness doesn't get you into Heaven. When do you know the will of God and how do you get it? *"We know that we have passed from death unto life, because we love the brethren. He that loveth not his brother abideth in death"* 1 John 3:14. The difference in life shows.

How do you prove love like the Good Samaritan did? Anyone can stop and help you. Ordinarily people often do.

Faith is more than how we behave; it's what we believe. We read the Bible. Some people think they believe, but they consult with no Bible. Do they really have eternal life if they show no proof and fail at Christlike love? We have friends with no religion who admittedly shun any claim of faith, yet they're admirable and generous. You know what that's like. They're in the dark. You see that the will of God for us is this brilliant kind of *love that works by faith*.

For a time back in 1970, I hung out with friends in Tacoma. We were young. There were girls, drugs, music, and trouble. I would travel between Seattle and Tacoma and stay at one place or another or stay with my mom.

One day, two black guys came to the door of an old house where I was at in Tacoma. They asked for Jimmy, who was a big drug dealer. I knew him, but had been told Jimmy was lying low, he was hot, and I was not to be saying anything. So I told them I didn't know. I thought somehow that this was an opportunity for me. I asked them if they were looking for weed, and they said yes. I suggested that I could make a phone call. Sure enough, my friend Wayne in Seattle had some.

We got into their black Mustang, which looked familiar, and hit the freeway. I can remember very well riding in the back seat, feeling pretty good about it. In a short while, we got to Wayne's house. It was an old small bungalow near the beach. Wayne's roommate, Bill, came to the door. He was not expecting us, and Wayne had left, but he brought out a pound of grass for us to try. Debbie, a teenage girl, then came out of the bathroom, and we all sat down and passed around a joint.

Bill was offering to sell them other drugs, too, like he was bragging. He was a friend of mine who had risen up the ladder fast by moving a lot of dope. He was making money too. We were getting high on a second joint, and a minute later, one of the men came out of the bathroom with a large revolver and said they were not paying. I looked over at the other guy, who now had a little derringer in his hand, pointed at us. This was not like on TV.

"Get out all of your drugs and money. We're taking it all, or we'll kill you!"

Bill said he didn't have it there. "Wayne took everything with him."

This plainly did not make a good story, and it made them mad. But Wayne was gone, and I had talked on the phone to Wayne at first. I thought about it later and wondered why they didn't ask Bill to bring out all the drugs and money before they pulled their guns. Now Bill refused them. He sat straight-faced in his living room on his kitchen chair. Debbie was on the couch near me. She wasn't yet out of high school.

I couldn't believe how cool Bill was. I knew he was holding a load of dope and drugs. They knew it. I'd seen these two around Tacoma—these two black guys in that black chromed-out Mustang. If I got out of there alive, if they didn't shoot us, they'd be caught. I had seen them.

The one with the big gun started searching around the kitchen cabinets, saying that if he found more stuff, he was going to shoot us. That's when I thought we were goners. He had hardly looked around when he got upset. He put the muzzle of his long revolver right up to Bill's temple and cocked the hammer.

Bill just sat in place. "I told you that Wayne took it all with him."

It almost sounded true. The man with the big revolver started slapping Bill in the face, grabbing his hair, and shaking his head, yelling and slapping him some more. The gun was up against Bill's head. It was unreal.

Bill was getting to him. My friend had a real slick personality. Everybody loved Bill. He was shrewd. Forty-five years later, he is still my friend. Last year, he was in town for Christmas, and he stopped by to visit me.

Anyway, when Bill didn't spill the beans, the bad guy told him to get over on the couch. With the three of us sitting there, the bad guy told his partner to bring the car up to the door.

"This is it," he said. "When the car gets here, I'm going to kill all three of you."

Then he told me to turn the stereo all the way up and sit back down. I thought that if Bill wasn't going to break, I wasn't going to say anything either. Like a sap, I turned the stereo up and sat down. I pictured the cops finding us full of holes. They had to kill us because I could talk. One more time, he threatened. He had the door open an inch, and one more time, Bill said, "I told you, it's not here."

The guy opened the door and left. Was he bluffing or was he too scared? Bill turned to me and asked, "What's the story?"

I said, "Call Jimmy in Tacoma and tell him two black guys in a black chromed-out Mustang just robbed you. He'll know who they are."

On the phone, Jimmy said right away, "I know them, and I'll take care of it."

End of call. They were turning onto the freeway south, and their number was up. They were given a chance to fix things, but in two days, they were killed by a bomb. They were looking for Jimmy to begin with, and he found them.

In Bill's freezer compartment sat packages of pills where I might have expected to look. Above the kitchen cabinets was a space where anyone smart would have looked and would have seen pounds of wrapped bags of marijuana. There was also a lot of money sitting in a spot—a lot of money. Bill was just too cool.

The way I see it, if I had died at the hands of these thieves, I would have gone to Hell for eternity. I think the Lord protected me until I was saved. Coming close to death makes you conscious of mortality. God let me see that. This is the way it's said in church. It was, more than likely, too late for those two gunmen.

To Know in Part Is to Know Our Part

> *Verily, verily, I say unto you, He that believeth on me, the works that I do shall he do also; and greater works than these shall he do; because I go unto my Father.*
>
> John 14:12

Those were forceful words Jesus spoke to Thomas and the others. They would do greater things than He did. What could be greater than what Jesus did? Though we try to be strong, we are weak. The Church has flaws. We get unhappy with each other. This new love we are working toward is only seen by faith in Jesus.

You and I haven't quite caught all the truth yet. The Lord Jesus Christ seemed to be a normal human being like us, and He wasn't respected for it. *"For though he was crucified through weakness, yet he liveth by the power of God. For we also are weak in him, but we shall live with him by the power of God toward you"* 2 Corinthians 13:4. This kind of love is not possible for us, but it is not impossible with God. We can have a way with people. God's way is understood by faith if we aspire to love.

It helps to know where you are going and how to get there. Exceptional leaders and teachers help. Spirituality is hazy *"in part"* 1 Corinthians 13:12. There is a benefit in churches where you find fellowship and gather strength. Pastors and experienced believers try to instruct us with wise counsel. They pray on our behalf with the Father's Holy Spirit.

You worry if you can't see where you are going. Life gets fuzzy. How are you doing? Most of us stress over finances. The Bible says a lot about money. You don't have to be an economist, but it sure helps to have a healthy understanding of money. Many ordinary Christians are not smart with dollars. It often happens in a marriage that only one spouse handles the budget, but they can be poles apart.

The same is true of politics. Some distrust politicians or hate politics. It helps to be keen in political science. At times, current events make us cringe. The Bible speaks of conflicts, countries, and rulers. The future can be a sore subject, so it's best to stay in God's will and act right.

Here is God's will: take His love into the world and make disciples. Does that thrill you, or does it trouble you? We live in a big world, but remember that the larger targets are easier to hit. Evangelism, in a sense, can be very effortless. Love is confusing, is it not? We have the love to give; greater faith will see it done.

Love believes all things, overcomes all barriers, and proves universal (1 Corinthians 13:4–7). Love is fair to all people. *"Wherefore receive ye one another, as Christ also received us to the glory of God"* Romans 15:7. No two people are the same, so I pray to be responsive to various kinds. Christians get hurt like anyone else, but we move on in a strong-minded faith that manages to work things out. Our lives are not on trial nor do we have a trial relationship with Jesus. Wait and see; firm faith does produce unfailing love.

I loved it when Jesus came into my heart. Don't you expect every friend to be as excited in their faith? It is not all that plain. Don't you see the will of God in Christians now, after we've received the infilling of God's Spirit? I want to win everyone else over.

"Whatsoever is not of faith is sin" Romans 14:23. We must be confident and determined. Don't be deterred. You miss the mark if you don't live by faith; you are on target if your life is led by love. All things are possible.

Salvation is a free gift of God, but people misunderstand this. Forced to turn to God out of our desperation, we are then drawn to Him by His provision. We are revived. Is life a test? We have answers. Every Christian should realize we are not working our way to Heaven. You and I depend on God. His hand is at work in our lives in a good way. We can't pay God back either. Our new life is a gift. We are not obligated.

If we believed everything about God, we would truly love. It has taken my entire life to begin to see the length of God's wisdom. Too often, people get intimidated when we try to explain that we want to sustain a lifelong walk of faith and love.

Be liberated from temptation, guilt, and condemnation. Our Father in Heaven calls us to be free, released from the "law of sin" (Genesis 2:16-17; Romans 7:21, 8:2). We ought to get along with this. Don't we have an idea of the way life works and where we fit in? So wherever and whoever, if our love isn't in Jesus and isn't of faith alone, it's a sin (Romans 14:23). Your heart must be in the right place.

I was really lost before I met Jesus. Seattle has been a left-wing town for a long time. It has persisted with the lowest church attendance in the country. I was raised in a broken home with little Christian influence. My mother's family back east was Christian, but here in Seattle, she took us kids to average churches where the salvation message was never given. We only went occasionally. What little exposure we had, though, might be partly why I came to Christ.

In the church youth group, we were warned to stay away from goofballs, but it's hard to impress a teenager. A few years later, while still a teenager, I began using drugs. Some very unruly years followed.

The drug craze of the late 1960s captured a lot of us. Some people today might not know this, but there was a time when America was not swamped with volumes of illicit drug use.

The highest birth rate in our history occurred after World War II. As people came out of the Great Depression and war, a new American generation came along. Then more warning signs appeared. Years were fueled with youthful energy and upheaval. The Cold War was going on. All at once, the civil rights movement heated up. The Vietnam War got hot. It was rough. Many manipulated the situation to get elected or to sell newspapers. Who avoided these unfavorable trends? The better part of our country denied the deadly influences and looked the other way. The youth suffered the most.

I started down the wrong pathway with marijuana, quickly moving on to LSD (or acid, as we called it). It didn't take long. I fell deep into sin, sinking to my very weakest at nineteen years of age. I staggered on the edge of ruin. My drug-sick mind fought to keep a hold. My brain was so stretched, it wanted to permanently snap. I was lost.

By age nineteen, I was in bad shape with LSD, speed, and dope, During high school, I washed dishes at a restaurant, so I looked for a job there again. My former boss, Carmen, was one of the best. He was tough but fair, and I thought he would give me a break. I went to the lunch counter and asked for him. He came out. I had long hippie hair, but he was glad to see me and got me a pop. We chatted. I asked if a job was open. He was expecting my question. He said no, turned around, and walked back to his office—with no goodbye. It cut me. I respected him. Few people could so clearly remind me of how far I had fallen. It's not easy to restore your pride and reputation.

I was driving down the street when my favorite high school teacher, Mr. Bentrott, drove by, going the other way. He had been a mentor to me when I was in school. He inspired me to do better. Though he didn't see me, strong embarrassment hit me deep down inside. The feeling stung. I had not yet felt the disgrace of how I was wasting my life. No way did I want Mr. Bentrott to see me. Could he have known how important he was to me in high school? Only these two men could cause me to feel like that. That was when I saw how little of my good self remained, and I felt ashamed.

I was living for me. The rest of the people in my crowd were living for themselves. By that time, I was pretty sad. I thank God that outside help came to reel me back in. There were a few adults with good lives who lent a hand. Along came charitable Christians who looked out for you know who. I was what we called "blown away" by them.

You see, I was doing what I had been taught—thinking of myself. I was thinking of myself, but I wasn't thinking for myself. I might have called it self-improvement, but it was self-absorption. A lot of us could have been termed overindulgent. I was self-absorbed, in a long tunnel with no light at the end. I was trying to find peace inside, but it was difficult.

It was new to me in my world to run across someone who was looking out for others, and I was outnumbered by a new group of good friends. *"Let nothing be done through strife or vainglory; but in lowliness of mind let each esteem other better than themselves"* Philippians 2:3. This thought could change mankind. It would revolutionize Christianity. What if instead of boosting myself, I lifted others up? Sure, I take care of myself, but the Bible says we should see others as more important. *"Be kindly affectioned one to another with brotherly love; in honor preferring one another"* Romans 12:10. This defines love.

A good gauge of life is to see how well we view others. What do you think? If you're always on the defense preoccupied only with yourself, you cannot see out over the top. Are there people in your life? People are key. Are we energetic and enthusiastic? *"Not slothful in business; fervent in spirit; serving the Lord"* Romans 12:11. The Bible tells every Christian to get involved and to take care of others.

Even after I was saved, it took me a while to climb out of hiding. Outwardly, I was extroverted, but inside, there festered a story not even I could figure out. Young people always have a lot of growing to do, changing to survive in this world. We try; we have to—and it happens. Someone advises us or makes suggestions or, to put it more strongly, someone sternly tells us outright what the score is. We become more responsible. The process of maturing isn't easy. Maturity is taking responsibility for your own self and others. God gives us a great deal of credit for our love on account of our faith. *"Look not every man on his own things, but every man also on the things of others"* Philippians 2:4.

In the early seventies, we called it the Jesus Movement. I met believers who spoke with authority. These friends were real and showed they cared. They were not trained psychologists or police, but were just regular people taking an interest. Dear people collectively spent countless hours with me. It must've been irritating for them. When they weren't with me, they worried about me. They persisted, withstood, and endured.

I didn't know much about big-hearted Texans with Southern hospitality until I got the benefit of their care and saw how it was more than a figure of speech. Change isn't easy, but much transformation came to my heart. I was healed in a big way. God made sure that the Holy Spirit worked in my life—and in theirs as well. They brought me to Jesus and to adulthood. Somebody was praying.

I thank God for every one of these wonderful people. Not all of them were Christians either. Jesus gets the credit for their generous help because the Savior brought love to my life. My recovery couldn't have happened without good Christian guidance. The friends we have when we are young mean a lot to us.

Seeing other young people come and go in our program made me think about what kind of Christian I wanted to be. How could I worship Jesus and then turn on Him? May the Lord bless and give credit to those good friends. Have you seen or been helped by a group like this? They liked me, and they loved me. Texas was the place.

I went back to Seattle to share what I had found. I wanted to open a halfway house. That proved unpopular before anyone saw it. I spent half my time trying to get others on board to help the helpless.

It wasn't happening. After a while, it became obvious: I needed to spend my time directly on needy people.

The Lord was shaping my life. People were especially patient with me. God says to *"exhort one another daily"* (Hebrews 3:13) and to encourage, support, and stimulate each other to stay together (Hebrews 10:22–24). The Holy Spirit blesses. Stay in the work of the Lord Jesus with full assurance of faith and never give up on love.

Now each day is still a new start. Just because I got it all figured out long ago doesn't mean I never get stumped in the present. With God's blessings, my prayers answered, and though I live to tell, you should know that doubts still plague me. Those early days were most precious.

A friend from work went out to dinner with me one evening. When we got back to the company parking lot, my car bumped the back of a hot rod and bent one of its fancy exhaust pipes to one side. It was a jacked-up old Chevy with big tires and dual pipes hanging straight out. My friend got out, took hold of the exhaust pipe, and bent it back into place. I didn't know who owned that car. Later, it bothered me, so the next day, I stuck a note on the windshield with my phone number in case the owner found an exhaust leak. I didn't want to forget it, leave it ruined, or see the owner mad. The guy called. It was all cool with him; he was thrilled and couldn't believe my honesty. Praise the Lord! You know—we should be bolder with the truth.

Our Race to Win

> *And I will very gladly spend and be spent for you; though the more abundantly I love you, the less I be loved.*
> 2 Corinthians 12:15

The Apostle Paul found it hard to hold on to people. Sin creeps into us the way rust corrodes iron. It can happen overnight. Iron is hard to break, but the purer the iron, the more susceptible it is to rust. Don't be too confident. Pride leads to a fall. Good friends help you resist sin. Friendship can backfire too. Pray to God for help.

A good man in ancient times named Job hadn't bent, tested, never failed. Satan went all out after him only because he was righteous. Job lost everything he had, even his children, his health, and his wife's support. His friends consoled him, but their words were critical. He had already suffered but these "friends" were painful.

God wasn't judging Job, so he held to his faith (James 5:10–11). He fully and patiently expected God to justify him. He was legitimate. Was Job hopeless? No. God was passing judgment on Satan. Job leaves us a strong example to follow. This story speaks to us in our hard times. When we are tested, are we like Job, holy and upright? God makes us as righteous as Christ, sanctified.

We live in a trying world. Life tests people to the limits. It vexes us. Anybody can get spun around or even leveled by what happens. This means that some Christians fall. It means that some sinners will be saved. Though a thousand disasters take place, you and I trust the relationship we have with our Creator, Redeemer, and Savior.

Just keep pointing the way to Heaven. If a number of counselors criticize us unfairly, don't forget that God loves us all—each one of us. Keep His grace in mind. See Jesus in your heart. We are consecrated. Christianity is an attitude, not a platitude. We are legitimate.

Heaven is not a dream, but it is a real place. After I found Jesus, I thought everyone was going to believe. I reacted by telling others, because they hadn't heard.

One day as I was leaving my apartment on the way to a company picnic, I glanced over at a pocket Bible sitting on the coffee table. The year was 1975. The little Bible had been waiting there for some stranger, and it hadn't moved. I grabbed it as I left, tossed it into the glove compartment of my car, and forgot about it.

Before leaving the city, I got off the freeway to buy some picnic food. I returned to the freeway with a package of hamburger meat and a watermelon for the picnic. A young woman was standing by the entrance ramp, so I stopped to give her a ride. She had been hitchhiking for two days and a night. Things had fallen through for her in Las Vegas, so she was on her way home to Canada, hungry and tired. All I had was raw hamburger and the watermelon. She wanted some watermelon.

Partly joking, I told her that all we had to cut it open with was a screwdriver in the glove box. Before I said more, my new friend went for it. She opened the glove compartment. What she saw was that small pocket Bible. It jumped out at her.

"What is this?" she asked, sounding like she had spotted a hundred-dollar bill. Her face just lit up.

"It's yours," I said.

She pulled out the pocket Bible like it was a special present. Then she went to work on the watermelon with the screwdriver. I invited her to come to the company picnic with me, and she did. Afterward, I took her to the freeway northbound ramp. The special little Bible went with her. I drove back to the picnic to make sure there was no suspicion.

Jesus has given us His approval, but after we become Christians, how lasting is this love? We run the hurdles. Life can be tough, but it's wonderful. The world is not usually a loving place. By returning again and again to the whole view of grace and recalling that our success is not our own, we are brought to see the power of Jesus' love. He is devoted to us.

Things are not always what we expect. For example, a few years back, I made a friend from the next street over from me. He was often gardening when I walked by. This conscientious and energetic fellow wanted to help the needy. He thought he would take a stranger to the supermarket to shop and buy groceries for the person. His church gave him the name of a woman who needed such help. My friend told me that when they went to the store, she overfilled the cart. It looked like she would never quit. I don't remember, but she might have gotten a second cart too. Anyway, my friend was furious. He just wasn't able to say "stop." The woman took advantage of him, but he couldn't speak up. It sounded like that was the last time he would offer to help anybody, but it probably wasn't.

It is funny how love works sometimes. You might have helped

someone and discovered it was a waste of time. Maybe after you gave a helping hand, it became obvious that the person you had helped was spending money unwisely or buying booze, cigarettes, and luxuries. Think of it: why are these people always destitute? You might help somebody in generous ways only to receive ingratitude, insult, or rudeness in return. You might give encouragement and receive resentment. You might give love and receive hate in return. Have you gone out of your way for somebody, only to have been ignored or not even noticed? It makes you want to give up.

The critical mind sees all that's wrong. The world complains. We wonder if it will make any real difference if we help. Thousands are starving to death and millions are diseased while agencies and governments siphon off monies. No matter how minor a contribution, every little bit is important. Doesn't everybody know that you help others because others have helped you? Every time stingy people pass others up, they grow more callous. It's an attitude, you know. Give and your heart gets stronger.

"I would give," says the doubter, "but who is going to help me?" There's is another way to see life. Jesus gave a guarantee in Luke 6:38: if you are generous, the reward will come back to you in your lifetime, and God will do so in a plentiful way.

Add up all the money given to all the charities in the world. They bring in hundreds of billions of dollars each year. Most of the world is blanketed with countless cooperative organizations, corporate programs, and government agencies. The US government gives more help than anyone else. Today, there is better education, housing, and health care than ever before. Individuals give time and money. Professionals and volunteers coordinate all that needs done. It means everything for those who receive. Everyone benefits.

Sharing does us good. Whether you give personally or through an organization, charity is what makes life tick. Contributing to society makes our world a better place, a sweeter place. How did we learn this? Kindness and consideration are basically human. It is good. Christians get a charge in their hearts and feel a lot better about life. It makes us cheerful givers.

God's divine presence in our hearts makes all the difference. Yes, this is His amazing love makes up for everything we're lacking. *"This is my commandment, That ye love one another, as I have loved you"* (John 15:12). Never be shy or ashamed to pray about your life. God's plan covers it all, but until we surrender to Jesus by faith, our love is nothing.

We struggle with unbelief, and we wrestle with our convictions. We're all sinners. We see that. Shouldn't believers get victory in their hearts? It is our understanding that Jesus was raised from the dead to give us new life. We believe in the name of Jesus. Heaven's glory should shine in our love. Regrettably, our love continues to be restrained even after we've turned from our sins.

You try to love, but you are tethered by bad habits. Have you ever seen a dog tied to a chain or rope in a yard when a cat goes by? A dog should know better, but it runs straight for the cat. The slack in the rope pulls tight. The dog's feet go right out from under him. The cat knows where the rope's radius stretches and sits out of reach.

It's just nuts to do dumb things over and over, always expecting better results. Similarly, do you stop one or two steps short of love? Christians are not born with naturally loving personalities, and we do not naturally love. Love comes in the person of Jesus. Love is not only a *characteristic* of Christians, but it should become our *character*.

Christianity is the only religion defined by faith. All other religions begin (and end) with the human effort of followers. Calling other religions "other faiths" is just a figure of speech. Christian faith justifies. "Other faiths" need effort to achieve merit. That's not faith.

Life's distress leads to doubt unless we believe in God's help to begin with. Plenty of good things do take place. Pessimistic people tend to reinforce a negative inclination at every turn. The charitable love of Jesus bolsters our faith.

I know that God is God because Jesus came to teach love. You and I can reach this better love. We can know Jesus as intimately as He knows us. Eternal love is available to us today because Jesus Christ died on the cross of Calvary.

Christian love does not rely on understanding, but it relies on believing. The heart has to be in it. Love is not just a feeling, but it is a true note registered in our consciousness of truth. The recipient may not know theoretically because of love they are receiving the faith. They don't even have to agree with us, but they know we are real. Beliefs must be trustworthy. That's why we need to avoid clever or false behavior. Be settled in your ways. People want to be able to pick up from you that God means everything.

You expect that everyone who wants true life will learn everything that's right in respect to Jesus Christ. We have to look at life on the bright side. Certainly, all of His riches in Heaven are promised to us who believe on Jesus' name (John 16:15). The Father gives to every Christian the same glory that He gave to His Son (John 17:22). The great love the Father above has for Jesus is the very same love He has for you and me (John 17:26). Also, it is automatic for Christians to accept the Bible as true to life. I may pray as I write this. Not only can God help you with the great wisdom of love, but He also sanctifies you. In the name of Jesus, the Wonderful Counselor, the Mighty God, faith is a green light to all of life.

Faith Loves Work

> *By this shall all men know that ye are my disciples, if ye have love one to another.*
>
> John 13:35

God has not called us to immoral love but to, no, a moral life and immortal love. When we're saved by Jesus and are taught to walk by faith, we are commanded to *love* by *faith* as well. God is great. In His great wisdom, He designed us to live. Is it possible to represent His greatness adequately in our regular lives? God's grace works right in the arms of His love.

People will notice. Let no one distract you. Let no temptation take you. The goal of winning the lost to Christ is achievable. God works His plan through the readiness of our hearts. It will be done by taking an interest in others and making them important to us. We win because of God and the fellowship of His Spirit.

Picture the powerful amount of love Jesus extended to us. Nothing could be greater. It is enough to believe. Can we put our hands on faith? This is nothing we can measure—not in terms of dollars and cents and not in actions. Our struggle is not carnal, but spiritual. How can you be certain of a place called Heaven or certain that your place is secured there? Just trust the way. *"And ye know that he was manifested to take away our sins; and in him is no sin"* (1 John 3:5). This is not a paradox. It is basic orthodox theology. If Christ had sinned, He could not have been the sacrifice for our sin. Through His death, our sins are removed—entirely!

Up until now, for so many, the path of faith has not been made clear enough. And if you are a Christian, don't let anyone tell you God will visit your sins on you. Read 1 Kings 17:17–21: *"to call my sin to remembrance."* These fears are what we all grapple with. We need to hear God's Word on this again and again. I study sanctification in every aspect to believe it. Faith will look beyond today and project something better; love makes it happen.

Thomas' story is a freeway on-ramp, an open road with no stop lights. Neighbors we talk to may respond to our message in one of two ways. Some will want to know more of the hope of Heaven and life forever in glorious splendor. If you offer a friend eternal life and convince them of such a hope, they will want to know how to get there, whatever it takes. Someone else who is bothered with sin, shame, and sorrow will first want to see how they can be forgiven and resolve their sins. We want to be able to tell the lost, "You can be forgiven, and the way of the cross is the answer." Heaven will be pure love, much more than ever imagined.

We don't want to tease anyone about how good it is with God in Heaven without telling them the way to get there. They may say that love will get them there. Yes, and if you tell them where we're going and how to get there, tell them about God's love.

Explain God's grace to a stranger. Have you seen anyone who thinks they could never be good enough to meet God? Let them know it's true. Many people need direction now, today! People want to know how they can stretch their money to the end of the month or how they are going to make it through this week. They are just scraping to get by. You may have to work with those individuals one day at a time, sometimes every day, patiently.

Suppose people come to Jesus Christ to get something. I was in a lot of need when I was young, so when I came to Jesus, I believed everything. I was really fascinated with love. Not everyone gets interested, and neither does every Christian.

Christians have salvation secured in Heaven. Our Father above would have us encourage one another in the hope of glory. God blesses my heart to love righteousness in the name of Jesus Christ. The main thing is to bring lost souls to salvation. Bear in mind that to help others, I myself have to be helped.

God tends the many seeds we plant. At times, we see quick results as someone accepts Jesus right away. Too often, we receive a weak reply or an argument. People are pessimistic. Friends and family often have poor reactions. Why be pessimistic? In such instances, we need to reflect on our trust in Jesus Christ and not get upset. Stay true.

Continue to pray. When it seems you have done all you can and it is not enough, your job is to plant a seed, water it, and watch. Only God can give life. All satisfaction comes in doing your best. Declare the gospel. Real faith does not come from a personal scorecard of good deeds or from things we obtain.

Most people have no idea what a true Christian is. You can't blame them if they haven't seen one yet. Can you blame them if the gospel has never been explained to them? The gospel is hidden to those who are lost, and the enemy blinds their minds. We don't want to trip anyone up or dampen their chances if they might be attracted later. Our bad habits won't cost us our salvation, but hypocrisy disturbs others. What do you think happens if we boast or fuss and leave a bad example? It hurts people's willingness to believe. On the other hand, our authenticity and sincerity are influential.

We aren't going to set the world straight, and we do encounter conflicts. If you and I are going to be a plus, we have to know where we stand, and then we must tell others where we are going. Is it enough to tell others that our goal is Heaven if we don't tell them the way there? It's a great disservice to proclaim the love of God when we fail to include the promise of eternity. It's an equal disservice to share our faith but leave out the love.

When we know where we're going and see how to get there, we live better lives. The hope of Heaven has a pull. It's like pulling a string on the table. You don't push it. If you pull on the end of a string, it straightens out. Such a future should straighten us out. We are being conformed to the will of God, confirmed, and comforted.

With our faith and God's love, we can bring others to safety. Jesus said we would have trouble in this world, so He gives us strength. Stick to God's perfect plan. We are secure in an insecure environment. Fear is not the cure. Anger is worse. Human nature is counterproductive. Hatred runs counter to the will of God. Everybody passes the buck, and we tend to ignore our own faults. That old nature in us is selfish. Christians need to be focused because *faith* is the agent of *hope*, and our message is *love*.

> *Thomas saith unto him, Lord, we know not whither thou goest; and how can we know the way? Jesus saith unto him, I am the way, the truth, and the life: no man cometh unto the Father, but by me.*
>
> John 14:5–6

CHAPTER 3

Appointed to Wrath

For God hath not appointed us to wrath, but to obtain salvation by our Lord Jesus Christ.

1 Thessalonians 5:9

None of us have enough confidence in our faith. None of us are fully convinced. It's a long way to go from being lost in sin to feeling safe in God. At one time, we were bound and condemned with the world, but now we've been brought near to God by the blood of Christ. We are citizens of His kingdom. Don't worry. We are no longer alienated, hopeless, or lost. God has said that no one should stay astray. The Holy Spirit of love is our life.

Eternity opens and all of the riches are free. You might think other people are appointed by God to suffer His wrath. You would be missing it right there. Who among us gives enough support or sufficient light to follow the rule of love and to love the lost? You see the difference to make a difference and be the difference.

Though we are made in the image of God and have corresponding qualities, it doesn't mean that our imperfections and limitations are seen in our Creator. God loves everybody. God's wrath is not irrational or sinful. His anger is in no way like ours. His ways are higher than our ways and so I would think our love is nothing like the love God has for us. A reaction to evil is necessary to the moral perfection the Bible has in mind when it tells of God's wrath.

This world has a reaction to God because His wrath is thought of as cruel. We can't call it cruelty when sinners are given a choice to turn toward God's salvation. It helps to have a clear view of the responsibility one's decision has for salvation. The Bible warns us of the dangers present in our world and the irreversible harsh consequence to come.

For a while, I met regularly on Thursday evenings with some Christian men. Our routine was to go to a Chinese buffet restaurant. It was an all-you-can-eat kind of place, and the food was delicious. We ate and fellowshipped, and as the restaurant quieted down, we would casually discuss the Scriptures and pray.

Henry, the owner, had an interesting story about how he had come out of the middle of Red China when the Bamboo Curtain was still standing. He was sympathetic to us since he remembered Christians in his youth back home. While he expressed respect for us, he said his main interest was his restaurant business. He was very friendly. He always encouraged us to eat more and to stay as long as we liked, which was often until closing.

One evening, a young Chinese waitress was ringing up my dinner ticket when she looked up at me curiously and asked if we were monks. She had watched us men come in over a number of months and had seen us reading the Bible together, talking, and praying. I assured her we were not monks.

"We're Christians," I told her.

"Do you believe in marriage?" she asked.

"Yes," I said. "Marriage is a gift from God."

"Do you really believe that?" She had an astonished expression on her face. She was obviously new in this country, and I wondered at her reaction. Then she looked at my friend Michael standing next in line. "Do you believe that too?"

"Yes," he said. "I believe that too."

"I believe that too," she said.

Then I said, "God gave marriage between a man and a woman

in love as a symbol to show He wants to unite us with Himself in a relationship of love. God loves us."

The light beamed in her eyes as she asked again, "Do you *really* believe that?"

I answered, "I believe that with all my heart."

She looked over at Michael again and asked him as well, "Do you believe that too?"

"I believe that too," he said.

Bobbing her head, she said, "I believe that too."

That is how we became acquainted with Du Ye. She was a smart, young college student from China studying here in Seattle. In the weeks to come, we would see her at the restaurant and talk to her a little bit, trying to get in a word of witness to her.

It just so happened that during that time, the *Logos II*, one of Operation Mobilization's book ships, made a rare appearance here in Elliott Bay, Seattle's harbor. The ship travels to many ports worldwide for ministry. My teenage daughter, Joy, was going down to the ship with her youth group, so I asked her if she would find a Chinese Bible. She came back with a copy of the *Jesus* video in Chinese. I couldn't wait until the next Thursday to give it to Du Ye. She was very grateful for the video. She assured me that she had access to a VCR and would watch it.

Then I went down to the ship myself. I found Chinese Bibles, as well as Chinese translations of several excellent books by well-known American Christian authors. A Chinese-speaking crew member pointed out that all the Bibles were printed in modern Chinese lingo except for one big one in the old language that probably had been printed before the Communist takeover. She said Chairman Mao had simplified their writing to unify the different dialects. She also said the Chinese people like to read.

Du Ye was turning twenty-one and one of the guys brought her over to our house for dinner. It was a special birthday. She was dressed very smartly with her cute smile, and she had a good time visiting an American home. She was intelligent, too, having had two years of college in China. I was impressed that she had ventured all the way by herself to go to college here. No one was at the airport for her when she arrived. She worked many hours at the restaurant to make money, and she was a full-time student. It was a lot for her to handle, and she was lonely and unhappy. For her birthday, we gave Du Ye a Chinese Bible and a set of Christian books by well-known American authors translated into her own language and a copy of my book in English, *Love Never Fails*.

At the Chinese restaurant the next week, I handed Bibles to the different workers. I asked Henry, the owner, if he wanted a Bible. He said he did not want a Bible for himself, but would take one home to his mother-in-law, telling me that she had asked for a Bible only the week before.

"You have a mother-in-law around here?" I asked.

"Yes, she lives in my home," he said.

Of all times for his mother-in-law to ask for a Bible, it was a miracle! Can you believe that? I gave him the big Bible published in the old Chinese language. It must have been of the Lord. Henry was very glad to take it.

Right then, another waitress walked by, so I asked Henry if she might like a Bible. She looked to be at least middle-aged. She took it with a big smile, bowed, and rattled off a bunch of words.

"What did she say?" I asked.

"She was most thankful," Henry said. "Her grandmother used to take her to church as a little girl in China. Her grandmother lived to be a hundred years old and had died very recently."

With 1.5 billion Chinese people in China, God led me to give this lady a Bible. This is when you know you are on fire for Jesus.

The *Logos II* sailed north for Canada and was scheduled to be back in Portland, Oregon, a few weeks later. Several of us drove south there to buy more Bibles and materials, and we were able to give them out in Seattle. Du Ye took some extra for her friends. We were foreign missionaries right here in our own city.

One Tuesday evening, Du Ye called me at home and told me that she had watched the *Jesus* video with friends. She said, "My friends don't believe, but I believe." We talked about her hopes, her discouragement, and her family far away. She said, "I have no hope, but you give me hope." She agreed to pray with me to invite Jesus into her heart.

A few weeks later, Du Ye was all smiles when she came over with a friend, another student. We had a good conversation that touched on a variety of subjects. These young ladies were very bright. The discussion rolled around to the gospel. After a while, I said to our new friend, "You are really enjoying our talk."

She nodded, smiling wide, and replied, "Du Ye has told me all about you."

"Then you may be interested in becoming a Christian too?" I asked. "You must be open to Jesus."

"I am."

With that, Du Ye suggested, "Would you pray for her like you prayed for me?"

I asked her, "Would you like to pray for Jesus to come into your heart right now?"

She nodded yes with her big smile.

Du Ye said, "Let's all hold hands." Then I led her friend in the sinner's prayer. You and I are God's greatest accomplishment in all of eternity, His greatest concern, and His greatest love.

It is simplistic to lump Christianity in with the common religions of the world. After undergoing this great salvation, we bloom with the bright light living in this eternal life we know today. We didn't come to Jesus unintentionally. We seek Him.

God is perfect. There is no other way we can please Him apart from surrendering. My best isn't enough. Everybody has that one wrong—everybody. We all try. If you don't make your mind up, to read, take Him at His Word, He says we sin; or you're lost.

> *But without faith it is impossible to please him: for he that cometh to God must believe that he is, and that he is a rewarder of them that diligently seek him.*
>
> Hebrews 11:6

Christians are still sinners until we get a new heavenly body. New believers need mature Christian friends to love them. I'm sorry, but I worry about the lost who come to Jesus. We don't know how their lives will go. These are the ones who embrace the gospel. Some people feign salvation, and when the going gets rough, they bolt. Everyone has to answer to our almighty God.

Love Seeks Not Its Own

> *[Love] doth not behave itself unseemly, seeketh not her own, is not easily provoked, thinketh no evil.*
>
> 1 Corinthians 13:5

Mature faith never looks to see what we get out of love. Give all you have in love and don't get angry or unhappy. Faith is our reply to God. Love has a witness—sharing what God has done, seeing what Jesus did for everyone, and doing what we can to live for Him. Jesus died and rose again to live, so we no longer live for ourselves.

We can live for God's glory and not just for our own selves. You and I have new Christian love. Don't be caught up in your problems. Skip self-interest and self-pity. But this kind of honesty doesn't always survive. If you're ignored, don't reject them in return. We can't look for road signs, omens, or stars as our guide. We should be careful. Our lives and the lives of those we know can change in a single crucial moment.

The odd shape of the ball makes American football intriguing. The ball is pointed. It bounces funny. It is unpredictable. That's what makes the game. Some win, some lose. Life won't bounce the way can't control people; we don't always control ourselves and what we say. We say something, but can't predict how someone will take it. That's the way the ball bounces.

> *Giving no offence in any thing, that the ministry be not blamed.*
>
> 2 Corinthians 6:3

LOVE BELIEVES ALL THINGS

You and I ought to regret it when Christianity gets a bad name. At least one person has said, "I would be a Christian, but I have met some already." That's why I try to live the best I can. We should worry only so much about what others say. You have a clear conscience. You may feel awkward about showing your faith, but Jesus said, *"Let your light so shine before men, that they may see your good works, and glorify your Father which is in heaven"* (Matthew 5:16). Our example makes a difference to others, no matter what anyone might think or say. And God helps.

Our choices are critical every day. Football is a game of inches. One play can determine the whole game, and just one player can make or break a play. Think about it like this: life is not a game.

Ask yourself if you are maximizing those dollars in your pocket for Jesus. Don't focus on your fear of messing up, but concentrate on the good you do. Bring some good to your family, to strangers, and to God. When you are salt and light (Matthew 5:13–14), you bless others and you'll see your reward.

The lesson here is that decency is not lost on people—not at all. A few people become standoffish. You might think it's getting increasingly worse, but it is no worse than at any other time. The world has always been rough, and eternity will be Hell for most.

Americans recall three thousand needless, horrible deaths on September 11, 2001, when merciless terrorists hijacked four passenger jets. But just a few weeks earlier, in August 2001, people here in Seattle made national news with our own senseless spite. During morning rush hour, a woman stood outside the railing high up on the I-5 freeway university span above Lake Union. She was getting ready to jump to her death. Traffic slowed as police arrived. A lot of angry commuters passed by, rolled down their passenger-side windows, and yelled, "Jump!" It became such a game that the police officers trying to talk her out of it had to close all lanes to keep cars away.

If the commuters were mad at being slowed down, think how it was when traffic was completely stopped. The woman did jump. If she had already wanted to end her life, how do you think she felt when people heckled her? The fall should have killed her, but she survived. What do terrorists think of everyone?

Jesus came for all of us. We are all lost sinners, and only a very few believe. Who was more irresponsible—the woman who tried to kill herself or the ones who taunted her? This was the general public, a sampling of American humanity, and not much better, I'd say, than the killers from the Middle East. This woman survived and then faced the world; it's too much.

Let's admit it—people, even Christians, can be unfeeling. It's time to bring in the clowns. Ironically, we more easily see others as coldhearted rather than ourselves.

Attitude is everything. We do not want to be perceived as superficial, but who is to judge? Satan's weapons of deception, intimidation, and temptation work to neutralize Christians. His empty death threats freeze hearts from loving as God commands. Satan accuses, but he never harms a believer (1 John 5:18). His words are hollow. He tempts, but he knows better than we do that Jesus saves. Christians trust in Jesus for the strength to resist the devil. Dedicated believers break down every stronghold that binds us. Why think things are worse today? We are set free. This being true, we can break down the walls that imprison us and those around us.

Our salvation is free in Jesus Christ, but it can be a burden to live. Generosity has a price. Our communities and culture foster a demonstrated unwillingness, a hidden darkness that prevents outside help. In the midst of such blindness, we work by faith to bring others to the light. Be an enthusiastic example. A bad attitude will put people off. Actions carry eternal significance. The blessings of the Lord are forever.

God brings His love to you and to others. Are you winning anyone over from sin? It is not enough to just avoid the negatives; we have to hit the positives. Life is more than fighting sin; it's living in victory. Believing is winning. A smart Christian witness picks up on this. God's powerful Spirit of grace helps all the way.

Yield to God's Spirit and never let down. His wisdom works everywhere, including at home with our families and at work with our friends. When we are busy with the Lord's work, we won't have time for trouble or things that bring harm. Carnal ways do cause problems. Look to live a better life.

Jesus came to be like us. He was "perfectly" like us. He understands us today. He met our same difficulties. God never shows these lofty goals to us without giving us the ability, opportunity, and possibility of gaining such eternal treasures. He desires our full success. God is not demanding anything of you. The fine influence of God's love is fluid; it's freely given. The Scriptures liken His Holy Spirit to oil or water. He doesn't necessarily push, but He draws you and pulls you in.

Jesus gives us blessed fellowship the instant we receive Him. We can walk in the assurance of His favor. He is working His plan, His character, and His will in our lives. Never give up hope, no matter how bad it gets. You will see your life bear fruit.

Those knockdown blows of sin and the anxious moments of grim times motivate me. I run to God and grow stronger. Trouble isn't an excuse and doesn't validate us or anyone else. Stop turning inward; turn it around. The peace we seek doesn't come from inside us. It comes from God above who fulfills and qualifies us; He alone justifies.

Failure is human. We're all sinners. Are you holding higher goals for a bigger life while harboring a weakness for temptations? We all see. Don't be too hard on yourself or others. People doubt that God really forgives. Do you wonder if He loves you? Do you worry if He will still love you the next time you fall down and mess up? If you are a Christian, God really has received you into His family and extends His care to you unconditionally and completely. If you fall, He still loves you. Jesus died "for the sins of the whole world," and He is our "advocate with the Father," always (1 John 2:1–2). See how idealistic expectations of faith can fade in the clashing trials of life. Be energized and renewed to live in righteousness. Why should you be discouraged in your poor inner heart because of disappointments? In love, we vigorously exercise a bigger faith.

Sin takes a toll on the outward expression of faith. Hope and patience suffer. Are we ashamed? We're being shamed unfairly. The accuser sits night and day assailing us. Are we to stand up to him? Of course we are—by serving Jesus.

All of us are forgiven equally—we are forgiven in everything! The point is not to rebel or sin even more. He who is forgiven much also loves much (Luke 7:47). You, a total sinner, are totally forgiven. It is to love all the more, warts and all.

Remember, someone had to get through to you! Graciousness will be respected, even by the bad guys. If you don't think the bad guys recognize your courtesy, kindness, and reverence, maybe you haven't thought about it. Jesus cut some slack for sinners when He met them and He was admired and popular with them.

Christians enjoy peace. When it comes with good interaction at school or work or with our families at home, life is good. Do you see how Jesus got involved with those around Him? Do you understand people as Jesus did? A cheerful "Hello" or "How are you doing?" can sure brighten someone's day, and it will also brighten your day to be friendly. That's just a small example of how to shorten the distance between you and someone else.

Maybe I am too sensitive about this and too negative. Actually, many people crave personal contact. Others may not. Some people are out of tune with what is going on around them. They're in a world of their own. They are unaware of how inconsiderate they are. Perhaps they have given up or have never tried. Oftentimes, people are very open, and we are the unfriendly ones.

Believers become partakers of God's will. We have escaped the corruption of this world. If some people think that it's much easier to fall into sin than to obey God, they should think again. Sin is harder to live with. It's like paddling upstream against the current. It gets tough, real tough. Those who think that sin is easier than obeying God need to turn their boats around. Jesus' love is incredibly easy, and likewise, we are better. He calls us to a lifelong vocation that continuously builds our character and blesses others the most. Pray that Jesus keeps bringing the many increasing rewards.

The Power of God

Let every soul be subject unto the higher powers. For there is no power but of God: the powers that be are ordained of God.

Romans 13:1

We can know who we are and learn what to do. God has a whole design for the entire world and everyone in it. Have you noticed how many people have never figured this out? They aren't listening to the right people. Maybe they aren't listening to anyone. In His abundant goodwill, our heavenly Father has raised leaders who point to better ways. Through these good people, your hopes and options are made possible. God has arranged rewards for those who line up with His plan, one person helping another.

God keeps our earthly estate in a perfect balance between chance and orderliness. Right in this sinful world, the Holy Spirit fosters decency. Civilization is somewhat civil. God hasn't left us to make our way by ourselves. No, He hasn't. Christians have helped me learn about God.

I came from the open vulnerability of sin and crossed the bridge of trust, finding salvation in Jesus. I understand much through faith. This vision was not easily formulated in my mind. This was the real deal for me, the belief of all things spiritual.

And whatsoever ye do in word or deed, do all in the name of the Lord Jesus, giving thanks to God and the Father by him.

Colossians 3:17

We achieve our potential by finding God's wise instruction. Why bypass His benefits? When we get out from under God's authority, we get messed up. He has influence over all things. Practically no one has heard about it. Virtually everyone is missing in action, both non-Christian and a lot of Christians. Times get bad. It's hard to go against the prodding of the Lord. How can people do that? It's hard to imagine how people can seem to do well without God, but they do. We have friends who push in the wrong directions, and they miss out.

Life wears us down. Our increasingly complex society is more strained with each passing day. The future seems impenetrable, as if we don't have a right to be human beings here on earth. Our problem is that we live here, and when the devil is our master, we live without Jesus Christ. *"Now if any man have not the Spirit of Christ, he is none of his"* Romans 8:9. We all start out with nothing, zip, zero. That's a problem for everyone. Finding a rightful place on good ground in God's divine plan is the goal.

The Bible is never outdated; in eternity, there's no such thing as never. There is only forever. The world doesn't know the Bible and is more distant from God. As we progress to the end of it all, the prophecies grow larger. The world wants a free society, one that is free for all, and it is going to be a free-for-all. Everyone is locked in sin. Sin restricts freedom and kills liberty. The depth of despair chills. Pessimism and pressure robs people of their normal senses.

Developments in the arts, communications, governments, science, travel, and other fields have improved the world. What remains to be reinvented is the human heart. We see a rise of prophetic events on the horizon hastened by the indifference in our thinking. Add it all up. The growing threat toward our anonymity as individuals has totally endangered us as a population. Acrimony and callousness decimate our very being.

Young people today are more challenged than ever. Youthful vitality is faced with pretty tough odds. A person may lose his life and his soul as well. Our times offer wonderful advantages with innovative skills and opportunities, yet produce compounding anxieties. The young person who falls behind has staggering disadvantages and is pelted with threatening risks. Older established lives are quickly replaced.

People in their twenties are entering a critical period in life. By thirty years of age, we have decided on a career, a philosophy, whom to marry, and where to settle. Where I live, just like all over the world, competent young adults often are opulent like no other time in history. But living in the mainstream gets harsh. Sometimes, we make a major shift in midlife, yet even that comes out of well-worn patterns.

Wisdom has to be handed down. I doubt youngsters listen clearly or early enough. There is an intrinsic ambition in youth to search out and question the world. Answers will never be found by abandoning correct and good values. Solid advice can come from unusual places. Learning to listen and stay objective with sufficient thought should be the aim of anyone interested in a future.

Honesty has a lot to do with faith. It's a healthy practice to build ties with people we trust, as all of us should have more resources to go to. It would be an indication that we are objectively seeking God's will. Are closed-minded people dependable? Everyone admires morals, but they don't always acquire the straightforwardness to ward off temptations.

Do not be misled: "Bad company corrupts good character."
1 Corinthians 15:33 NIV

We must spend time with unbelievers if we are to reach them, but don't be led astray by keeping bad company. Not everyone is open to God's truth. If I expect to convince the whole world of God's love, I am going to be disappointed. Does everyone need to be positive to do better? I want to stay optimistic and be patient at the same time. When others show bad manners, I try not to make it my personal problem. I pray.

Biblical evangelism is lived in the context of church life. Our lives are not our own when we give everything to Jesus. Working together is worthwhile. As our motives stay pure, our direction becomes clear and godly principles are held dear.

We cannot make people believe. Can you make a person love others? Some have hatred. Behavioral science works to turn criminals into law-abiding citizens. Preachers seek to make converts. Teachers live to motivate students. Wives want their dull husbands' attention. You can never make anyone love. It is simply not in the definition. But you can win them with a smile.

If you can talk someone into doing what they don't want to do, it doesn't mean they'll automatically appreciate it. A bad little boy can be made to sit down in a chair, but in his mind, he is thinking that he's really standing up. How can you make someone else love? To gain a friend, you must first be a friend.

God has His way. He is using me even if I don't understand. Are we going to see everything God is doing? You and I can do the right things and reach out and help, but still have no visible effect. Don't question the intentions of unbelievers by wondering if they're compatible or contemptible; instead, ask if we are committed to the task. Be bold to give your complete all to the lost, and in so doing, give yourself to Jesus Christ.

I have a secret that I should tell more friends about: my prayers get answered. Honest, I have surrendered my life to Jesus. My life was so bad that I felt as if suicide would be better. When I got saved, I felt it was like spiritual suicide to resign and allow Jesus to take over.

We Christians are confident that we have eternal life in the name of Jesus Christ because when we pray, we get answers from God. *"And this is the record, that God hath given to us eternal life, and this life is in his Son"* (1 John 5:11). If I went this long without ever having a prayer answered, I'd be real tired of it by now.

One thing God asks us to do as much as anything else is to win someone over. If you can hear Him, pray for this. *"Likewise, I say unto you, there is joy in the presence of the angels of God over one sinner that repenteth"* (Luke 15:10). Shouldn't we be excited by this? Feel it in your heart. If we only knew the truth of it!

We are fairly thankful for ourselves. We appreciate all grace received through Jesus' atoning sacrifice, and we should feel this strongly for others. I do not need to write anything to you about sin. Need I spell it out? A body quits, yet you hear we go on.

Be generous. Be a Good Samaritan. Wounded souls die all around us without the benefit of a better explanation, one that is backed by a good example. Slow down and help a stranger. Jesus seals your future in Heaven; would you resent anybody's salvation? Work harder to do your part here on earth to bring the light of day.

With times as rough as they are, it can be hard to love. Life is a long journey, but it's worth it. Everyone needs Jesus. The world craves love. Why does life scare us? That's because we lose at love, and it's a confusing experience.

Young folks start out romantic and naïve. Progress suffers interruption, which can happen at the worst times. Tragic accidents and permanent injury can strike and destroy loved ones. Debilitating diseases take a slow toll on a promising future. Financial security evaporates unpredictably, leaving you nowhere to turn. Few of us start out with the know-how to deal with loss or, worse yet, with sudden loss. Death comes early—always too early. It hurts the ones left behind. Most loved ones survive grief and move on. A few lose heart. Amazingly, some live long, full lives with healthy marriages and successful families.

Christians represent the way of love with hearts of compassion. Does God want us to quit loving people after we think they've turned away? We cannot predict outcomes. A spiritual battle may come to you, or you may have just started a fight. I meet someone new, and I want to invite them in and get to know their story. You and I should not run away. God creates miracles. When you see a friend foul up, you might come back later and find that the story got better. Expect God to work beyond your expectations, with no restraints, and accept His command to live. Don't give up on people. Pray.

Faith in the New Testament does not take the nerve it takes to learn to swim or to get on a bicycle. Gaining love is more than breaking annoying habits. Spiritual maturity is not achieved by cerebral deliberations or repetitious exercises. Good life comes in Christian faith, not the other way around. The tag of discipline doesn't necessarily define us; however, faith does take practice.

Maybe you've heard the term "sloppy agape" used disapprovingly as a warning. The bad news is that multitudes of Christians have not yet caught on to the wonder of grace. We are painfully inconsistent in applying Scripture to life. This is good news and bad. The criticism indicates the message is getting out. Sharp Christian teachers get the accent on grace. The promise in the New Testament is the power of the resurrection; it's first summoned by the blood of Christ and the calling of God. Love believes all.

Our faith and God's love don't always unite us. Jesus hands life to us to prove what is true. We are meant to be of one mind and fellowship in accordance with God's way. Fights come from believers as much as from the unbelieving and disobedient world. Jesus has taken authority over evil in order to give us life and love.

Reprove Them

> *Have no fellowship with the unfruitful works of darkness, but rather reprove them.*
>
> Ephesians 5:11

We have conflict among ourselves, yes; you needn't be afraid of that. We have conflict in our minds. Who do you know who doesn't have fights? Love separates people every day.

Sometimes, difficult people become unsafe. If they pose a threat to us or to others, then we ought to find the appropriate response. For instance, we might call the police. But there are reasons. Concerned for the well-being of others and fearing serious consequences, we might be obligated to disapprove, dissociate, or otherwise correct a person or persons and avert some grief, doubly so if we encounter obstinate Christians. Then, arriving at a good, sound resolution, it is incumbent on us by faith to take action and correct a bad situation.

But now I have written unto you not to keep company, if any man that is called a brother be a fornicator, or covetous, or an idolater, or a railer, or a drunkard, or an extortioner; with such an one no not to eat (1 Corinthians 5:11). A young man started coming to our church with his girlfriend. Both had fallen into youthful temptations. The two seemed to be making progress toward recovery. She had been in our church with her family as a young teen, but then she fell into trouble and stopped attending. When she started coming again regularly with her new boyfriend, this guy was very polite and said all the right things. We were pulling for them both.

Bob, a widower with a heart for helping needy people, rented out a room to the young man. Not a dime was paid the first three months. Bob was one of my good friends. He had lost his wife to cancer. His diabetes was voracious, and he had a very bad heart. He needed help at home, and he needed the money.

The new friend found his way around the house and used Bob's credit card to open porn sites on the home computer. Of course, the hooligan quickly disappeared after that. All the credit card companies had to be called, numbers changed, and billing blocked. A few days later, it was discovered that hundreds of dollars in cash was missing from its secret hiding place. The damage had been done.

The young woman and three more women like her were all made pregnant by that loafer. He probably had no conscience. This was a low-down bum who opened computer porn, abused credit cards, and instead of paying the rent, he stole the cash. It hurts to think that Bob, in his kindness, had been taken advantage of. When panhandlers or homeless people ask for money, sensible people think it's wrong to give.

Bob continued to open his home up. He allowed several other young men to live under his roof. He suddenly got an extremely rare medical condition that doctors could hardly figure out. While Bob was in the hospital getting both of his legs amputated at the shins, his house was trashed. He was still in the hospital when a police officer came one day to ask questions. He showed Bob a pistol that he admitted was his. Bob was told that one of the young guys had taken it and killed himself. It seemed like double the shame soon after that when Bob went to glory.

I want to tell you that before Bob died, he recovered. His medical complications began in early 2002, and he was in and out of the hospital and nursing homes the rest of the year. He was eventually fitted with two prosthetic legs. Bob learned to walk around on his new feet and took his place back in church. I will always remember the time when we deacons assembled to serve communion. Not to be denied and without anyone talking to him, he just stepped out of his pew and rounded the corner. I just stepped out of his way. Bob also returned to teaching his Tuesday evening Bible study at an assisted-living residence. In fact, he moved into the place. The group soon tripled in size.

After church one Sunday evening as I was leaving, I told Bob a joke. He had a big loving laugh. He was waiting for his ride to pick him up to take him home. When I left, Bob was alone in the lobby. Everyone else had left, and the youth pastor later found Bob. He'd fallen asleep and was no longer breathing. I heard about it the next day. God sure blessed him in church that evening. Bob fell asleep and woke up in Heaven with the crown of life.

Someone may have thought Bob was careless with those bad characters he met. Faith takes a stand against sin or faith chooses to help. Picking your friends is a big deal. Have no kinship with unfruitful works of darkness, yet having friendship with people who are dubious or who differ from us keeps us alert and alive. We can't expect everyone to act alike. Our Christian friends can act like sinners. Life is more than having sinners accept our ideas. The first act is to convert their hearts to Jesus.

It's not always easy with faith to be able to love and to be wise too. Some couples in our church with good homes and good thing to offer have taken in troubled teenagers. They were able to have young extended family come stay months or years. These teenagers came to church and participated in the youth activities. At the end of their set time they went back to their families. The reports that followed were not good. Once home, this teen followed the crowd with drugs and sex. What did my friends think? It broke their hearts. We hold out in the hope that in the years to come, our prayers will be answered.

Good citizens are wary of being hit up by freeloaders. Can we contribute to such messes? The Bible says to stay clear of any Christian who refuses to work (2 Thessalonians 3:10) or who won't take care of their own family (1 Timothy 5:8). What do we do? *"A man that is an heretic after the first and second admonition reject, knowing that he that is such is subverted, and sinneth, being condemned of himself"* Titus 3:10–11. They have their own minds about things. We wrestle to be reasonable.

Leave the expenses and consequences to God. Does love fail? The Lord says that His Word does not return to Him void (Isaiah 55:11). He convicts the world. He wins the lost. The One who judges knows all things. Express your faith. Help the cause. Infectious love is contagious. God commands us to love our neighbors, and we can only comply with this in faith.

Christ Shall Give Thee Light

> *But all things that are reproved are made manifest by the light: for whatever doth make manifest is light. Wherefore, he saith, Awake thou that sleepest, and arise from the dead, and Christ shall give thee light.*
>
> Ephesians 5:13–14

Our state laws free convicts too quickly, yet somehow, the prisons stay overcrowded. One well-established minister asked his church to welcome an ex-offender into the fellowship. Knowing of the man's past, some members of the congregation disagreed and decided to leave. The energetic pastor stuck by his beliefs. The man in question attended regularly. He was a new Christian who continued to grow in a remarkable way. The church saw a number of new people come to faith.

It is not easy to get people into church or get them to stay. We each pay the price for crimes in our communities and for the weaknesses of our churches. There is an association between revolving doors of churches and a famed recidivism in prisons. We know people say Christianity is a problem. They are not favorable to us. But if churches won't teach the right things the right way, there you are.

There has been a fight in Christianity between liberal and conservative ideas. It has been characterized, depending on who is talking, by strong words that split those who stretch the truth and by some who would define it. Often, it parallels politics. That being said and having been pretty much settled for half a century or more, we have fallen short. You can look back two hundred years and see the division. In some respects, we have reached the top of the curve; after that, the falling away is measurable. I believe there is more to go for us to reach the end of it all. To say that love believes all things is not to say that everything goes. That of course pushes out the strict truth, but let's focus on all that God has said. This brings in His love.

We are enveloped by danger in the greater culture of the world. Christians wake to the realities of sin and arise to the call of faith. Fight sin head-on. Understand how righteous living exposes evil. The Bible counsels us to combat the ills of sin with a hearty thrust in God. Let's not react out of frustration or act defensively in anger. That can get touchy. Instead, let us look to the Scripture's practical principles for the right course.

Living is difficult, and therefore, people are difficult. If an individual's character does not add up, we tend to give up. Solve the impasse and show you care. Do you care? You would not be the first to love and be let down. Do you think your love is irresistible? Not even God's love is irresistible. Satan resisted God's love. We literally find ways to resist love, absolutely. Wisdom is first found in the Scriptures and takes precedent over personal experiences.

God tells each of us to examine ourselves. Where would faith be without the guiding principles of our Scriptures, and it can shape a rapport with others. Facing a person up front may bring a reaction. Say your prayers for a better effect.

We can go so far in our attempts to keep the unity of the faith that we compromise New Testament admonitions that teach us to separate, not so much from sinners as from troublesome Christians. Sincere love does not count any sister or brother an enemy, because confronting disobedience directly can bring repentance. Hopefully, we keep an honest, firm grip on our own walk and find our path through life.

Devoted Christians aim to stay consistent and sensible. Be zealous, but be true. Is what we say and do really who we are? Not always. What is significant is who we are personally. It's vital. Christians should be of one mind. The way you relate to others tells where you are in relation to God's program.

More than words, the fruit of the Spirit in our lives is what impresses people. Strong love is able to say no. When we part company with anyone, we should leave a clear opening for restoration. Restoring a reputation, healing the injuries, and working for harmony all happens in the way we tell our own story.

God commands Christians to rise up. The Apostle Paul points out that salvation means we rise up from the dead. Christ's resurrection has come upon us and He gives us light. Quickly, then, wake those who sleep. Are you waiting for somebody else to do this big important job? You and I have to take the initiative.

What is not immediately perceptible is the harm that is done. To our shame, Christians can be lax or even conciliating to a fault. Does Jesus help if we do nothing? Peacemakers must take charge and make change. Sometimes, less is best. Passivity can be a proactive thing and a strong thing. Our role requires rational insight. "Rational" here describes *rationed action*, a more judicious response in ratio to a situation. The fine line in forgiveness can be misunderstood as a little consent to sin.

On one side of a city, everyone is watching television in their living rooms, while real people on the other side of town are fighting real-life dramas. That's poor. Instead of challenging these fantasies, people with no substance of character soak up soap operas and fill their lives with vicarious thrills (as if no one should think about what is true or try to turn this world around?). The world is turning around, all right, every day. God will one day cancel their programs and take the phony actors and actresses off the air!

As a dream when one awaketh; so, O Lord, when thou awakest, thou shalt despise their image.

Psalm 73:20

Thousands of people have seemingly nothing better to do than to just sit around playing games, reading, and watching movies. This is especially harmful with children whose parents have less involvement. And the parents are not assertive. They're just living for today. New technologies have higher stakes. Jesus Christ is coming again to establish His truth in righteousness.

We live in a Hollywood society. Thank God we are no longer part of it. Christians who lack a thrill can get involved to help struggling souls. Why live in pretend theater? Traveling to Disneyland isn't bringing us closer to the realities of a responsible life. Join in the good efforts to stop the social ills around you.

Cynicism fuels society's apathy. Generations of atheists have taught half-truths of ignorance. Unbelief creates ugly feelings of despair and mistrust. The learned and trained alienation of the soul invites doom. Which one of us, then, will get pulled into crime, depravity, and rebellion? The ridiculing of good values has surely cranked up the other side, they profit in their mockery and malign our culture. Comedians have risen to prominence simply because they glorify absurdity and vulgarity. What is left to protect? Alarmed believers run up against a paradoxically unarmed pacifism that is, nonetheless, destructive. Rich and poor, young and old, men and women have basically lost purpose with no direction in life.

Public figures are too often self-serving. Political leaders command and speak without specifics, filling their redundant positions with nondescript rhetoric. Dedicated citizens serve with distinction, but everywhere you go, the powers of government are being tested and the levels of control are questioned. The enemy of our soul pushes on us relentlessly.

The American dream has prided itself on advanced education, yet students today show less ability to reason than previous generations. Politicians are faced with complicated problems. They are saddled with committees demanding more and more expensive solutions. The same issues are fought year in and year out. These are potentially exciting times, but an apprehensive, unappreciative public is mired in dejection.

The strong and capable are on top. At the bottom of the heap are the weak. The poor are smothered under great suffering. The intense social pressures and crushing requirements of technocracy prove an unbearable weight for too many hearts. Though we speak the same language, they are too defensive and don't hear. We throw out the lifeline, but they panic and flounder and can't see. Hysteria is a contagion that spreads undesirable speech and dangerous ideas. It takes the stronger ones to pull out the fragile before it's too late.

For those of us who have increased in awareness, it has become painfully clear and obvious that others have not. People have understandably succumbed to the dullness. The blind-hearted soul is removed and noncommittal. Many of us try and are rejected.

People may act like they don't need you, but they do. Can you get through to them? You might disagree with that picture. Will your kindness and patience really pay off? When at first you don't succeed, try and try again.

Let no man seek his own, but every man another's wealth.
1 Corinthians 10:24

Love puts others first. This one piece of advice put into practice would turn the world around. Believe it. Everybody wants to be loved. Even if there is that one rare person who claims not to want to be loved, suppose we take the person and treat them well. Return good for evil, for instance. What happens when you give a lot of your good attention to an undeserving person? The walls come down.

People want to know if you like them more than if they like you. It is our basic human nature to test others to see if they like us. Do you think it is more important to people what they think of you or what you think of them? Someone may or may not seem to like you. People want to know, "What are you going to do for me?" Deep down inside, people are interested to know if you like them.

Everybody likes to be liked. It's human nature to think of ourselves first. Let me put it another way. If someone did not especially like you, but you showed them well enough that you liked them, would they begin to like you? People want to be appreciated. It's hard to like somebody who doesn't like you. It's hard to dislike somebody who likes you. How long does it take to win a person over? When people show they care, it's much easier to like them.

You are working for your own benefit, and I am working for mine. That's the way of the world. People think it's foolish to live for the benefit of others. People judge us by what we do wrong, but we often miss what's right. We see good things at times. How much good is there? "Do unto others as you would have them do unto you." This requires us to pay attention to the lives around us. The practical side of life demands that we take care of ourselves and take care of others. At its worst, life can be pretty vicious. The world seems to be that way, for the most part. Don't you feel like you should be different—not selfish and self-centered? The human condition is such a pity, but don't look down on others.

One time, I had a vigorous conversation with a friend who was very interesting because she liked communicating. She had a wide-open mind, but was a bit unsettled. I asked her if she was doing all right. She said she was. We talked for about an hour. She had different views than I did, but I didn't argue. At one point, I asked if she felt that God was in control. I don't know why I asked or why she said yes. It just seemed like a great question for her. I didn't get her thinking on it. The Lord gave it to me. I simply left it there for her to chew on. A little reinforcement is good to give to someone.

If we believed our own thinking, we'd fail. We get deluded and then disillusioned. Dependable love is improbable. The carnal nature fights against God, between people, and within family and church. We don't know how much Jesus is doing.

With great care, our Creator has hidden us in the body of Christ, protecting us. Christians are hidden in Him, and our sins have been covered. We are seated with Him in the heavenly places (Ephesians 2:6). Our citizenship is in Heaven, even though we are here (Philippians 3:20).

God declares Christians *holy* by His justification and salvation through Jesus Christ. Have we yielded our hearts *wholly* to God in His work of sanctification? Sadly for us, the Church's record is more *holey* than Swiss cheese.

The message is barely getting out. God is the source of truth. We Christians have hardly made it news among ourselves. Throughout the centuries, societies have tried to define a reason for being. How many know that the way to God is free and that the only way to be made right is to become a part of who He is, to be in Christ? From Genesis through the Book of Revelation, the Bible says mankind is fallen. Are we left to suppose that the gospel is only for Christians?

That's a contradiction; anyone can be reached.

Edify each other in the faith and in perfect love. Full of all hope, God's plan of grace gives Christians an extended mission. In the time we have remaining, we must stay firm in our conviction and remind others of the eternal future we'll share. That being said, love is always attainable from the hand of our all-knowing God. Jesus teaches us to show how this is our purpose in life. We witness God's message that love works, but only by faith.

Working with Faith and Grace

And the Lord direct your hearts into the love of God, and into the patient waiting for Christ.
2 Thessalonians 3:5

While we wait for His return, pray for the Lord to direct hearts into the love of God. This is our faith. It is to believe that Jesus paid for the sins of the whole world—not for us only, but for everyone. It is vital to say again that for all who will receive it, He paid the *penalty for our sin*. We rejoice with each other in the thought. Not everyone professing Christ as Savior is sure. Much of the poor preaching and teaching we hear and read casts doubt among God's followers. It's not right that we doubt; believe in all the things that are right.

You and I can be extremely glad to know that the Savior is returning for us. Your attitude improves more than 100 percent if you just accept this by His word. Be equally pleased also in the knowledge that our Lord has saved us from the Hell to come. Why is Hell written about in the Bible if there is no Hell to avoid? People could suppose dead bodies just decompose, dissolve into the ground, or evaporate into the air. If every person across the world eventually arrives in Heaven, then what would be the point of Jesus' death? If Hell is merely academic and nobody ever actually goes there, then what was the purpose of His suffering? We want to trust the Bible the way it reads, see what it says, and listen to God.

None of us receives enough support for our faith because none of us are thoroughly convinced of what we believe. None of us gives out enough of this encouragement or are sufficiently enlightened to properly honor the Lord and love each other. Church is not always a safe place either. Sin and suspicious behavior preoccupy Christians who are not strictly consistent. It's good to challenge the wayward if firm correction might turn the backslider back to God. Remember that Paul warned the Corinthians to forgive and not be too harsh when one of their own was overly corrected and overly sorrowful.

The Apostle said that Satan might get the best of them. You and I know of the devil's devices. *"Wherefore I beseech you,"* Paul warned, *"that ye would confirm your love toward him"* (2 Corinthians 2:8). We don't want to see anyone destroyed, but instead, we want to see them restored in their faith.

> *For God hath not appointed us to wrath, but to obtain salvation by our Lord Jesus Christ.*
> 1 Thessalonians 5:9

We are saved. Then it should be no worry. We know we are going to Glory. Christians never get lost along the way. What could be our hurry if eternal life is forever and we know we have it in hand? When you are unclear about this, especially after receiving Him into your heart, you are going to be confused. You might be unclear about where you are going, or you might know you are going someplace but are uncertain of the way. Christians, though, are never lost. In an odd-shaped world that doesn't make sense sometimes, feeling secure about Heaven helps; it's a perfect place. Remember, Earth is not perfectly round for reasons. Christians will continue to ask, "What is the will of God?" The first command of Jesus is love, so love is clearly at the core of God's heart. People associate obedience with various things they think. Disobedience will take us away from love every time, because love is what's right. Yet love is tolerant.

When we're more thankful, it shows in our love to God and to all others. Why don't we want to believe, receive, and give God's unparalleled, pure love? Each of us accepts this ministry upon profession of faith in Jesus Christ.

You have to love this work. Why is it so hard? Jesus said life would be easy and your burden light (Matthew 11:30). If you have to work at love, check the directions. Do you want it to work? Say it this way: "If it feels like work to you, you might not have fully accepted it." True faith is a labor of love.

Once people taste and see that the Lord is good (Psalm 34:8), their hearts might produce faith, but the world today is seriously hooked on all the flavors of negative and repressive emotions. All the bad things people do may seem entirely harmless—until these things possess and consume them. How can we prove to people that God loves them? The power of an undeniable love must draw them like no other.

Someone demonstrated this good news to us, and so we, too, declare it out loud. Salvation is a free gift; we could never earn it and can never pay God back. Therefore, true repentance is not ever geared to achieving a place with God nor regarded as a way of staying right. Our better conduct must be extended out of pure gratitude. They who are forgiven much will also love much (Luke 7:47). Our faith is held by attachment to God. There is no other way.

When I really see how much my Father in Heaven loves me, I will be transformed. Faith acts out of a keen awareness of Christ's redemptive work. This is full, free, and clear, apart from our involvement, and results from the uttermost atonement of our sins. A subtle note distinguishes lives lived in subservient obedience to commandments from lives lived in peace. The Savior's teachings are obeyed as God anticipated; we follow according to His calling. And love responds in kind. We seek to please the One who has saved us.

If we allow life to defeat us, we will grow indifferent toward our neighbors. The times require us to live and interact with difficult people. There is no use in being defensive or offensive. Demanding that others fit into our specifications keeps us from appreciating their worth. Presume they have potential. Respect their short time on earth. I come across many decent and kind people. The good ones help me to tolerate the few bad apples. We should often give others the benefit of the doubt and accept them as they are. You meet few who are so intolerable that you cannot put up with them. We seldom know very much about our friends and why they act the crazy way they do. You and I must prepare for any direction God leads in and energetically bring out more gains.

Time goes on with or without us. The world goes 'round. You have your burdens, and I have mine. Do you know people who withdraw into their own space, floating about, adrift, or hooked on one craze after another? They may be going someplace all right, but they are missing God's blessing. They are losing more than they're winning. With the last diet they were on, they gained more than they lost. God can bless them.

Christians should study the Word of God to help what they know to do. God's love can be perfected in us. We read the story, but can we live it? Here is the rub: love doesn't come from others, and we fall short of it also. Doubt comes in the absence of love. Because of their own contradictions, unbelievers wonder if they are worthy of Heaven.

LOVE BELIEVES ALL THINGS

But whoso keepeth his word, in him verily is the love of God perfected: hereby know we that we are in him.

1 John 2:5

There's a direct connection between salvation and perfect love. If you have been forgiven much, you should love much also. Many Christians feel they are not forgiven much because of their own goodness, or they think they don't have a lot to be forgiven for. Others fear that their sins are too great to all be forgiven. How badly do you want these doubters to be saved and just outright justified? Christ died for every sin of every sinner, so don't you expect to see the love of God in every Christian? Bad conduct in fellow Christians is disruptive, harmful to others, discouraging, and disparaging to the name of Jesus.

The Prodigal Son had an older brother who was all about duty. He stayed at home on the farm. That story was not about him, but it was about repentance and forgiveness, which in itself brings us back to faithfulness and obedience. You and I have qualms about phonies. They look like they're headed for Hell. God knows.

When I get out of sorts or feel discombobulated, I pray. I ask for a fresh start and fresh blessings, and I tell Jesus that I need Him to answer my prayers. Somehow, then, I get a chance to help or encourage someone, and this fills my heart. I come away with a better connection to Jesus than when I started. When this kind of love springs up, I feel like praying nonstop.

When you begin to doubt the reality of Heaven or the validity of faith, take another look at the cross. Absolutely, one only needs to read the narrative of Scripture for the full record of all Jesus Christ went through to accomplish our salvation. Jesus is eternal, yet He died. This is the record. This is inconceivable, illogical, and unexplainable. God wrote it in such a puzzling way that we must accept this truth by faith.

Jesus was entirely righteous, and the sins of the world were unfairly laid on Him. Unbelievable! His divine nature took the ugliness and stench of all impurity from start to finish, from birth to death. Was

Jesus so completely compressed by the weight of sin on Him on the cross that He could not think? He was deserted at one point. He cried, *"My God, my God, why hast thou forsaken me?"* Matthew 27:46. Jesus bore the weight of the Old Law nailed to Him on that cross (Colossians 2:13–14). That which He held perfectly, but which judged sin entirely—every sin ever committed—was all in the Law of Moses piercing Jesus' hands and feet more painfully than words can say. All at once, as life was bleeding from His sacred body, our sin, the Father's judgment, and the law of commandments impaled the Messiah. He took our place.

> *But blessed are your eyes, for they see; and your ears, for they hear.*
>
> Matthew 13:16

Think of those people who directly witnessed the life and death of Jesus Christ and His resurrection from the grave. Even more blessed are those who were not there but believe just as much. You know friends who don't care. Do I just occasionally tell others about Jesus, or do I live to tell others? Love is slowed by our sophomoric hearts. Think about what we have now. You and I have to go the distance to rescue the losers and the lost where they are.

To verify something, you prove the opposite. You have to see that there is a Hell in order to get to Heaven. You must see that you are lost before you can be saved. In math, you double-check your subtraction problem by adding in reverse, from bottom to top. One must see a need before asking for help; see how something is broken in order to fix it. People first see that their future is futile and therefore fatal, and then they look for the answer.

The Bible says we are born in sin, dead in trespasses, without hope, and alienated from the kingdom of God. Trying to obey the Law of Moses was like trying to climb a ladder to the stars. Adding more laws to try to make it work wouldn't help you obey the laws you break any more than adding more rungs to a ladder would help you reach the sky.

> *But that no man is justified by the law in the sight of God, it is evident; for, The just shall live by faith.*
>
> Galatians 3:11

We must prefer to ask God to make a way to Heaven. It is an escape from Earth. There is no hope here. If you look inside yourself, you will find something smaller and of little value. What's in your self is finite. What is in God is infinite. You and I are limited, but the One who made us is unlimited.

People have lots of choices, but God gives us one choice—to believe. We are really at a disadvantage. I think people are gambling all their lives to get them through. The mourners at a funeral celebrate the love of their dearly departed. This lingering love might last or carry them on for now, but it does dissipate in time. It has to. Love disappoints us in life; it cannot sustain us after death. We are mortal, so our love is not a portal. People better look out. They can't see what's ahead.

For us to foresee the worth of Heaven, we must look at the price Jesus paid. We don't know, and what we do know, we might not understand. Nevertheless, God has placed death in front of each and every one of us. Isaiah said, *"The chastisement of our peace was upon him, and with his stripes we are healed"* (Isaiah 53:5). Each of us must reserve the time needed to study and ponder His death and life. To see and appreciate the durability of our salvation, be aware of the standing we have now simply for believing, for we have come to *"the measure of the stature of the fullness of Christ"* (Ephesians 4:13). God the Father expects that we are able to believe it all.

> *For the corruptible must put on incorruption, and this mortal must put on immortality.*
>
> 1 Corinthians 15:53

CHAPTER 4

Increased Faith

And the apostles said unto the Lord, Increase our faith. And the Lord said, If ye had faith as a grain of mustard seed, ye might say unto this sycamine tree, Be thou plucked up by the root, and be thou planted in the sea; and it should obey you.

Luke 17:5–6

I look at trust; it has more muscle than faith. It takes simple faith to believe in God. We don't know much about spiritual things in the beginning. Mastering the Word of God, getting prayers answered, and bringing fruit builds stronger experiences and better expectations. It's one thing to say that you believe. Will love come by itself? Maybe you've had bad experiences. As we begin to rely on life, we get assurance and see what's possible. Life needs to be right. Maturing means we learn to trust love—love that's really real. Increasing faith is no longer satisfied to just say we love, but we want to see.

You can't leave faith alone. Believers want God to make love happen. Think what you could do with a deeper faith. Love is an intentional decision. It's built with trust and truth and grows with time. Will anyone want to come to Jesus if you say nothing? Ask Jesus to increase your faith to show more of His love.

As a boy here in West Seattle, I played on the green wooded hills overlooking the harbor, staying slightly aware of the city's downtown buildings. In my late teens, sitting at a place called Hamilton Viewpoint, I became curious of the adult world across the bay. I felt a lot of emotions as I took the time to sit there and ponder.

In past years, I did my serious thinking at this viewpoint. Late in the evening, I'd watch the distant headlights of silent cars gliding amid the sparkling city lights. The trains run along the waterfront, twinkling in the darkness. Brightly lit cranes load oceangoing ships. They come and go at all hours. The city hums the sounds of industry. From my lookout, it was an exotic mixture.

There is always something going on in Seattle. I've gone in the evening to Hamilton Viewpoint to watch this beautiful city. You can stop in the middle of the night to have a look. When you sit long enough, as I have done many times, you see the resourcefulness of society. The multitude of lights exhibit various interests and the industriousness to build up with complex design and efficiency. I think of the families of all those people—their lives and the many generations.

The city never quite sleeps. I especially remember late nights around the time of the summer solstice. I stayed until the early sunrise awakened the city. I watched the darkness fade and the colors lighten. The night workers go home and the day people go to work.

Jesus made the difference in my life. As a Christian, my thoughts went to prayers: *Where do I fit in? Who am I, Lord? What is life all about?* Praise God, I found the whole answer in Jesus. I didn't know how or see where to get in, but then I found out.

I look out at my city and wonder about the years, the history, and the innumerable lives and their stories. How many of these people know the joy of the Lord? Probably not many. How many are happy? I would say a majority of people are usually happy. Are half as many unhappy? Let's say that you could know which ones on the unhappy side are miserable, troubled, hurting, depressed, and misguided. A smaller number in that group are in critical need, in crisis, and on the verge of losing it all—and I worry about their future. There's a different future for those who are happy and those who are sad.

You may know people who have lost everything. How many are in that small group? I don't know. They're in every town and city. Here's what I am getting at: they want help. A fewer number of those who are chronically miserable and in crisis cry for help; they are ready for help, but don't know where to find it. I find them. At one time, I was in such a state myself, wanting help but not knowing where to go. Jesus came into my life when I was ready, willing, and desperate.

I was only able to find the way to Jesus when I realized I was lost. The modern portable culture takes us far from home and family. There is no way back. People think decisions come from thoughtless impulses, societal influences, or the spiritual domain, as if everything is fed to us. It is conflict and resistance. Time keeps us moving on. Anyway, at the end of the day, average people are made to feel that they have no choice.

People have let themselves think of each other as only a tooth on a gear or a lobe on a cam in a cast-iron machine. We think we are fine just sitting there going around in a little circle. We are finally used up and replaced. Is there nothing we can do to help our situation? The fastest way out is to break down. Throw a wrench into the works. Going bad is all anyone can do to make news. If you go really wrong, that's even better. What's worse is that people act on these urges and strike out. They're alone and on their own. It all appears like a big conspiracy, more than an impulse. Why throw a wrench into it? You can behave yourself. Why not take that wrench out, join in, and fix the system? The very best thing is love.

A growing faith has guided me in making wiser decisions. We can help others with our God-given love. Hope is at hand to believe and to achieve. One must be convinced to be convincing. As a recovering sinner, I have learned to turn hardships around. On tough days, we might feel prone to give in, but we should look to God in prayer.

There's never a reason to fall down. Sadness, sickness, and troubles are all reasons to keep going on. Beer at the grocery store has no magical magnetic pull. People get a weakness for it. Make no excuse to sin. We either shift blame or we take responsibility.

The calamity of life motivates us toward love and faith in hope of righteousness. Trust the Spirit. *"The word is nigh thee, even in thy mouth, and in thy heart: that is, the word of faith, which we preach:"* Romans 10:8. *"How beautiful are the feet of them that preach the gospel of peace"* (Romans 10:15). The answer is offered. The message of God's love is getting out.

Ministry of Prayer

> *I exhort therefore, that, first of all, supplications, prayers, intercessions, and giving of thanks, be made for all men.*
> 1 Timothy 2:1

First of all, it doesn't say pray for only one person. The whole world is our mission field. Pray standing up, sitting down, on your knees, or prostrate on the floor. Do everything you can, and do nothing without prayer. Please—pray intercessory prayers to Jesus for every conceivable person everywhere throughout the whole earth.

God wants *everyone* saved.

> *Who is a God like unto thee, that pardoneth inequity, and passeth by the transgression of the remnant of his heritage? He retaineth not his anger forever, because he delighteth in mercy.*
> Micah 7:18

Every Christian is ordained to advocate for our fellow human beings. Jesus paid the price for every sin. I once passed a church that had a sign out front that said, "The more love we share with others, the more love we have." Anyone can think they can take the wisdom of that modern saying and live it. If the common sense in it helps somebody see more love in life, let it never be without the truth of Jesus and the fact that He shed His blood on the cross. An imagined fanciful "goodness" permits a sense of security and prevents souls from seeing their sin. Love is when the Holy Spirit lives within, when the more we give, the more we have.

It didn't take long after I became a Christian for the gift of prayer to amaze me. One prayer early in my life was answered even before I said "Amen." I was still twenty and praying for a job. God knew I didn't like to work. I was living at the halfway house in Victoria, Texas, when one evening, I bowed my head and prayed. *My money has run out, Lord. I really do need work. I will walk from one end of town to the other. I will look for weeks if that is what it takes, and I mean it this time. But it seems to me that if You give me a job right away, then all the time and energy can be used to make money. I will even shave my beard off if that is what it takes.*

I always felt it was the part about shaving my beard off that persuaded the Lord. My eyes were still closed, my head was still bowed, and I was not finished praying—when the front door swung open. First thing out of Mike Busby's mouth was "Kyle, I got you a job!"

Mike had just been hired for a new job with Dairy Queen, so he told me to go to Car City, the used car lot where he had been working. I was hired the next day, and I didn't even have to shave. The owner's name was Roy. Praying harder got the answer.

A couple days after I had started, Roy called me to his little shack he called an office. He said, "Kyle, you've been working in the heat, so come in and cool off with the air conditioner for a bit."

When I stepped through the doorway, I saw a big guy sitting down in one of the metal chairs.

"Sit down over there," Roy said. "I want you to meet my friend, Block."

Mike had told me about getting cornered by this guy in Roy's office.

Block started in on me about the Bible from Genesis to Revelation. He finished, looked at me and, with his head tipped a little sideways, said, "Let me ask you a question. Do you want to ask Jesus into your heart?"

LOVE BELIEVES ALL THINGS

I told him I was already saved. He looked over at Roy, who shrugged his shoulders as if to say, "How would I know?" It must have been the beard.

Block asked me why I hadn't stopped him. I said, "You sounded so good, I wanted to hear you through."

We were fast friends after that. He came by regularly, always with some great word to share. How did he do it? Soon, I figured out that Block read his Bible every day. So I started to read more, too, until I had something so exciting that I just had to tell somebody about it. In the weeks that followed, Roy's ring of friends dropped by often. We stopped work and sat down in the office. As they shared their stories of faith, I got the burden to witness. Soon I was winning souls for the Lord.

Roy was Southern Baptist and became a real friend to me. He was a little too old to be a brother, but not old enough to be my father. He was a friend. From 9 a.m. until 6 p.m., six days a week, we worked on cars in the Texas heat with no shade. I was not in shape for it. Each morning, I would sit on the edge of my bed while the room spun around. It took five or ten minutes before I dared to set my feet on the floor. Then I walked down the highway to Car City.

Roy taught me more about determination and work than anyone before or since. He never gave up on anything he tried to do. He'd say, "There's really nothing to it. All ya got to do is do it." He had two thick calloused hands always fresh with scabs from fixing cars. He taught me the connection between earning and giving. Most of all, Roy and his sweet wife and their friends were the best examples of Jesus' love reinforcing me with their encouragement.

Roy taught me to be capable. He taught me to work hard and not to shrink back from the challenges. Roy had a car there one day that he could not start. So he tuned it up with his bare hands. He put the key in the ignition and turned it to the On position. Then he stuck a screwdriver in the number 1 spark plug wire and had me pull the fan belt around. I reluctantly rotated it so the number 1 piston came to the top of the stroke, and *bam*—Roy got all the electrical charge in his hand. With his body leaning over the fender, he jumped straight up two feet off the ground. He had me pull the belt the other way, and he jumped off the ground again. Then he said, "Back again." The third time he jumped, he tightened the distributor, and just like that, the car started right up. I had never seen anything like it.

A few years later here in Seattle, an old car of mine ran so rough, it wouldn't start for anything. It was still in the days when I was young and poor, and I found myself desperately working to repair the car in the evening after a long day of work. It was critical for me to fix the car. I planned to go someplace important the next morning. The clock was ticking. The trouble was most aggravating, and I got so tired I couldn't think straight. I tried to figure it out in time to get a neighbor to drive me to the parts store before it closed.

I remembered that my shop teacher had told our class that if we get a problem we can't master and we're working on it too long with a lot of frustration, take a break. He said to go sit down, drink coffee, or do something to get your mind off it, and when we come back, the answer will suddenly be there.

This one time, I had to make the pressing decision to take a break and waste the moment because I was so pushed that I couldn't think right. I just went into the apartment and lay down on the bed for a quick nap. I fell asleep. I woke up after about five minutes—with the solution smack dab in the front of my mind.

The answer was the condenser. *Yes!* I said to myself. I had a condenser with a set of points, and since the car wasn't running, I hadn't put them in. However, the old car was not running because I hadn't put them in. Mechanics always time an engine with it running, but I thought I could set the points by eye before starting the engine; then, with it running, I could turn and fine-tune the distributor by ear.

I ran out the door, opened the hood, and took the distributor cap off. In the middle was the old set of points—so worn that they were welded shut. I put the new points in. Using my feeler gauge for the gap, rotating the engine by pulling the fan belt by hand, I set the cam high on the lobe and attached the condenser. I tightened it all down. The car started right up. I drove it around the block and then adjusted the distributor a little left and right to smooth out the vibration; it ran perfectly.

A problem might be big only because it seems big. My whole car was rendered inoperable by a five-dollar set of points. Big problems can have a quick fix if you can figure it out. Nine-tenths of the answer is in identifying the snag; the cure itself is only one-tenth of the trouble.

It didn't take long for God to grant even bigger blessings to me. After having friends like Roy and Block, I try to return thanks to God through my service. My life continues to be filled more and more with love. I have worked harder and harder to serve the Lord. Yet as much as I try, I can't keep up with His love.

The Salvation of Love

> *For with the heart man believeth unto righteousness; and with the mouth confession is made unto salvation.*
>
> Romans 10:10

Believe in your heart, and love with all your strength. Your head is necessary also, because you hear the gospel with your ears and confess it with your mouth. *"Whosoever shall call upon the name of the Lord shall be saved"* (Romans 10:13). How can you hear if no one tells you? Paul asked, *"How then shall they call on him in whom they have not believed?"* Romans 10:14. Think about it. Where is faith? You hear it. Faith in a heart comes from hearing, and then salvation is accomplished by verbally confessing. We know the love of Jesus and must tell the world!

Susan was twenty-one when I met her in the late fall of 1981. She worked in a preschool where my daughter attended. On one cold dark evening, I saw Susan leaving, so I asked if she would like a ride home; after a short hesitation, she accepted. Once we were in the car, I asked Susan about herself. She started talking, explaining that she felt bound by invisible chains that were of her own making. This ended up being more of a ride home to the Lord for Susan.

I don't remember everything Susan said to begin with, but we had a talk about God. With my little girl riding in the back seat, I took our conversation in the right direction. She later told me that although we were talking about God, she had known that I was a Christian, and she had mentioned Him first in some small way.

Susan said she was mad at God because her dad had committed suicide. You could say she had a load of mixed emotions. Her dad was her hero, but he drank too much and was extremely abusive to her. Then he killed himself. Susan was now living in sin out in the world. I stopped the car and switched on the dome light. She spilled the beans wide open and cried a bunch. She told me how upset she was at God for taking her father from her and from her brothers.

"God is not to blame," I said. "He is your only help. If you push Him away and fight Him, then how can He comfort you? Jesus is your Savior."

She was crying hard. Opening my Bible, I asked Susan to read aloud a passage about God's salvation love. Midway through her reading, she was totally overwhelmed by the Spirit of God as He was coming into her heart. She was sobbing, but managed to finish reading.

We prayed together for her salvation. This, she will still tell you, is when she got saved. She had grown up in a church and believed in God, but had not received Him in her heart.

Susan felt so good after we prayed that she wept like a child. That empty, lost, searching feeling was gone forever. Instead of resentment, guilt, and pain, her faith in the heavenly Father brought intense joy to her soul, heart, mind, and body. She realized He had always been there loving her and had never failed her.

The void inside Susan was filled with real love and forgiveness. She now has a very special love in her heart for Jesus and for all of her family and friends. Other Christians have doubted her sincerity because of her instability over the years. My heart aches for Susan because of her monstrous struggles, yet I am tremendously impressed by her resilient faith. She assures me that God's love is there for her all the time. It's evident how much Susan prays to the Father. Real happiness is attainable for each of us, and life is healed by the progress. God touches us for certain reasons so we may grow and learn. You can lean on Him more and more in confidence.

We are created in God's image. God is never changing, immutable; does that mean that people never change? You have probably heard that expressed. After God made man, He changed His mind about that. Do you recall what God said in Genesis 6:6? God does change His mind, and we can change our mind. Is God able to change you? The answer is—only if you let Him. Have you made a personal decision to receive Jesus into your heart? Then faith does mean something to you. I pray that His love increases in you until you believe with every bit of your heart.

Christians with an applied faith will find out that God lights their inner being. You look at life from a better perspective as you mature. Believers develop in God's wisdom and decide to think happier thoughts. They feel and act new. They have changed their point of view.

You and I want to have a better love. It helps if our temperament is steady. Rejoice in hard times and be all right about things when you are tested. Can you keep that in mind? We are automatically part of the sufferings of Jesus. Think about that when you are accused, mocked, or ridiculed. Would you be ready to die for your faith if you had to? Jesus sets us free from anger, grudges, and revenge. Most of the time, our problem is not the agony of life because many of us enjoy the ease of life. We get so spoiled that it reduces our reliance on God. Riches can be another one of Satan's tricks. We must learn how to grow dependent on prayer whether we are in poverty or in wealth in sickness or in health.

Study the Bible and decide what you could be doing for God. There are boundaries on our responsibilities. The question arises of *how much* we could do for others while taking care of ourselves, our family, and our everyday duties. We can't run other people's lives for them. What can you do? You can make a difference by being different yourself, to make your life better.

Labor that Bears Fruit

> *Be kindly affectioned one to another with brotherly love; in honor preferring one another; not slothful in business; fervent in spirit; serving the Lord; rejoicing in hope; patient in tribulation; continuing diligently in prayer; distributing to the necessity of saints; given to hospitality.*
> Romans 12:10–13

God gave this new life to me and straightened me out. I was young and saw a crowded Seattle and prayed, *Lord, they are out there. Please give me one or two people, as many as I am able to help. I do it for You.* I could have wasted a lot of time trying to teach people who would never have accepted the truth, but there were those who were open. There were also floundering Christians in need of support. *Please help me, God, to find them. You know who they are.*

God graciously answered my prayers to live with a purpose. It's my calling. While holding down a regular job, I have been developing ministry. I work forty hours a week, so I can afford to meet people in the evenings and on weekends and minister to their needs. There is not much indication that I am wealthy by Seattle standards, and I do not often get broader cooperation from other Christians. Since moving back from Texas in 1975 to start, God has been the ever-present guide and provider.

I wanted to start a halfway house here in Seattle to rescue people from drug abuse. The idea never caught the broad interest and support of other Christians. I've talked to all kinds of people about their need for Jesus. I have taught Bible studies, rounded up believers for rides to church, and hosted many meals. After a time, I found myself visiting and picking up friends in various secular treatment programs and halfway houses to come for fellowship. I always tried to take someone with me to visit friends at residential programs, mental wards, and nursing homes. Sometimes, we lead a person to Jesus. We've handed out Bibles and books. We've had impromptu group Bible studies and prayer meetings and made lasting friendships.

I began to see that I didn't need to start my own halfway program. It didn't have to be a structured deal. There are already shelters staffed with professionals and all the red tape. They are often run by unbelievers. I don't have to have a license, inspections, budgets, rules, reports, or even a schedule, and I don't have to have a fire extinguisher on my wall to meet code. Let others do that in their places. A halfway program where people stay isn't what I wanted anyway. I want people to fully recover all the way.

Freelancing with the Lord gives me plenty of time and independence to work. A lot of the time, God wants a deal that is unofficial, Spirit-led, and with no strings attached. Just show up and make friends. We go for rides in the car. We drive to the city parks or go out to the countryside. I bring some people home to my place for a visit. We have gone to visit their families to encourage their unity. We've sorted through the bigger issues of life with them. Many of us remain in touch years later, and we are still at it in many ways, even though we've ended up in different churches in other parts of town or even in other states.

Someone asked me, "How do you make contact with these people?" I just put myself in places where I can make connections. When they accept the help of God, they frequently lead me to other friends in need. I'm just guided by God's grace. "Go out quickly into the streets and lanes of the city, and bring in hither the poor, and the maimed, and the halt, and the blind" (Luke 14:21). God is in this verse.

When desperate souls see one dependable Christian who isn't easily frustrated, they reach out for help and open up. Are you afraid of overcommitting or having them take advantage of you? God protects us and supplies ample provision for the ministry at hand. I want them to take advantage. By talking about Jesus so often, as He is in my heart and on my mind, the crowd gets thinned out. Those who hang on want more. In some circles, a decent friend is hard to find. It's wonderful to meet friends years later who are mature in faith and doing better.

One faithful brother in Seattle is Paul. In the 1970s in what we call the Capitol Hill neighborhood, Paul made a living for many years selling pot—until the local church folks knocked on his door. Paul set out to win his old crowd to Jesus. When I met Paul, he was leading a Friday evening meeting in his apartment. All were welcome. His place had the best fellowship. I don't know of a better example of a Christian who changed so much in life while living in the old environment.

Paul became a carpenter. He took people into his apartment, and it became a regular thing. After having lived in a couple different apartments, he rented a house with the help of the guys. They shared expenses, counseled one another, and grew spiritually. They became a growing group who met together just like a couple of churches. Paul married a like-minded woman from the area, and together, they helped some of the neediest people you'd ever see. It was not a program, but many recovering friends have passed through Paul and Lyn's door. Paul and Lyn opened their cupboards, and they opened hearts too.

We won't necessarily receive anything in return for assisting the disadvantaged. It's too bad that successful folks have so much business of their own already with their homes, families, and jobs.

Neglect leads to helplessness.

We have commitments regarding relatives, recreation, and sports. We have grandparents and grandkids, college and military obligations, political activities, and vacations. These are important, worthwhile commitments. Good folks who are busy have a need to relax more than others. Rest is valuable. Some dedicated believers, though, are looking for ways to cover the needs of hurting people and those less fortunate we need to help.

Suppose you went to a big birthday party for someone special. You would expect to see lots of fun and many presents. Imagine that among the presents, one very special gift is unwrapped. Everybody is taken aback by the generosity. It's very special! You're as impressed as everyone else. That is, everybody except one friend, who later explains to you the ulterior motives of the giver and the scheming behind this exceptional gift. It wasn't apparent at the time, but when you hear of the egotistical intent of this one partygoer, you agree it was definitely poor judgment and pathetic taste. Likewise, it's tragically sad for us if our service to God is predicated on anything less than altruism. It's ministry.

Growing Stronger in Love

We then that are strong ought to bear the infirmities of the weak, and not to please ourselves.
Romans 15:1

God, with His power and preeminence, will raise you up to help the less fortunate. One good reason to maintain our health is to help those who are not in shape. Too many Christians hide behind a list of old cliché excuses. Many times, I've heard church people say they don't reach out enough beyond the confines of their assembly, home, and work. Christians might have a few unsaved friends, but we don't know our neighbors well enough. Sometimes, a ministry opportunity is right in our church, but we miss the signal. If we stay alert to God's leading, we can win souls. Our labors are not in vain when we stick up for those who are truly in need.

Years ago, a mom from the area attended church with her small kids. Her husband never came. I thought that the mom was pretty, but she looked dark and sad. She was depressed and quiet. They were always in church. She looked worried, but she came regularly with her children and sat there with them.

Eventually, the woman stopped coming to church, and it appeared to be the end of the story. She came to church only once or twice after that. I did not think her kids were coming anymore. I heard she was out of the state and being treated for depression.

It oddly escaped my attention over the years that the young good-looking boy in church who sat front and center by himself was from this home. He still lived in the same house with his dad. The boy, Devin, was now bigger.

I had casually admired this guy who came, this boy from the neighborhood who stayed after Sunday school for the worship service. He also came to the Wednesday evening kids' program. I failed to ask about him and hardly noticed him sitting up front every Sunday nor did it catch my attention when he quit. The fact that he stopped coming escaped me.

Now I am sorry I didn't get acquainted. Devin's dark eyes and dark hair were just like his mother's, but I never made the connection. Our church has always had kids who came without their parents. There have been too many children in church for me to keep up with. I try to be friendly with everybody, so I should have known this young boy.

Devin was fourteen when he committed suicide one Saturday afternoon. The dad found his son dead. A letter had come from school earlier that day saying Devin had been caught cheating. There was a father-son confrontation. A few hours later, life was over for this precious teenager.

Devin's parents and his two sisters were left hurting. There was incredible sorrow. They cried for weeks. The pain must've been unbearable. Do you know how hard it would hurt your loved ones if you killed yourself? I pray for this family. Each of us should realize how much we are loved.

A large crowd attended the memorial service. Devin had been in eight different sports and was on many teams for years. He had lots of friends, so many kids and teachers from school and people from all over the area were at the memorial. In our kids' Bible club, Devin had worked on every one of his Awana books and had memorized all the Scripture verses. He loved church. Who knows what this young man suffered that pushed him to his death! Everybody wondered how a sweet guy who was as well liked as Devin could come to such an appalling end. There was a larger family there for Devin after all.

Praise God for the ministry our church has had with this broken family. Who can explain it? If it seems to you like everything is a losing battle, know that Christians have been there all along where they were needed most.

Those at the bottom of society have their pressures. Stubborn problems have long and involved precipitating circumstances that are not easily or quickly remedied. It takes time. *"We then that are strong ought to bear the infirmities of the weak, and not to please ourselves"* (Romans 15:1). Love is helpful. Dramatic improvement may not show in a person's life right away, but love with faith proves the validity of Christianity.

Unhealthy minds build barriers and walls on the outside, like layers of an onion. Defense mechanisms wrapped tightly around and around keep people out and let nobody in. People are unprepared and ill-equipped, but a trained psychologist applies technique to roll back the years of hurt. What do therapists offer if allowed in? Troubled people need credible respect and recognition, and they need to know that you won't hurt them.

Part of Christian ministry is dealing with disappointments. People let each other down. Haven't we all been let down? The hardest cases go from bad to worse. A tough challenge will also reveal our weaknesses. We have places in our own selves where we have more serious work to do.

I told one very troubled young guy, "I have good news and bad news for you."

"What is it?" he asked.

"The good news is I don't think you're crazy," I told him. "The bad news is you're lazy."

In the following years, he married and became a dutiful husband and father.

If you manage to get to the heart of someone, even if they are unhinged, they want to know that someone really cares. If they let someone in only to get hurt again, they will suffer even greater damage and shrink into further reluctance. That rebellion or defiance means they will not let themselves be open again, no matter what.

Life is too painful. What a success when you carefully gain access into someone's troubled world and prove worthy! Trust can be restored. The only thing this person wants to know is that you see them and you'll do no harm. Let them know it and prove that you care.

With help from Jesus and His love, take your time, and you may see miraculous results. God's love makes people want to repent of their sins. People need people. We all need encouragement and support from others.

People don't learn very well how to face what comes. When you convince someone that you are willing to stick with them through their difficult times, forgiving the revolting episodes, they become more willing to see life through. All of the despair is caused by lingering feelings of abandonment, and in adulthood, emotions are exaggerated. Self-deception leads to self-destruction. The heavy scars of steady grief remain permanently painful. Cry, and you cry alone. It's hard. People can be inhuman. We want a better world. Prove reliable and the fever breaks. When you simply stay in effective prayer in the name of Jesus, you may help reestablish **love** with ***faith***.

From Least to Greatest

> *If ye then be not able to do that thing which is least, why take ye thought for the rest?*
>
> Luke 12:26

When we're not doing things to help the world, we're running away. We get anxious. We hate ourselves for what's around us and fail to deal with our own faults. Let's take it from the baseline—admit we're sinners and say that nothing in us is good. The progress needs to be demonstrated in your own heart. Stop blaming others, and start working with them. Each one of us, from the top to the bottom, can trust God for ways to change.

LOVE BELIEVES ALL THINGS

And he sat down, and called the twelve, and saith unto them, If any man desire to be first, the same shall be last of all, and servant of all.

Mark 9:35

It starts with you first. Be faithful with the little things, and God will give you more of the bigger things. We ought to do our best. People freeze in fear. God has a strong hand in this world; nobody stops Him. Why lose sleep? We know the world isn't so kind. I trust that you are growing every day in His Spirit.

It doesn't take long before people see that you are sure in your faith. Christians who are relaxed and secure offer a better life to the grim souls who are harassed by doubt.

Nations rise against nations. A staggering number of closed societies remain uncivilized and estranged from the Spirit of God. How many countries wrestle with unrest? It's around and within. Your security of faith reassures others.

Way back when I was eighteen or nineteen and on drugs, my mother took out a life insurance policy on me. One day in 1977, I got a call from Mr. Hall, the life insurance salesman. He asked me if we could meet to discuss my policy. He picked me up from work for lunch. He told me how much I was paying and he asked what my needs were. I thought that he must be a busy man with more important things to do than fuss with one small customer like me. He was a likable man, but I felt like telling him he didn't have to come to see me if there were no issues. I liked the personal attention, but I didn't want him to waste his time.

His reply caught me off guard. He said his job was to take care of his customers. He had sold enough policies to perpetuate business, and all he had to do was follow up. He called on his customers, explained their present coverage, and anticipated any changes. His territory covered a couple hundred miles. He only had to keep his files up to date. Mr. Hall got new sales when a person would buy more insurance or refer a friend to him, and that's how it worked.

He had a good thing going. I liked it. In the talk we had over lunch, we decided that his company could automatically tap my checking account and save me the chore of writing a check each month. I was glad he came by. I thanked the Lord for him. Not knowing if he was a Christian, I prayed that in some way I had made a good impression on him for Jesus. It was a worthwhile lunch hour.

Later that day, I realized the value in what Mr. Hall had said. His sales technique could work in my life in Christ. Here was a truth from the Scriptures made alive. You live with people all around and coordinate times of ministries for the Lord. A top priority is to relate to Christians. *"As we have, therefore opportunity, let us do good unto all men, especially unto them who are of the household of faith"* (Galatians 6:10). The goal that we know is to have a network of good fellowshipping friends with whom we interact. We share Scripture in the same way that Mr. Hall talked about the benefits of a life insurance policy, such as how much we put in and what we have coming.

The promises of eternity are today's blessings of joy. Just as Mr. Hall explained the value of a policy, so the Bible holds ideas for Christian community. We depend on each other. Needs do come. We tell the good news to friends and make it known that we are here for them.

If the only thing to do is lend encouragement and prayer, we are led by God to visit friends. People like to get together. We also introduce friends to others so they can link up. We must be diligent, knowledgeable, and willing. God's love fills us so that we are ready on time, and the Holy Spirit moves through us when called upon.

If we work at it, we can establish a winning outreach. It's a special blessing from our heavenly Father to gain the trust of others. We must know the Bible as well as we can, follow God's leading, and expect Jesus to orchestrate these adventures. The Holy Spirit also amplifies the prayers we offer up to Heaven. Let us leave no doubt with anyone that we are genuine Christians. You don't want anyone thinking you're phony.

If someone says in their heart that Christianity is out of the question, they're wrong. There have been conversions of sinners.

Should it surprise us? It's a mistake to think some people can't be saved. Are we against salvation? They're the ones God wants.

Mr. Hall was an accomplished salesman. We must be good testimonies for Jesus. With dedicated time, we can practice serving one another—and maybe find a few new customers. Someone will be searching for a way out of trouble, for salvation, and a friend will refer him to you. After seeing the example of Mr. Hall's approach, I worked to be better at my day job and to stay devoted to my ministry daily, and it continues to increase. What you capture with faith and love may be uniquely yours.

Before Jesus Christ came into my life, I never considered any of the places He has taken me—like nursing homes, mental wards, and jails. Do you answer your telephone in the middle of the night? That is often when desperate people call for help. A woman called at two in the morning to talk small talk for a while. I listened. We talked a bit, and she let on that she was thinking about ending her life. She called because she was lonely.

I am writing here mainly about the most difficult types of people to get to know. They are the angry, the blind, the disabled, the elderly, the loners, the misfits, the rejects, the sick, the smelly, and the ugly. They wander all around us. You may be one of these people. We need helpers. You say, "I'm not qualified." If you care, you're qualified to do what you can. To walk this road, it's essential to love, to be accepting of people, and to be patient. Be sensitive. Let's talk in the bravest ways we can. Combine faith and love. Trust in the Lord; it's His way.

Long-Suffering and Doctrine

> *Preach the word; be instant in season, out of season; reprove, rebuke, exhort with all long suffering and doctrine.*
> 2 Timothy 4:2

We have the wonderful message of *love* and *faith* to carry us, enduring to the end. We love God. We are grateful for what He has done by bringing His salvation into our lives, especially since we were less than deserving. We were in the red. Say it and display it every time, in all circumstances, to anybody, at every opportunity. It's work. Let's show our appreciation to God with a full commitment.

> Our ministry in the Lord takes much prayer,
> And such prayers rise when we really care.
> We have more love than we are able to share.
> It is a load we are willing to bear,
> And so an unbroken plea to God we air.

Gladys first came to my notice when Gladys' daughter killed herself. Gladys' husband also had committed suicide some years earlier. I remember what was said about him: he was active in church and nobody saw it coming—yet people said afterward, that all the time, he had been quietly signaling for help.

I got a phone call one evening from Gladys. She had heard about me through the circle of friends, one of whom referred her to me. Gladys was remarried now, and her new stepson, Jeff, was her concern. She talked for an hour on the phone about the young man's many troubled years.

Jeff's life was tragic. Jeff was literally run over by a garbage truck on his way to school in the fourth grade. It crushed his pelvis and left him with serious debilitating problems and a series of operations. In the hospital one night, his brother died in the bed next to him from an asthma attack. His mother suffered with psychiatric problems and died during Jeff's youth. You can see why he had trouble in school.

Jeff's family had taken him to church as a child, but when he had gotten out of hand, his dad took him to see a psychiatrist, just like his mother had seen a psychiatrist. Jeff had been in a mental ward and in a group home for teens. He dropped out of school at sixteen. He had been drinking, taking street drugs, and abusing the pain pills that the doctors continued to give him.

This young man's heartbreaking life was as unhappy and unproductive as it gets. Gladys gave me Jeff's phone number, and

I promised to call him. I waited a couple of days, praying that the Lord would prepare our visit.

We must move or our light will go out. Christians may somehow believe that God is so determined to save the lost that it just gets done. Yes, God works. God is sovereign. Revival won't happen until we conquer our own doubts. The harvest is great, but the workers are few (Matthew 9:37). Our own erroneous thinking is the holdup.

When I called him, Jeff seemed friendly and said he would meet with me. He was twenty-two years old. I picked him up after work and took him out for a burger. I told him that I was not a doctor or a psychiatrist, but I could be his friend. He did not need a psychiatrist "friend" who, for a fee, would quickly write another note for drugs; that type of friendship was not working. He needed a friend whom he could like and trust. His situation was not that uncommon. He was an adult without a real friend. He prayed with me that evening for Jesus Christ to come and save him.

After I took Jeff home, I thought about how easy it had been to win Jeff over. It seemed too good to be true. God told me that if I expected the young man to come to Jesus by faith, then by the same faith, I should be confident of his decision. Instantly, I got a sweet feeling in my heart for believing it.

In church, a notice was posted about an upcoming evening baptism service. I asked Larry, an elder, what we needed to do to get my friends baptized. I had another new friend, Phil, who had come to the Lord when our church ministered at the old downtown rescue mission. I'd stuck around for an opening with someone and won Phil to the Lord.

Larry told me to just show up at church with towels. As soon as they saw us at church on the night of the baptism, a couple of the elders scooped up Jeff and Phil and took them into separate rooms. Jeff and Phil soon returned to the meeting and sat down. A decent message was spoken on baptism—that we didn't have to grow up in the church to qualify and we didn't need to know a lot about Christianity, but we just needed to profess a saving faith. The pastor said we didn't have to be faultless, because we were forgiven. Then a succession of church teens passed through the water. Jeff and Phil stayed put.

I held my seat until it was over, and then I jumped to my feet. My two friends said they were questioned about their smoking. They were asked if I had brought them and if they would be there if it was not for me. Probably not, they said. Neither could they say much about faith. They were told not to participate, no further explanation given.

Right away, I asked them both where they would go if they died that night. They both answered, "Heaven." I asked each one how he could be sure. They each said, "Because I believe in Jesus." My church friends came up to assure me they had seen what the elders had done. They asked me not to overreact. I assured them I wouldn't.

I took my wife out to the car, along with Jeff, Phil, and another friend named Glenn. I then went back in to speak with the two elders who had refused us. They explained why these guys were not ready to be baptized. I was all right with that. I said, "I am here to help fill this church. I go to work forty hours a week so that I can go another forty hours in evenings and on weekends to bring more people to Jesus. Will you help me? If you are unwilling to baptize them now, please work with me until they are ready." That never happened.

I only saw Phil one more time after that. I got him into an apartment with Glenn. I asked Phil to be patient and hang on, but he left. Then Glenn was told at another Christian program that he would never recover. He melted down at the sheltered workshop where he worked, lost his job, and also lost his apartment. Jeff continued to attend church. I even saw him talking with one of those elders at a potluck dinner. We didn't go there much longer though; that ministry wasn't happening.

It was a good church with sound doctrine, and it had a remarkable history here in Seattle. I had made some real nice friends there, but over the course of a few years in the late 1970s, it was the fourth church I had found unsuitable. You might expect to give new Christians a chance. Maybe a lot of people don't change. Maybe I was wrong and disappointed, but I start with the perspective of my own experience, that I had changed with the groundwork of a lot of other Christians.

Life didn't turn around for Jeff. He was soon in another hospital, another mental ward, and another program house. He was on and off the pills he got from more than one doctor. At times, he had a drinking problem. Christians will ask, "How can this man be saved?" I can't help him without better support. The lack of leadership in Jeff's life was hurting him, but he didn't latch on to strong teachers to stick with it. I think a new convert should attract help. Jeff's spiritual growth was dubious at best, but you and I must learn to leave the verdict to God.

Some believers we know can't tolerate or value a backslidden Christian. Alcohol, drugs, and pornography are very serious problems, but so are church elders who are too proud. Congregations tolerate elders who are puffed up in their own goodness, yet reject a novice who is unstable in his ways. But then attendance drops off. We who are strong in the faith ought to support those who are weak in the faith (Romans 14:1, 15:1–3). I am not condoning sin and I am not gossiping, but I am affirming righteousness and service.

I sympathize with my friend who says it is not right to take money and time away from youth programs with good young kids who prove smart, only to sink it into lost causes like Jeff or Phil or Glenn. But can you understand my point of view? Good kids need to be introduced to tougher ministries to prepare them for the world and the future. An ounce of prevention is worth a pound of cure. Get them before they get in trouble.

I got saved in a Christian program, a local effort staffed in part with high school kids and dropouts. With Omni House, we went to schools, churches, and secular service clubs to speak to the community. I was online recently with a friend who was involved in this program decades ago now; she says she got into it not because she had a drug problem but because she was devoted to God and is still devoted. Drug abuse was rampant and robbed our youth. Today, drug abuse kills people of all ages—now more than ever before.

I had hoped Jeff's story was going to have a happy ending. My friend didn't grow as I had hoped he would. He was inconsistent. I tried to help him the best I could. I had him in our home and introduced him to different fellowships. In his late twenties, he was frantically trying to grow up. He was progressively compulsive and angry. He couldn't break out of the gravity of "delayed adolescence," and it was sad. I was sorely wounded in trying to help him. He was short on progress. Unfortunately, in the end, I was most dissatisfied with the more mature Christians. Their lack of attention did little except crush Jeff.

The last time I saw Jeff, he had shown up at four thirty in the afternoon to where I work to hit me up for money. I took him down the street to my car, and while driving him to his place, I told him there was nothing more I could do for him. He was obviously stoned.

I told him, "I don't blame you for the inability to overcome, it's bigger than you. Other people have let you down. I know you have tried." You can disagree. God knows.

Jeff said, "You have always been square with me, you've tried. You have been a true friend. It's not your fault."

We parted as friends. I encouraged him to do his best, but gave him no money. Addiction is tough. It's very, very difficult. It's absolutely real. I'm relieved to know we had that last talk. It was a gift from God for both of us.

Jeff was found dead in his apartment at the age of thirty-two. Our close friend Paul phoned me to say he had been summoned to the morgue to identify the body. In Jeff's pocket was a piece of paper with Paul's phone number. In view of Jeff's erratic life, I had doubts about him. Immediately, in a moment, the Lord gave my heart the same sweet feeling: "You asked Jeff to receive by faith, and with the same faith believe that he did." God blesses me even now with tears; my friend is safe, a whole person now.

My experience in working with drug-abuse problems is that the years of neglect perpetuate these disturbing events. The problems are deeply rooted. It was my friend's father, a Christian man, who was paying the bills all those years, ruining the boy with ungodly doctors whose cure was always the same: "Take these prescriptions and come back next month." A time-out for an honest self-examination can and will prove beneficial. You and I too often see the desperate solutions people dream up. Someone capable should come in to intervene.

We can step in the way of cruel patterns and change the course. With Jesus, we can influence people and lead them to a healthier way of life. Christians do work hard. It takes a huge effort, a lot of time, and a real commitment.

God will lead you to try helping if you will follow through. When a sad person is down, really down, failure certainly accumulates. How are we going to fill such a tall order? We can do so by being a friend. It sometimes takes super endurance to teach another person how to care for himself, how to take responsibility with a car, to help him fill out his income tax form, to tell him to take care of his teeth, to coach him to relate to people, etc. You have to make visits, share meals, buy groceries, and give other essentials.

Looking back, I am glad I took Jeff to visit his dying father who was suffering with emphysema in a nursing home. It was his only visit before his dad died. I also visited his dad there on another occasion with another mutual friend. I've had no hard feelings toward Jeff. God gives these openings for a purpose, and I take my turn.

You don't know how many people have asked me if drug addicts want help, or if they even can be helped. I say, "They want help whether they know it or not." Besides, I want to help. I am more concerned than they are, and I am worried for a safer neighborhood too. Drug abuse doesn't grow on trees. Heroin addicts weren't fated to be heroin addicts. Beggars down on First Avenue weren't born on First Avenue.

Life changes whether you like it or not. You might want to stay the same, but when everything around you moves, you will appear to be different. Change is coming. Can you alter the outcome? You might get blamed if you do nothing about it. Take the blame. If you are sitting in a mess, just tell people it was a mess when you got there.

> *For there are some eunuchs, which were so born from their mother's womb: and there are some eunuchs, which were made eunuchs of men: and there be eunuchs, which have made themselves eunuchs for the kingdom of heaven's sake. He that is able to receive it, let him receive it.*
>
> Matthew 19:12

The old argument between nature and nurture is settled right here in the words of Jesus. We didn't choose the chromosomes we were born with. We can be influenced by other people. Or people can choose some things and decide for themselves. It's obvious.

Change is so slow that you would say it doesn't happen. Watch the minute hand on a clock. Sixty seconds causes *minute* movement of the big hand. Most big things get done slowly, like watching the sun going across the sky.

Unbelief says you can do nothing for yourself. Even without being a Christian, a person can try and do well. People make progress. So why try if it's so hard? We want a better life. How does it occur? The Declaration of Independence explains it: "We hold these truths to be self-evident." It's our duty to remove tyranny and live to serve society. Change is likely. God is good, and there's reward in His work.

It amazes me when I hear people say that there is nothing anybody can do about anything. If that statement is only true sometimes, then it's not true at all. Wisdom sees when to change, when to stay the same, what can change and what can't, and it sees what has changed.

Love is a choice. People can embrace better desires. This is the bug that bit me and made me write all these thoughts. I wouldn't dare say God told me what to write, not totally. Realistically, He seems to have reasonably compelled me, of course, with my willingness. The Scriptures are all about these various factors molding our lives. God has prepared a big place in our hearts for our reactions, our responses, and our true responsibilities.

Love can be a passive verb if it makes the recipient the subject of the love. When *love* is a noun, it is passive, a thing to be described. *Love* can also be an active verb. Is the love in your life active or passive? If you hate the evil of the world, for example, you might find it hard to do things, but you can still feel love and act on it.

Passive love requires an active faith.

Servants of the Lord

And the apostles said unto the Lord, Increase our faith. And the Lord said, If ye had faith as a grain of mustard seed, ye might say unto this sycamine tree, Be thou plucked up by the root, and be thou planted in the sea; and it should obey you.

Luke 17:5–6

Jesus said we only need what little faith we have. If He gave His original disciples a hint more to increase their belief, would it take a lot to obey? Ask yourself if faith can increase. Maybe you'd say set levels of faith are a given (Romans 12:3, 14:1; Galatians 5:22). If we can help someone's unbelief, we should do so. *"Lord, I believe; help thou mine unbelief"* (Mark 9:24). Everyone needs the Lord's help to reduce the doubt.

As a young Christian starting out, I was told I was never going to be ready for service until I learned to be disciplined and mature. I didn't take the advice. I had to win souls to Jesus right away while my head still remembered the old sinful world. God had wonderfully saved me. My conversion was still a fresh recollection. Call it "first love."

I was asked by another elder, "Do you think you can lift others above your own level?" Think about that. I wasn't ready for that question. We could wait and try to be perfect. Jesus told ten lepers to go show themselves to the priests. Read Luke 17:14; all ten were cleansed of leprosy on the way. While nine went to the priests like they were told to do, one leper got excited about it and went back to thank Jesus. If we start out, God works along the way. We are not all the way there yet.

The passage above, Luke 17:5–6, containing "increase our faith," continues on to the next few verses. In fact, although not a trendy passage, the following part brings the needed conviction. It's a big injunction that starts with a little conjunction.

> *But which of you, having a servant plowing or feeding cattle, will say unto him by and by, when he is come from the field, Go and sit down to meat? And will not rather say unto him, Make ready wherewith I may sup, and gird thyself, and serve me, till I have eaten and drunken; and afterward thou shalt eat and drink? Doth he thank that servant because he did the things that were commanded him? I trow not. So likewise ye, when ye shall have done all those things which are commanded you, say, We are unprofitable servants: we have done that which was our duty to do.*
>
> Luke 17:7–10

Serve the Master first. This is your duty. Do this first, and then you can eat later. Love can move mountains. Jesus wants to see to it that every Christian loves exactly as He does. When serving the Lord, we are more powerful than anybody expects.

After a day's work, serve God in your community. You can come back home to your own life later in the evening. Or you can go home after work, sit down to dinner, and then go out to serve God. You can enjoy your own time another day.

If only we could get a better handle on our position and humbly see our station in life! We are the Master's obedient servants. God is the manager. Which is easier: to lift a tree with a wave of an arm and throw it into the sea, or to love? Genuine humility is not impossible, and love is great gain in this world (Ephesians 4:2). We aren't here for ourselves.

God never promised to give us all we ask for, as if He has no discretion. I'm afraid we don't understand Him. Don't take for granted that you're doing everything right. Leave the ninety-nine right now and go find the ones who are lost.

> *I say unto you, that likewise joy shall be in heaven over one sinner that repenteth, more than over ninety and nine just persons, which need no repentance.*
>
> Luke 15:7

There is much to get excited about when one poor, disheartened soul comes home to God. Jesus would assemble the ninety-nine plenty-fine folks to save the one. Some are awfully lost. It takes many hands to help reach them. It oftentimes doesn't seem to make sense for us to squander love on those whose chances grow slimmer. Churches want to attract newcomers who can provide help (like money, naturally), not souls who need help. Whether you are helping a child or a criminal, try to give your extra effort every time.

On the weekend, when you want to take a day off for yourself, give someone some attention. We need to take care of ourselves, but don't be self-indulgent. The world's culture pulls Christians into sin. Research says service is good for your health. You don't have time to feel sorry for yourself if you're meeting the needs of others.

God is our King. We believe, but we don't stop there. Faith comes to understand that God is sovereign. *"Let the peace of God rule in your hearts"* (Colossians 3:15). Notice how God rules in hearts with peace and not by force. Allow Him to rule in your heart. God is perfectly able to govern lives with love.

One of the beauties of the Bible is the way it prescribes the distribution of truth, not forgetting that God paid for our sins and now helps us in life. We love other people in a subtenant way. God doesn't just passively give love. He works through us. We see God's love defined when it's His work instead of our meager efforts.

The tremendous stress and circumstances of life require my very best to go on and live. What does it mean to live if the life isn't making progress? The last enemy is death. My life must last beyond death. I want to do more. I want to have more. What can I take with me? What can I leave behind that is going to last and be worth something? A rocket takes extreme effort to break out of earth's gravity, but *"Who shall ascend into heaven? (that is, to bring*

Christ down from above)" (Romans 10:6). We have the blessing and consent of Jesus, and His Spirit is coming through to others. *Please, Lord, increase our faith and love.*

Sometimes, the people who truly do trust Christ in their hearts don't show real promise because they are slow to grow. God knows they are His. Do they not see our Father's concern for the world? The truly saved person who starts out right, but then falls away because of the allure of the world, social pressure, and personal issues, is no less of a Christian.

Seek God's filling and feel His rejuvenating life. Do you look at the better loving Christians and say that you are not like them and that you feel incapable? God has set us apart, and His love for us is supreme. You must do better than average, if you expect God to move in more remarkable ways. Live your life for Jesus in service to Him.

Jesus Christ looked to the hope of eternity. Did God select a certain few people to save and then forget about the rest? You are special and you are forgiven. Trust in His will and give your life so that others also may believe.

The goal of the victorious Christian life is to fulfill the Great Commission. This is why we see *love along with faith in Jesus Christ* as the principal thing. It is the very most winning combination. God had it in mind for Christians to believe all these things.

> *For whether is greater, he that sitteth at meat, or he that serveth? Is not he that sitteth at meat? but I am among you as he that serveth.*
>
> Luke 22:27

Our Prerogative

Do everything in love.
(1 Corinthians 16:14)

CHAPTER 5

The Approach of Christ

We love him, because he first loved us.
                                   1 John 4:19

God has a new approach in Jesus Christ: it's love. It's correct to say that we didn't love God; He came to us. Now we love Him with this new love. Our love was not His love. From the start, God is above us in everything—righteousness, strength, and wisdom. His thoughts and ways are higher than ours (Isaiah 55:8–9). He loved us first. God took the initiative so we can be open to love others.

We have all been at a loss. How does God decide who to pull from this world and who to leave in sin? God loves each and every one of us the same. Did God in His plan decide our fate back in the beginning or even before that? God is sovereign. You can guess how far back. Imagine—back in time immemorial.

God ordained the judgment to be centered on the cross, and a decision rests in us. When is judgment day? It is in the future. Eternity is yet to be decided. God calls on all hearts today. We must define *faith* and *love* together here in this study.

Before time began, long before anyone appreciated God's grace, we weren't in the least bit deserving; Jesus was destined to give His life. *"He first loved us"* 1 John 4:19.

Judgment carries a load of condemnation for a sinner. God strikes fear in the person strictly out of His concern to save. People seldom see this point. We are not ever saved by our good deeds nor rejected from His kingdom for our bad deeds. It's not our righteousness that counts, but His righteousness. *"The goodness of God leadeth thee to repentance"* Romans 2:4. He is ahead of us here. God works His will in our lives after we receive His Holy Spirit. True repentance acknowledges the sinfulness, which Christ turns to godly character.

Wisdom places things in the right order. Everyone has temptations. Christians can be the first to help those who flounder, when the sinner needs it the most; God wants you and me to step in with prayer. This is something we do. We live by faith alone, and love doesn't need to be repaid or rewarded. With no visible sign, we read and believe the Bible and act on it. The responsibility is with us.

Jesus Christ accomplishes His will every day. Ask yourself how much of your world is transformed. His Father's will was accomplished on the cross. Fix in your mind that God was the first to love so that you can love. Everything else will follow.

> *But God commendeth His love toward us, in that, while we were yet sinners, Christ died for us.*
> Romans 5:8

Without exception, every biblical doctrine has to come together here. Judgment pivots on this point—Jesus bore our sin for us on the cross. The crucifixion and the resurrection are the most potent events in history—even in all eternity—including from eternity past to eternity future. The everlasting Father gave His only begotten Son, whose body they laid in a tomb. Since the Holy Spirit raised Jesus for our justification, all those who believe and take hold will

Some people are afraid to pray. Do they think God can't forgive them? So if this is stuck in their head it won't come out. What's not said is Christian's slim view of a sinner's way of life.

Our Father gives His unfailing love, filling us with His Holy Spirit. God's Word leads us to the safest place with Him. Christ not only came to save believers from damnation, but He also came to move us from alienation to intimacy with God.

You know Him by following Him to the foot of the cross. Buried in baptism and raised in His likeness, you live in the world each day in just the same way as He lives right now in heaven.

> *He that believeth on the Son hath everlasting life: and he that believeth not the Son shall not see life; but the wrath of God abideth on him.*
>
> John 3:36

We had the wrath of God bearing down on us. We didn't begin as believers. God's love is the catalyst in this formula, and it prompts a response. The moral of the story is to give God's love to the lost, even if they loathe you. And suppose they might love you.

The cross is like a prism separating light into colors. Believe it or not, man's free will and God's sovereignty strike the crucifixion to give a verdict. This is what God is doing here: he has created a situation. The outcome is either salvation or damnation. Here are the four most critical concepts surrounding the crucifixion of Jesus:

1. Our Father's sovereign plan is revealed.
2. Man's free will is shown for its real worth.
3. The way to Heaven is offered.
4. Mankind's rejection of hope is their condemnation.

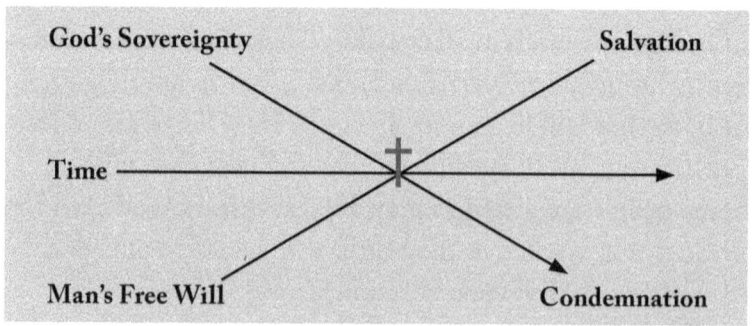

To better understand any one precept in the Bible, we should compare it with the complete look of Scripture. If we mess with an important doctrine, our entire theology slides sideways. We want no detours. Take God's words from the pages and apply them to your life in practicable, loving ways.

The teachings of the Bible are relationship with Life Himself. Believers who read the Word of God and love Jesus faithfully see the broader picture. The Church belongs in this present age. All is arranged to illuminate the power of God's love. Unlike in Adam's time or in Moses' time, love is inexhaustibly complete in our time (Ephesians 3:9–11). Jesus certainly loves each of us all the way, from beginning to end. This is what this study is about. Jesus is Lord. He is one with the Father, totally equal. He created all of this for love. The amazing grace of God, even if half hidden, is shown by the glory of believers in the name of Jesus.

The Sovereignty of God

Blessed is he, whosoever shall not be offended in me.
Matthew 11:6

Lost souls are often offended by one little mention of the name of Jesus. It's okay to say "God" to people, but don't say "Jesus." Their old nature resists. We all shy away at times. The only hope in life is Jesus Christ. All who believe and receive are saved from their sin. *God* is spelled with a big *G*, and we are only people, spelled with a small *p*. Blessed is the heart that is not ashamed to say that Jesus Christ is Lord God.

God sits above the confines of time and sees everything all at once. He anticipates our salvation. God decides who to save. How does He differentiate one of us from another? I see now that God's hand worked in my life in a special way, especially in the months just before I was saved.

God's foresight has never prevented anyone from coming to

Christ. The Bible says that the judgment day is ahead. In our time-bound perspective, judgment day has yet to occur. We believe that God is working the same in everybody's life, at all times, and in full. The One who knows all never acts arbitrarily.

God's decrees are right. He rules with indisputable power. There's no reason for people to fight God. We even work against love. Why fight what's right? Everybody tries to run their own lives. It's hard to deny that God is there, hard to argue with His wisdom or His Word. Those who go with another plan outsmart no one but themselves.

The Father in Heaven is sovereign. He chose the way to save us. With whom did He consult? We read about Jesus' time on earth and glimpse a bit of God's heart. We study the life of Jesus and wonder about His death, burial, and resurrection. He converts us from sin to righteousness. Jesus is "seen" in prophecy; we interpret the Bible in its own words as a whole and learn from it. The Bible gives the direction to the one and only hope in life; our Father in Heaven sent Jesus because He loved us so completely.

> *For the promise is unto you, and to your children, and to all that are afar off, even as many as the Lord our God shall call.*
>
> Acts 2:39

God first called Israel to believe, and then the gospel came to the whole world. Who has God called? Only Israel? Only the few? The verse speaks of the promise *"to all"*; that is to say, it is *"to all that are afar off,"* to the Jews first (this is very important) and then to the Gentiles. We can count on God's promise to Abraham. It's the good news. People are hearing it.

> *And the times of this ignorance God winked at; but now commandeth all men every where to repent.*
>
> Acts 17:30

Look at this verse. It's a statement of God's commandment. Not everyone comes, and not every Christian, sorry to say, understands this to be a blanket calling, but it's the New Testament in the blood of Christ. God commands the whole world to repent. His call isn't just to a few, but to all. This mandate remains today. Why would anyone think God cannot be sovereign and give us a free will; we can accept or reject? We sin freely, obviously; all a sinner has to do is to take the free invitation to salvation. It's not only imperative to give out the good news—our testimony is necessary as well—to tell others out loud.

> *For the grace of God that bringeth salvation hath appeared to all men.*
> Titus 2:11

God gives this offer to everybody, but not everyone is open to it. God hasn't ever lost control. He draws everyone, but He gives each of us this choice. Does it take anything away from God? He is honored. He doesn't give deference to any one person over another. Go read the record as found in Deuteronomy 10:17; 2 Chronicles 19:7; Job 34:19; Acts 10:34; Romans 2:11; Ephesians 6:9; Colossians 3:25; and 1 Peter 1:17. We were lost, and the Father sent Jesus to bear our sin and guilt in His death. Sinful as we all are and saddled with our lower nature, God leaves it strictly up to us to ask Jesus in.

Life tests us to see what we are made of. God is there and we have our life. We each suffer here for sin in this world. Everybody wants an out. Don't we suffer from the sins of others also? You wanted a way out, and so does everyone else. You would think so.

Our Maker knew us well enough to predict a result when He offered us salvation. Jesus *"was foreordained before the foundation of the world"* 1 Peter 1:20. He made provision for our sins and paid for them Himself, but I don't think He decidedly bent us into shape. Instead, God loves us. Do you think the God of love would send His Son to die as a blood sacrifice to recover us, and then press us into submission? Our Savior said, *"And I, if I be lifted up from the earth, will draw all men unto me"* (John 12:32). Is God's choice of whom

He is going to save decided apart from the cross? You and I react or respond that is, all men, everyone.

God *"so loved the world"* (you can insert your name) that *"he gave his only begotten Son"* for you (John 3:16). Jesus is now preparing a home for us, with His love and it's already paid for.

The way some Christians think, we have no decision in the matter because, they say, God is King and is totally sovereign, in charge. They say, "Since He made us, He made faith in us too." God is in charge and made the world as He did, but He is not the author of sin. So why the sin? They say we're handpicked by God, and "That's that." Then why? Do we deserve Heaven? No.

God sure rejects far more people than He receives. None of us had ever done one thing right. We should know God *"hath chosen us in him before the foundation of the world"* (Ephesians 1:4). They put a lot of stock in their own worth. We didn't sin before the foundation of the world. Think, "If God has chosen Christians ahead of time, how did He decide whom to choose?" These people admittedly don't know! "What criteria has God applied if it is not our goodness or superiority?" My reply is *"Today is the day of salvation"* (2 Corinthians 6:2) and *"Whosoever shall call upon the name of the Lord shall be saved"* (Romans 10:13). God gave us free will and a decision to make.

A few unbelievers think they have been left out on purpose; just ask them. Lust is their issue and other sins. The Scriptures repeatedly say that we are not judged by our behavior, our sin, or our goodness for salvation. It's His goodness, His favor, and His grace. We have this whole freedom to come because God is Lord; this isn't in question. He protects this idea. While His forgiveness is powerful, remember that God made the rules.

The standing commandment in the words of Jesus is to *"Love the Lord thy God with all thy heart"* (Luke 10:27). Our longing for God is a steelyard of righteousness. With our hearts we believe, and with our mouths we confess (Romans 10:9). We are *"fearfully and wonderfully made"* (Psalm 139:14). God's plan in creation called for a family to be like Him, just like Jesus—and He made no mistakes along the way. We need to show this love to others.

Made in His image, we were given a conscience and a free will by God. (Some may balk at the term "free will" because they defend the doctrine of eternal security. Please don't confuse this with Arminian theology, which says we freely accept Christ and so can freely drop Him.) We decide, feel, hate, love, think, and repent. Our loving Father never alters our humanity; He defines humanity as He secures us in His plan.

Christ Jesus is *"the man,"* the only mediator who could save us all (1 Timothy 2:4–5). The last thing God will do is force people to believe. Every knee will bow and every tongue will confess that Jesus Christ is Lord (Philippians 2:10–11). Jesus is Lord. He calls us "the Church," as a group. The Father confers all judgment to Jesus (John 5:22). God *"hath put all things under his feet, and gave him to be the head over all things to the church, which is his body, the fullness of him that filleth all in all"* (Ephesians 1:22–23). God has chosen "us" (Ephesians 1:4) and "you" (plural) (John 15:16), which never ever annuls an individual's "response-ability" in the least.

God does not make hearts already with faith, but He makes them all ready for faith. He does not place faith in our hearts, but He places in each person a heart able to see.

In His sovereignty, God chose the nation of Israel as an example to the world. With Moses, God said He would punish sin and reward obedience. The religious leaders at the time of Jesus' very much expected to please God by their good works. God first showed the Israelites their inability to keep the Law of Moses, wherein there was mercy if they turned to Him, but it was at the appearance of Jesus that they failed big time and they nailed Him to the cross. They unjustly handed the Lord Jesus Christ over to foreign oppressors who together drove Him outside Jerusalem and, with more cruelty, crucified Him. Israel rejected their Savior. Jewish priests, rulers, and a Roman centurion with soldiers stood watch at the crucifixion.

> *Him, being delivered by the determinate counsel and foreknowledge of God, ye have taken, and by wicked hands have crucified and slain.*
>
> Acts 2:23

Israel performed the will of God, though they did not understand what they did. By their own wicked devices, they condemned Jesus to death. God chose this nation of Israel to be His people for a reason. They killed Christ. At times, Israel pleased God. He loved them. At other times, they rebelled and angered Him. How frightful it must have been to have been punished directly by God! God was prepared for their sins, though, and made provision. Even when Israel rejected their Savior, God knew that too. If all people are liars, does that make God untrue? Ultimately, Jesus was in the hand of His Father.

The dull Jews expected God to magically remove their enemies and bring peace. Make sure you know your Bible well. "*Study to shew thyself approved unto God…rightly dividing the word of truth*" (2 Timothy 2:15). The book of Romans was written to separate the New Law from the Old. Chapters 9–11 expose Israel's efforts to justify their ways. In Romans 9, Paul dismisses the letter of the Law to embrace the Law of faith. Compare Jacob and the Jews to Christ and Christians. God hasn't changed; love is the New Law.

When God loved Jacob and hated Esau, it wasn't an illogical whim. Judgment is not in question. It's foundational. Works becomes the direct opposite of faith and grace. Paul's point is that it is "*not of works*" Romans 9:11. He rightly divided the Scriptures in two—in half, as God put it, from the Old to the New Testament, from Jew to Gentile, and works versus faith.

> *He took his brother by the heel in the womb, and by his strength he had power with God.*
>
> Hosea 12:3

Even when he was in the womb of his mother, "*by his strength*," Jacob had real pull with God. This indicates and illustrates how God saw Jacob's desire. Even now our strength of faith has "*power with God.*" (By the time it's all over, everyone will know God is on His throne.) There's a gigantic jump in Romans 9 from the self-righteous rebellion of the Jews to finding righteousness in the Gentile church because through faith in Jesus, we are heard.

A lot of the wording in Romans 9 deals with how God judges people. Israel ignored the heart of God. Religion became a custom. They were too anxious in their sorry inability to follow the letter of the Old Law. That is the very reason they fell into decline, and ultimately, "by the determinate counsel and foreknowledge of God" (Acts 2:23), they killed Jesus. These are two opposite implausible things. Jesus came to save them, to forgive them, and His own people would not receive Him.

Paul stressed in Romans and in all his letters how Israel as a whole did not seek righteousness by faith. What, then, is faith? It's the reverse of external conformity to the written code. It is not faith in one's own self or in one's own capability. Faith rises in the soul with unhesitant trust in God's guidance and provision. The Old Law condemned. We are justified by faith in the blood of the New Testament. Paul shows over and over, the disparity between works and grace, just as far as between sin and righteousness.

God could never move away from His inherent righteousness, not one iota, jot, or tittle nor surrender His perfect sovereignty, not one bit. God had the difficulty of turning us back from sin while defending the precious free will He gave us in the beginning. How could He save us? Jesus declared, *"For many are called, but few are chosen"* (Matthew 22:14). God calls all. This is not commonsense. There is something in us He looks for.

Jesus is the Judge. By what one method or standard does He retrieve anybody or reject others? If He allows one person into Heaven, He opens the door to all. *"God hath dealt to every man the measure of faith"* (Romans 12:3). Has God picked you or me because we are nicer than someone else? He didn't make us any better than He made others. In God's supreme plan, in His great love and wonderful wisdom, He orders that anyone who willingly receives Him receives complete pardon of sin and then is given eternal extensive reward.

Free Will

> *But Israel, which followed after the law of righteousness, hath not attained to the law of righteousness. Wherefore? Because they sought it not by faith, but as it were by the works of the law. For they stumbled at that stumbling stone; As it is written, Behold, I lay in Zion a stumbling stone and rock of offence: and whosoever believeth on him shall not be ashamed.*
>
> Romans 9:31–33

It was odd to hear a radio preacher say, "You must believe God is sovereign! You aren't trusting God if you depend on your own decision and your free will to be saved." He contradicted himself right there by saying that you have to trust God. It is our call.

Paul was writing about Israel and the Old Law. What it had to do with faith was Israel's obedience, it was their willingness to comply or to rebel it was their downfall. Sounds to me like a choice, sort of like faith means a decision to obey the gospel.

Here is the bottom line of Romans 9: "*Whosoever believeth.*" You can see it here in the King's English: it is free will. Any "*whosoever*" applies to Jews and Gentiles alike, we are held to the rule of Romans Chapter 9. Yes, we must do something. We definitely have to believe. "Believe" is the verb. The predicate "*believeth*" is what we do. You and I make that decision resolutely and aren't ashamed of it.

Jesus didn't say, "God so loved the world that He gave His only begotten Son, and whomsoever He chooses." He didn't say that. Jesus said in John 3:16, "*whosoever believeth in him*" lives forever.

Paul wrote "whosoever believeth," of Israel or anyone, won't be ashamed. It's difficult today to see what a big culture shock it was for the Jews, who saw themselves as "God's chosen people." They were the chosen ones. Then some Gentiles got obviously saved.

Jewish Christians tried to stay in Israel and pin the Old Law on the new Gentile believers. Paul wrote to Rome to warn of the danger of this course to emphasize the fact that Israel no longer fit the program, particularly since their program had ended.

Jesus changed the discussion. It's something we want. *"Blessed are they which do hunger and thirst after righteousness"* Matthew 5:6. We hunger and thirst. God is good. We want salvation.

We see the world make sin fun, like it's good, "Stolen fruit's sweet." Has it escaped everyone's notice how many times people actually want to do right to have a good life? If the truth be known, most of us want to do good. We should say so. You and I understand what is best more often than we practice.

> *What shall we say then? That the Gentiles, which followed not after righteousness, have attained to righteousness, even the righteousness which is of faith. But Israel, which followed after the law of righteousness, hath not attained to the law of righteousness.*
>
> Romans 9:30–31

As Christians, we wrestle with faith as well as with our conduct. What son is not corrected by his father? I don't think that anyone could choose to reject the Savior if they understood Him and saw His grace right in their own sight. Would you give up your place? God loves people. Jesus *"is able also to save them to the uttermost them that come unto God by him"* (Hebrews 7:25). Follow this, we come to God. See the new principle of the *"law of faith"* Romans 3:27. Believe and come to God; He will come to you.

You don't have to live in fear of commandments, condemnation, or temptations. We try to obey. *"For what I would, that do I not; but what I hate, that do I"* (Romans 7:15). Saul was a zealous Pharisee, and he was also a failure at that. He knew it. The good news is that we can live the way God wants us to. We can live the way we want to. This new life, the new mind, appeals to us.

God's approach is inviting. It's love. There is willful sin with you and me and a lack of willpower. This is why we gave our hearts to Jesus. He overcomes.

Your faith and mine is very much separate from the Old Law. How did we come by our faith? People need a genuine faith if they want to meet God. Having a huge faith helps even more because this world pulls hard. In Jesus, it isn't works righteousness; it's faith. It's New Testament. *"This is the work of God, that ye believe on him whom he hath sent"* (John 6:29). Heaven was opened wide by Jesus' birth, death and resurrection. There's no denying the truth.

The Scriptures put sunshine on the seed of faith and warms the ground. We've had to ask Jesus in. Each person must believe to receive; there's no other way and nobody else.

Paul was a minister of the New Covenant. It's essential to see how this Apostle systematically outlined theology in the Old and New Testaments. He layered verses with verses, positioned Jews and the Gentile Church separately. Romans 9 puts the spotlight on Israel. *"They sought it not by faith but"* (Romans 9:32). Paul said, if possible, he would have left his soul in Hell to save his countrymen, Jesus had given His own life. Paul recognized Him, *"a stone of stumbling, and a rock of offence"* (Isaiah 8:14 and Romans 9:33). But to the disobedient and guilty, to the stubborn-hearted (1 Peter 2:7–8), Jesus meant death to them.

God places the truth of Jesus Christ in our way. He waits for our answer. In that case, faith begins with us. We admit we are hopelessly depraved, and we turn to Jesus for mercy. This is the plan of salvation. He gives this decision to us. The sinner brings glory to God. We are created in His image. Our faith now brings His glory to us.

God commands all to love Him. That means we must draw close and desire Him. As virtually foreseeable, we have it from Him—a free will. There is no doubt about it!

Our heavenly Father wrote the plan of salvation to give it outright to the Church. It is like the mathematic laws we learned in school. In junior high, it took a step of faith for me to learn the rules of algebra since I thought algebra was abstract. We had repeated exercises in solving problems. How did they fit? For example, algebra says that a positive number multiplied by a positive number always produces a positive. I was good with that. But a negative multiplied by a negative produces a positive. Then, if a negative number is multiplied by a positive number, the product is negative every time. These things made no sense to me.

In an equation with a small negative number, such as -2, multiplied by a very large positive number like 1,000,000, the answer will still be -2,000,000. Why doesn't a big positive number get the little negative one out of the doghouse? God made us. He made us with a free will. Is free will a negative idea to you? When the decision to believe, predicated on the free will of a mustard-seed faith, is multiplied by God's immense omnipotence, logic says that God definitely gives us a powerfully huge free choice.

To get along in life, sometimes we have to solve problems with our understanding, and sometimes we must use the instructions. I have to use the reverse gear in my brain to try to understand why the lowest score wins in the game of golf.

John the Baptist exclaimed, *"He must increase, but I must decrease"* (John 3:30). Humility works best with less. Faith is our decision, without visual perception, to rest securely in the Lord our God. The Bible says, *"God is love"* 1 John 4:8. Solomon said in Proverbs 3:5, *"Lean not unto thine own understanding,"* because we have to trust.

We are too human. A young man is not going to win a woman's heart by telling her that God told him to marry her. What is free will without righteousness? We sin. God doesn't force our love or obedience. You and I should feel the same way as He does.

Some Christians are afraid to own up to a free will, and they run from the idea that individual converts decide of their own volition. The same teachers turn around and warn against sin, as if we can stop it. They take a stand on compliance and obedience. We need God. He made our hearts for faith. Please understand how God works in us to obey Him. You and I choose our eternity, and after that, hopefully, we will influence someone else's future practices.

Many Christians say God, in His sovereignty, decided/elected who is to be saved. Would God in fairness have us think we choose to believe only to find out when we get to Heaven that our faith is ultimately His prerogative? These Christians say the doctrine of election is incomprehensible, like the doctrine of the Trinity, with conflicting ideas that are separate but true at the same time. That's what they say. Is it just semantics? It's not taught in the Bible. God wants to reach us to teach us. You and I do want to learn. We can't teach those who won't learn. Believe in the "plan of salvation" that puts the ball squarely in our court. God persuaded us to be willing. Remember, He loves us.

God wants everyone back. Suppose our individual salvation was prearranged, like Calvin, Knox, Luther, and others said; that would be catastrophic, to my definition of faith. My idea of what it means to disobey, repent, and abide would have to be readjusted. If God's sovereignty actually controlled the choice in my heart, my idea of love would have to change too. From my perspective, that twists the word *faith*. People connected to John Calvin brutally killed somebody who was dissenting. The Doctrine of Calvinism claims that sinners are so depraved that the choice to believe could not come from us. Did I hear that right? God's love is not autocratic or unemotional, but it is wonderfully affectionate. His caring nature compels a response.

It shakes me up to see Christians differ strongly, at times violently. John Calvin had an impact. Look it up. If God chose us before the beginning, why does the Bible place the judgment day afterward in eternity, beyond the end of the world? Look it up.

God is not the author of sin nor does He lead us into temptation. He commands all to repent. He grieves when we don't see. What registers with you? All these years, I have seen my life in Christ as a very willing, personal, and mutual relationship. The word *faith* denotes a cognizance of responsibility. Does God decide who is going to be a Christian before we get a chance to believe on our own? God is not a bully. He wants His love to be returned in kind. Jesus said we are His friends, not His servants (John 15:15) because we know His plans. Since the beginning of time, God has allowed everything to happen as it has. God intends for us to have an understanding, give our consent, and to accept Him.

Jesus promised to fulfill all things. Jesus, *"the author and finisher of our faith...is set down at the right hand of the throne of God"* (Hebrews

12:2). That is not to say, though, that the author of faith compels each person to fall in line. God commands and we obey.

We look to none else, only God. I believe what Paul wrote: *"because we trust in the living God, who is the Savior of all men, specially of those that believe"* (1 Timothy 4:10). Not every person believes, because that's their decision.

God could not accept anybody today by works in the Old Law. There was never enough good in any of us. Can we boast in anything such as intelligence, power, strength, or wealth? This is not a beauty contest. By this world's standards, there are too many issues and differences to judge by. He who is Judge either condemns or forgives—not randomly, but fairly. God has done absolutely everything in His power; we must grab on. Our decision is the mandate of the New Testament.

It is our faith that counts. How many times does the Bible have to say it? The Philippian jailer asked, *"Sirs, what must I do to be saved?"* Acts 16:30. If God did our thinking for us, we would all be saved in a second, and we would be obedient too. What must you do? Let's be honest. We have our free will, although far too often, we exercise it in a poor way. God wants us to exercise our free will His way, in the best way. The jailer was given the answer, easy: *"Believe on the Lord Jesus Christ"* (Acts 16:31). Salvation was predicated on his believing, The jailer (subject) had a responsibility to believe (predicate). It was his choice, (prerogative). His salvation was predicated on his believing.

The original sin of Adam brought sin and death upon the human race, so sin is the issue. After Adam, everyone was born enslaved to sin and can only be set free by God.

No one was bound to get saved. All of us were bound for Hell. Born of a virgin, no inherent sin, yet Jesus learned obedience, Hebrews 5:8), was perfect in all His ways. His righteousness canceled the power of sin, giving His life, saving us from death.

With the Old Law removed at the cross (Colossians 2:14), we are face to face with God. The only question left is: Do you believe? God's holy and sovereign position stays intact, while man retains his free will. Amazingly, at the same time, the shed blood of Jesus atones for everyone's wrongdoings.

Everybody is lost. Everyone has the same potential to get saved. Yes, God has elected us, but to win elections, you have to enter the race. How would faith and salvation look at the start of it? We want God. *"Seek, and ye shall find"* Matthew 7:7. Many of us who came out of a distressed and starved background thirsted and thought God was there. We expected He was benevolent. *"He is a rewarder of them that diligently seek Him"* (Hebrews 11:6). What a wonderful thing God does! I was aimless, lazy, and lifeless, but now my days are full.

Salvation

> *For the which cause I also suffer these things: nevertheless I am not ashamed: for I know whom I have believed, and am persuaded that he is able to keep that which I have committed unto him against that day.*
>
> 2 Timothy 1:12

"I am not ashamed." The phrase is packed. Paul was not ashamed; he believed. Paul was persuaded and was committed. God was committed to him. Who would be ashamed of the gospel? Some view God suspiciously since He will send them to Hell. They think God is hostile. They expect God to take away any fun, rob them of all rights, and punish them for their thoughts. We prefer to look at God in a positive light. Not only do unbelievers fight God, but they make life harder for the rest of us.

> *To declare, I say, at this time his righteousness: that he might be just, and the justifier of him which believeth in Jesus.*
>
> Romans 3:26

Here it is again: "him which believeth." The "him" here is me, and guess what I do? I believe. In the days before I was saved, I was very burned out on drugs. *Burned out* is more than a phrase. I felt dead. I saw myself going to the gates of Hell, feeling the heat and smelling the sulfur. Even then, God still believed in me.

My friends and I wanted out of sin, and we struggled to find a way out of the pain. We were confused and wanted help. Isn't that clear? Those temptations were sucking us faster and faster down the drain. The world is tricky, sin blinds, and the devil snares us in his old net. Did you have a time when you were falling and thought you were a goner? Jesus had to be my salvation, or it was all over for me.

God was pulling hard on me, but so was the lure of lethal sin. Right when I sank to the bottom, drowning, and couldn't find the bottom, I saw God's hand reaching out. When I was a little boy wading in a lake, I slipped off an edge, and the water was over my head. There was no footing, and I couldn't swim. My dad quickly jumped in to save me. Without God, there's no hope. At a proverbial turning point, the choice had to be made in my heart.

I was at a crossroads. I was standing in the crosshairs. I had been young and gullible. In 1969, drug dealers walked the streets in the University District, openly calling, "Acid, speed, weed." I didn't see the danger. After two and a half years and nearly fifty acid trips, my mind was going to snap so permanently, it was not even funny. By 1971, my world turned heavy psychedelic ugly. There were more rising trends like cults, heroin, homosexuality, pornography, and Eastern religions.

Temptation drew strong on me, but so did God right then. After I heard the word of truth, I trusted, and after I believed, the Holy Spirit sealed my salvation permanently. God has promised to "save to the uttermost" all who will come to Him by faith in Jesus (Hebrews 7:25). I think a lot of Christians are in denial about how much sin has tempted them.

> *In whom ye also trusted, after that ye heard the word of truth, the gospel of your salvation: in whom also after that ye believed, ye were sealed with that holy Spirit of promise.*
> Ephesians 1:13

Christians have the confident assurance of eternal life. You can say that we are predestined of God here, for it's now a promise. Salvation isn't complicated. Skeptics think the hope of Jesus is too sketchy to be certain. They dismiss us. That sounds convoluted. From out of the blue, people affix stipulations and insert egregious regulations that put you into the red. To simply believe and be secure is inconceivable to everyone.

It should be difficult to grasp eternity. It's not plausible that the great riches given in salvation are free. What's the problem? Here's the knock: "easy believism"—but don't be put off. Simple faith is producing good Christians.

God knows how hard it is for each of us to cut loose from the old ways of sin. Unless you have kicked drug addiction, you don't know what it's like. That's what it's like to repent and beat sin. If you think that to quit drugs, all you need to do is simply stop taking them, you're wrong. It's not that easy. It starts a fight. Withdrawal hurts. It goes against us hard, against all we have inside of us. To flee to Christ is just that—escape; it's hard. To emerge from the corruption, one must expect something exceptional in the future—like Heaven itself. The goal of our faith is more than eternal life; it's love.

We started out in God's image. Then our minds were deadened by sin. What dark thoughts still haunt there! God accords us a lot of credit for trying. Our Savior knows the distance we cross to move into faith. He restores us to the loftiest position with Him and affords us huge rewards, all because we come to Him. God gives us His very greatest love because our human faith is the whole thing to Him.

God draws us with the magnetism of His engaging presence. His approach has never been to compel anyone to believe. He does not "predestine" unbelievers to be saved. God brought His plan more down to earth than that.

You can diagram the different models people have of theology. If in advance God granted us predestination when we were ignorant, settled it before we first breathed let alone believed and had us while we were lost, we would be as good as saved before we were

Christians. In the view of those who believe this way, predestination would mean salvation.

In the Bible, *predestination* is just a fancy word after salvation for eternal security. Any time the word *predestination* is seen in Scripture, it refers to believers, not to lost sinners. Take the term *predestination* off the BC side of Calvary and send it over to AD—from the day we receive Jesus as Savior, forward; we had no part in Him, He did not have us, *"Now if any man have not the Spirit of Christ, he is none of his"* (Romans 8:9). That's lost. From now on, His loving Holy Spirit is our security.

Christians are predestined to be like Jesus in Heaven. If we can lose eternal life, it's not very eternal or predestined, is it? If salvation is free and is not of works, we can't do anything bad enough to lose it. Anyone can have Jesus. Nobody is barred in advance. Christians are never barred now. We were first persuaded and repentant and then predestined. The goal of creation is perfection. God draws us and He holds us for good.

> *I am persuaded, that neither death, nor life, nor angels, nor principalities, nor powers, nor things present, nor things to come, nor height, nor depth, nor any other creature, shall be able to separate us from the love of God, which is in Christ Jesus our Lord.*
>
> Romans 8:38–39

We are saved. You and I meet people who think that God is unfair. With God's kindness, we have become His heirs; we who were slaves of sin. What a great guarantee! Our Maker has power to say, "You can take the high road or the low road; take either one, Heaven or Hell." God didn't ask for our advice. He has no counselor. He figured enough of us would make the right choice, so we aren't pressed into believing. The Word of God develops freely in our hearts. It's about conditions and circumstances.

Christians desire to carry the message of Jesus as far as possible. Let's get back to the Bible basics. Save me from the muddled theology of endless study and the many confusing opinions contending out there. Take legalistic doctrines like election or total depravity that, frankly, stifle compassion. Forget the doctrines of predestination and Calvinism, which stray from the gospel. Fatalism is a square peg in a round hole. The message of Jesus is a clarion call.

> *I can do all things through Christ which strengtheneth me.*
> Philippians 4:13

The word *can* carries the idea of ability, that we are able. The thought is subtle. It is not that we might or will, but that we can. People can see. If all things are possible, love is entirely possible. We have God's permission and His help. If we are linked to Christ, we will love. I hear "No" from people when God says "Yes!" The question is: Will you? The little word *can* is loaded. Locked in this familiar word is the meaning of faith. Don't just memorize the verse, but memorize the word *can*. If you memorize this word well, it won't be hard. Meditate on it. See your potential love—if you can.

Those who have Jesus *can* see that our love was flawed before God. People generally know the why and the how, but they want to know if they can. We cannot, because we ask not. In reading the Scriptures, I have discovered that with God, we can love, and surprisingly, we can be loved. It's not in ourselves. I wanted Jesus because I needed to get along with others. Ask yourself about what you want.

We do not save ourselves. We are saved by grace, and it is *through faith*—not of works. Who can boast? (Ephesians 2:8–9). Grace is the issue. Salvation is the free gift. Faith is not the gift. New life is the gift. God doesn't give us faith. He requires it of us. Faith isn't the goal. Eternal life is. Faith is merely the step that's needed. *"Now faith is the substance of things hoped for, the evidence of things not seen"* (Hebrews 11:1). Thank God for His unsearchable and "unspeakable gift" of eternal life (2 Corinthians 9:15).

Amazingly, out of your dark heart comes this desire to be made right—to love. "Blessed are they which do hunger and thirst after righteousness: for they shall be filled" (Matthew 5:6). Glory to God!

How many are desperate to live in righteousness and hunger to live this way? Too few choose to do so. More important than just thinking about it, we must decide in our will, in the back of our minds, and from the bottom of our hearts that we need to be free of our sin. But we can't help ourselves. We turn and allow Jesus in. *"Ye have obeyed from the heart"* Romans 6:17. Refusal is the inexcusable blasphemy.

> *For the love of Christ constraineth us; because we thus judge, that if one died for all, then were all dead: and that he died for all, that they which live should not henceforth live unto themselves, but unto him which died for them, and rose again.*
>
> 2 Corinthians 5:14–15

Man looks at outward appearances, but God sees the inner heart. One died for all, so then all are dead. Now that Christians have died to sin, the love of Jesus compels us. *"Knowing, therefore, the terror of the Lord, we persuade men"* 2 Corinthians 5:11. This is why we persuade others, and we should never be ashamed of this.

God invited us. He put the cross of Jesus in our path, sacrificed for us. It is incumbent on each person to seek. Everyone should know God is calling, Romans 10:8–9; we all have it in us to believe. Confession is on the tip of every tongue. Jesus turns nobody away. But people turn Jesus away.

Condemnation

> *Jesus said, For judgment I am come into this world, that they which see not might see; and that they which see might be made blind.*
>
> John 9:39

The light of Jesus' life shows the darkness of all hearts. None of us are godly. Folks have many sets of values, varying opinions, likes, and dislikes. What's right? There is something else by which Jesus judges us.

Many of us do not come to the light for fear of what would be seen in our behavior. What if you suppose that nobody loves you? We love if we are loved. We are the sinners and the cynics, the pessimists and the unbelievers of the world. Do we know we are blind? In a nutshell, the self-centered person thinks, "People should love me." People less often say, "I should love others." Love in a mortal heart is fleeting like an image in a mirror. We think we see love, but the moment we look away, it's gone. It is no more.

Many in the world talk about love. They write about it and sing about it. Do they get it? They are branches without fruit, clouds without rain, doomsayers and pessimists they discourage others. Hearing the story of the cross, they stiffen.

Married couples hit a few holes in the road, see some seasonal bad weather, and yikes—they're done. Their union is gone. They sharpen their tongues, take a jab at each other, duck, and quickly run off.

Everyone sees what is wrong, but they give up on what's right. Nobody knows how to do right all the time. There is not a single one of us who is righteous. Not one of us is able to walk the road to Heaven on our own. You need the righteousness of Jesus Christ. God is help, and He only faults those who refuse Him.

God planned what He was going to do from the start. When engineers build a bridge or building, they first diagram a design. Their calculations are tested indoors before they begin. They don't want to invest a lot of someone's money to see a building fail.

The University of Washington in Seattle had half of their stadium rebuilt. It rose from the ground up. With the large superstructure near completion, it suddenly fell down in one motion. The awesome crash was recorded on film. Something in the drawing or fabrication went terribly wrong. They had to start that one over. The new stands were completed, and the trusting fans pack in. Usually, engineers predict an outcome. God has not made one mistake, period.

Seekers will still question if God cares or if He is in control on Earth. Agnostics ask why He allows terrible killers to run loose in the world. They wonder how a loving God can send hordes of people to Hell. But what have you and I done to stop the dangers—protect the children and rescue the perishing? We fight evils, but not necessarily for the right reasons or for the purposes of God. If we don't confess Jesus out loud to people, He won't confess us to His Father in Heaven.

We see people every day who haven't found it in themselves to open to God. Their silence is unnerving. Is the light of God's Holy Spirit going to wake them up? You would think God would have to crack their hard heads to save them. We pray for them, hoping God will do things a bit easier, gentler. It causes me to think how all of us have been more obdurate. God moved our way first. People can take the next step.

I understand why some Christians feel that we couldn't have believed even a little bit on our own unless God first put it in our soul, but He is not leaving anyone out. Yes, He is fully sovereign, and we are fairly stubborn. To that end, God moves first.

Assume God ultimately intervenes, of course, which explains how conversions happen and city revivals spring up. This is why Christians pray for the lost to be saved. The fact that we are born blind explains unbelief. We grapple with a grim unalterable society that has grown around us. God isn't autocratic or mechanical. Is God's sovereignty versus human free will a circular argument? There is no excuse to sit back, do nothing, and watch God do it all. Christians are accountable to God. This is not that hard.

> *But we preach Christ crucified, unto the Jews a stumbling block, and unto the Greeks foolishness; but unto them which are called, both Jews and Greeks, Christ the power of God, and the wisdom of God.*
> 1 Corinthians 1:23–24

We take up the cross of Christ to become the testimonies that convict. We return kindness for rudeness. To the ones who are sympathetic, we appear to be committed to the Lord, but to others, we look as if we should be committed to a mental ward. Count the cost. The truth is that the payment has already been made.

God gives us His truth and the freedom to proclaim it. This is the truth that turns people away from sin. Read the words carefully: truth, liberty, freedom. We remain silent to the insults. What you see in the world is a struggle.

Truth is freedom. Believers know the truth. Our friends will have Hell to pay, yet there's no buying their way out and it costs nothing to get in. They are simply frozen in sin. They just get swept into the crowd as easily as they would fall off a log.

Love should be shared as coming directly from God. Can we pass along the fresh love of God if it's not settled in our hearts? But the burden is in our heart and the battle is fought within but then, "Who is sufficient for these things?" (2 Corinthians 2:16). No one is adequate in themselves to carry this all. The point is that Christ paid for the sins of the whole world.

> *For we are unto God a sweet savor of Christ, in them that are saved, and in them that perish: To the one we are the savor of death unto death; and to the other the savor of life unto life. And who is sufficient for these things? For we are not as many, which corrupt the word of God: but as of sincerity, but as of God, in the sight of God speak we in Christ.*
>
> 2 Corinthians 2:15–17

To those who believe, faith is the free ticket to eternity. Unfortunately, I can't forget my fears for the lost. To this world, our words are "the savor of death unto death." Who can argue with them, warn them, or win with them? You and I can't walk away from what we know. The appeal of the gospel has been passed down through centuries. Faithful souls have carried the Word of Life every day and every mile.

God is all-knowing, all-seeing, with an endless capacity, and we are all-believing. God knew from the start that Jesus would gain a following. People give their lives to follow Him. Christians have lost their lives to dangerous unbelievers. Do you think that God would have allowed His Son to suffer on the cross if He knew that not one person would respond? God should not have ever sent the Messiah if that were true. Christians live their lives right to win the lost around them or give their lives and die for others.

God's Sovereignty Salvation

                                                  LOVE   FAITH

Time Plan of Salvation †   **Predestination**

                                                  SIN   UNBELIEF

Man's Free Will   **Condemnation**

Everyone starts out condemned. God has saved us from the power of darkness. (Colossian 1:13). You and I have had to have repented. We have this promise of Heaven. But Christ died for everyone. All of us start out on the bus bound to Hell, but a few get off before the end of the line. The Word of God brings faith.

God commissioned the Church to spread the gospel. We can see how central our role is. *"How shall they believe in him of whom they have not heard?"* Romans 10:14. They won't—unless we let the secret out. People are normally kind and loving. So what sets Christians apart? Let's be quicker to love and faster to tell the good news. We witness to win them; remember, too, that our life and testimony convicts the unbelievers.

We long for a better world. The message we carry is most important, but it's blocked in a world fettered by fatalism, behavioral science, and obstinate unbelief. The culture is ruled by a determined hostility. They are working on us and our weaknesses.

There's only one way to break free: look for God, enough to give your life to Jesus. Work hard for God's kingdom gratefully and zealously. You and I need to strengthen each other's faith in Jesus to make our love stronger. This is not just about some of us, but the reason why God made us all—is for Himself. We have a need in our lives that only God can fill, something that only He fits. Give God credit for creating us with minds that want Him, for designing us with hearts big enough to receive Him, for making us with hands capable of serving Him, and feet to take the word to all the world over. If everyone saw that they were forgiven, why wouldn't they believe and want to get saved? Sin has drilled a big hole in life.

Christians who really try to improve realize that the only chance of succeeding comes by surrendering their lives to Jesus. As loving as God is, we won't be good enough for Him. He is 100 percent righteous. He asks for our best. Do we get righteous by straining ourselves or by training ourselves? We don't do either. Well, we do, but we don't.

Abraham is the father of us all because he believed and then acted on God's call. Are you getting into Heaven? The doctrine of faith is damning to the holier than thou who believe in their own goodness. The odd thing is that rigid, religious folks can be an unruly bunch, some think the same about "New Testament" Christians.

Our God was patient with Paul, putting up with him until he was ready to believe. Paul learned the wisdom of patience by example. He said, *"Not that we have dominion over your faith, but are helpers of your joy: for by faith ye stand"* 2 Corinthians 1:24. You see God had Paul. Though God is preeminent, He is long-suffering, and He never wants to have dominion or dominance over your faith. Rather, He helps your unbelief and puts joy into your faith to give you confidence.

> *And the servant of the Lord must not strive; but be gentle unto all men, apt to teach, patient, in meekness instructing those that oppose themselves; if God peradventure will give them repentance to the acknowledging of the truth; and that they may recover themselves out of the snare of the devil, who are taken captive by him at his will.*
>
> 2 Timothy 2:24–26

We *can* work for the salvation of everyone around us. Consider these four factors:

1. The sovereign, perfect will of our Maker.
2. The independent free will that we possess.
3. Our influence on others who oppose us.
4. The devil.

Do we try to push unbelievers into Heaven against their will? That would bend the rules.

Jesus taught us to pray for His will to be done on earth. We must hope to move people. We can also influence God by prayer (2 Thessalonians 3:1). God is omniscient and alert to our pleas. He is moved by our concerns and touched by our affections. Our God has given us this great big love even toward contrary people. The devil deceives people.

God is good. Paul said in 2 Timothy 1:12, "*I know whom I have believed and am persuaded*," because we all have a free will. Really, would God refuse anybody? It's evident that everybody counts on God's goodwill. Would He say, "Today is not your day," taking pleasure in seeing a person go to Hell? If you think God has given grace in the past, you will soon see the place He is preparing now in Heaven. God is able to do anything. Nevertheless, He doesn't drag us to faith, He doesn't sin, and He doesn't force people to be good.

Jesus teaches us. He wants us to care, to put others first, and to put Him first of all. In chess, a good player anticipates several moves ahead both for their own and for the opponent. As a Christian, I not only watch my moves, but I also carefully consider what others are going to do. It isn't that we see everybody as opponents, for I think it's just the other way around, spiritually, opposite what's normal. Put yourself in another person's shoes. What do they see? Be wise by knowing what needs doing before being told. With experience and maturity, you can see around the corner to know what is coming. What would you want to do for someone if they were in your place? The wonderful character of *love* with *faith* looks out for others.

The light of God's love is inviting. As truth is more powerful than lies, darkness retreats from light; love is superior to hate. The hope of Jesus Christ has been made known to us, the Holy Spirit does His work, and God the Father is glorified.

The Reproach of Christ

If ye love me, keep my commandments.
John 14:15

Some of us have been saved so long that we have forgotten what it's like to be without Jesus. The rebellion in the human race shows that God gave us a free will. Way back, the prince of this world sucked people in, and now he offers countless counterfeit solutions to supposedly elevate us out of our predicament. That's like the guy who sets a fire, calls the fire department, and then runs in like he's the hero. We, instead, bear the reproach of Christ.

God provides real restoration that works and lasts. It happens simply because we agree with Him. What's so hard about this? People can say yes to God; it's all He asks.

Jesus leads us to live righteous lives by the rule of His wisdom. Think of a writer who labors to capture love on paper. What changes hearts and minds? This does not come through any ordinary love. The world accuses and questions us. There will be those who refuse to believe no matter what. True miracles occur when people surrender their lives to gain the love that lasts—and then live to pass it on.

It's very important that we are prepared for the work God has these days. If we walk as God would have us walk, we cannot lose. The Bible says so. The fruit of the Spirit in our lives is *"love, joy, peace, longsuffering, gentleness, goodness, faith, meekness, temperance"* Galatians 5:22–23. We have in our hands the perfect love to give, and we have daily victories because every Christian has God. We become servants to God, to other believers, and to the world. You ought to win a lost person to salvation. We must love.

LOVE BELIEVES ALL THINGS

Love is the strongest of all influences. What is exceptional in our life with Jesus? Christians can be good at love. You might fail often. Count on God's sovereign will to override. God's expectation is getting accomplished here on earth the same as it is in Heaven.

Let no lost soul go and say they didn't see. Sometimes I believe I'm dreaming because I want to impact everyone in the whole world. It's not a game. We're hoping they feel the heat. You could be the first real Christian someone actually meets.

People argue. It doesn't necessarily mean they think we are wrong. They may not agree with us, but they might know we are right. They might. Rumor has it that we are to be avoided. Why is that? Are we delusional? No. God gives us more authority than we are aware of. Don't assume God controls everything. We make a decision to believe and decide when to speak out. Jesus calls. People are without excuse. What's obvious is they do know something about us. It's God's love that moves us and others too. His charity is powerful. We are known for helping our enemies, certainly our friends, and especially our families. But people have other ideas about faith. Talk is cheap, yet actions speak louder than words.

Imagine a person who takes it for granted that belief is something static. Our faith doesn't hold an inert proposition that we must affix faith and then that's it. No. Faith that lives is the difference between getting on a train that is stuck on the tracks or getting on a train that's picking up passengers. Not only does this train go, but if we get on board, we travel with it. We are getting on a moving train headed where Jesus goes.

If we are uncomfortable, that's because the Holy Spirit prods us. He transforms us into the likeness of Christ. If anyone believes in their hearts that God raised Jesus from the dead and confess Him as Lord, anyone, they are saved (Romans 10:9). We proclaim the true gospel.

Our faith is defined. This train has a destination. Modern society shuns dogma. We attain the goal of salvation not by mental assent alone, but by active faith. We must get on this train whose destination is Heaven. Tell your friends to get on board!

We drove out of Seattle one Sunday afternoon to sightsee in North Bend and the Cascade Mountains, and our old car overheated on the steep highway. After cooling it down with water, we made it to North Bend, but the radiator was shot. I got Louise, my wife, and our friend to a bus stop where they waited while I parked the car at a repair shop. Walking back, I asked people when the buses ran on Sunday afternoon. "They don't" was the answer.

They don't run on Sunday afternoon! The young woman I just talked with caught up to me and offered us a ride to the next town. Struck by her kindness, we all piled in. She talked about her trouble in life. Her young son was her saving grace. It seemed she was a believer, but didn't know the gospel. We had an amazing talk, and she drove us all the way, an hour to Seattle. We had a powerful conversation. By the time she let us out, we were all sure the Lord had it planned in detail.

God in heaven saves. It's each individual's prerogative or privilege to accept. It is our part now to give a witness in fear, yes, but more importantly, in love of salvation. The Church is crucial to God's plan by explaining, sharing, and showing the way. We all have our own choice. Christians all should know everything by now.

God's approach in the instruction of the Bible leads us to the cross. How we pick up on God's love makes the difference in how well we affect others. Some people seem to be unlovable. They remain unloved. It may be that you are the first person to ever truly love them. With a strong belief in Jesus, we can love others before they love us. This accurately defines *love* with *faith* in all things. Love people even when they don't like you. God loved us first; we can now love others.

> *Herein is love, not that we loved God, but that he loved us, and sent his Son to be the propitiation for our sins. Beloved, if God so loved us, we ought also to love one another.*
>
> 1 John 4:10–11

CHAPTER 6

Choosing or Rejecting

And many other signs truly did Jesus in the presence of his disciples, which are not written in this book: but these are written, that ye might believe that Jesus is the Christ, the Son of God; and that believing ye might have life through his name.

John 20:30–31

The best reason to believe in Jesus Christ is to have His love. Life baffles us enough, but love is even harder to figure out. Can we believe it? Imagine how much the Apostles could've said had more been written. The earth couldn't hold all the books (John 21:25). That thrills the skeptics. How optimistic it is to expect to inherit Heaven's boundless riches and live with the wonderful One who has it all to share. We should try to tell everyone we meet. What a pity when unbelievers turn us down.

Five words of love and understanding are worth more than ten thousand words we don't know in a foreign language. Now that we believe, we do everything we can and we retrieve everyone we are able (1 Corinthians 4:9 and Ephesians 3:8–9). Love and understanding are able to do more than we ask or think.

In all that Jesus does, God gives us plenty of reasons to believe and to choose. Jesus gave His all for us in leaving Heaven to die here so that when we leave here, we can go to Heaven forever. Jesus made us and saved us to give us all that's His, even Himself.

There was a young couple associated with the halfway house where I was saved; we were getting acquainted, and I thought they were Christians. We were walking to the car together when I said something "Christian" and got a reaction from them. It caught us all off guard. I was new in the faith and pretty well living in an idealistic bubble. I assumed at first that everybody was coming to Jesus.

Anyway, I then asked them, "Well, you two are Christians, aren't you?"

Charles cranked his neck around and indignantly replied, "No! We're not!"

That caught me off guard. I found myself saying, "You've got to be!" It's surprising that we stayed friends after that. I said something every chance I got. Charles was on the board of directors of our program, they belonged to the Jaycees, and Janis was the secretary of the halfway house. She couldn't escape me, and she said later that I bothered her a lot. She said I had been a slouch and that I sat around all day doing little but talk about Jesus.

Pastor Chuck gave them each a Living Bible for Christmas. A few weeks into January, Janis and Charles were talking with each other, when one said, "I have been reading my Bible. About a week ago, I asked Jesus into my heart, and I haven't told you about it."

"Well, I have been reading mine, too," the other one said, "and I asked Jesus into my heart about a week ago." They both figured they were saved at the same time.

Our part isn't very hard to figure out. Obedience is impressive and reverence is admirable. Is it enough? Be a good witness. How do we win lost souls for the kingdom of God if not by His love?

Be sure to allow some space and time for God's love to work. His generous ways give people a wide opportunity to come and be saved. God set an example.

In his book *True Spirituality*, Francis Schaeffer wrote that God provided enough for us, it is "substantial"; he said it's plenty. Friends stray from their aims when they aren't satisfied. The way to rejoice in our Maker is first pray and be thankful that our Savior redeemed us. It is important to be happy with God. Contentment is essential to our relationship with God. People see this in us.

Responsibility begins and ends with the individual. God has done His part entirely, but He's not in the business of breaking anyone's will. Likewise, it's wrong for us to impose or force our beliefs on others. We can say something appropriate and pray. It helps to have a person's attention to develop some rapport and some discussion. The gospel is a load for believers to hear, and it's a pressure on unbelievers as well, especially after they have been told. They do think about it.

It's not easy to convince people. How do we get through to the lost when they are hooked on sin? Talk to an addict, but they're not listening. They are like a bucket with a hole in the bottom: they have no retention. I may be 100 percent right based on God's Word, but people don't know that. What's the hitch? I want a small button to push or a switch to flip somewhere inside those stubborn hearts. The wrong tactics will drive off those who are hardened.

Love requires tolerance. It's presumptuous to thrust one's own views, values, or compulsions on people. We are pursuing a love that's helpful and even influential, but to push myself or my demands unfairly on others is certainly not love. We do take advantage of people and overstep another's space, and there's little gain in that. Will they give in to us? Love is honest and wins respect. Love is kind and does not demand its own way.

We aren't going to convince everyone in the world that what we believe is true. Besides, sometimes, we're not right. Our prayers to God aren't always correct either. It's important to align ourselves completely with God from the start.

We impose our thinking on people—and even on God Himself. Why don't we come to Jesus with our whole heart? There are blind spots in our lives where we do not allow the light of Jesus to shine in. We have reservations. We have desires and lusts in the back of our minds. Can you drop them, let them go? Twisted thinking steals life. We don't know why friend and family can't hear us. We may not be aware of what's keeping us from responding to God's Word. Even if Jesus isn't visible, love is viable if we value the Bible. Let's focus on the significance of its precepts. Life thrives in the expression of our faith.

Our old nature, the flesh, is in conflict with our new divine nature. New believers enter salvation with preconceived notions of what life is about. The bias can range from misshapen viewpoints to extreme fantasy. We aren't ready to be so forgiving of ourselves or others if we haven't seen the depth of God's pardon—the excusing of every sin thanks to His mercy poured out on Calvary. It's not what we personally feel that defines Christianity, but it is what God says in Scripture and everything He has put in the meaning.

We sometimes demand from God what He is not willing to give. What God gives is substantial; it is sufficient. It is, in fact, just right. When we come to God with fanciful expectations, we miss the true blessings and lose much of what He gives and wants to give. In our greed, we want all or nothing. We often settle for nothing. That is the way it sits.

A Christian might get discouraged if life isn't what was expected. Consequently, our faith wavers and spirituality is blurred. When we crave empty things and go from one fling to another, we hurt ourselves. Everything doesn't have to be a life-and-death urgent decision, since what matters most is life after death; plenty goes in between.

God makes salvation sure and secure. He hasn't just bailed us out, but He has pardoned us. If you're good with simple food and clothing, don't let people, things, and times upset you. Here's the point: when you allow these things to upset you, you're getting away from your *faith* and your *love*.

Many people think they're Christians when they really haven't the first clue to knowing God's heart. You are a Christian if you've met Jesus personally. This is my understanding. Most have either low expectations or fanatically huge designs regarding religion. You've heard people say they were flying in three directions. They're missing something. There are four directions: north, south, east, and west.

One guy told me he'd been saved more than once. If you pray four different times to get saved and only once receive Jesus, then one out of four isn't bad. Someone might tell you they used to be a Christian. There are actual Christians who aren't sure they are saved, and there are unsaved souls who think they are. The general public is seldom convinced by the confusion, and many refuse to listen anymore.

Most people are not Christian, but nobody should openly reject God's promise of salvation. Not only incorrigible people, but many average folks sincerely doubt that God would ever accept them. Oh, they know. They have heard. They are in denial.

They can't cope with disapproval from other people, much less from the Almighty. People who repeatedly suffer broken relationships and tend to develop a rejection complex. The ego says, "Reject others before they reject you." Bitterness grows like weeds.

Syndromes set up early in life, and people go from overbearing to depressed to hypersensitive. It could be in their attitude, or on the contrary, it might be that their personality is unlikable and so they are mistreated, and then they become more unlikable. Multiplied rejections will amplify the dilemma, build frustration, and perpetuate the sense of disgrace, and so they're prone to anger. You have met someone who has fits of rage. They are hurt; that's why they harbor lifelong hostilities and volatility.

Pessimists put huge demands on life with tough, tortured ideals that mostly fail. Then they run and hide. Nothing alleviates their conscience. "What conscience?" you ask. Can an obdurate heart be honest? Sinners continue to sin. Does the subjective mind have objective thoughts? The dejected spirit cannot feel accepted.

If doubters and scoffers ever did apply themselves to agree, it would be difficult for them. Inflexible people live with these feelings. They learn to struggle with their handicap of inadequacy. Time and again, they suffer disappointing rejections that make every explanation empty. It's basic. How can they see clearly to improve themselves? Though they harbor awful regrets, they continue to push love away.

Lost people don't come knocking on your door. Finger-pointing doesn't get in with anyone anymore either. Love learns contentment and sheds the resentment. Getting our own act together attracts people. Accepting and respecting the impenitent ones gives disbelievers a better chance of considering the truth. You may not look impressive to people, but it's important for you to live your faith. You mirror God Himself. Love is the most important thing, more than anyone says. Believe everything in Jesus.

Accepting or Denying

> *Peter seeing him saith to Jesus, Lord, and what shall this man do? Jesus saith unto him, If I will that he tarry till I come, what is that to thee? Follow thou me.*
>
> John 21:21–22

We sometimes fret about those around us when we really should be focusing on our own things. Jesus told Peter, you "Follow me" (John 21:19). Peter was bothered by this answer. After what he had seen in the previous few days, Peter was apprehensive.

Jesus, brought back from the dead, faced Peter here and questioned his love. Peter had said he would never deny his Lord, but he had denied Him three times in a row. Jesus asked Peter three times, "Do you love Me?" Three times, Peter said yes. Jesus told Peter, "Feed my sheep" (John 21:16–17). Is Peter accepting or denying? He was still denying. Peter didn't get it. He was on the fence, not quite on board.

John adds that Jesus predicted that in later years, Peter would suffer an awful death to glorify God. John outlived him to tell it. What irony: Peter, who denied Jesus to protect his own hide, ultimately followed Jesus to death.

Peter looked at John and asked Jesus, "Lord, and what shall this man do?"

Jesus scolded him and said, "What is that to thee?"

Peter didn't understand what Jesus had just told him.

Peter very much represents our weak human nature. By being preoccupied with everybody else's business, we lose our own way in life. We aren't helping. Ambivalence, apathy, and mediocrity come from the very same people who criticize, meddle, and transfer blame. I should fret less about the next guy's stuff and be mindful of my own priorities. There seems to be no escaping our old complaining attitude. It's a bad habit.

> *Thou hypocrite, first cast out the beam out of thine own eye; and then shalt thou see clearly to cast out the mote out of thy brother's eye.*
>
> Matthew 7:5

Get your own act right and be aware of others as well. You can help in constructive ways. If we clean up our lives, we will be better to others. Though we think of ourselves as altruistic, it happens sometimes that we enter relationships toting an agenda. Suddenly, unknown to those we are trying to love, our egocentric mentality and unhealthy thoughts become the bugs that get in our heads. Unsaid thoughts, misunderstandings, and the fine print and clauses cause relationships to blow up in your face. A hidden motive may be secondary to your sincere purpose, but the lower self surfaces and bites in the end. We like to blame others for that. That's bogus. Steer clear and stay on course.

Those who take no responsibility will make gains at other's expense, yet they shortchange themselves. Predictably, relationships don't last long, and everyone ends up more cynical than before. You break promises, spread bad feelings, and find a way to hurt people. Disliking becomes disrespect. We get along with each other a lot better when we let Jesus guide us.

Find peace in God. Prayer grows. Do you move through life and know the right way to go? Some of us have insatiable emotional needs. When difficult people hamper you, God can give you elasticity and flexibility. Resistance vs. existence: it is part of God's plan for us. It motivates us.

We can get the grace to correct someone's error. Can you imagine how you might do that successfully? Without thinking about teaching them a lesson, you can reach those who oppose you. Be patient (2 Timothy 2:25). How do we turn things around and see people more optimistically? It takes time. Also, if someone so uncaring rejects you, your faithful uprightness in the Holy Spirit convicts them of their unrighteousness. Practice persistence sympathetically and live joyously.

Remain under God's direction, and He will watch over you. Being crucified with Christ, submit daily to walk with Him. Selfishness attacks like a disease and takes over. When you come to Jesus and stay with Him, you are genuinely changed and your prayers get answered. Catch your potential in God, take less from others, give more, and bloom abundantly. There's no substitute for victory.

You will be a loving person before you know it. To the degree that we operate in the flesh, we are vulnerable to others who are operating in their flesh. When we invest ourselves in the carnal nature, we reap corruption. The fruit of the Spirit is peace, which is not necessarily measurable, but by faith, we see the blessings appear.

It is God we are seeking to please. Christians can go beyond what God calls us to. We overshoot the plan, oversell ourselves, and burden others with unrealistic expectations. We don't need to have everybody's agreement on everything. We want God's approval. I get in trouble trying to get into someone's corner. We don't always fit people with our better ideas.

Our mission is to bring God's Word to the world. Be as powerful as His grace allows and be straightforward, as is polite. We must proclaim, and you want to tell everyone. Paradoxically, being new and sticking extra hard to God's guidance brings our efforts to nothing. Frantic actions become counterproductive and self-defeating. What is realistic? If unbelievers reject Jesus in their heart, they are without excuse. Just go to them. Love people. We don't want them to go to Hell.

Everything about God's love works. It requires a growing, fresh lively faith to endure. Man is a fallen creature. People are prone to prejudice and reticent to change. The harder I try, the more I see that the truth of Jesus isn't easily accepted. People aren't going to get it unless they're given to repentance. Christians have wasted a lot of years.

We hear it from people who say they can't see Jesus. They don't see why they should live differently, and Christians make it too complicated. We doubt as well. When we get a better message, some of our friends see it and some get defensive. Try to make it clearer. Wanting to communicate and be accepted can get a little touchy. I am met sometimes with big trouble; nobody likes their intelligence questioned. Not only do I try to run others' lives, but I also have a tendency to interject my ideas into God's plans. Yet if our intentions are honest in the course of our approach, the attempts at love get stronger and stronger. The impact lasts longer and longer.

Proclaiming or Disclaiming

> *Jesus saith unto him, If I will that he tarry till I come, what is that to thee? Follow thou me. Then went this saying abroad among the brethren, that that disciple should not die: yet Jesus said not unto him, He shall not die; but, If I will that he tarry till I come, what is that to thee?*
>
> John 21:22–23

After Jesus gave this advice to Peter, it was repeated that John would live until Jesus returns. Evidently, this rumor was so widespread that eventually, the Apostle John wrote it into his gospel. John's long life made it harder to dispel such a reputation because first-century believers expected Jesus to come back in their day.

The possibility that God would preserve one of His Apostles for two thousand years still passes through the mind of some novice Christians. It passed through my mind when I first read this passage.

Some years later, a friend told me he had entertained the same thought. This human tendency raises a question to give it some odd meaning. Wild notions should be avoided.

Watch for false prophets, Matthew 24:24–26 *"For there shall arise false Christs…Believe it not"* Why compare yourself with others? Walk your walk in His Spirit. Don't swallow the awful rumors that circulate from deceivers. John no doubt wrote to correct the account of Jesus' words, *"Follow me."* An ordinary levelheaded testimony will lend greater faith to believers and will better test the unbelief in others.

This story warns about the many crazy exaggerated claims that twist our thinking. God teaches us faith. The gospel is sufficient. It's substantial. Believe Him in everything, but don't believe everything you hear. Refrain from excess. God's love extends a level of courage and kindness, but God doesn't want us to overextend ourselves or read too much into things. This is the conservative side of *love* with *faith*.

Prayer isn't like you can rub a magic lamp, then Jesus pops out to grant you three wishes. Some Christians think they can trust God for everything while they do nothing. Others pontificate with self-assurance, willing to do everything in their own power to take the world on. They pry into people's lives. We need God. Let's be sober and realistic about life. Get more focus on the Bible.

God gives Christians the right help, but we invite trouble. Our problem is that we stray from God's goodwill, individually, corporately as churches, and even as nations. This increases all the way to international and global warfare. Continuing to deal with the everyday realities here on our own street and we are inept, we inflate our egos by worrying about world-size problems. People feel no duty toward society, while others feel that the universe is sitting on their shoulders. In proper order, our Maker has judiciously arranged His great principles, to which every person is answerable.

Churches work together, so the gospel shouldn't be exclusive. The peoples of the world are hurting for salvation. Help at least one person who is down. Give them a little lift and more hope. Give honor and decency more credence. Take Jesus at His word, follow faithfully, and pray for the world.

We can't grasp all our Maker has said the way He intends us to.

It's because we have only half a brain to live our beliefs. Our other half, biologically, won't function religiously, not quite. This is the way we are. Our carnal side comes to salvation with natural motives like covetousness: "What do I get out of this?" We are selfish. We are illogical. Death and Hell wait. Our doubting side has idiosyncrasies and quirky-like traps. Give Jesus more. Be more thoroughly convinced of God's good character (1 Peter 3:15). Godliness is so uncommon in a dishonest world; it's a challenge to be honest.

I believe in focusing on *faith* with *love*. It will save us from a whole lot of foolishness. You can test the so-called wisdom of all teachers anytime by this one rule found in Galatians 5:6 (NIV): *"The only thing that counts is faith expressing itself through love."* It's very seldom that we biblical Christians align the doctrine of salvation—faith alone—with the one powerful first commandment of Jesus—love. When I listen to a preacher delivering a sermon or a Bible teacher teaching, I want their words to line up with the true message of *faith* with *love*.

Good Judgment or Bad

> *If any man love not the Lord Jesus Christ, let him be Anathema Maranatha. The grace of our Lord Jesus Christ be with you. My love be with you all in Christ Jesus. Amen.*
>
> 1 Corinthians 16:22–24

Keep on loving by the grace of the Lord Jesus Christ. We face rough times catching heat from people, even those closest to us. We get distracted with many issues and temptations, and we allow all those unfortunate disbelievers to go down the tube to eternity without Jesus. We have days without the sincere love and acceptance of others, but it's not wrong to freely give. Even when we ourselves are hurting, shouldn't mean we can't give more and love more. Let love be unconditional. It's not idealistic or unrealistic to have sensitive compassion for others. Keep the faith and lean on God's love. A starry-eyed man came into the Christian coffeehouse downtown one Friday evening and walked around pronouncing loud warnings of condemnation to the patrons at various tables. It was in a large busy room. For a while, I watched him stand over Christians, browbeating them with an ominous voice and calling them to repent. He seemed to have little effect as he moved around, hardly interrupting anyone.

I was still enjoying the fellowship at our table when suddenly, a blast of religious polymorphous foreboding spilled over on us. The man was now holding his arms above our heads.

"God sees your works," he nearly shouted, "and they are wicked!" It went on and on like that, unceasingly verbose. "Do not think you will escape the judgment. I tell you that you will not escape, but you will receive your punishment. Repent of your sins now! Forsake your carnal ways!"

He looked down for a second, paused, and went back to his zone. I prayed to God for a way to deal with this disruptive character, and I stared up at him until he stopped. I could barely get a word in edgewise with him because he would take a breath and go on with another angry outburst about Hell. When he let up for a second, I broke in.

"Will you pray for me?" I asked with a sheepish voice.

He barely broke stride in his rant and denunciation. I was afraid of the scene he was making and the sorry impression he might make on newcomers.

"Will you pray for me?" I asked again. "I need prayer."

He stopped, somewhat surprised, but then he continued. I guessed nobody had taken him up on his preaching. He was tall and handsome, but he was putting everybody off. He had his arm stretched out at me like a football player carrying the ball.

"I need prayer," I insisted. "Please, will you pray for me?"

His peals of thunder dropped to a stutter. What could he do? He had to answer the need of a sinner, but with what? He raised up with more warnings. "Your sins have found you out! You must repent!

No one will escape the wrath of God!" He blabbed on with no end. "Everlasting damnation is reserved for you because your deeds are evil! I see your heart, and it is dark!"

"Will you please pray with me in the prayer room in back?" I had him. "Please, I could use somebody to pray with me."

He calmed down and agreed. It was not easy for him, but he was unable to refuse. We walked to the room set aside for prayer ministry. Once inside, he again began to announce all of the bad news God had for me. At least his poor behavior was out of the crowd's view. In a meek tone of voice, holding my Bible out to him, I quietly asked him, "Will you please read to me from the Scriptures?"

He glared at me. This really rattled his cage. Would he even read a word? Was he a real Christian? I think he probably was. He was neatly dressed, appeared intelligent, and I guessed he studied his Bible. I figured that with his head in this condition, he had not been reading the Word lately. I was going to hold him to it, so once more, I calmly repeated my request.

"I need to hear the Word of God." Then I got more specific. "Will you please read Romans Chapter 6?"

He couldn't refuse, but he found reading nearly impossible. The first verse came slowly, and then he got into more loud prophesying, so I encouraged him to read on. I had asked this mixed-up man to read Romans 6 with its stronger doctrinal statements. The Apostle Paul wrote it to correct the misconceptions among the church brethren.

If you do not love the Lord Jesus Christ, you have cause to fear. He is coming! Apparently, neither the promise of Heaven nor the threat of Hell moves people. Those who fail to accept God's love will be condemned by Him and will suffer in Hell forever. If anyone stays ignorant, then let them be ignorant (1 Corinthians 14:38). However, one reason others might believe is because of your *love* and *faith*.

Like a spoonful of water to parched lips, my new friend read a little more, but he began stumbling over what he was reading. I asked him to continue reading. *"Therefore we are buried with him by baptism into death, that as Christ was raised up from the dead by the glory of the Father, even so we also should walk in newness of life"* (Romans 6:4).

My friend's voice was unnatural, and it took him a painfully long time to read the whole chapter out loud.

This guy came in to pour dark condemnation on a Christian crowd. He was posing a real problem. You and I can't make perfect Christians out of anyone. God doesn't turn anyone into perfection just like that. It takes some time. God made a way and gave us the opportunity. How did we think to become Christians? We were justified by Jesus' blood. It's incongruous for us in Christ to try to drag others through a knothole, expecting people to see our thinking. We can't even clothe our own selves with godliness.

I then requested the man to read the entire fourth chapter of 1 John. He hoped I was done. I suggested it was for my benefit: "I need it." I wondered if he could read it through. Was he a Christian or not? *"Beloved, believe not every spirit, but try the spirits whether they are of God: because many false prophets are gone out into the world"* 1 John 4:1. That's hard.

The man stuttered at first, but continued reading steadily toward the end, completing the entire hard-hitting chapter. I asked him to read every verse of 1 Corinthians 13. He felt that he had to, and he sounded like he knew the Bible. I requested Galatians 3. He read most of it before he started crying, falling to the floor on his knees.

"Pray for me," he said. He cried big time and let out his heart to me. All his troubles and his marriage spilled out while he cried like a child. He was overcome like a house on fire. The Holy Spirit came over us, I was able to minister the love of God to him, and we prayed.

On an ordinary day a few months later, I happened to be in another part of town at a bank when this same guy walked up to me. I wouldn't have recognized him, but he knew me. He told me how well he was doing, and he wanted to tell me how God had blessed him since that evening at the Christian coffee shop. He told me that his life and his marriage had been put back together. He looked real fit. Praise the Lord!

Essentially, what God wants for us is to believe. Why attack the simplicity of the gospel? Many Christians pitch warnings, correction, judgment, and punishment. I can't count how many times I've heard

Christians say they want God to come right now to obliterate the wicked. Why not be positive? All people need consideration and sympathy. The Bible teaches us to love our enemies, and if we love them, we should warn them about the wrath to come. Help believers. How do we bring these two approaches together? When you are eager, you want to criticize, but when you care, it's usually best to keep quiet and pray.

> *There was a man sent from God, whose name was John. The same came for a witness, to bear witness of the Light, that all men through him might believe.*
>
> John 1:6–7

A few Christians have the idea that we should preach the gospel the way John the Baptist took it to the people. I don't think God wants us all to lose our heads this way. God does not say in His Word that everybody is going to land in Heaven. He said, *"all men through him might believe."* Anyone can believe, *"as many as received him"* (John 1:12). You and I are to bear witness to "the Light." Many prefer their darkness and sin. They refuse to come because their guilt would be revealed. Some will be slow to believe, but nevertheless, they might change their minds. We hope for ourselves to sustain the love to win them over.

Jesus brought the message of grace and holiness and peace. He said it would be difficult to win over the world. What is going to change its stubbornness? The facts aren't good enough. We can practice patience to express our faith with love in the simple directness of our speech.

Be confident of what God wants and what He doesn't want. God has taught us to help others with lots of prayer (2 Corinthians 1:11). Sincere faith sorts out the misguided ideas so that our genuine love can come into practice.

Loving or Losing

> *But woe unto you, scribes and Pharisees, hypocrites! For ye shut up the kingdom of Heaven against men: for ye neither go in yourselves, neither suffer ye them that are entering to go in.*
>
> Matthew 23:13

Jesus called the Pharisees hypocrites. How did Pharisees shut people out of the kingdom of Heaven? Their Scriptures were the commandments of God. Obedience was the only option. Ask yourself why God laid out so much instruction for sacrifices and atonement. All that sacrifice and atonement would not have been necessary if the people had obeyed. Does not one mutually cancel out the other? They were commanded to obey without fail. Did they expect their sin to be covered by sacrifices? Now the question is reversed. Has Jesus forgiven us so we can sin? God has rectified us to righteousness.

Sometimes, we say it's our fault if someone goes to Hell. Let no one blame others for their unbelief. Should we feel as guilty as Pharisees when the opportunities come to save lost souls and we fail to share our faith? We are each responsible for ourselves. It is true that we can put a stumbling block in front of people, and on occasion, we may cause someone to fall. Who's perfect? Do we gauge our holiness by how often we win lost souls? Goodness is a fruit of the Spirit, not of us. We may be credited for more good than we expect yet it is of God.

We cannot earn our own salvation nor do we earn salvation for anyone else. Each of us has God-given free will. God's purpose in the Church is to give witness to the gospel, leaving the choice to each person. Christians have a mandate to witness. One person will plant the seed and another waters, but it's God who saves souls (1 Corinthians 3:6–7). We must back off, give people slack, and give God time.

Since the work of the cross is finished, God looks at our faith. Hope rests in the sufficiency of Jesus Christ's blood. Before we confess our sin or do one good deed, it's up to God, who knows our hearts, to determine whether we're acting in good faith.

Sadly, domineering church leaders with legalistic attitudes exert their influences. They add fine print to the canon of Scripture, which both expands and limits God's province. Any deed considered to earn sanctification is just another sin—artificial good works (Galatians 3:3). A few Christians, even pastors whose fellowship I've enjoyed, have fallen back to think of good behavior as required for God's grace. That's a contradiction. It's hard to get away from such language.

Here's where I get into splitting hairs. Do we have to *do* good things to be saved, or are there things we must *not* do in order to stay saved? We go ahead and avoid doing wrong. There definitely needs to be more stern ministry to sinful Christians, not less. Jesus Christ is our great High Priest, not by the Old Testament Law of carnal commandments, but as it says in Hebrews 7:16, "after by the power of an endless life." There is no way we are losing, we just might not be winning enough. The ministries that please God the most are the ones that spring from new hearts with *faith* and *love* in Jesus Christ.

In the same gentle wisdom with which God saves, He puts the call of service on us. We don't want to see anyone go to Hell. How is it that some Christians are proud to say they wish whole populations damned into oblivion? You've heard it at different times. Does God leave it for any of us to relegate another person to the eternal torment of Hell? A simple solution: "We should just bomb them to Hell!" So true we think that way, or are these words from those who only claim they're Christian? Friends complain they haven't had success in ministry lately. If you ask me, attitude is important.

Sometimes, I hear old Christians say they can't win souls to Christ anymore. Then we'd better work more among ourselves.

Missionaries go to remote parts of the world because they make inroads there. Regional cultures are bonded by ethnic, tribal, and family rule. They're closed societies that reject outside influences. Once penetrated, though, these people groups may come to Jesus as a whole, and this might occur when the first to come is their leader. In the meantime, while we see the ignorance in distant places, our own neighborhoods have lost souls who are small, forgotten, and unseen by our churches. What's the destiny of these strangers? They hear the gospel and they may believe.

We're not going to convert anyone. Jesus does this. It is possible, though, that we can be influential. They can repent. Remember the way *love* promotes *faith* in others.

God is just. He takes into consideration those who've never heard. Many believe in God though they've never seen a missionary. Not one person is left out of Heaven unjustly. God cares about our world. According to the Bible, God judges nations. Some may question His fairness in that. Those who hear the gospel and refuse will be more guilty than those who haven't heard (Luke 12:48; Romans 3:2). Psalm 103:1–2 says, *"All that is within me, bless his holy name. Bless the Lord, O my soul, and forget not all his benefits."* One reason God wants us faithful is so our laziness and apathy won't be their excuse.

We wouldn't say that bona fide believers have faith alone. After we accept Jesus into our hearts, we get the urge to win over the lost. When we act out of obligation, it's no longer faith. We don't have to save anybody.

God is wise in all matters. Not for a second does He miss anything or anybody. The call to spread the gospel is simple. Don't manipulate lost souls into imitating. If you're pushy, people turn away. Your faith must spark a fire to reveal Jesus' love.

The greatest period in the Church's storied history is facing us today, and many people have not yet seen an example of a real Christian. Moral values are debatable, unable to produce any more than a veneer—a thin surface shine. Christian love should be extremely different. We bloom and bear fruit. How do people know we are here? We must pray to befriend them, respect them, and not be afraid of them. The Church is always here for real. Love is strong when it's given in the name of Jesus Christ.

If people expect to be ready for Heaven, they're mistaken. Their lives lack God's approval. Have you ever been caught? Picture yourself stopped on the road with a police car behind you, lights flashing. You have a quick moment to think back over your last few minutes. How did you drive for the last mile? Were you going the speed limit? Did you use your turn signal? You think you were driving as well as ever. What could the officer cite you for? He asks for your driver's license. He talks with you as policemen do, listening for irregularities. He tells you your license plate has expired. You might be a good driver, totally safe and courteous, and yet get ticketed for driving illegally.

Faith registers, and God gives us carte blanche to love.

God gives discernment to Christians. We have wisdom. Share the plan of salvation and be willing to allow all the results and the judgment as God works. Without undue stress, we show others their responsibilities, staying honest and direct. We ask, "Why not?" There are reasons. We ask out of our love.

We can step up and confront sin. Sometimes, we don't know exactly what to do, whether to push or to give someone space. Wisdom understands the difference between right and wrong and knows how to be an example of righteousness instead of being combative. Jesus is pleased to award us peace because we are guided by righteousness, moved by the need around us, and people are searching.

Throughout the Bible, we read many stories of people who corrupted the truth. The percentages haven't changed today. In the New Testament accounts, false teachers attempted to lead people away from the truth. They added all kinds of pseudo-religious rules to the message, as if people would come out better. Oddly, they passively removed truths such as the burden of faith and the responsibility to love. We owe our time to God who watches, He knows who sees. *"Therefore judge nothing before the time, until the Lord come"* 1 Corinthians 4:5. When you see the Holy Spirit asking you to reach others, don't make it hard.

God sees the thoughts and intents of our hearts (Hebrews 4:12). Have you surrendered your life to Him? Do you relinquish all things and wait for His blessing? *"Delight thyself also in the Lord: and he shall give thee the desires of thine heart"* (Psalm 37:4). Jesus wants you first of all, totally, and then He fills you with the answers. He will help you. Praise the Lord for His grace, because we never get our part perfectly right by ourselves. With Jesus, we do get our part perfectly right and it's great!

Contentment or Resentment

> *The Lord is my shepherd; I shall not want.*
> Psalm 23:1

There's always so much to want. Could you be happy with what you have? It takes a lifetime to learn this. You've walked in a dark room before with no light—faith is like when it moves. Contentment means you settle with what you have to work with.

"The Lord is my shepherd." He doesn't do everything I want, as if He has no discretion. With our old human nature, the more we gain, the more we want—and there's never enough. We always want more. You think that a little more would do it. Things don't have to be sinful. If we don't get what we want, we resent it. Learn to be happy in the Lord. "I shall not want," because Jesus is all I need.

The lesson in Psalm 23 is to be at peace with God, to be at your best. The Lord tells us to pray so He can bless. He sees what we need and knows what would please you (Matthew 6:8).

It's good to be ambitious. There's nothing wrong with trying to improve your situation. Our prayers help. *"But seek ye first the kingdom of God, and his righteousness; and all these things shall be added unto you"* (Matthew 6:33). Put God ahead of everything else before asking for anything. This is a principle. But remember that you can't bribe God. Don't try to make Him your top priority just to get your wishes granted. God does not work that way. He wants you to want Him.

> *He maketh me to lie down in green pastures: he leadeth me beside the still waters.*
> Psalm 23:2

LOVE BELIEVES ALL THINGS

There is a certain composure that follows the willing believer. We enjoy tranquility—like the flourishing peace of a summer afternoon meadow—*"to lie down in green pastures,"* no matter the circumstances.

Picture yourself like this. See the idyllic pasture the psalmist paints. You are on your back in soft green grass under a clear blue sky. However hard the winds may blow, "he leadeth me beside the still waters." It isn't a raging river. There are no rapids, not even a babbling brook—it is a place of placid rest. Life's a picnic, not a panic, *"in the presence of mine enemies"* (Psalm 23:5). This description could fit anybody you know.

We like to go out to the country and escape the stress of city life, bringing that sense of peace back home, so it stays with us into the workweek. Why can't we have this feeling all the time? It's our choice. We learn by repetition and practice to have a better attitude and enjoy these healthy emotions regularly. Get a better attitude to work. Learn to lean on God.

The Good Shepherd does not have us rely on our feelings alone. He leads us to those greener pastures where sheep feed in plenty. God takes us to the waters where we drink safely. He provides all we need every day. Life is easy. Anyone who takes refuge in the Lord in their heart finds that other people are easier to live with. Whatever the condition or circumstance, Psalm 23 speaks contentment. We have it made.

Notice that David says the Lord restores his soul first. After this, he comes to the path of righteousness. What is great is that He does restore my soul. From this one day forward, *"he leadeth me in the paths of righteousness for his name's sake."* Allow God to lead.

We can start doing the right thing right now, but not without the Good Shepherd. You can't fix everything in the world today or change all opposing opinions. You can't correct your past to get on the path of righteousness. Is there a connection? We have failed.

David puts it in the right order.

We tend to think of it the wrong way; all our trouble is not in the past. Maybe when we act better today things turn out better. Jesus takes and leads us to a beautiful life.

Unhappiness and resentment don't lead anywhere. They take you on a road with no end. You don't want to go down that way. Some people take that road and never return. The farther you go that way, the farther it is to come back. If a person is disappointed with things and the old thinking builds up, it will boil over. If you don't change now, who's to say you will ever turn around? It may never come.

What God gives us today is enough. Where this psalmist says, *"I shall not want,"* he's written a play on words—a double meaning. Does God give us everything we want until we ask no more? It would be naïve to think He overindulges His children. David's thought expresses true contentment. It is not as if things are good the way they are, but it is more likely that we see that the Lord cares and we are good with this. What He gives is substantial. He gives us manna in the wilderness every day. It is enough to live on. Contentment is not complaining.

> *Not that I speak in respect of want: for I have learned, in whatever state I am, therewith to be content.*
> Philippians 4:11

You hope that acting right and being good will bring happiness. That's not the way it works. Things may sour. Happiness is not our highest goal. We can't make everything turn out the way we want. Learn to be content. We can be satisfied—even if things go wrong.

Find better friends. Bad company corrupts good morals; people don't always make us happy. Lasting relationships and healthy lifestyles are important. We get along nicely when we are more dependent on God than on people, pleasures, or sports. Will others do as much for us as God does? Christ is doing everything to make us happy, and He will establish a good place for you and me. His ways bring joy.

> *But godliness with contentment is great gain.*
> 1 Timothy 6:6

In the Lord's Book, contentment leads to godliness, which in itself is great gain. This is spiritual. God prepares us a feast in the presence of our enemies. Jesus said that if He went away, He would prepare a home for us in Heaven with Him. *"We brought nothing into this world, and it is certain we can carry nothing out"* 1 Timothy 6:7. Whatever befalls us here in our time, remember to be grateful, a far better home is waiting somewhere on high. What a great glory it is to receive more in Jesus Christ! Believe in God. Believe also in the love of Jesus.

Love is contagious. We need good character. Is faith enough? This is not contradictory. People must be able to see in order to receive. When people shrink back, we want to urge them on.

Doubters crave the carnal pleasures and things of this world. You can see what attracts people. Give the kindness you have in Jesus. It's rare. When anyone suffers in life, we offer understanding. If someone seems blasé about the message we have, we can try to get their attention by our concern.

An American missionary in Bangladesh was crossing a river on a boat when a local man noticed him and asked what he was doing there. The missionary answered, "I have come to bring the message of Jesus Christ."

The man asked, "What's in it for me?"

"Come to Jesus Christ, and you'll have your sins forgiven, you'll spend eternity with God, and He will bless you forever," the missionary answered.

"Is that all?" was the man's reply.

It's what you're looking for in this life, I guess. To me, Christianity sounds like the best thing possible. I like Christianity for the way it's written.

My wife and I went to visit an unsaved friend several times in a nursing home, and we were able to share our faith with him. He was relatively young to be in such a facility. His parents had moved him back to West Seattle near to family because he was near the end of his life. When Louise knew him in high school, doctors found he had a brain tumor. They operated more than once. Over the years, his condition worsened. Eventually, he became severely disabled, immobile, nearly deaf, and he had terribly skewed vision. To communicate with him, we had to write on a big drawing tablet.

We tried to ask him if he believed in Jesus.

In a garbled voice, our friend asked, "What proof do you have?"

That was an honest response. It's a tough question. We were hoping to bring him to faith. We both scrambled to find an answer he would like. Louise pointed to the evidence in the authenticity of the Scriptures, with more manuscripts than all other ancient writings and with thousands of documents to back them up. I told him how a lot in my life had changed for the better since I received Jesus.

He then asked a very fair question: "What difference has Jesus made in your life?"

"Before I became a Christian," I said, "I didn't get along well with people. Love is in my heart now, so Jesus is truly alive in my life. Now I connect with Jesus and I connect with people. That covers faith in Heaven as well."

He looked at me a long while through one eye, and I supposed he was thinking hard. Maybe he thought I was weird. I couldn't tell what this meant to him. Louise was busy writing and explaining the basic plan of salvation in big letters. He was obviously open. I was considering his situation. He was probably lonely and he was worried.

"God answers prayers," I said. "God can make you a happy man."

More details of our conversation escape me, but he enjoyed our visits and talks. We vigorously shook hands a couple times at the end of our exchanges, giving every indication that he wanted to talk about life's great issues. All of us are basically alike. It's reasonable to expect that anyone might respond to some caring attention. Forgiveness and Heaven can sound a little like "pie in the sky, by and by." Everybody wants fulfillment in this world, and we all long for genuine relationships.

Experience teaches that time passes faster than we realize. A few months after visiting our friend, his failing health began drawing him closer to death. We rushed to see him to present the gospel once more again to him. Other Christians came too. After his death, we talked about our times together with him. We solemnly remembered these visits.

Our friend in the nursing home had a good heart. He was touched by our visits. Like the man in Bangladesh who wondered what he would get out of knowing Jesus, our severely weakened friend might have wanted something in this life. We all might. Troubles can crush people's spirits. When the people seem to have nothing going for them, pray. We hope that both our friend and the Bangladeshi man received what God offers, what everybody needs.

Jesus makes life full. You will be content. Is what you want or what you ask of God really what you allow yourself? When you have arrived, the carnal pleasures of this world are less tempting, and your troubles become bearable.

Jesus speaks to both the happy and the hopeless. His good news is for the rich and the poor—for any and for all, those who are poor in spirit; the rich do not have an advantage, and the poor are not at a disadvantage. The message of Jesus isn't radical. All of us can have real hope, peace, and love from day one with no waiting or we get the grace to wait.

Your troubles may actually signal that God is now with you. He chooses to bless, in whatever condition God has found you and in any way; be more willing. The Bible is given by inspiration of God for good doctrine, conviction, correction, and instruction (2 Timothy 3:16). Our reconstructed lives are now connected to God's will.

We need to step back and watch Jesus work. We are the Lord's servants. Who stops God? The Lord will direct us to care for the down and outers He has placed in our path. God will lay them on our hearts. Our love has to be bathed in prayer and washed in the blood of Jesus.

Think about this when you feel you can't put up with this world any longer. Jesus died for us; indeed, Christians believe He died on the cross for everybody. There might be someone you think is impossible, but your kindness makes a difference in every one of those encounters.

God's unique prescription in the Scriptures is the best clue.

The dynamic love to which a Christian aspires requires the hope of Christ—life after death—life before death. When the only consolation to our souls is simply to trust the light of His glory, our eternal life is pretty awe-inspiring. We have found no life in the universe outside of this thin crust on our little planet. As tragic and sad as times get, it helps to see more of Jesus in order to keep going. Leave the future in God's hands and make more of every day now.

Consider our human estate and why we go bad and do wrong. You've become more aware of God's plan. Remember His love when life gets punishing.

When life appears to be rolling along smoothly, it doesn't always mean things are good or will stay that way. Just because times look bad doesn't mean there is no good or that things won't get better. Your disappointments and discouragements may be for your good.

A bird sits on the ledge of a tall building or on top of a telephone pole and looks around. You and I would be frightened stiff up there, but birds have no fear of heights. Jesus Christ frees us from the curse of the universe (Genesis 2:11; Romans 8:2, 21). What changes in our lives? We can hear what He says when we go to God in prayer; we are changed into new creatures.

Someone can be helped by you if they haven't given up on life. They'll get along with some word or two from you. The gospel is able to save. *"It is the power of God unto salvation to everyone that believeth"* Romans 1:16. It's easier to reach others when your faith is strong. It moves you to reach out. You can be distracted by certain ideas or inhibited by uncertain thoughts. Others are too. Even if most people say no to Him, God cares what happens. Try.

One morning, I awoke from a vivid dream that seemed very real. I dreamed that I was tied up facing a firing squad; for what, I don't remember. At that time in my life, I was experiencing terrible stress. In the dream, I was asked if I had a last request. As I remember it, the firing squad held off. I answered that I just wanted a minute or two more to look around and savor this world one last time because it's been so good. Though tied to a post, I still knew the beauty of life and thought how glad I was to have been here. At that moment, I awoke. Some people resent life, others enjoy it. The dream reminded me of how truly grateful I am and I love life.

Each day is a gift from God. A day is a present to be taken, a present to live in, and a present to be given. Every dawn is a package to be opened like a flower to be picked. Be glad you're alive. Enjoy life. Don't be in a hurry, but remember that time is short. We are in a race to the end. We push and press to do God's work until the harvest is ready.

I have had some awfully rough times and some losses, but I wouldn't want to have missed the experiences. We must stop and watch. It is another day above ground to be around; don't misuse it. Life is big no matter what, even in death, we are witnesses of God.

Accepting or Rejecting

> *And there are also many other things which Jesus did, the which, if they should be written every one, I suppose that even the world itself could not contain the books that should be written. Amen.*
>
> John 21:25

Jesus performed many miracles, and many more stories about Him have been left untold, but enough has been written in the Bible for us to accept it all. Life tells us of the need to believe in something greater than ourselves. Life has innumerable wonders to fascinate the human mind that the information is still being collected. We haven't even begun to know God.

God is illuminated in all wisdom, and His love is obvious. God's way becomes dominant in our hearts. Our Maker never slows. He loves us continually. Christians have yet to get a handle on this wonderful promise—the best promise ever. God's unstoppable love never fails us. Our love wants to believe all these things.

Some people say they can't believe in God. Ask them how we got here. Say, "Do you remember being born?" When they say they don't remember it, ask them, "Then how do you know you were born? Did somebody tell you about it?" Imagine all of us arriving here on this dangerous planet, yet we can't say how we got here. Few scientists will spend an entire career searching for clues to our origins. We just woke up here together with only a trace of history and fragments of prehistoric life. We can imagine only little of our future, and it is a loaded situation. It is frightening! How can we find any means of escaping the inevitable end? We appear to have no remedy, either, for the depraved condition of the human heart. This liability cries out for a power beyond us. Do we look for any other power beyond ourselves? What a thought! We have a huge need for a trustworthy, loving God who knows us and wants to help.

God's love alone will pull us through, but we must have the faith. Mankind generally rejects our account of Jesus Christ. As in the beginning, the question before us in the Church remains the same: are we who follow Jesus accepting of others? Just as the moon circles the sun, the moon circles the earth. The bigger object would pull the smaller into itself by gravity, but centrifugal force keeps it pulling out and speeding around. The point is to love others as Jesus would have us love them. That's how things work.

Peter worried about what the next guy was going to do. Jesus said emphatically to be concerned about yourself. He said, *"Follow thou me"* (John 21:22). Skip the excuses, and let's just plain go to work for Jesus. There are Christians you know who do fine with accepting Jesus Christ, but they circle around in apathy and express no interest in others, rejecting different people and picking apart their flaws. If we understand this well, we will start with ourselves.

It is too bad that we waste time struggling with unrealistic expectations. We turn anxieties into counterproductive behavior. Life is illogical. It's not what it should be. I've had to learn that it's healthier for my own physiology and better for my peace of mind to trust God—and it allows me to be of more use to the rest of the world.

We don't have to be upset by horrible people or troubling things. God has been infinitely patient with you and with me; we simply don't appreciate it enough. Think how your heart connects with those who appreciate you.

Mature faith will allow every fellow human being time to find their way. We can support them with generous love. Let's take our animosity and worry to Jesus and leave it with Him. God has carefully planned our lives, even using our imperfect friends and situations. He takes the fractures among believers, and He fashions ministry. He turns the friction we face with nonbelievers into outreach. We can expect catastrophes. Doesn't it seem only natural for us to try for harmony? Ambitions can be driven by selfish motives, so Jesus said there will be offenses.

People want approval and they feel let down if they don't get it, but they pretty much do what they want. We look at appearances and gauge others by what they do. Attitude sets emotions and behavior follows, good or bad. You are what you think. Our minds process a series of choices, and we decide which buttons to push or which levers to pull. Time takes mulling things over and making good decisions to work in life. When it's all said and done, the core element in your life is your will. We need more willpower with self-discipline. It is not easy to confront your own unsafe heart. God reproves us, and we must obey. Do we cut out the bad thoughts or entertain them? We're bothered by spiritual battles that could be avoided. The reality is that they are won or lost within our own muddled minds.

Tolerance gives a sweet liberty to Christians. We could become happier people and more likable. We can be comfortable around unbelievers, accepting them as they are, and the Christians too. Sure, we'd like to change people, but we have to be smart. Hopefully, they'll be attracted by our love. God doesn't coerce us into believing nor force us to obey. We can become more willing and do better. This is what's most important. Do you encourage those around you or do you discourage them? We need to be more positive. It's permissible. It's realistic.

Start each day with renewed vigor. Pray for God to open the eyes of your understanding. We are the objects of His calling, the beauty of His glory, and the beneficiaries of His inheritance. We are the saints. It takes a lot of getting used to. Our little bit of faith allows God's eternal wisdom into our souls to change us from carnal to spiritual. The realization of faith will take us through the rest of our lives. God intends to transform us to recapture the world. Before we even ask, God has prepared all of this. He furnishes us with His Spirit, changes us with His preeminent power, and makes us His in order to fill us all the way up with *faith* and *love*.

We are accountable collectively, individually, or both. We must stay close to one another, even more so in these tough times. We know to pray. The Church works best corporately in an atmosphere of *faith* and *love*.

Those who reject the message of salvation do so of their own volition, knowingly and without excuse, even if in denial. How quickly the wrath of God will come on them! Many will not accept the Savior when they understand that Jesus bore their sins on the cross. Pity them; spirituality is not tangible. There will be no escape from Hell.

It might be obvious to us, but it's not that easy for people to believe. They are blind, and sometimes, we do not give a very clear answer. You probably feel that love by itself can't carry the day, but it does with faith in Jesus. You have believed. And Christian fellowship is important to you. Know that your time with those around you also means a lot to others.

> *Seeing ye have purified your souls in obeying the truth through the Spirit unto unfeigned love of the brethren, see that ye love one another with a pure heart fervently.*
> 1 Peter 1:22

CHAPTER 7

Love vs. Lust

From where come wars and fightings among you? Come they not hence, even of your lusts that war in your members?

James 4:1

Lust violates God's New Testament Law of *faith* and *love*. It makes Christians look like the foxes guarding the henhouse. God wants us to know that besides the sin that was covered at the cross, we still harbor the old nature. God has taken the Old Law away. We are nonetheless hounded by temptation, but we who are in Jesus Christ now have a new nature. The Holy Spirit does more than fix our lust; He gives us His love. God works from beginning to end to make a new life for us. He wins the battle we fight. He has our inconsistencies made over in His glory. Trust Jesus. Stop fighting Him. Stop fighting. Let God give you your life back again.

Evil rules a lower nature deep in our core. Self-control by itself isn't able to overcome our thoughts or deed of envy, greed, impulsiveness, and selfishness. Self-will says, "Everything for me." Our disguise doesn't erase hidden desires. *Selfishness* could be our real name. To sin is to miss Christ's first and second commands.

Lust is a synonym of sin. It's the opposite of love. See how low people can go. The Dead Sea is the lowest point in the world. It contains no noticeable life because any water that flows into the basin can't flow out; it evaporates due to the heat. Deposits of salts and minerals collect, so fish and plants don't survive; hence, the name *Dead Sea*. Israel's Dead Sea is almost 1,300 feet below sea level. Death Valley, California, by comparison, is 282 feet below sea level.

Death Valley is an uninviting place. It also has its name for a reason. It is the lowest dry land in the Western hemisphere. It has a negative altitude, a relatively low latitude, and its heavy air is insufferably hot. Most residents are only seasonal. Death Valley has little to give. God speaks in the character of this harsh and desolate terrain.

If we can't get what we want, we fight to get our way. People are like that when they have less regard for others. Friends have conflicts. Some people steal from their families. Citizens betray their own countries. Depraved souls will kill just for money. Even while helping each other, we might end up combative. We should be harmless.

Lust says there is no death. How shallow are the lust of the eyes and the pride of our flesh? We want to be first, even before God. Can those who place their unchecked ego ahead of God ever expect hope in their future? Time is finite; make it count.

We want Jesus to clean up every mess we make. Our attitude adjustments and paltry methods don't get us new hearts. We abuse the gift of God's mercy when we allow sin. God's children are naïve to think only of their self and then expect blessing.

> *Ye lust, and have not: ye kill, and desire to have, and cannot obtain: ye fight and war, yet ye have not, because ye ask not. Ye ask, and receive not, because ye ask amiss, that ye may consume it upon your lusts.*
>
> James 4:2–3

Sin is rooted in lust and things like the love of money. That's where hate and wars begin. We can easily start a war, but it is more difficult to stop one. James speaks to all readers. Who understands how completely sinful we are? The helm is a small part that steers a huge vessel, and though the tongue is little, it is, in truth, incalculably destructive. It's untamed because the heart is impossible to satisfy. More is not enough, and baby, you aren't the only one.

Love does not seek its own gratification, but self-centered people are lost. Aren't you a bit afraid that nobody cares? We don't face up to the harsher realities. We are progressively more sinful. It grows. Look around and see how inconsiderate people are. You can lose your mind if you think about it too much. Count the ways we hurt each other, but don't overlook our numerous acts of charity and kindness. There's encouragement. No community works together entirely, yet all of us care to some extent; societies are amazing.

In this world, it would be much better to follow God in faith and in truth. We are partial to our own thinking in many ways. Isn't it handy to lean on those closest to us? Instead of taking, we can be giving. We can afford to be charitable. Adultery, lying, murder, and stealing begin with coveting. It's dreadful how low and callous mankind has to be. Doesn't the break come from going our own way and doing wrong? Can we be fair and objective and helpful? Our Lord grants us our prayers for doing what is right in His sight.

> *Do ye think that the scripture saith in vain, The spirit that dwelleth in us lusteth to envy?*
>
> James 4:5

Modern economies have grown more affluent, and people have grown more self-serving. Myth-like hedonism has more and more become the norm. The devastation of moral problems mounts up over time. We should see how lust is at the root of it. Reverse the trend. In contrast, love is generous. Drunkenness and adultery bring superficial contact, not togetherness. Sin is basically antisocial, selfish behavior. Immorality never benefits anyone. There's no way for that to happen. Love does no harm; it helps. Love increases and abounds and is fruitful.

The old human nature measures itself and counts what it possesses.

Desire and frustration are evident early, as when babies cry if they don't get what they want. Kids are allowed to be demanding and unruly, hysterical; they get older and throw adult-sized tantrums. Their rage gets explosive. All that people have in life is nothing except growing emptiness. This generation strives for too much, for ambition, for excess of success, for self-indulgence—and they end up hooked on these things without being at all satisfied. So in the wake of shattered dreams, we come to despair and disappointment.

Love leaves town on a late flight, gone from the lonely hearts of the travelers. Lust runs your life and then ruins it. It doesn't have to be abnormal, illegal, or immoral, just habitual. Like an addict, you're hunting for your next fix. Consuming appetites have costs. To keep paying, you have to take from somewhere else. If a habit uses all your recourses, where is giving going to come from? There'll be no investing and no saving. People become shortsighted and as ruthless as poison. Selfishness has no limit to what it extracts from us or takes from others. *"But godliness with contentment is great gain"* (1 Timothy 6:6). Get peace.

The economy doesn't have to keep growing to be strong. Do we have to keep buying to stay happy? Something jumps out at us, and we have to have it; something in the way it moves attracts like no other.

Come and Follow

> *And he said, All these have I kept from my youth up. Now when Jesus heard these things, he said unto him, Yet lackest thou one thing: sell all that thou hast, and distribute unto the poor, and thou shalt have treasure in Heaven: and come, follow me.*
>
> Luke 18:21–22

We must give our all to Jesus. This is a message for each of us. The young man's question was, *"Good Master, what shall I do to inherit eternal life?"* Luke 18:18. Jesus quickly reminded him of the

Ten Commandments. The young man said he had obeyed them all his life. Jesus then told him to sell everything he had and come and follow Him.

This is bigger than the Law of Moses, and it's a departure from the Old Testament. It set a standard for salvation that few can follow. Up until then, this young man only followed written rules, but now, he has come upon a leader to follow in person: the Savior.

He said he'd kept all the commandments. What's more important? The account says this man couldn't part with his wealth because his personal worth was too big. He went away sad. This fairly defines the New Testament.

Jesus felt very sorry for this young man who had been careful to keep the Law his entire life. The Savior could identify with this young man since He, too, had carefully kept every commandment. Jesus loved him because He, too, was tempted. All the young man had done was obey without questioning God. Keep the whole Law and God will bless and prosper you. Be good and you'll be rich. He had always been rich. Is that why he was obedient? Now he was asked to leave it, give it away, and follow Jesus. Was that a commandment or a question? This kind of obedience is subordinate to something new now. It is a choice—a new commandment. It is to accept and follow this new person, Jesus.

Many of us could envy a rich young ruler for the simple reason that he is young. Older people sometimes resent the younger, if for no other reason than they are younger. You can see the man did not want to give up what he had. People a little higher up on the ladder sometimes dislike those on a lower rung. Be aware how many of us are enthralled or trapped by the things we have. Remember, it's wrong to be possessive; it's contemptible as being envious of what others have. Really, it's a kind of a shame. There is no doubt that any ruler can abuse authority, and those who are ruled can rebel just as unfairly.

This rich young ruler fought the idea of becoming a follower. The best leaders are those who have learned by experience to follow happily with confidence, humility, and integrity. This short story expresses our human nature, exposes it, and defines Christianity.

I'm afraid we are totally human—and maybe less Christian than we ought to be.

Riches get to be a burden. Life gets dark when that happens. What became of the well-to-do young ruler? He went away sad. Did he quickly dismiss this conversation and think nothing more of it? He asked Jesus how to be saved. He must have been touched by Jesus in some way; was his question simply a passing thought? If the truth worked on him, his thirst may have turned bitter and eaten him up. Whether he got angrier or more curious, he had to think about it when a short time later they killed Jesus. It did happen. What then, came of this poor guy? Things do work on us, either for or against us.

We don't know this man's name. Nothing more is said about him. Use your imagination and fill in the future. Whatever became of the man who walked away from Jesus? To fill in here, I am reminded of Saul, another figure in the New Testament. What was eating him? He took up this fight against the Christians. Remember, Saul was also a rich young ruler at that time.

Who asked Jesus, "Good Master, what shall I do to inherit eternal life?" There is no scriptural evidence to suggest a connection with Paul, but there is nothing to say it's not him. Did they know each other? The case had been building in young Saul for some time. His emotions could well have been the same. His heritage, lineage, and prestige were all endangered by this new preacher-prophet. One after another, Pharisees came out to every road and synagogue to ask questions of Jesus or to try to trick Him with words.

There is a chance that the rich young ruler held a religious position in the theocratic society of Israel. If he had money, he had family. It was hard to break ranks with family, especially where there's money and an inheritance. Young men have their own wills. This rich young ruler had family, just like the prominent family Saul had. They had this in common; the Bible doesn't say what in their background brought them out.

Saul was zealous for the righteousness of God and for Israel too. He later wrote that he had kept the commandments perfectly, blameless. Standing in front of Jesus, the rich young ruler had this same confession. Saul apparently had the power to command, the money, and soldiers to persecute Christians. He saw it as a righteous cause.

Something in the Christian message was extremely aggravating to Saul. It made his blood boil. The followers of Jesus were reputed to have left their boats and nets to give their lives to be with the Messiah. The message was told everywhere, *"How hardly shall they that have riches enter into the kingdom of God!"* Luke 18:24. Those who heard this were certain that no one could be saved, for everyone has a degree of greed. It's possible that Saul had this big grudge with Jesus personally from somewhere. His good intentions became a smoldering sin.

> *It is written, My house is the house of prayer: but you have made it a den of thieves.*
> Luke 19:46

Sadly, religion turns into just what we are already. Here is the big story: we turn green with envy for more money. Will we who have come to Christ advance far enough to become what Jesus wants us to be? It is not only the possessions we own, but it's a secret longing to gain more, like a reputation. Obsessions absorb us. It is temptation. It is lust. It is the root of all evil. We call it upward mobility, but God calls it descending to the depths. Money is controlling. It's influence. If you have it, the growing anxiety is deadly. When you have money or position, you're desperate to hold on to it. If you don't have it, you have little control or influence. Our heart's lust can be traumatic. In all likelihood, this is the place Saul found himself—traumatized.

No one could think to earn their way into Heaven any more than they could think money can buy happiness. Saul, the rich young ruler, was not going to follow Jesus. Saul took it upon himself to go after those followers. He got the consent, money, and swords to round up the believers and to confiscate their belongings and separate their families. The new doctrine the Christians were teaching had to be stopped before it spread. How many died because of Saul? When they stoned Stephen to death, he was there. As Stephen was stoned, they laid their coats at Saul's feet (Acts 7:58). How much of the blame fell on him there? *"And [Stephen] kneeled down, and cried with a loud voice, Lord, lay not this sin to their charge"* Acts 7:60. Is this why God saved Saul? Maybe Stephen's words of forgiveness grated on Saul, who found no mercy within himself, but Jesus considered all this. We don't know.

Saul's lower nature took over. There was no end to his fury, and he couldn't stop himself. Maybe he saw he couldn't save himself. When we don't get what we want, we seem to blame people who we think stand in our way. Who's really stopping us? Our problem is not so much the people who bother us as it is the things we want and take.

You see nothing wrong in what you want, but find fault in everyone else. You and I must learn to be less defiant, more transparent with ourselves, and more satisfied with things the way they are.

Honestly, you and I could destroy one another. Love keeps no record of wrong. Paul wrote, *"Blessed is the man to whom the Lord will not impute sin"* (Romans 4:8). Paul really needed this. God sees no sin in us because of Jesus. Do we need to see the sin in others? Believers in the Lord can afford to be forgiving and less judging; that's God's job.

You and I today love more powerfully than anyone can see. Christians have bad days and good days, and there are always better tomorrows. When there are losses and sorrows, we must know that life will be good again. Express the pain and feel the hurt, but keep the faith. Don't forget to count your blessings. Think about the more pleasant things in your past. This is all the more reason to believe in your future. Don't be bitter.

Reaffirm our faith in all things true. Keep in mind what you've learned through the ministry of reconciliation in Jesus Christ. See how you've matured. Believe it all, if you can, the future in Jesus. Nothing in eternity will match the wonder of what God is doing on earth by grace with your faith.

The story of the rich young ruler appears in the first three gospels. Then we see in the book of Acts that Luke himself traveled with

Paul. Do you suppose it was known among the brethren at the time why Jesus loved Saul and saved him? Then what else do you think could have come of the rich young ruler who met Jesus? The Bible has no further word of him. We know, though, that he and Saul—Paul—had something in common: they were guilty of coveting. Nothing really cures an insatiable personality; there's no filling that can meet their needs.

Consumed with Sin

> *For the flesh lusteth against the Spirit, and the Spirit against the flesh: and these are contrary the one to the other: so that ye cannot do the things that ye would.*
> Galatians 5:17

Saul the Pharisee kept every commandment of the Old Law until lust trapped him. In his actions, Saul seemed holy. He was single-minded, dedicated, and obedient, even if nobody saw. He was "blameless," he later wrote (Philippians 3:6). He meant it. Saul's cravings were the sin of covetousness (Romans 7:8). Even in his mind, the more he tried, the harder it became. When did Saul first see the way that no amount of zeal could have kept his mind from lusting? There was no forgiveness in life with the Ten Commandments.

An awful passion struck Saul's soul. The Christian message of mercy incited him. While he was ruthlessly hunting believers, he must have yearned to be stopped. These acts couldn't have earned him a hero's fame. Did it hit him when he saw the grace with which Stephen died? Jesus met Saul on the road, blessed him with the Holy Spirit of God, and enjoined him to preach the very unique New Testament message of *faith* and *love*.

Wherever they can, the enemies of the cross hinder Christians and hurt the faithful. Murderers have tortured and killed untold numbers of innocent believers. How can human beings do that?

The prince of this world, the devil, has a death grip on them. Satan fights to hold on and blocks our hope. Jesus is the only way of escape.

> *Submit yourselves, therefore, to God. Resist the devil, and he will flee from you.*
>
> James 4:7

As the light of Christ disarms sin in our lives, the world and the devil are convicted. Unbelievers strike back against our message of love, but God's light overpowers their darkness. Do we wrestle only with our own carnality? We engage the world too. Don't kid yourself: if you're living for Jesus, people will be tempted to interfere. Satan is here to steal and to destroy (John 10:10). He uses deception and temptation. We ought to prefer to walk in the Spirit and not in the flesh, for only then will we have peace.

Jesus has come to save us from ourselves. We're impulsive. Self-control is very difficult. Simply because we're not able to feel respect for ourselves, we fail to get support from others. Our inadequacies provoke resentment. Hate becomes one's choice, doesn't it? When we walk in the Spirit, we appreciate other people.

I eat too much and I don't pray enough. Can overeaters like themselves? A diabetic falls off a stringent diet not so much for the flavor of food, but because the appetite is out of control, and maybe also for the lonely latent wish to debilitate one's self. Smokers get addicted to smoking, and they're haunted by a tendency toward self-destruction.

The reasons are clear. Addiction to tobacco is deadly, but many people just cannot find it inside themselves to quit. Marijuana is even more carcinogenic. Gamblers are fascinated by the chance of winning, but why don't they quit when they're ahead? It's losing, really, or they would be satisfied with their winnings. Gambling is classified as a vice. It proves vicious. Winning the jackpot, money, can also fetch tragic results.

Child abusers often act out of the very contempt they feel for their own selves. Those who hurt children emotionally, physically, or sexually show how extremely wounded and desensitized they are.

Finally, violent people in one way or another destroy themselves.

Lust universally lowers people's self-worth until they're useless. Do sinners get condemned by God, or does their behavior bring death in and of its own shame? The devil's main aim is to demean human life and dehumanize the prey. Adam's first reaction after his fall was naked embarrassment.

Sin's degradation is grossly portrayed in the dangers of modern society. Why do perverts inflict repeated pain for their pleasure? Those in gay pride parades have marched their mocking lifestyle down the main streets. They call it pride, but seated in the will of their fallen souls is the mysterious impulse to sully one's own ego. Why fly down the road to ruin? The lower nature reduces us and pulls us down.

Prostitution is better described as debasement. A person who hires a prostitute degrades the one employed and one's own self. It's lust in want of love. It's sick emotion. Its satisfaction isn't in the sexual act as much as in the darkening of character. In the healthy right way, romance is appreciative, fully committed, complimentary, and supportive; it elevates dignity. Bad carnal nature lures people into a downward spiral like waste being sucked down the drain, through the trap, and into the sewer.

Those life choices deride the self. Rape has been re-categorized as a crime of violence since its rage originates in an irrational drive to violate and defame. The victim is wounded, but the perpetrator suffers intensified guilt and shame.

The Lord instructs us to edify others and to lift each other up. Those other revolting behaviors aim in vain to disgrace God Himself. But don't worry: *"God is not mocked"* Galatians 6:7. God lifts us up and makes us examples to the world and even to angels above.

Of course, our sin offends God. Sin is offensive to people as well. You can think of lots of examples of antisocial conduct. Sarcastic remarks are painful insults that fly so low they are not worth answering. People injure their families or break ties with others for odd and illogical reasons. Love makes a good connection. My songwriter friend, Max, said, "There is no defeat in withdrawal from a point of contention." There's victory in this. We need to add more confidence to our faith in order to hold each other up in love.

I have constantly studied to find the key that unlocks self-centered hearts and what opens them to the Lord. They are stuck like dried glue. Sinners will still remain sinful, cursed creatures dying in dishonor as long as bad habits and sins dominate. Everyone must repent. It's very hard, and again, it's very hard to turn to the perfect way of Jesus.

True lifestyle evangelism is a living dialogue of continuous, conscious prayer. Changing the way you live could mean a change of address. Some of our friends are not good for us. Jesus said it would be tough. Your enemies could be those in your own home (Matthew 10:36). Christians sometimes have to choose between family and faith. Following Jesus could take you to new places to serve. Any location will be better when you know that Jesus takes you there. And it may be hard to stay there, maybe not.

People probably don't know how low they can go until they sink. Sin depersonalizes. Most of us haven't a clue what it would be like. We're comfortable. We live side by side with neurotics who are frenzied to death. It isn't pretty, but it's a pity. They are eaten alive in sin, and they're not usually very friendly either.

Ministry takes fortitude. You must be brave to try to rescue people. You'll face insults, hard words, and scores of quarrels. If anger is a problem, don't make it yours. Spite is venomous. Wisdom can end the bickering. It's a fight between contempt and love for neighbors and for yourself. Darkness hides. Faith rules the day. A quiet answer works wonders.

The sweetest part of life is the way that God loves us, eternally and forever. How can people see this if they haven't been shown? Everyone has been told about their failures multiple times. We all fall. We fail to receive encouragement. How often do our good points get recognized? One definition of *love* is "appreciation." We need to

LOVE BELIEVES ALL THINGS

reflect our Savior in constructive ways and value one another more than we do.

Don't let others go. Without question, we all want approval; there is nothing wrong in that. Each one of us feels it. When we're faithful, we help others do better. We won't let friends down. There are things we can do or say or show; people should know that we love them, and we shouldn't keep them guessing. Love cares to correct—not to hurt, but to help. Pray that we can bring love home to them. Let's be representatives of the Lord. With God, it means knowing for all time who it is who loves us. How is it that we fall short? The Bible will help us avoid enticing sins, to save us from the deadly world.

The quicker we get right with God, the sooner we can have our lives improve. I once saw an electronic combination lock that was creatively designed. Every time the code numbers were incorrectly punched in, there was a penalty delay. If a wrong number was put in, you had to wait a few seconds until the penalty time expired, and then you could start over. If you kept pushing numbers while the penalty was in effect, even if you put in the right combination, you just racked up more time in the penalty delay. A person who had no business trying to enter and who was unfamiliar with the door would not think to wait a minute before entering the correct combination. Any stranger trying to guess the combination would be at it all night because more penalty time would be added each time a number was entered. That's why there are good reasons to let the penalties clear from our spiritual locks and clocks. You might have the way all right; wait before trying something again.

You must know the pattern. If you know what is right and it's not working, pray. The grace to wait is wisdom from the Lord. You may get excited, but it's to your benefit to give yourself fully to the Lord before you do anything more. It opens a door.

Taking time for prayer will help. Stop, relax, and wait for God to clear your mind. He will answer. As God truly blesses you, you will give Him His deserved glory. We give God so little of this kind of time, and we should give ourselves a break.

The new life God gives us shows we are saved. His love grows in our hearts with space to make a place. Our behavior improves. We are pure and perfect spiritually, sanctified and made holy with the breadth of His immutable righteousness. Situations change, the days go better, and we endure beautifully by faith. We haven't necessarily sensed the change we've undergone or seen the big blessings that are promised to come, yet Jesus helps us in our labors and prayers, even with our neighbors and friends.

The Love of the World

> *Love not the world, neither the things that are in the world. If any man love the world, the love of the Father is not in him. For all that is in the world, the lust of the flesh, and the lust of the eyes, and the pride of life, is not of the Father, but is of the world.*
>
> 1 John 2:15–16

You and I would have had to have been there to witness Paul's conversion and to see him switch from the Old Law of Moses he'd been raised in. John, the fisher of men, saw it. He left the nets behind to know Jesus, to touch Him, and to stand there at the foot of His cross. That came with a lot of grace. They saw it all and were the Apostles of the New Testament.

Maybe the harsher realities and finality of the Old Testament have faded into the past since it's been about 2,000 years now. Do we adequately appreciate the fact that Jesus redeemed us from that Law? Read Galatians 4:4–5 and ponder the contrast Paul tried to describe. Sadly, we've accustomed ourselves to God's forgiveness. In the same way, Christians minimize their first love. Let's exercise better faith in Jesus. We can again bring these surprising new expectations and express God's love a little better.

The Apostle John warned us of the past, present, and future of this world. The media today watches our movements, assesses the economy, and follows the money. John said it is the "mark of the beast." We assume this world runs on wealth. The markets use dollars to gauge productivity, but we only prosper with good, honest work. In that case, it's unrealistic to jack up false profits. Everyone ends up paying the cost.

Such excesses put us into debt and despair. Credit card abuse, spending more than we can pay back, has gotten to be the routine. Businesses charge expensive lunches and drunken parties. Alcohol and dope drain society of energy, money, time, and lives.

Headlines frequently report traffic deaths caused by drinking, and the cost of destruction and injury resulting from drunk driving still accumulates. Who keeps track of this? Our government and institutions have added up the liabilities of alcohol and drugs, so several generations have amassed plenty of factual research for our continuing education. Insurance companies pay out for the damages. They find causes of compulsive behavior and offer programs to get people straight and keep them at work. They have statistics on crippled lives, emotional and medical costs, lost production, lost wages, death benefits, and their company profits. It's not a popular issue when so many politicians and rich people are hooked themselves and they lower our standards. They average it out for everyone, so now we all suffer.

The war on drugs is a worldwide effort costing nations untold fortunes. Drug lords are the people's enemies. They tie up resources of drug enforcement, military, and other government administrations. The medical community and disease-control centers can rack up billions in the fight against substance-abuse health problems. It no longer alarms people. Most of this flow of information passes us by. Over the years, it hardly registers. Everybody can repeat the six o'clock news verbatim, unable to voice any answers for these threats.

The prisons house thousands of inmates who are waiting to get out and get back to getting high. Those with a lower level of education often get into crime. Babies are born into poor circumstances, raised by various parents or guardians and few dads, while passed from home to home. Some are born addicted. Again, kids drop out of school or college because they get high.

My friends would rather talk about other topics. They don't want to hear facts about alcohol or drug abuse ("That doesn't apply to me," they say) and would rather forget that these plagues have ruined so many neighborhoods. Our homes, schools, and streets aren't safe. Don't forget that most crime is committed while under the influence, so that's why millions of men and women are locked away. The burden has broken the criminal justice system while everyone wonders why we're bankrupt and in debt. Innocent elderly and disabled people have less help.

There are intelligent civic leaders who are legalizing drugs as a "positive" step. They say that will lower arrest levels. Yeah, right. Remove more laws so there'll be fewer criminals. They point to the old prohibition days in the 1920s. America called it a failure. The opinion that organized crime grew during the decade of prohibition meant they had to legalize alcohol again. No. That move to legalization set a bad policy. The damage is done. The precedence has streamed in more permissive policies in the decades following.

Prohibition in the 1920s rose with well over a hundred years of the temperance movement and evangelistic revivals. Most families went to church back then. What became of the national consensus that led up to the constitutional amendment prohibiting alcohol? Our dark side grew with the likes of Charles Darwin, Margaret Mead, and Sigmund Freud. After certain politicians turned booze loose again in 1933, organized crime became a powerful influence in the mainstream. Crime is big business, and it gets political. Beginning with the Roaring Twenties, there was a big swing from prosperity to depression, from prohibition to decadence, and from peace to war. People today should know their history better. How much have we legalized in the name of freedom, and how much corruption do we tolerate? By decriminalizing vice, we have seen more crime. More crime causes more harm. The question now in front of us is our future—if we have one.

The high school dropout rate is one thing, but the church dropout rate is another. I have friends who dropped out of church to drink. The last time I pulled the top off a beer can, I couldn't touch the contents. It was not because of social pressure, but I believed that the Bible told me to abstain—and honestly, it was also due to my broken heart seeing the lives of my dear friends ruined. You don't want to contribute another nickel to the alcohol industry.

It took decades of dedicated struggle for Christians to win the battle against slavery in America. Even after the bitter bloody Civil War, prejudice continues against people of color. If every action has a reaction, then the larger problems really start with revenge and retaliation. Sometimes, Christians have been named in these injustices. Pray that the spiritual truth of Jesus can rule every thought and action of true believers.

We cannot turn away and ignore the fact that well over one million unborn babies will be aborted in the United States this year.

The Nazis kept their slaughter more secret than we do in our country. Abortion is a bad choice to control population. The conscience accommodates the taking of these innocent lives as if it were a common thing. Adultery is widespread in our time, but abortion has become commonplace and excessive. Neither adulterers nor murderers shall inherit the kingdom of God. Satan wants to reduce us.

This is where we need to take a stand on God's righteousness. As opportunities arise in social conversations on contemporary issues, we might bring up the topic of abortion and approach it from a spiritual standpoint or in terms of science. May God give us the courage to speak out (Acts 4:31). Pray for God to move. Perhaps people would respond better to speaking with us personally rather than hearing lectures from a podium. It will require further educating of our community if we're going to stop abortion. Talk to people one on one. If the Church doesn't speak, the call for change won't come from any other place.

The pro-choice fight has spread from abortion to the prevention of birth defects. Is carrying this baby to full term a complex moral issue? If society denies the right of mentally or physically challenged individuals to be born with full legal recognition, we all lose in part. The thought behind this new question is an outrage to civilization, starting with all the handicapped (the handicap-able really). Society has only recently made progress in legislation, building codes, schooling, and job opportunities for the disabled. In the last fifty years, this has been a physical, as well as a philosophical, struggle. I've found it not uncommon to hear certain "normal" people say, "If I were injured and left in such a condition, I wouldn't want to live." This is not a realistic statement nor is it constructive, but it is repeated. Could the reluctance to accommodate disabled people be bigotry? Does it deny their very right to exist? Life is tough for a lot of people, but you and I might be their biggest obstacles.

There is a new type of hero in our day—a disabled individual who overcomes and triumphs. Books are written, movies are made, and newspaper stories are printed of how one physically challenged person rises above the odds to achieve a wonderful accomplishment. While we celebrate disadvantaged champions and glorify their grit and hard work, we might be overlooking the very ideals embodied in their feat. All handicapped people have potential, and their biggest hindrance is the attitude of the community in which they live. By and large, these victories are treated as exceptions rather than examples.

Books, documentaries, medical science, and our current state of legislation would have us believe they're leading us in the right direction. It's immoral in their opinion, however, to make a truly decent decision about the right to life.

Please help save babies. Why is it that we have federally funding for the arts out of fear that we might not give opportunity to a van Gogh or a Picasso who may otherwise fail, yet we abort literally millions of unborn babies with all of their potential? Is this democracy or hypocrisy? Make your choice. God knows.

After a seed is planted, it comes alive when it germinates. This occurs before it breaks above ground. Even so, our lives begin at conception, in secret, before our parents are aware of it. We call this pregnancy. These are the facts of life. By definition, we say that a new life begins when cells split—at conception. Most of us won't cry out for the truth that abortion kills. It's not simply a religious notion that has no place in the market of ideas. The science of child development begins with conception and even with the environment in which children are conceived.

We could expand the language of the Constitution to include "the right to life, liberty, and the pursuit of happiness for the unborn," as it is stated in the Declaration of Independence. Yes, each one is at the most defenseless, vulnerable stage of life. This is self-evident; they have the right to life. They have no say. Who will protect these infants? If it's a mandate to support human rights, then let's recognize human life from the start. Do the laws in our courts ever reach or include unborn children? In some cases, they do. The law can go further still. Often the very same people who push children's rights oppose the unborn child's right to life. The harm falls hardest on blameless babies. The harm of this sin hurts women. Amendments to our United States Constitution insured justice in the American government with the Bill of Rights, emancipated slaves, granting them with citizenship and voting rights, and gave women the right to vote, etc. Let's stop abortion. America has led the way since the "shot heard round the world," but there's much more to be done to protect lives.

Many people get along without Jesus. They have accomplishments and reasons to be happy. What can we tell them? It's easy to stay in your comfort zone by playing it safe. Who can blame you? We are fine when everybody acts nice. You compromise. You pay your bills and taxes and drive the speed limit. Most people live good lives without a lot of trouble.

It may be a sign of the future when neighbors in our communities live well. Isn't that a frightening thought? *Utopia* literally means "no place," because there is no perfect place. The devil would love it if we didn't think that we're sinners in need of reform; imagine if we attained all that we needed and got it properly. People today sell their souls to get all they desire. We dream of a day when everything is free, no money; it all just comes to us like it's ours for the taking. It's in the back of people's mind now.

Lots of us build financial comfort and convenience lawfully. War is too costly as nations grow affluent; it's unthinkable to steal, fight, or kill to get rich. Why steal when you can gather more by conforming? Imagine how sweet it feels when you have everything you want and you earned it. How would anybody need a salvation (2 Timothy 3:5)? Life goes on, but don't be duped; cultural whims aren't a trustworthy guide. Needs will be met in the new world order, yet nobody will know Jesus. Can I win anyone over if they all live right, lack nothing, and take it easy? How Christians are going to act then is anyone's guess.

Give Your Life

> *He that findeth his life shall lose it: and he that loseth his life for my sake shall find it.*
> Matthew 10:39

It is quite a contrast when I think about how far down I was before I came to Christ and how gratifying my life is since. I marvel. God must have known back then how good my life would be with decades of Christian living. My life has been especially happy because of the blessings Jesus sends my way. Jesus loves me, and I love Him for it.

The goal of the "Me" generation of the 1960s was to find one's self. Young Americans would say with real pride, "I'm out to find myself." Just exactly what was it that you might obtain if you really did find yourself? It wasn't necessarily a crazy image. Prior to this, our country had turned into a materialistic modern society. We had arrived. Then we heard that we arrived when we got outside of ourselves and looked to the welfare of others. Better yet, if I get outside myself living for Jesus and loving my neighbor, then I really do find myself, and I read it in such Bible verses as Matthew 10:39. I sure did. I found *love* with *faith*.

People get to know themselves only by getting to know God. Some people back in the day got all enthusiastic about the concept of loving themselves. Reality is not found when we learn to love ourselves, but it is found in loving our Lord and Savior and learning how He loves us. Self-esteem has been emphasized in child psychology and for adults. By knowing God, we see our worth and inspire this new hope in others.

It was about "self" in the late 1960s. The buzzword in culture was "turned on." All you had to do was, as Timothy Leary said, "tune in, turn on, and drop out." You would've had to have been there. Listeners were directed to get stoned, go fall down on some freshly mowed grass, and daydream life away. "Turn on." It was really about awareness. What good is life in a plastic world of make-believe? The thing we'd say was to "get real." A lot of us shook off the revolting turned-on effect and never went back. We didn't go back to the original state of nonexistence either. We went straight to Jesus.

In the 1970s, the gospel was freely given and generously received. Many heard for the first time that they had to meet Jesus and be "born again," and this became well known. The "born-again" revival spread. The emphasis was on a personal relationship with Jesus—not in merely hearing about Him—He changes everything in us (2 Corinthians 5:17). It was a peer-driven youth movement in a financially expanding, booming time. The surge was unstoppable.

The conservative evangelical fundamentalist wave (which actually began in the early 1920s in response to liberalism) undoubtedly made its big mark on the century. Christians have been out preaching that the love of Jesus is more than a religion—it's a way of life.

When I was much younger, the television news made the end of the world seem very threatening. We had the Cold War, the Vietnam War, the war on poverty, the *Population Bomb*, endemic disease, and starvation, etc. I turned to Jesus Christ and found out what the signs of the end meant, in the Bible verses. They made us think the second coming was approaching. Christians still speak of their conviction that Jesus must be returning soon; the increasingly sinful conditions of our world say so. Sin has caused ruin since the fall of man. There's been chaos and killing all along.

There was a news report the other day that a woman had consumed too many drinks and smoked a pile of marijuana before she drove the wrong way on the expressway, killing herself and others. You could say, "She didn't feel a thing," but don't take comfort in that thought. The next thing she knew, she was in eternity, likely where it's not good and where there's no turning around.

After I found Jesus, I loved the way the Bible addressed all my situation. Christianity had to work for me. I struggled to take hold of the answers. I was at the end of my rope when I got saved. Not every Christian has come to that crisis. Jesus asked me for my life, and I had little to hang on to. Well-meaning people have asked me to take my talk elsewhere and to feel satisfied just in myself. They know I'm doing well. They want me to ease up. They don't want a Christian to rock their boat. Really now! All who really love themselves will seek salvation, and they'll not give up until they find Jesus Christ, and all they have to do is ask Him into their life. Don't despair. You're not alone.

> *And forgive us our sins; for we also forgive everyone that is indebted to us. And lead us not into temptation; but deliver us from evil.*
>
> Luke 11:4

Jesus has saved us in two ways: from our sin and from our righteousness. We're not any better than anyone else, so we should be forgiving of others. Besides daily irritations that we encounter, what festers is the deeper anger and nagging animosity brought on by an appetite for purpose, realization, and a justification to live. Life is a competition, and we want excitement. Instead, we have resentment. We're in anguish for fear of not getting everything we want. Fulfillment in Jesus means an abundant success in life that produces generosity.

When you pray and get blessed, you will want this for others. You do have to want this. To our betterment or to our detriment, we choose which direction our hearts turn. Christians want to be blameless, harmless, and never offensive. God delivers us from evil. Our old nature would return evil for evil. We have offended. We age with bitterness, or we mature with God's forgiveness. It is not insignificant that Jesus preached this grace. In Jesus, this new transforming power of grace does work.

We must trust God and not place anything or anybody above Him. Learning to be content and curbing our speech adds to godliness and brotherly kindness. Who are we hurting? *"A soft answer turneth away wrath"* (Proverbs 15:1), but too often, we get antagonistic and a little knowledgeable and start blistering others with accusing words of criticism. Disapproval and guilt whet the appetite for sin.

Once again, we find ourselves in sore need of God. We've been looking to satisfy ourselves in the wrong places. The germ of malice is a contagion to which Christians are not immune. It's an infection that corrupts even the best of our plans. Bitterness and cynicism go like a plague, if allowed to spread.

Just as drunkenness is a consuming sin, bitterness also ruins lives. Anger will hit ever deeper in the soul with addictive hatred and spite. You may not suffer it in your family or mine, in your neighborhood, but violence hits everywhere. The fabric of decency is ripped apart in many places by these forces. Who helps? Many of our educators, philosophers, and politicians are increasingly driven by dark motives.

The hearts of unsuspecting souls fall into subjection to fears. There are myriads of counselors and other professionals who give empty answers to broken people because they themselves lack any hope of healing. Capable analysts with lots of training and skill are helplessly lost, and they're not objective; their goal is their own profit.

I talk to young people who've come out of sin and lead others to Jesus. The only thing is that many turn back to the world again. Later, I find these same people confused by their further wrongdoing. Obviously, anyone can go crazy abusing drugs. Who is immune? My advice to those in recovery is to wait.

When you go on a big ride at the carnival, you might get real dizzy. When you walk off the ramp and onto solid ground after the ride ends, the world is still spinning around. Why is that? When I'm too dizzy after a ride, I look for a light pole to hang on to, and I don't take a step until the whirling stops. My friends may walk away without me, but I'm not taking a step. Friends in recovery should do nothing more until their lives calm down. Then move on. Since we live in the Spirit, we want to walk in the Spirit so we better wait for Him.

> *All things are lawful unto me, but all things are not expedient: all things are lawful for me, but I will not be brought under the power of any.*
> 1 Corinthians 6:12

A bolder faith sets us free from our old habits. Some of us already have so much wrong to correct in our lives that it takes a heap of courage to face these painful debts. We feel too anxious and frustrated to see. We pay a bigger price for holding on to the old ways.

Our difficult days drain us and leave us disposed to doubt. Satan wears out the saints with lust and temptation, *"And he shall speak great words against the most High, and shall wear out the saints of the most High"* (Daniel 7:25). God gives rest. The Bible contains wisdom to help us make better decisions, as difficult as they may be. God will fill our lives with the vitality of His glory.

We must be honest with ourselves. If you're sliding downhill out of control, get help. We grow and mature, either for good or for bad. Sweet is the heart set free from self-centeredness, shame, and old grudges. You have to learn to be grateful. We may have to learn it over again.

We find ourselves incapable of change and unable to escape. Turn to God and pray for mercy. Many people would rather complain. Since things are what they are, they may stay that way. God's love could move through us without difficulty, but we have all of our worries. We fight with people because we can't see straight. We get mad and give them no room to improve, even though they may improve with time. We will know that we have progressed when people continue their ways and troubles remain, but we stay unperturbed and unruffled. Righteous anger is all right if it dissipates and does not hang on too long.

We find no peace pursuing the pleasure and sordidness of old desires. Lust bends people like the young sapling planted on the side of a mountain when it grows up against a rock and is bent for life. In time, the tree grows more deformed, or it might straighten up as it turns toward the sun. Is there a time when the sinner comes to God? Some people are crooked. Does it make any a difference to depart from sin and live right if we are still unforgiving? Love believes all things are possible with God.

I worked with a Christian woman who was fun to joke around. I would tease her by making stuff up. She would always try to correct me with words like, "Christians can't lie," and she would act indignant.

I would say, "Yes, they can," and that would really bother her. Then I would tell her another lie. It was fun. She knew I was kidding, but I hoped it relayed a message to her because she was part of a small strict following. Christians can lie and we do. It's not impossible. We are not perfect. So what? Is it a sin to be nice to someone who sins? Sometimes, we need help. This is difficult news for a few believers I know. I sympathize. So where exactly do we draw the line between judgment and mercy? It is hard to verbalize the idea since none of us live up to God's level of holiness, but this is His stated goal for each of us: *"Because it is written, Be ye holy; for I am holy"* (1 Peter 1:16). It was hard to be perfect before we were saved, and it is still impossible now. There, I said it again. We have a ways to go.

The Lord's Prayer directs us to confess our sin and to forgive others. This is when faith counts. We have to think by faith. We must forget our old mentality and open up to a greater understanding: *faith* with *love*.

The inability to cope with frustrations and regrets causes despair and depression. Eventually, it develops into chronic emotional problems, physical illnesses, mental instability, and immorality. You hurt your own well-being by getting belligerent and vengeful. Who enjoys fighting? Bitterness can become so ingrown that it entangles our lives, devouring the fruit of our labor and stealing love away from our families. Inevitably, as the years go by, this rut becomes a trench. In over your head, you cannot see a way out. People burn out of control with hatred and turn against those who are most important in their lives, it crushes them. How is anybody able to step in and rescue you? Only Jesus Christ, our Savior, is able to help with His life-changing forgiveness.

Our behavior can stay with us. We can't always help ourselves. I've had to learn to relax. Driving on the freeway in the city is a proving ground for emotions. The flow of traffic in my lane can be interrupted by one single car. It might be a stalled car on the other side of the highway in the other direction, but it slows down my side. It will probably happen as long as we ride on wheels.

The same feelings bother me about people. They allow distractions or temptations or even one person to hold them up. Let the love of the Lord flow freely as He intends, in and through His grace. Absolutely nothing is standing in your way. Is that the way you see it? But you are slowed down. Whether tempted by sin or tempered by guilt, *"Christ is become of no effect unto you"* Galatians 5:4. The world, indeed, goes the other way, blocked and bottlenecked by what's going on. Our old mind is terribly fascinated by it. We are stymied. God sees us victorious.

We punish ourselves more than anyone else. Fuming Christians complain about others, asking, "Why are all these people so bad?" We get preoccupied with what's wrong. Call us protectionists or perfectionists. We get depressed, telling ourselves how unbearable things have been. Besides, you ask, who are we actually hurting? *"He that diggeth a pit shall fall into it;"* Ecclesiastes 10:8. The lives of people are burning up like in a fire—so run in and rescue the survivors. Do we care to try? No, because we're worried about what everyone else thinks.

This world gets rough. We believe we should have nothing go wrong and no pain. Maturity knows that problems are common to all, one after the other. We all have our share. In a sense, no one person is worse than any other. You can argue with that. You can see how the hurts in your life are able to increase your faith and let everything strengthen your love in Jesus' name, when you understand He cares.

Pray for God to send more love. Life could be different than it is. We complain and then we run away. People who refuse to believe are ripe for the harvest, and God needs more workers—so we should reach lost souls as a team; the time is critical. We all want to see life change, everyone—even the most difficult people. Perhaps most of us give it less thought. A few might want to know why a big commanding God is not doing more. Jesus has promised that with His Father's love, He will accomplish every potential blessing. Our Savior longs to grant lots of blessings and to save as many people as possible. His glories in Heaven are infinite and eternal. God's love never fades.

From Fiery Trials to Fiery Love

> *Beloved, think it not strange concerning the fiery trial which is to try you, as though some strange thing happened unto you: but rejoice, inasmuch as ye are partakers of Christ's sufferings; that, when his glory shall be revealed, ye may be glad also with exceeding joy.*
>
> 1 Peter 4:12–13

A Christian of strong conviction won't think it's strange when fiery trials come, as if strange things should never happen. Life is a test. We get more experience. What kind of Christian do you want to be? At times, I feel like I'm a hex on God's work, but that's why we need to pray and allow the Holy Spirit to rule. What we see isn't a hoax. Our faces do not need to be so dejected nor our hearts subdued because of trials. Love is a test, and we are tested.

Let's support the work of the Church, share the faith, and give more true love. Resist temptation and the devil will flee from you. Don't let a guilty conscience be your guide. Love springs out from a clean heart and the bright hope of Heaven.

We need to be fervent servants. Jesus commands us to give all we have with all of our mind, all our strength, and all our heart. We are underachievers. Find room to improve. Time is running out. We must bring our talents together and gather determination as in an emergency. Even in the bad times, true believers always rejoice in what's ahead.

There must be Christians you know who love God joyously. Can you think of some who stand out—not as haughty, but humble. You want the type who know Jesus better through reading their Bibles. Life isn't about having all our problems solved, but is about learning to cope without complaining because God has it figured out. How do we communicate this? I will not be bothering other people if I love God, believe in Him, and I'm trying to do my best.

My friend Stan answered the question, "Who loves God?" He named David, a kid who was baptized in our church but later went to prison. Soon after David got arrested and was sent to prison, Christian prisoners pressed him to repent; he knew he had to surrender his heart to God. Many of us received mail from him. His fervor never let down during the years he was locked up or since. Dave was released after a long time. He then went to college, got a job helping others who were getting out of prison, and he got married to a lovely lady. God can use men like him. Dave's work now has inspired others to follow his example.

If you know my friend Stan, you know he loves God too, and his wife Dorothy is also devoted with all her strength and time. Believe me, they are a team for years together. We love God; we count our blessings. We give Him praise for His power, truth, and wisdom. We thank Him for His care, His provision, and His surrounding protection. Loving God, counting on His everlasting ways, and praising Him will perfect us. It reflects on Him.

Just as the hot summer sun wilts flowers, our devotion faints in the heat of this world. We waver. We have second thoughts. We doubt. Can we remember to pray when we've been so careless? We love God more or less, sometimes more and sometimes less.

God knows if you love Him. How do you show it? Say, "I love you, Lord!" Our God is beautiful beyond words. He created everything there is. God made everything out of nothing, and He made it more marvelous than we can see. How do people argue against Him?

Remember also to love God for the wonderful God He is; imagine how big He is!

God is bigger than outer space. He designed the earth precisely to cultivate life. If we were in a different orbit closer to the sun, we would be scorched. We would freeze if we were too far away. The odds are extremely improbable that the universe could support life, not even on another small planet like ours. We are placed in just the right place and are set like a fine watch. Scientists know that if the earth were 10 percent bigger, gravity would squish us. If the atmosphere were made of any different mix, we couldn't exist. The earth's axis is tilted perfectly to give us seasons for the crucial changes in the wind and weather. If the earth's axis were tipped one small fraction of a degree more or less, we couldn't last. How precarious can it get? People take life for granted. Likewise, love is not to be taken lightly.

Our normal body temperature is 98.6 degrees Fahrenheit. If it goes up or down five or ten degrees, we become sick or even die. On hot days, we stay at an even temperature because God gave us a cooling system, like a car radiator. Our bodies transfer heat away rapidly by the laws of physics, when our perspiration evaporates off our skin. We lose weight on hot days not because we burn more calories, but because we shed water. We cool down by burning fewer calories as our metabolism slows. We are our own refrigerator!

We also have a built-in heating system to warm us like a furnace, a thermometer, and a thermostat. Each of us has a fire going on inside us. We literally do burn calories. If we have no thermostat, what prevents the body from heating itself through the roof? I don't know where exactly the thermometer and thermostat are located, if it's in the skin or lungs or a vasodilator, but we correctly sense temperature, and our metabolism increases to burn more calories so we stay warm. My wife says she thinks I'm right about this. We are our own furnace!

We don't catch colds from being cold. We already have cold bugs before we step out the door. When we get exposed to low temperatures for too long, our body can't keep up, so as we lose a few degrees of body heat, the cold bugs gladly multiply. When the virus symptoms manifest, our body smartly runs up the temperature in a fever to kill viruses and infections. Our brain knows how to turn the heat up on the bad invader bugs, and they don't survive. Then we flush them out in fluids and sweat. The tiredness comes as our body's energy is taken up in the battle and spent for heating and healing.

We really burn extra calories in the cold to stay warm, but we temporarily sweat water off in the summer to cool. This process is more fantastic than any refrigerator or air conditioner. We have a cooling system, a heater, and an amazing autoimmune system.

We take God for granted the way we did to our dear old dads. God has tuned our bodies to these environments and vice versa. Do we think about it much? Neither do people see God and heed His love, even if they know to do so. All creation is defined. With no doubt, we can move around with our lives and with others also without thinking much about it.

We bring sinners to salvation and cheer them on in faith and in grace. Genuine Christian character comes only from God and is strengthened by our sober evaluation, humility, and a bit of intelligence. Our mental facility to assimilate can improve. Plain godliness can be imitated by the carnal mind (2 Timothy 3:5), but holiness is pure and righteous. Since grace and truth come by love, authentic values aren't based on one's ability to keep up external appearances. We give our lives to God, and He gives us some slack to take out the tangled knots. We should all want to relate to God and to get along with each other better.

Whoever wants to do so can learn to open the door to Jesus and find the right way to see things. Whatever the situation or condition, let's work to promote this positive transformation in others, beginning with their empty hearts. How many Christians will go that extra mile? Even one's own family might feel threatened by a big change. Converted we are. After being a Christian for so many years, I believe the truth of God's love more today than ever.

Bona fide love transforms attitudes. Why would we ever find it necessary to tear someone else down in order to build ourselves up? It's because we're trying to get ahead of others. It's safe to say that this is a habit. You may not do this often, but we all know people who find fault in others without being that honest about themselves.

There are many ways in which we work to make ourselves look good or try to better our position at the expense of others. We are selfish. The list could get long with a cosmic variety of accusations, conversations, and situations if we tried to write them all down. If we persist beyond what's relevant, we could end up back in the same old trap of fault-finding. That's what we're trying to avoid. Unfortunately, a lot of us needlessly hide in defeat, and nobody else suspects a thing. If people say anything, they say it in the wrong places, in wrong ways, and it's bad.

More than once, I've caught myself in the middle of a discussion defending my actions by accusing someone else. Why do I have to make someone else look bad to make myself look good? In other words, I think that I must discredit someone else in order to justify myself. Can I really come out a winner in a trade like that? I should want to be generous. It's my mistake to try to advance myself to begin with. Other people will see me for what I am.

There are times when an explanation is in order. Jesus answered those in the crowd who questioned Him. We should be sure, though, that we are in the right place—and that we are also in the right. If we're doing better with good things to begin with, we will seldom have to defend ourselves. However, when it becomes necessary, we should defend our position. We should, though, be able to disagree over differences without vilifying the other person. Too many times, we speak without thinking, and we hurt one another. A critical disposition can be habitual. Pray to be pleasing to God with each word spoken. Be an encouragement to others.

I was talking to a sales agent recently. She was a real nice, friendly person. I said, "You must be a Christian."

"Yes, but no," she said. "I am spiritual."

Strangers listen to our hearts and hear God's love. Do we have the character to solve issues and resolve differences of opinion? Stop being a pain. With Jesus, yes! Jesus said He would draw *all men* unto Himself. Do we want to leave anybody out? To help, start reminding

Christians of their higher spiritual position and their possession of Jesus. We overcome the darkness and help others strictly by God's grace. I would like to have more time with people. Right now, it's more about the unbelief out here and the light up there.

Overcome Evil with Good

> *We know that we have passed from death unto life, because we love the brethren. He that loveth not his brother abideth in death.*
>
> 1 John 3:14

We get in trouble regularly because we all are born in sin. We might think too much of ourselves, better than others would say. We think of ourselves more highly than we ought to. Maybe you feel less of a person than you are.

Any overdependence on people and overindulgence in food or material possessions makes our predicament the worse for wear. God is breaking us away from these patterns. We can place Him above all. He wants our love. After that, He brings good relationships and enrichments in their proper order.

Christians are set apart from the rest of the world. One of my favorite times as a Christian is making new friends in Bible study groups. We make each other feel important, and we have fun too. We love to see the Scripture verses light up with discovery. The look of enlightenment on someone's face shines as if someone has found gold. We need more Bible study than we're getting. Learn how to reach out. We should be studying and teaching others. When discussing the Scriptures with someone else I get other points of view that I have not thought of. I get the most from studying and teaching when I'm doing what the Bible says. Nothing quite does it better than studying God's Word and seeing it at work. This follows our Lord's New Testament call.

Our steps of faith set us apart as disciples. Jesus asks us to work in service with elders and other church leaders. This takes faith. God meets us in the offices of our pastors. Ministers utilize counseling skills quite a bit. Much of the counseling in America is done by clergymen. Good Christian therapy is available in cities and towns. A lot is gained by discussing problems honestly with our everyday friends. We are the counselors and teachers and tutors. Bible study groups, church associations, and special events help us grow. We have reason to hope.

Another thing that sets us apart is the love we have for our enemies. We don't have to return evil for evil. We have a license to love. If you wait long enough after a war, you might find the old combatants coming together in respect. "There but for the grace of God go I." On rare occasions, friendships develop. In many parts of the world, you'll find poisonous hatred that's lasted decades and generations. It affects us all. Christian, we must pray to our God in Heaven to reconcile the grudges a few people proudly harbor.

Let's give up our hurts and anger along with all the old desires and lusts. Love is basic. That means it will reduce problems. What we need is a lot of faith, hope, and patience in order to love. Christians have a good history of building each other up in constructive and practical ways. Jesus is in Heaven. We are here. He will give us stronger ties with each other and friendship toward the unbelievers, even toward those who don't deserve it. To know God's love solves everything for me.

We are not God, but we are commanded to be like Him. It's in us now to change. God is not man-made. God made man. He made us able to change. That is, He requires us to change. "Lord, I can't change," you might say, but the New Testament teaches repentance. Our awe-inspiring God sparks inner longings to create spiritual fervor. Prize the dignity you have, and you won't hurt yourself or anyone else.

God's commands are moral. He requires us to cooperate. Whether we sense it or not, sin has lowered our morale. We get warnings in life. I get told not to do something, but I go ahead and do it anyway—and then I learn why I should not have done it. Do you feel you're fighting the battle by yourself? Maybe all your old friends have moved away. When you're lonesome, make friends. If you have no family, make your own circle. God always loves you. Unfortunately, when you have nobody, that's when people grab what's yours for themselves. Respect what belongs to others. Lust is at the heart of a lot of grief.

People usually think that guilt and shame make us stop sinning. That's not always the way God works. At some point in a sinner's life, any reason to care drops away. The doubt deadens any sense of decency, responsibility, or self-control. Common sense is diminished. Inhibitions are abandoned, along with any idea of true pride. Do you know what it is to feel so guilty, you end up doing the same wrong things again and again? Those who reject help spend money they don't have, eat more donuts, or smoke more cigarettes. Internalized disapproval causes pain. It pushes folks further into sin and condemnation. It's covetousness and greed, we say little; they end up out of control. External pressures and disgusting feelings only push people further out. Can love even come close to touching a situation so stinking toxic?

> *For the love of money is the root of all evil: which while some coveted after, they have erred from the faith, and pierced themselves through with many sorrows.*
> 1 Timothy 6:10

This study on lust makes me think. What became of the rich young ruler who asked, *"Good Master, what shall I do to inherit eternal life?"* He walked away from Jesus. He could only have fought with himself. The Bible hasn't given his name or said where he went. Just suppose he was *pierced through with many sorrows*. Have you ever had friends walk away from faith? Maybe you've stumbled. Even if not, put yourself in their shoes. This is what love and empathy can do; it's the opposite of lust. This why it's in the Bible, to teach us to care.

You can't avoid the idea that this man's riches brought sadness. Imagine if he became the young vicious Saul, the persecutor of the early church. Left to our own devices and chasing our desires, we come to a frightening scenario.

People hold on to whatever it is that holds them. Whether it's something bad or good, when it takes a person away from Jesus, it is only a matter of time before their fate will be disaster. Jesus told him, *"Sell all that thou hast, and distribute unto the poor, and thou shalt have treasure in Heaven: and come, follow me"* (Luke 18:22). What will happen to us if we walk away from Jesus? It's not hard to see what it means here: help the poor or else you'll suffer (Proverbs 28:27) and be sad. The attitude Jesus confronted applies to us.

Catastrophes and emergencies may shake the addicted sinner into temporary sobriety, even to prayer, but the cycle of depression, escape, and recidivism returns a short time later. It's a pattern that gets to be a syndrome. Do penalties deter offenders? Hooked, obsessed, in denial, and facing looming liabilities, minds are numbed, blind to the tougher consequences. They're ignorant of their subconscious links to sin. When old enticements hit, sin runs its course, finishing in death. Christians do well to remind each other of the dreadful fate we've avoided so we don't fall back, but it's quite another thing if we fail to reach more sinners while there's still time.

God is totally concerned about the details of your life, big things and small. He hears you pray for the lives of people. He is the Sovereign One who makes the delicate flowers so pretty, the mountains so strong, and the colors of the sunsets so awesome. Hundreds of thousands of miles of shoreline around the earth have been constantly lapped by waves every minute, year after year, since the beginning. God loyally watches over each of us night and day. We ought to be devoted to our Maker, but we need to be changed.

Times do get troublesome. People the world over don't have the hope of prayer in their lives. Many twenty-year-olds these days will say life has passed them by. Lots of our elderly look back at their lives and live in the past. They do not live in the present, let alone see any future. They only see a blank wall ahead. Billions of people the world over spend their lives without salvation. God places us in

Jesus Christ, and He makes all the good improvements in us. Jesus is changing the lives of Christians to reach the world.

You feel better when you're giving instead of taking. Drop an encouraging card in the mail to a friend when you are on a holiday—or any time. Better yet, drop in to visit—soon. Go to visit at a nursing home. Donate money to a cause, church, missionary, or to research. Help a poor stranger. Give a hug. Tell your mom you care. Deep down inside, you need to love.

Christians have the ability to live life right. We are blessed, and we can instantly reach others with unselfish, effective love. The whirling, cold vortex of deceit tries to pull us down into an early grave. Look upward to Heaven to get the strength of Jesus' love. The supernatural love of Jesus expresses the very highest point of God's incomparable character. We are extraordinarily bonded to Jesus as disciples, and it shows. Everyone knows the voice of love when they hear it. Tell them it's Jesus.

Instead of putting it on others, we Christians bear more than our share of the load—and we don't take out our frustrations on others. Developing the good habits that fulfill God's everlasting purpose requires a lot of patience and practice. We need to rehearse all these good things with each other. We need quite a bit of reeducation and a lot of help from above. The law of supply and demand says that when there is less of it these days, a little good is worth a lot more.

First take hold of the truth, get it in your heart, and attempt to love. Don't fear. Jesus has greater power. You can give up the old desires of the flesh. Jesus has you cornered and surrounded, but have you surrendered? A light shines brightest in the dark. Our problems of sin are overcome by faith. God's love wins.

> *Forbearing one another, and forgiving one another, if any man have a quarrel against any: even as Christ forgave you, so also do ye. And above all these things put on charity, which is the bond of perfectness.*
> Colossians 3:13–14

The Impasse

For there is not a just man upon the earth that doeth good and sinneth not.
                                        Ecclesiastes 7:20

CHAPTER 8

Opposite-Phobia

For all have sinned, and come short of the glory of God.
Romans 3:23

The human race is at odds with God. Our world is out of control in an inverse universe. When we know and understand, we still can't help ourselves, and it makes us mad like crazy. Do we see how far we've gone astray? To be sure, your fears will find you out. Faith is the good sense to think right. Life here isn't like being in Heaven where all things are clear, but *faith* gives us today a foretaste of God's *love*.

Things end up opposite of what we want. Sin is a mystery, and we give up on love right here. There's no question that it's the vexation of our old nature. People complain of getting exactly what they hate. You and I yearn to return to a former time when all was innocent. Our chronic frustration takes more of what we look for and gives us less, as this inner turmoil prevents our accomplishments. What's our perplexity? Let me describe it with a new term: opposite-phobia.

We can break away from that cycle.

By resting in the Lord, anybody can overcome snarls and come out ahead. What is the mechanism that makes panicked drowning people thrash and splash, when all it would take for them to be safe is to relax and float? So we get swim lessons. Jesus would save us from any illogical "opposite-phobia" and help us to overcome this.

We look at other people and say they are backward. The truth is that the whole world is going backward. It might be acceptable to be a little wrong once in a while, but God sees life from a much different perspective. He sees it the way it is, and we see it the other way around. In fact, we look at everything from our own point of view. God wants us to see things His way.

We end up exactly the opposite of where we should be. It's just as if all of us have our heads screwed on backward and our shirts buttoned up the back. Our left shoe is on the right foot and our right shoe is on the left. We're standing the other way around too. Tell a person to go left, they go right; tell them to go right, they go left. We're not off course by a little bit; we're 180 degrees off. We're going the opposite direction. Do you think we're following God? People confuse what is right with what's wrong, and wrong becomes right.

We want God to do something big, and He's asking us to do something small. Have you seen cars on the freeway race to the front of the line and cut in? It's as if no one else exists. It happens. They make believe. Would you do that in a store? What is it in the lower nature that says you deserve to be in front? People are afraid they'll miss out. We certainly do miss it.

Fear Is a Snare

The fear of man bringeth a snare: but whoso putteth his trust in the Lord shall be safe.

Proverbs 29:25

In 1980, here in Washington State, Mount St. Helens was rumbling and steaming. As the volcano swelled up, experts warned of an increasing chance of an eruption, so it was surrounded with roadblocks and the area was evacuated. The governor was asking people to cooperate by staying away. I remember saying at the time that even with all the warnings, there still would be someone needlessly killed up there when it erupted.

This was a live 10,000-foot volcano in the middle of the countryside giving every sign of going off; you'd expect people to give it all the room it needed. Still, I said there would be some geologist or photographer who would get hurt when it blew. We never expected that there would be over a hundred enthusiasts in the red zone. The top of the mountain suddenly exploded one morning with the force of fifty atom bombs. Tons of it turned to powder in an instant as it blew sky-high. A path of destruction sped downhill for miles with heat and high pressure, leaving forests of trees strewn like toothpicks, and it was even stopping rivers. More than fifty people were horribly killed. Many more ran for their lives. The ash from Mount St. Helens rose in the air famously, and by noon, the east side of the state was as dark as night.

I never had any inclination to go near it because of those early warnings, but that crowd was drawn by some strange deadly attraction. It was opposite-phobia. It was startling how many curiosity seekers were camping out on the volcano. There were families with children. Was it history they were seeking or maybe the intrigue of danger? The onlookers had come from as far away as Utah and Texas. The people were not killed by the volcano as much as by their own impulse to court death by challenging the red zone.

We get obsessed by threats. We give in to intimidating situations. Growing fears will consume us. When does it become a complex? As we are hurt time and again, our pain is compounded. How can we not focus on it? Wounded, we only feed each other's fright. We fixate on our hang-ups; we're engrossed and enslaved.

Fear itself is ugly. It causes us to take all our frustration out on others, and we ridicule them. People resent life. More than that, human nature shortchanges itself; it's self-defeating. Cooperate with God's help. Hope to recover. To escape our old nature, we have to get a new nature; put our faith in the Lord and try to please Him.

You can be your own worst enemy. There are those you know

who hate life. One way, it starts is that we work for attention and approval from people who have status. It is very annoying to not have anyone's acceptance. It's unrealistic to maintain that act. It's an unhealthy level of dependence on other people. That's hard. We get edgy and drive people away. We probably don't see how foolish we look. Put Jesus first in your life. Boost your success rate and that of others, and rely on God's wisdom. Love works in our faith.

It's all right to enjoy the fruit of your own work and rejoice when others do well. On the other side of the coin, opposite-phobia has an image of fear. It is not a fear of losing, but it's like a fear of winning. We fear what is unknown. Do we inwardly think if we excel, others might criticize us? We ought to see that our achievements rob no one if we're doing right. We should also see we are not deprived by the accomplishments of others. God is our sanctuary, a fortress, an ever-present salvation to those who trust and believe in Him. It's a pleasure. God's will is very much alive in the heart and lives of every Christian.

We should recognize how God is at work in everyone, both believers and nonbelievers. I have a few friends who doubt the veracity of this statement. It's a given. There are Christians who feel insecure in their relationship with God. A few people tell me they are borderline Christians. What does that mean? You can understand how hard it must be for those who live in dread of losing their salvation. It neutralizes any movement and prohibits their growth. The lost soul shows no blip on their screen. I trust God is at work with them. If you suppose life has passed you by, look again. God's Spirit is the biggest gift of all. If people are floundering in their walk with Jesus, maybe they are simply unaccustomed to victory. They could certainly be instructed by you if you put together for them a stronger connection between *love* and *faith*.

We all have our dreams in life. Why can't we win? Birds fly through the air with the greatest of ease, and fish swim underwater like it was made for them. God did make it for them. We are also now good to go. *"Consider the lilies of the field, how they grow; they toil not"* (Matthew 6:28). Just wait. Good things will come to you.

If love is going to build, it needs a firm foundation. I heard a man describe the process of constructing tall skyscrapers. He said that the higher a building goes, the more expensive it gets because the costs rise exponentially with every story added. The extra expense is not so much from adding to the top, but from adding to the bottom to make the ground floor stronger to support all that's above. I wouldn't have thought of that. The first floor and foundation must have a beefier design with every additional level. The top floor always costs less than those below. This analogy applies to our love. Our love has to be strengthened on the base level to be able to support the rest, rather than having the load piled on top and weighing things down.

Pray to God. Your greatest longings may never be fulfilled. Your dreams may be reduced to nothing and might, without God, become only your poor decisions. You wouldn't know if they were your delusions. Surrender to Jesus all your heart's worries and cares. Yield to Him even your most terrible fears.

Jesus knows how to help because He expects us to fall short, and He knows why: sin. He wants us to trust Him in all the details of life—in trifling tiffs as well as in monumental mistakes. Don't get bogged down in trivia, because small things can bite back. Allow God's goodwill into your plans and see His love appear. Grow in grace and patience by remembering that none of us are able to cope effectively with our hurts and losses on our own. And think of others. All of us are able to rise above, but we do it with true *love* by *faith* in Jesus.

What we fear the most defeats us unless we place ourselves more fully into God's care. When something as large as Mount St. Helens comes to life, you should try to stay clear away from it. The things in our lives that pose these threats will pull us in and injure us. God tells us not to react with fear. He says to respond with more confidence in His love.

> *There is no fear in love; but perfect love casteth out fear: because fear hath torment. He that feareth is not made perfect in love.*
>
> 1 John 4:18

Defensive people are so worried that they don't tune in to others. Nevertheless, people do affect one another. Opposite-phobia is antisocial. Our Lord is sworn as our everlasting High Priest to prove His great love by mending our failures, healing our hurts, and yes, straightening out the social disorders infesting our world.

By so much was Jesus made a surety of a better testament.
Hebrews 7:22

We can put more stock in Jesus. For some reason, Christians can be particularly gullible and susceptible to the world's pollution. We try, but we are not always very impressed by God. This is precisely why we are prone to temptation. We feel unsure of our relationship with our Maker. Each of us should know our Bible and see that Jesus surely is the minister of *"a better testament,"* the new covenant, the New Testament.

Resistance to God translates into mistrust and strife. Nervous people make others jittery. People project fear in more ways than one. We all worry. Faith in Jesus is sacred. We frighten others when we look scared. Faith fixes it.

In the past, we've succumbed to sin, but we can be turned around to Jesus's way. He favors us, transforms us, and helps us guide friends through to their victories. God makes peace on earth possible—even among the hatred, the rivalries, the violence, and every other wrongdoing. Are we repulsed by crowds? You might fear people. This world is definitely dangerous. We're bound to repeat failure only because we are not aware of God often enough. What gives? God tells us not to worry. He watches over us day and night. Faith cuts through all the contradictions. God is going to do His work in His way—both in us and in this world.

For all the promises of God in him are yea, and in him Amen, unto the glory of God by us.
2 Corinthians 1:20

Jesus justifies sinners. There is no need to fight it. The way God deals with our sins is changing us for our own good—into holiness. God is not as concerned about situations as He is about people. He isn't bothered so much whether people are cohabitating, divorced, or homosexual as He cares that they are lost. Their dysfunction indicates a failure to the core. God forgives all sin in order to bring us to His righteousness and peace. Give God more credit. He has our lives. He's creating awesome, amazing blessings more than we know. Our soul fails us. Trust God, and you will see a love like you have never dreamed of. This hope is the opposite of what the world is headed for. It's in the back of their mind. Contrary to what they say, they're going to get something they really don't want; we'll have every good thing to keep.

The Failed Soul

> *I opened to my beloved; but my beloved had withdrawn himself, and was gone: my soul failed when he spake: I sought him, but I could not find him; I called him, but he gave me no answer.*
>
> Song of Solomon 5:6

Solomon wrote a poignant song about the love between a man and a woman. With only a few words here, a lover tells the full story. It's a vivid picture of this moment, a snapshot. Here we can see human love. The distress in this verse captures the hesitation in the woman's love and in the man's withdrawal. Our lifeless soul laments such a pitiful reluctance to respond to God when He comes to us.

Saying how we really feel can sometimes be the most difficult thing to do. The more important a thing is to say, the harder it becomes to say it. For far too many, stepping forward and admitting our true feelings seems like it's near impossible to get around. It shouldn't be hard to say what we mean and to express our hearts. What are we afraid of? A little open honesty wouldn't be the end of the world. Too often, I've been caught on the spot when my nerves failed, although the words were in me—and I regretted it.

A shy young man has a real battle with himself over a girl whom he would really like to ask out on a date. After worrying for some time, he rustles up enough courage, finds his voice, and asks the big question. She hesitates. Then she makes some excuse not to go out with him. She may've had her eye on this guy though. She might have told someone else what a real dreamboat this new boy is, yet in her shyness, she turned him down, and she hates herself for it. She thinks to herself that the next time he asks, she'll say yes, but he never asks her again. Then suppose young man asks her several times before she agrees to go out. She could go a long time before telling him her true feelings.

Imagine if our friend doesn't get the courage again to ask the cute girl for a date. Instead, she goes out with someone who doesn't really care about her. What she perceives as genuine caring in this other guy is just slick talk to take advantage of her. What does she do when she finds herself in a place she doesn't want to be? Meanwhile, our first young man is completely powerless over his own insecurities, jealous but intimidated by that other guy's bold moves. What does he do when he's not acting the way he feels he should? This is a clear case of opposite-phobia, and we all have seen it.

Let's see if someday, the shy young man gets his date with this girl. With the right amount of moonlight, they fall in love. This does not mean that opposite-phobia has been detected, diagnosed, or cured. Often, this is left unchecked to grow into its advanced stages in adulthood and in marriage. Thereafter, we can find some of the most profound contradictions, sad as it gets.

It's true that opposites attract, especially in marriage. People often marry conflicting personalities, but don't realize it until later. Being different isn't wrong in itself, but how we handle it is what counts. Opposites can balance each other and actually be better together, because one will complement the other. It can be beautiful. People, though, tend to harm one another if opposite-phobia is an issue.

Spouses find themselves yelling "I hate you" at each other. What they mean is that they disagree and are disappointed with each other on a few points, they are too dependent, and they feel that they very much need their mate's love and support. That's traumatic.

Another classic line repeated in haste is "I'm sorry I ever married you!" The big mistake is not necessarily the marriage, but the divorce. Someone who spouts off with such language is seldom taken seriously. The frequent use of these barbs, the lack of content, and the poor timing come off as pretty immature. It takes a small person to act that way. Married couples come to where they're unable to admit they love each other. People really are extremely sorry that their marriage has not worked better.

Feelings in a frustrated marriage are not only expressed in bad taste at home, but they may be talked about in public with friends and family. People are quick to add on to gossip, so the "advice" given in return is often doubly negative and counterproductive. What started as stories descends into wrong moves with bad motives. Poor advice makes things worse. Neurotic people work on each other like spontaneous combustion.

Strong negative emotions show we are acting with bad judgment. The angry feeling of bitterness has no end. Too much for one is not enough for another. Focus your eyes on God and quiet these racing thoughts. His grace will calm your mind.

Tactfulness is the ability to criticize or advise someone without raising an eyebrow. If you are smooth enough, they listen to what you have to say. One rule I use for seasoning my cooking is to put in just enough spice to flavor the food, but not enough to tell what it is. If somebody tastes a dish and immediately notes what exact strong seasoning overpowered the recipe, it's embarrassing to me. You want the guests to say that you made great beef or tasty chicken, without commenting about the garlic, oregano, or pepper. Here again, you and I can always employ taste in what we say. Try getting love alone by cutting out the digs and saying something positive with faith.

> *For that which I do I allow not: for what I would, that do I not; but what I hate, that do I.*
>
> Romans 7:15

The odd things we do are not permissible, and what we simply should do, we don't. We find it in ourselves to say or do the wrong thing. I have heard it said, "He lied where the truth would fit better." We get so absorbed, we say things that are quite damaging, completely different from what we intended, and so we step right into the very snare that most frightens us. Then what happens? People who are particularly keyed to our difficulty will turn and pull a stunt we surely dread. Can you understand that? We're backward. We're prone to turn a situation into what it's not out of a fear for what it might be.

There are times when other people do or say something wrong, and we jump on their case, thoughtlessly adding fuel to their fire. Whose side are you on then? We could ruin them. Instead, let us act in love (2 Corinthians 2:7–8). Can't we limit ourselves? We're quick to condemn, but we fail to remember how much we've had to learn ourselves—the hard way. We forget what we know, and sometimes what we know, we don't or won't admit it.

From Bad Talk to Good

> *Brethren, if a man be overtaken in a fault, ye which are spiritual, restore such an one in the spirit of meekness; considering thyself, lest thou also be tempted.*
>
> Galatians 6:1

A little humility helps us all. When we get a better view of our own fallen nature, we look at each other's faults and consider that we must restore and not destroy others. Ease up and reach out. Show some care and concern and look out for the well-being of all, but if left unchecked, opposite-phobia leads us into brutal battles with those exact fixations we fear the most. Paul said, "*lest thou also be tempted.*"

In the same way, our biggest resentments are sure to overtake us, and they will do so to the same degree that we allow it. Christ's love, on the other hand, brings us back to our senses, back to faith.

For some unnatural reason, it bothers us to discover our own faults in others. We don't know why we get mad, but we react adversely to those who reflect our very own failings and weaknesses. Haven't you criticized someone for something and then found yourself doing the same thing the next day? You've been criticized by someone for some odd deal, and you noticed that they do it too. Pray to Jesus for His loving grace. He can help. Instead of meddling, do the mending. Our clumsy tongues are tricky. They like to be constructive or destructive. The Holy Spirit replaces caustic comments with helpful hints.

Finding faults in others is normal, but singling out one person or focusing on one thing and blowing it out of proportion is a sign of opposite-phobia. Obsessing on the faults that others have becomes mentally unhealthy. You think you are trying to help, but you end up doing just the reverse. You do more harm than good. Don't throw water on an oil fire or it will spread. We have the option of a restrained comment; reduce your response, and after a careful word, quickly let it go. "A soft *answer turneth away wrath: but grievous words stir up anger*" (Proverbs 15:1). If you have to yell to be heard, then you aren't very close. Get next to people and build rapport, or you will only push them further away. In case of disaster, minimize the damage. If a ship is already on fire, we're not talking about prevention, but about minimizing damage. Nobody moves me to their point of view when they're trying to make me look bad.

In football, they say, "Don't give up the big play." Sometimes, the defensive squad plays so tight on the point of attack that when the ball carrier breaks through, there's nothing but daylight to the goal line. I like the old "Bend, but don't break" defense concept. It's tough to coach players to stay close enough to their opponents to stop them, while at the same time, leaving enough space to prevent the big play. If you're too hard and rigid with not enough give, you will break. Oddly enough, flexibility is stronger.

The *Titanic* was built to be unsinkable, but it sank on its maiden voyage. The wreckage was recently discovered and explored. The investigators concluded that the hull was made of such hard, pure steel that it shattered like glass when it hit the iceberg. It had not bent, had no give. Like the old cliché about dancing on the *Titanic* unaware of the iceberg ahead, the crew ignored caution, assuming invincibility. Then, sudden catastrophe struck in the night. The party was over in a New York minute, like a glass jaw. We can make our lives harder by assuming that we are invulnerable, acting buoyant, and who's the last to know how fast we might sink?

> *Confess your faults one to another, and pray one for another, that ye may be healed. The effectual fervent prayer of a righteous man availeth much.*
>
> James 5:16

Believers have grace to embrace truth, and God is close enough to hear us. "*With the mouth confession is made unto salvation*" (Romans 10:10). Our lower nature is contrary. It holds us back from God and each other, and then it takes us into various sins and temptations. Jesus draws us by His Spirit, "*speaking the truth in love*" (Ephesians 4:15). We pray as one and get heard. Sometimes, the truth is obvious; sometimes, it's not and is left unsaid.

I don't mind talking about my problems or a few crimes I've done. We're unwilling to talk about the most significant things, about what most needs to be aired out. These secrets are the last to surface. They're locked up deep in a dark dungeon, on the lowest level, at the end of the row in the last cell. When we bottle up those foibles inside, they fight and struggle awfully hard to come out. They fight to stay inside.

Verbal confession isn't easy. The fact that I believe something is unmentionable doesn't mean it is. Holding these words in can make them damaging. Smelly garbage needs to be taken out. Sometimes, it's difficult to get out. The mouth and heart are stopped. Nearly everyone, including me, is ready. Just get it out. The Holy Spirit is living in fellowship with us. We have faith in God, and He brings miracles. The ministry of confession is powerful and important, but it's trying for us.

Since we tend to look at life backward, in hindsight, we should yield to God and allow Him to direct our ways. Name it "opposite-phobia," and we can even watch out for our own syndromes and see when we're headed into danger. Pray, study, and work with the development of God's will in your life. By knowing the Bible and applying its basic principles, this can be extraordinary; we can detect opposite-phobia early to keep life from backfiring.

Things in the world are tough, but it's possible to cut through the complexities. We can cross a frontier and move to heights we never dreamed of before. God gives us the freedom. This spiritual life includes people, or it's not spiritual. We need to open up to one another, let God in, and look for the best—and it happens in surprising ways.

Christians walk by faith, not knowing why things happen as they do. God tells us not to worry. He gives love to live. Faith sees through people problems. Serenity is flexible. Joy is a light. *"Now the God of hope fill you with all joy and peace in believing, that ye may abound in hope, through the power of the Holy Ghost"* (Romans 15:13). Have hope. Whether we confront sin or confess it, love has no fear; God has grace.

Confession of sin is for our sanctification, not our condemnation! God has forgiven us for our sins, so we have absolutely nothing to lose now. We can be honest with ourselves and others. Government witnesses are granted immunity to testify in court, so they will tell their full story. Strangely, these criminals or suspects do talk, and their word is accepted. Though they may have killed or committed treason, they get on the stand to serve a purpose greater than what they've been accused of. This is good.

You may suffer from the opposite-phobia complex. I call it a complex when it affects so many aspects of our lives. Trust God in Jesus Christ. We are justified to claim victory. Watch God build your world anew with more integrity and stability.

God's Love Is Too Good

When Simon Peter saw it, he fell down at Jesus' knees, saying, Depart from me; for I am a sinful man, O Lord.
Luke 5:8

Peter and his friends had been fishing all night, and they must have been really tired. Jesus came along drawing a large crowd. The people were pushing Him. He saw the fishing boats, got into one, and asked Peter to shove out a little way from the land. *"And he sat down, and taught the people out of the ship"* (Luke 5:3). Jesus finished speaking and then told Simon Peter to let down his net into the water. Here's the catch: insisting that they had fished all night and had caught nothing, Peter did as he was asked and brought up the biggest load of fish.

Peter's reaction was humiliation. "Depart from me," Peter pleaded. He was totally devastated. As you might think, he should have been impressed. There's no way of knowing why he told Jesus to go away from him, but he admitted right there that he himself was a sinner. So why did he want Jesus to depart from him? Jesus was supposed to save him. You might think Peter would cling to Him, and he did indeed follow Jesus from then on.

Ask yourself why this fisherman told Jesus to leave him there. Did Peter want to keep on sinning? Is that why he tried to chase Jesus away? People don't always avoid Jesus simply because they crave sin. People have issues.

After failing to catch even one fish, the fishermen were almost ready to give up, leave their boats behind, and look for another job.

Peter was obviously overwhelmed by the miracle, but he told Jesus to leave him. Was he afraid of Jesus? He might've gone along for the loaves and fishes, like so many others had done. Peter heard the message right there in the boat. Was he repentant? Maybe Peter felt like a failure at fishing—and even at living. Maybe he didn't blend in with the crowd, but he did become part of the story. If Peter couldn't trust the success Jesus offered, maybe he had a case of opposite-phobia that held him. The whole thing was too intimidating.

Jesus may have spoken about emptiness and the hole in everyone's life that He could fill. Nothing is said here in Luke 5 about any of the words of Jesus' sermon. Just prior to this story is Luke 4:43, and in Mark 1:15, we see Him there as the Messiah preaching the coming of the kingdom of God. If He was telling this gospel message again from the boat, what was Jesus saying about brokenness? The end of Luke 5 contains the parables of the cloth and the wineskins, which speak of tearing, like the tearing of nets that couldn't hold all the catch and the two boats that began to sink with fish, one belonged to Peter.

Jesus often preached the need for a new life. He said we need to do more than simply improve. We are sinful. Peter was uncomfortable with that. He was reluctant to resign and rein in his life in order to gain a place with Jesus. This is a tough decision to make.

Jesus has so much good to give, yet out of fear, too few accept Him. Nobody wants to die. Doesn't everyone want salvation? I think so. Is the pull of sin that strong? God's love is good and powerful. Is it also scary? We're crazy. Sin disappoints and its results deadly.

> *If ye continue in my word, then are ye my disciples indeed; and ye shall know the truth, and the truth shall make you free.*
>
> John 8:31–32

Out of a sense of vulnerability, we remove ourselves from the presence of God. Christians come within view of God's truth where He makes us winners. We should hang on and walk in His Spirit, but it is so intense that we can hardly stand it. If He were to open us to the full measure of His glory, we would drop dead from its power. Do you think we shrink back from God for the immorality of this old world or because of our own mortality? His love is so excellent that we have to back off.

Do not quench the Spirit (1 Thessalonians 5:19). Allow God time.

Make more room for thought and prayer, for reading and worship. Feel the emotions of His love. Increase your capacity for God. We don't know enough or see how to rest in the hope of our Savior! Get nearer to people. Be friendly. You're not spiritual without others. I love to remember times with close Christian friends when we just gloried in the Lord together and sort of shined. Other Christians help. God gives more to us in proportion to our faith.

In our walk with God, we occasionally come to a place where we begin to shy away. We're like the teenager who'd love to get close to that special girl, but she comes down the hall and he gets weak in the knees. We're like the married couple who has true intimacy, but they find it too good to believe and too wonderful to hold on to. Getting in with God is simply too much, it seems. That's when temptation knocks on the door. It's not like God has the plague. A closer walk with God does have benefits.

Nicky was a young lady who worked in our office. When she started there, she had a refreshing spirit. She was young, bright, and cheerful. She was also very pretty. Maybe her outlook changed when the guys paid too much attention to her, but I saw her get ugly with her boyfriend on the phone. She sounded too harsh to be joking. Her attitude toward the rest of us got frosty.

One day, she came over to me and said that I had dented her bumper with my car in the parking lot. I was totally unaware of any contact. She showed me the damage. No way did my car line up to what had happened to her nice, expensive car, which belonged to her boyfriend. She said she was afraid of what he was going to say.

This was not my problem. Was I going to own up to it and pay for it? She came off rather miffed. In an instant, by good faith, I told her to ask her boyfriend what it would cost to fix. He was a repairman in an auto body shop.

I thought about what it would be like for my daughter to ask me for help. You see, Nicky had grown up not knowing her father. When she was a baby in 1975, her parents put her on a boat in Vietnam with her aunt.

I took one of the guys out to show him the two cars parked side by side. He agreed there was no way my bumper could have rounded into her car in that parking space and hit it to cause that dent. He said he wouldn't give her a dime. There I was, not wanting any trouble. I wanted to win her to Jesus. Was she playing me for a fool to take my money? It didn't matter what others thought. None of us knew what went on with her and her boyfriend. I just gave it to the Lord.

The next day, Nicky came out of her office to tell me that her boyfriend said he wanted two hundred dollars. It wasn't that I had all that much money, but I told her she could have it. Once again, I surrendered it to Jesus and prayed for her soul. Peace came into my heart free and clear, settled.

About half an hour later, a man came in and asked for me by name. I kid you not. I said I was Kyle Hester. He handed an envelope to me and said it contained two free tickets to the Seahawks football game that Sunday. It was a gift from one of our company's vendors. It had happened to me before. I had once given two tickets to one of the guys, and he took his son with him to a game. Now, just minutes after telling Nicky I would give her two hundred dollars, in walks a stranger with two passes to the game with "$130" printed on each ticket.

I thought about it and then went into Nicky's office and told her to ask her boyfriend if he'd rather have those tickets instead of the money. She said she would phone him. Sure enough, she came out and said he wanted the tickets.

That was the year the Seahawks stadium, the Kingdome, was demolished so that a new stadium could be built. The Seahawks played one season in the University of Washington's Husky Stadium. I suggested to Nicky that they park in our company lot on Sunday and take the bus from there directly to the game. It would easily take them right there without the expensive, crowded parking situation. The traffic is horrible at the games, but still, I was afraid that she or her boyfriend would ignore my suggestion.

On Monday morning, she told me that they got there but didn't go in to the game. They had driven directly over to the stadium and gone around for a long time looking for parking. Sadly, they drove home without seeing any football. Does that describe human nature? You don't want that to describe your relationship with Jesus.

You don't have to be left out. Loneliness is as common as any pain you name. If people talk about being lonesome, they think about being without love. My definition of loneliness is having a big love with no place to go and nobody to give it to. Learn to care for others unselfishly, regardless of the cost or trouble it brings. When you give, you have more love for others and you gain more yourself, thanks to Jesus.

After Jesus was arrested in the garden, Peter followed from far behind (Mark 14:54). How many Christians follow Jesus from a distance? Some would figure it to be a safe distance. Some pray long distance and only when needed. If we walk in His Spirit, why not run with Jesus? Let's throw aside every weight of sin that so easily weighs on us and slows us down (Hebrews 12:1). Christians miss an inestimable amount of blessing, throwing away their lives.

> *And Simon Peter followed Jesus, and so did another disciple: that disciple was known unto the high priest, and went in with Jesus into the palace of the high priest.*
> John 18:15

That other disciple, John, went into the court of the high priest with Jesus. You know John was not afraid. It was Jesus who was on trial. The closest disciple of Jesus was there by His side to be with Him. John stood boldly in the court of the high priest. "*Draw near with a true heart in full assurance of faith*" (Hebrews 10:22). John was never the one on trial, but stood in the eye of the storm where he was perfectly calm.

Peter stayed by the fire in an outer courtyard, denying the Lord. John, on the other hand, was recognized by the high priest, and he had the wherewithal to go and see that Peter was let in the door. Jesus was about to be sentenced to death, and John had the run of the place. Did anyone take note of John and his quiet courage in the middle of the night? We can remember this when we're tested for our faith and also when we go before God.

> *But Peter stood at the door without. Then went out that other disciple, which was known unto the high priest, and spake unto her that kept the door, and brought in Peter.*
> John 18:16

John, standing with Jesus in court, had the presence of mind to see Peter outside. John was identified to the high priest, but Peter preferred to stay anonymous. It's a lesson for you and me when we're afraid to show ourselves to be Christians at crucial times. The only one actually on trial here was Jesus. If we have our hearts centered on Jesus, seeing the centrality of His death, our relationships with other people more often stays right. We hold ourselves back; the avoidance separates us from our important responsibility to others.

> *Then saith the damsel that kept the door unto Peter, Art not thou also one of this man's disciples? He saith, I am not.*
> John 18:17

The gospel of John, in particular, records the way these two men acted differently. There's also a parallel here. Upon news of the resurrection, both John and Peter raced to the tomb. John got there first and stood at the threshold, perhaps out of respect, while Peter burst inside to see that Jesus was gone. He went right on in. The tomb was empty.

Your faith and mine behave quite contradictory, yet we may well be on par. You hear some people say they believe in God, yet they think He is hard. Christianity isn't easy for them. It is too bad that so many people have not had the brighter side of faith explained to them. It is worse yet if they refuse and refute the good news. They don't let me in their corner. Can I remain more optimistic than that? I can, if I rely on God.

People don't really know just how unhappy they are. Do they

get to me or do I get to them? What's weird here is when people like their misery. Misery loves company, and they'd rather make me unhappy. Reality is what you make it. Those people will find someone convenient to commiserate with. We call them losers. I win if I stick with Jesus.

Hope in the Lord

Delight thyself also in the Lord: and he shall give thee the desires of thine heart.

Psalm 37:4

Putting the Lord first in life is more than a Christian cliché; it is the uncommon invitation to receive your cherished goals in life. When you focus only on what you want, you forget the Lord. Why serve the Lord halfheartedly? We have desires in our lives, but when unfulfilled hopes are too compelling, they become fixations that deter us from achieving anything else, or they could allow us to achieve nothing. These overpowering distractions can diminish the appreciation of any good news. See the good you already have. Insecurity and fear keeps us from progress and real love.

The mere threat of losing something troubles people so much that they actually do lose it. A fear of failure holds us back from our greatest ambitions. Doubt kills, like the way timidity by itself can hurt a marriage. Your aim might not be a bad thing to try for, there's nothing wrong if it's nothing abnormal or sinful. The fact that you place an unusually heavy stress on a certain thing or that you take an object and place it above all else and romanticize it does make it dangerous or doubtful. The best future seems impossible too.

People go nuts when they are attracted or attached to those big goals and ideas. Pushed by demanding impulses, every square inch of life becomes a pressure point, and every minute of the day bears up under loads of weighty anxiety. These strong misplaced desires are driven further from us by the various ways we take. We're used up in the frantic, seemingly inescapable clash of cosmic irony. It's straight up a vertical climb, too steep a penalty. For whom did Jesus pay the price? God wants us to see what He offers, and He wants us to join with Him to work for the good of everyone around.

> *Commit thy way unto the Lord; trust also in him; and he shall bring it to pass.*
>
> (Psalm 37:5)

We get so occupied with our needs and prayers that when the answer comes, it escapes us. The example of Peter comes to mind, when he was freed from jail and those who were praying for him couldn't believe that he was knocking at their door. Don't miss the answers.

After the resurrection and ascension of Jesus, thousands became believers in Christ. Let's go back to the time when King Herod wanted to strike the Church. He killed John's own brother, the Apostle James, and that prompted the king to imprison Peter also. *"And because he saw it pleased the Jews, he proceeded further to take Peter also"* Acts 12:3. People went from the resurrection of Jesus to persecuting and even killing the new leaders. That's a big jump. Imagine how horrible it was for the followers of Jesus to face losing Peter also.

The believers prayed most seriously to God because Peter was in a bad fix. The very one who had been so afraid for his own safety that he had denied Jesus now sits in jail and has the executioners coming for him in the morning.

> *Peter therefore was kept in prison: but prayer was made without ceasing of the church unto God for him.*
>
> Acts 12:5

Peter is now completely different. He is changed. He has a team of Christians praying their hearts out for him. Great things have been happening in Jesus' name. That night, the chains fell off and an angel led Peter past the guards to freedom. Peter was out of jail, and he couldn't believe his eyes. When he returned to where they were praying, they were too busy to let him in—too busy praying. These Christians were bent on their knees imploring all of Heaven; a miracle took place, and they didn't know Peter was at their door. Earnest prayers get heard. This is especially true when it counts, when you're praying about people who truly matter, and when you're together in a fervent fellowship full of friends.

> *And as Peter knocked at the door of the gate, a damsel came to hearken, named Rhoda.*
> Acts 12:13

Once again, the all-too-human Peter comes knocking, and another young woman is there at the door to open it. This time, Peter is not arriving to deny the Lord, but to tell of his astonishing deliverance. A wonderful transformation has taken place. Do you ever experience this difference in your life? Living for Jesus Christ is about more than quitting old habits, falling in line, and getting it right; it's about gaining the victory. Peter's story did not end there. He and John were just getting started.

We have to rest in God's grace that emerges in the revelation of our Savior. *"Let this mind be in you, which was also in Christ Jesus"* (Philippians 2:5). Jesus was broken because we were broken, and until He returns, we are still very incomplete. What kind of person would question the ways of God? Don't let imperfection stop you from going forward.

A lot of Christians caution that generous teachings on forgiveness, grace, and love will lay people open to uncontrolled immorality and sin. This wonderful biblical doctrine of grace in Christ is our religion. People see the problems; they should also see the solutions.

Jesus bore our shame outside the city limits of Jerusalem (Hebrews 13:12–13). Christians really could venture out more. We can love sinners, among whom we were once numbered. It may seem outside of our purview, but it's very much our business.

Our goal is to follow the Lord's plan on earth. We are working under God's "law of faith" in gratitude, which makes for grace (Romans 3:27). The rawness of our old nature is laid bare by the potential of God's enduring blessing.

Be prepared for life ahead. Work a good plan and do what you know is right. The devil wants to come and undermine you and interrupt your church to prevent your ministry—or has he done so already? This is all the more reason for Christians and church leaders to find fresh ways to share the wisdom from on high.

In review, Christians get the infinite power to live victoriously. We have friends who love as Jesus loved. We really do have His life. In patience and persistence, we lift others up to God, and He wants to offer sinners hope and fill us up with more joy.

> *Whither is thy beloved gone, O thou fairest among women?*
> *Whither is thy beloved turned aside? that we may seek him with thee.*
>
> Song of Solomon 6:1

The Song of Solomon is a passionate love story about a bride who hesitated when her man knocked. By the time she answered the door, he was gone. Her heart was stirred by him. Her hands felt the love, but before she could open the door, her beloved had withdrawn. Her soul failed when he spoke, but then she didn't find him. She called and there was no answer. Do you know a story like this? Do you know of believers who miss their calling or those who avoid a calling with Jesus and experience nights of darkness and disappointment?

Solomon tells how the bride wandered the city in the night looking for her love. The watchmen came down the street and found her. They assaulted her. The keepers of the walls took her veil. Can anyone find her bridegroom and tell him that she still loves him? She is sick with love. Nobody cares. There must be someone who feels bad for her.

The women of Jerusalem question her, not only about the love in her heart, but about the object of her affection. Solomon's story is timeless. It's this way today when a wife doubts her husband. A wife is often told by others that her love is wasted on her loser husband. He needs her, though nobody considers this part of it. What nerve to tell them their marriage is doomed!

People desperately need help to find love. In the Song of Solomon, the bride tells how wonderful her man is. He is chief among ten thousand. With thick black hair and eyes like the eyes of doves, his cheeks, hands, legs, and mouth are altogether lovely. He is her beloved and her friend. She pleads, "Where has he gone?" Then she gets help.

The real world chews people up. People are really contrary, brutal, mean, and violent. It's easy to see why thieves take advantage of the elderly, the poor, and the weak because they can't defend themselves. It's hard to get help before it's too late. Love is a sign of God's Holy Spirit. Alienation is of our own doing and of our own choosing.

I once heard a lot of yelling coming from outside, down on the street corner. A very young man was sitting on his haunches, crying and screaming at his girlfriend who was trying to walk away. I watched them for a bit. It seemed to me that she was splitting up with him and he was in a panic. He couldn't take it. They were pitiful. She was scolding him. She was fed up with his immaturity for sure.

He didn't want to lose her, but he was driving her away with his hysteria. My heart broke for him. If they would slow down and forget their frenzy, I thought they might have a chance, but she was in hysterics as bad as he was. She wanted to get free of him. It might be that he loved her. This is a normal question here: Are there things you and I can do, or that she and he could do, to mend the relationship, fix the split, iron out the wrinkles, and rescue their love, or does the whole thing have to get chucked? Potentially, they will both possibly mature in time to be good mates, affectionate and respectful. That could also happen with someone else, somewhere else, and in some other way.

Christians study to know Jesus better, and we can't wait to be removed from this evil world and go to see Him in Heaven. *"Lift up your eyes, and look on the fields"* (John 4:35). *"The harvest truly is great, but the laborers are few"* (Luke 10:2). I could quit this effort because of the lack of help and support I get. I stay busy laboring for the ones who need my help. It's hard to love people. I try to be realistic without sounding cynical.

> *My beloved is gone down into his garden, to the beds of spices, to feed in the gardens, and to gather lilies. I am my beloved's, and my beloved is mine: he feedeth among the lilies.*
>
> Song of Solomon 6:2–3

You can get a spot right next to Jesus anytime, and you can talk to Him all day while you work together. Solomon's story here had a happy ending. Writers write books and put out movies to make a statement. Real life is not clean and easy. We walk a fine line, a narrow road. Most people have a terrible ending: Hell! It is in fact only a beginning, the start of pain so extreme it will make today's hurts look like Heaven on earth.

When we were boys at our grandmother's house, Dad went into his old boyhood bedroom with my older brother. The door was shut. I remember that very well. I didn't know why they were in there. The sight of them coming out also struck me. My brother later said that Dad had explained the facts of life to him. He almost giggled in front of Dad, but held back. We should be more mature when hearing the facts of life in Jesus Christ.

Know the truth and do what God has spelled out. He will faithfully guide you through. Have you met older Christians who testify of the many ways God has blessed them? God loved each of us tremendously while we were still sinners. Think how much more He loves us now since we have expressed faith in Jesus and we are saved. God loves Christians. We've received reconciliation and have access by this marvelous grace in our Lord. At the same time, this is true. There are people doing what's bad. They turn life upside down.

The Grace to Persevere

And many shall follow their pernicious ways; by reason of whom the way of truth shall be evil spoken of.
                                                             2 Peter 2:2

The lies of this world are overpowering. All of us have failed to love God because of our roaming desires. We have gained little and missed a lot. A few of our wrongdoings are innocent and naïve, while our compulsive nature flirts with dirty sin.

It is too bad that a few preachers warn us not to go overboard with the idea of grace. We need grace. How far will they go without it? Some ministers limit their remarks to keep it simple as a rule. They avoid grace, afraid their congregation will leave and not come back. They have little peripheral vision and come up short on the vertical reach. When they dodge the topic of grace, they haven't much *faith* in *love*.

By my count, legalistic preachers are more often the ones discredited by their famous scandals. It's odd how it happens like that. They call it cheap grace, but Jesus doesn't think so. He paid for it with His life. Jesus made it valuable, amazing grace.

I heard a reputable Seattle area preacher on his national radio spot scolding proponents of grace, comparing them to the long-past Nicolaitans mentioned in the Bible. The Nicolaitans were a sect in the first century who abused the message of the Church and lived licentiously, even openly shameful. This famous pastor had the largest church in the region when he became front-page news with his out-of-state arrest for several counts of lewd behavior. Men in his church here then came forward, saying that he fondled them when they were boys, even during their baptisms right in the front of the church. What filth! If sin is just the bait, guilt is the trap. This man was in denial, blind to the cost of his actions.

He lost his ministry. Are there Nicolaitans anymore? The Love Family Israel in Seattle sinned openly, as did the Manson Family in California and the Branch Davidians in Texas. They lacked normal emotions. Everyone I've heard who teaches grace in Christ testifies or professes to typify virtue. The Bible says *faith* and *love* cover a multitude of sins. This is true.

We need to be rescued by God from the habits and practices that are so hard to conquer, and Jesus frees us from them. We've become too comfortable with conditions that are unfavorable. Our "churchianity" repeats itself over and over again so monotonously that we lose any feeling and suppress the forward progress we once enjoyed.

We have to do something to break these logjams. Convicts imprisoned for long terms actually get to where they fear freedom. Used to their confinement, they feel safer under that security. People with long periods in a program or halfway house get an institutionalized mentality. It's a tendency. Pray for a fresh vision if you want a renewed mission.

The enormous growth in world population has caused some nations to boil over. Some of us at home have a real fear of crowds. Have you noticed the pace at the grocery store? You get bumped into. If you hesitate at the checkout stand, others quickly push in front rudely, speeding like it's the freeway. Don't we view others as objects that get in our way? Shoppers avoid eye contact as they walk up and down the aisles, studying rows of boxes and cans. Nothing is more evident than this evasive apathy which tends to dehumanize us. Maybe it's just me. Top-heavy advertising, competing colors, and the drone of piped music overwhelm us and make us feel insignificant. The Holy Spirit of Jesus must be offended.

> *But seek ye first the kingdom of God, and his righteousness; and all these things shall be added unto you.*
> Matthew 6:33

God's eternal promises exceed the dreams of our hearts. For now, life requires us to endure and persevere. Devote yourself to the Lord, and "all these things shall be added unto you." Don't be afraid like Peter the fisherman. Jesus puts us in places to expose well-hidden spiritual inadequacies. We have a greater new spiritual capacity. It is too bad that fear has slowed us down in our own lane. It's time we pull out to pass.

I was at my brother's place up in the mountains one time, and late on a dark evening, I took the dogs out for a walk. Have you ever been scared stiff? There were woods at the edge of the property where I was standing alone with the dogs. As I was watching the dogs sniff around, I was listening to the winter wind swirling overhead between the sides of the mountains, creating an incredible stereophonic resonance. At once, my ears tuned in on the high-fidelity sound of crackling branches. Right in front of me, it seemed like a large animal was coming right through the woods in the dead of night. I listened and convinced myself that something was moving my way. I turned to go back, but my two feet seemed to weigh three hundred pounds each, and my legs could hardly move. Nothing like it had ever happened to me before. I tried calling the dogs, but my voice had no air. I was paralyzed in fear. It took all my strength to lift each foot every step back to the door.

After I got inside the house, it hit me that the wind caused the bare branches of the leafless trees to click against each other, and all the trees together made a ferocious noise. What was I thinking? There was nothing to be afraid of.

We will win them with love. How much do we believe this? Paul lists the fruit of the Holy Spirit with love as the first fruit (Galatians 5:22). Believers accept injury without retaliation, not returning evil for evil or insult for insult, but by showing we care. The meekness of love is the promise of our calling, "that ye should inherit a blessing" (1 Peter 3:9). We get abused, hated, and rejected. God gives the fruit of gentleness and patience. We treat opposition with thoughtfulness and faithfulness since self-control is also a part of the fruit of God's Spirit. Christians give troublemakers more consideration than they deserve. As bad as the world gets, love will bear fruit.

Souls surrender to Jesus during life's most painful times. Are we a help to others or a hindrance? Those in despair may need a correction, but they also need to hear this new direction. Isn't it intellectually dishonest to call ourselves Christians if we don't live our lives to help others? If all we do is worry about fighting sin without ever emphasizing love and good works, we do a terrible injustice to the truth. Jesus said, *"Blessed are the poor in spirit: for theirs is the kingdom of Heaven"* Matthew 5:3. The bigger half of the story is *faith* and *love*.

We can stand by the helpless with *faith* to be a bridge of *love*. People are falling all around us. Christian stewardship is life at its best. This inspired movement God brings out tells of His eternal power and endless life. He wouldn't have given us all we have if this is all we get. Many people doubt that His miraculous love is true or even right. Not all Christians are convinced, but right now, there are lots of wonderful young servants preparing to follow the Lord. Tested workers are routinely proving themselves. They'll go to the end. God places His power in the hands of ordinary saints. Our faith fails, but God's love works.

Accept God's forgiveness. You've chased a magnet around a table with the flux and force of another magnet. When we were kids, we pushed magnets like this. As fast as you go, without ever touching, you could not catch the other. My dictionary defines magnetism simply as anything that attracts, a phenomenon that exerts a strong attractive power, or the charm of a magnetic personality. My dictionary doesn't say a word about magnets repelling. Every magnet has two poles, a negative and a positive on either end. Magnets repel half of the time—if they're backward. Check your dictionary. A magnet attracts, but if you turn it around, it repels. This is what makes motors work. This is how easily God can turn lives around with love alone.

Fears and obsessions hurt us, and opposite-phobia makes us all overcompensate. We get flustered and cause ourselves to overreact. We are God's children. We can beat our dilemma. Think how carefree you were as a young kid. Your parents looked after you. They paid the bills and did all the worrying. Our Father in Heaven never frets because He knows and cares more than anyone. Come near to the heart of God today. With every bit of His strength and all of His mind, His love has more power with your faith.

> *For God hath not given us the spirit of fear; but of power, and of love, and of a sound mind.*
> 2 Timothy 1:7

CHAPTER 9

Marriage

For we are members of his body, of his flesh, and of his bones. For this cause shall a man leave his father and mother, and shall be joined unto his wife, and they two shall be one flesh. This is a great mystery: but I speak concerning Christ and the church.

Ephesians 5:30–32

This passage is a wonderful revelation of Jesus Christ and the Church. Where in the Bible do you find a more beautiful reflection of our spiritual marriage to Jesus? We give ourselves to God in the name of Jesus Christ. He gives Himself to us. Marriage between a man and a woman is the expressed image of God's total love.

To be enraptured in love is Heaven on earth. I hope you've been there and know what I mean. The harmony of love gives witness to the devotion that Jesus Christ has for us. The attachment a man and a woman have in marriage typifies our eternal bond to God in His Spirit. Pray for the unsaved to find beautiful love in their marriage that will inspire them to seek and find the Lord God. The intimacy of marriage testifies to believers of the magnificent intimate love that Jesus has for us.

Linking our personal connection to God with the Bible's tradition of marriage lets us learn helpful and meaningful concepts. Our faith says that God's forgiveness goes beyond our understanding. The acceptance we seek from our spouses means everything to us. The support we enjoy from other believers in church can also have lifelong significance.

Marriage can be our biggest disappointment. Pray that we don't see love as our biggest failure, but our highest achievement. Thinking that no one loves you is not loneliness; it is selfishness. But how often does love bring true happiness? It's rare. The fallen nature has weakened us and threatens our future. Sin disrupts our pursuit of true fulfillment. Jesus draws us to Himself and closer to one another in church, family, and in marriage.

Having hope is not a bad thing. Love with faith triumphs with extra boldness of heart. The longer we know each other, the more our differences bear out, so boldness is required to go on for a powerful love. Each of us is different; uniqueness is an asset particularly when seen as an opposing support. Opposing support is a term used by builders. This is a good thing.

We fall in love with someone who has familiar and similar qualities. You and I may agree about life, but we are still going to have a variety of styles, some very unusual. Define love here. Think about it—God is able to manage everyone's separate story all at the same time.

You might think that no two people will fit together unless they are the same. However, separate pieces of a puzzle can't be straight rectangles or equal-sided squares, but they have to be odd shaped in order to interlock and stay together!

We each have our own experiences, preferences, and strengths. Our families have left big impressions on us. God made each of us ourselves. It's only natural to have associations and memories that are individually yours. How do you fit? We each have our very own particular way of handling life. It could be a good way or bad, for better or for worse.

Courtship days are a time of romance, so couples may not see where forgiveness will play a big role in their relationship. Those who fall in love lose their heads, thinking only of their captivated hearts bathed in complete adoration. At first, we allow each other a new portion of confidence with seemingly perfect acceptance. We've received much reinforcement from each other. You can let life go when you are in love. Later, with the agitations of life, your warm love cools and the feeling of passion fades. You try to add more loving perks to cover the failures, but it becomes an effort. We won't reject each other so quickly if we're quicker to trust God no matter how difficult the times get. Mature Christians know what the grace of God means to a relationship.

Love can be very illogical. What will enable us to get over these hurdles? If the going gets tough, it very much helps to get along with each other. Don't kick up a storm. While we retain what's valuable from the past, wisdom knows that new things need to be added. Whatever comes, Jesus promised He is going to win in our lives, so be thankful. You have help, and encourage those around you.

Love can be defined by forgiveness. It starts with the forgiveness that saves us. Grace gives us new life in Christ. God places us in His body, the Church; we belong. When Jesus comes into our lives, we get a fresh start with high expectations—but we aren't perfect yet. Forgiveness is always a stretch; in our minds and in our guts, it's an irrational act or a step of faith to accept what's wrong. We have to take a long look and take a real hard swallow. Love, it is said, is an irrational emotion. We have a new mind in Jesus to grab hold of *love* by *faith*.

We come to Jesus with the hope that He can satisfy all our longings and prayers. Following the teachings of Christ definitely leads to abundant life and also to a lasting, loving marriage. We have to see each other through many hurts, losses, obstacles, sorrows, and sins. As two people join in marriage, they are not aware at first of impending problems. They are wondrously love-struck and oblivious to the long tough road ahead. They cannot see flaws in each other. Think how preoccupied we are with romance from an early age. Young people paint an ideal picture of love, so they can't imagine how their poetically expressed appreciation of each other might get lost during future years. Are we selfish or generous? Marriage is for giving love, and love is forgiving.

Our Father in Heaven instituted marriage as a sacrament to be a witness of the bond we have with His Son, Jesus Christ. What better place is there than at home where two kind hearts accept each other? Negotiating life together is a part of marriage. Our union of love has the capacity to share God's love. Husbands and wives who adore each other have passion and more compassion every day.

The Bible's typology of marriage parallels Christ and the Church. This is why it's a sacred calling to marry and to live the rest of life together, representing this eternal hope Christians have. Why does this lost world need to flaunt immorality? It distorts the pure image Jesus gives people in connection to Him. It cheats life and obscures the truth. Believers live as one and as one with God. There's no doubt He wants us to have the right kind of marriage to reflect Him. We shine with the righteous new life He imparts to us. But let it be the hidden man of the heart in that which is not corruptible, even the ornament of a meek and quiet spirit, which is in the sight of God of great price 1 Peter 3:4.

Forgiveness Makes Right

> *There was a certain creditor which had two debtors: the one owed five hundred pence, and the other fifty. And when they had nothing to pay, he frankly forgave them both. Tell me therefore, which of them will love him most?*
>
> Luke 7:41–42

Christians become more willing to love as they learn God's grace. Without His great and powerful pardon, we could not have come to salvation and to stand in His presence. We were lost and without a clue. We were bad, sinful, and wrong, and now we have been made right. As we come to life and rejoice for this forgiveness in Jesus Christ, we love all the more. Only by God's forgiveness can we have His love.

The power of love is found in the blood of Jesus Christ. The biblical teaching on forgiveness must be held in the very highest regard and be repeated. Love does not keep count of wrongs nor does it imagine faults. It does not return evil for evil or tit for tat. Love does not pick and choose when to forgive. It doesn't rejoice in the iniquity of others. Instead, love hopes for the best in others, coping with their failings until the real good is formed in them. It takes time.

Love is renewed when quarreling couples affirm that they want their marriages to work. Confession and forgiveness produce miraculous wonders. Pardon actually reduces the blunders. We should move on, considering all our own faults and don't stay hung up on your partner's carelessness. It helps to talk about the hurts. Why dredge up the past? Patiently wait for Jesus to accomplish His will in your own heart as well as in theirs. Spouses have to share their sincere feelings, tell their thoughts, and listen carefully.

The thrill of a new song or pride in a new car wears off, and it is the same with marriage; it can get boring when the proverbial honeymoon is over. That fantastic feeling you had at the start of something good turns off. The taste goes flat and you tire of it now. You can understand why people fade from a once-bright faith in Jesus or how the hot flame of romance loses its glow. You didn't expect that so then don't know how to fix it.

Getting hired for a new job is exciting, especially since most times it is a step up. When it begins to be less thrilling, you see others complain and tell stories about the boss or the work. Misery loves company. It doesn't take long to become bored or sour. We can quickly grow into rebels, just like the other employees. We soon misplace our enthusiasm.

Don't forget how important life is to you. It's said that the two best days in a boat owner's life are the day he buys it and the day he sells it. People have always expressed similar thoughts about their marriage.

The hope of fulfillment in marriage is not unrealistic. We say our vows with a great optimism for our better half, yet we want to stay reasonable since nothing here is perfect. Are you bitter with disappointments? You must remember to cherish your spouse and love your own self (Ephesians 5:28). Keep your desire in marriage, never say die, and be more alive. God knows what we want better than we do. We'll never lose out in life when we give ourselves over to God's direction. These are very good reasons to believe in our good faith, willing to risk our love on others and our mates.

We can't comprehend the extent of our sin or visualize how bad we really are. Nor can we thoroughly apprehend God's holiness. We cannot fully appreciate His forgiveness, turn our full restoration to righteousness, or approximate the terror in Hell that we have avoided. Our sin is that we aren't thankful enough; we're ungrateful and sometimes angry or even vengeful.

How odd it is to tell our darkened world that God has set aside the guilt of sin! You and I need grace and power from above to speak the truth of this great mystery of Christ. Who among the billions of unbelievers can value the sacrifice of Jesus at the cross? It's a surprise to be saved. God's Spirit comes to reveal all this to us and to enable us to grow in this knowledge. The unsaved need Jesus. You and I need a better view of God.

Words fail to communicate the New Testament ministry of reconciliation. Good Christian marriages represent Jesus. In the same way that each kind of animal got off Noah's ark two by two, loving couples fill the world. Jesus sent the disciples out in pairs to proclaim His truth. If a sad soul can be comforted by one person, then two people are even better. A lonely heart is healed by the care of two, and *"a threefold cord is not quickly broken"* (Ecclesiastes 4:12). Loving Christian couples simply walk into the room and beam with their radiance.

I love older married couples who have cheerfully served God together for years. Healthy Christian couples can come alongside those who are hurting. Hurting people see that we want to help. Troubled souls recognize the joy and peace in our hearts. Don't you know what you want out of love? You don't want to get hurt. Sometimes, we get close, and then, for no good reason, fail in ourselves to hold on. Seasoned Christians are able to relay the hard-earned wisdom to help the younger married get over their troubles.

There's not often much support in this world, so our reality check comes from reading the Bible. The Scriptures come directly from God. They tell us what we should know, what we want to know, and that everything is going to work out. This world is difficult, so we need to be forbearing. Life can be hard and unforgiving, yet we can't run away every time. Love consists of more than just emotions. You need to be settled, more down to earth. We better remind Christians of the joy by encouraging both the strong and the weak.

The Holy Spirit gives us glad hearts, even in trying times, and the greatest joys in marriage are free for the asking. Marriage is the biggest joy. We must work at it. Durable marriages are maintained by energetic cultivation. *Love* is an active verb. We feel better when we have clean consciences and exercise prayer. God is here to help. A loving pat on the back from the most important person in your life is beautifully reinforcing.

To accept others just as they are while making adjustments in myself and staying patient can be a wonderfully rewarding endeavor. If no one else changes, at least I can be happier. Demanding that others have to change is counterproductive. Allowing them space and time for their own growth develops a relaxed, less stressful place where voluntary improvement is more likely, and my own attitude matures in the process.

Faith in forgiveness is one of the best examples of how Christian love works. Obedience and forgiveness are difficult for us. It's never in us or in our flesh to overcome. Christians are supposed to forgive; it's our eleventh commandment, so I've heard. Have you read that in your Bible? God's rule of forgiveness is another act of righteousness that we simply can't do on our own. You might call that kind of forgiveness works righteousness. Ironically, you can say these same words another way: forgiveness works righteousness. You get a better result. If we look honestly into our hearts, we would admit our incapability to pardon others completely. How could we do this with our human hearts? Pray for God's Spirit to overflow so you cannot help but to forgive others and forget about yourself; thank the Lord for doing everything.

Another Law

> *I find then a law, that, when I would do good, evil is present with me.*
>
> Romans 7:21

Another law is working in my flesh, warring against my mind and enslaving me. The Apostle Paul wrote similar to what I often think: *Sin is not what I want, but it is what I get.* The righteousness I hunger for is found now in faith, and I thirst after the perfect love of Jesus. It comes in the hope of Heaven. If righteousness is what you truly want, you will be blessed. Jesus has already secured this for us in His plan. Jesus justified us in His resurrection. We are righteous sinners stuck in the flesh. We are being sanctified and perfected, but only in Heaven will we be all the way alive in His presence.

The last thing married people want to do is hurt their partners, because they sincerely promise to help and protect each other. However, we say and do things that hurt the ones we love, and we hate ourselves for it. Many couples war with each other. Our fallen nature is sowing the seeds of demise everywhere throughout our lives. On every side, we are engaged in psychological warfare with our neighbors. Now the war has come home with us.

> *Now then it is no more I that do it, but sin that dwelleth in me.*
>
> Romans 7:17

If we stop long enough to consider that we all sin, we do not need to be so hostile. We could be sympathetic, but we are sinners, so we are hostile to each other. Some people feel they are the only ones with problems. There are the people who can only find the faults in others. We recognize that all have sinned. Being realistic with ourselves and with others does not mean that we condone sin.

Instead, we very much need to reassure the ones we love.

He says she does this, and she says he did that! Too many of us give up, and many have fought to the end. God is certainly fully aware of our present temporal terrestrial situation. For this reason, His Holy Spirit helps us to mature and to grow together. We need each other. First, this battle of sin makes it rough, and secondly, Christians know that it's tough on everyone, so we continually wage the good fight of forgiveness and move along.

> *For I know that in me (that is, in my flesh,) dwelleth no good thing: for to will is present with me; but how to perform that which is good I find not. For the good that I would I do not: but the evil which I would not, that I do. Now if I do that I would not, it is no more I that do it, but sin that dwelleth in me.*
> Romans 7:18–20

It is not that I sin, but that sin is in me, so I'm not the one who is winning over sin, but God who lives in me. God doesn't blame us for our sins, He knows we were born in bondage to sin. That is why He was willing to save us. God's pardon is for any of us, if we will only accept it, and we can all do this.

All the criticisms and condemnation, and even our own feelings of guilt, cannot make us refrain from that which we should not do. We feel guilty at heart, undeserving and hopeless. Then we turn right around and blame others. And we sin again. We need God's forgiveness to vindicate us and stop the recriminations, freeing us inwardly to live right outwardly. This only happens after we admit the truth that sin is in us and it is we who sin.

When we can be open, we can be more honest in marriage. Life gets murky. Forgiveness finds liberty, not only from feelings of guilt, but from guilt itself. We are freed from condemnation. With God's permission, we set out and move on in love. In forgiving us, God gives new life to our hearts. In the grace of His love, Jesus is restoring us to His original plan—to be glorified with God. When we lead others beyond superficial friendships and past old vain conceit, then God can fully bless. Life requires an extraordinary amount of bravery on our part. We live confidently, choose to see the good, and fix what's broken.

Ambassadors for Christ

To wit, that God was in Christ, reconciling the world unto himself, not imputing their trespasses unto them; and hath committed unto us the word of reconciliation.

2 Corinthians 5:19

Jesus' blood was shed for the sins of the world, the whole world, even for all those who never believe. This is inconceivable. Only the God of the Bible could speak this into existence. This is not just a cliché, but is every bit the true story. We should feel sorry for the ones who are lost. We are duty bound to invite everyone to come to salvation. God does not use His list of grievances anymore in this age of grace. Anyone who simply believes in their heart "I am a sinner," and confesses with their mouth "Jesus is Lord," and sincerely repents will inherit eternal life with God.

People receiving Jesus as Savior, aware of being completely forgiven, respond with excitement and give this straightforward effort to please God. Understanding the condition of sin and this unconditional pardon, Christians should want to work in every way possible to bring all others along. For this very purpose, Jesus gives to all His church—all of us—His powerful love. This is what's needed to get everything done.

We each differ in our level of development. Some people try too hard to improve. Others might actually be improving, but because of their stress, they get ugly toward others. You know you have truly improved when you're getting the grace, wanting to reach out with your heart, and are always blessing others. That's not just talk.

We might correct flaws in ourselves before we correct every last sin in others. You and I aren't fixing everything. A civil society requires a certain amount of tolerance. Other opinions have a place. Even though we disagree with many in our country, we believe that the divine liberty we cherish in America permits differences. The notion of freedom holds that good values naturally rise to the top. True conservatives and true liberals both believe this to be our understanding. But we take exception to something or somebody and blow it all up.

The government has laws. We should want peace and order. We aren't talking about accepting evil, but we're talking about accepting people. If we set out to squelch every infraction, we'll demolish ourselves in the process and become the dictatorial country we would loath. Our energies should be spent in building up better things and defending truth, not being so easily dissuaded. Such tranquility must start in our hearts and homes.

The real beauty of marriage is not necessarily found in our physical strengths. Too often, we use these same strong traits against each other. Think of how time steals our strengths away. When you are driving your car down the road and realize that the road is too narrow for an oncoming car, the courteous thing to do is to yield and allow the other car through. Generosity brings youthfulness and longevity to our lives.

Couples get down with troubles, and their tensions increase. Hostilities and insecurities creep in. Partners become hurtful to each other. Their mate suddenly becomes mean. You want to turn the trend.

Divorce seldom solves problems; it often makes life worse. It especially hurts the kids. The pain in the aftermath of divorce may not be immediately evident. Was the marriage a mistake? After a temporary relief, the years bring realization that the divorce may have been a mistake. Perhaps the marriage is not really the problem; it's the people, the ones who can't face their own dumb faults.

Christian parents are the ambassadors for Christ to their children. Do you know the very last verse of the Old Testament? It is a building block of theology, and I want to refer to it here. You might expect something like "Obey the Lord in all things," or "Fear God," or some other foreboding warning of judgment. It's really not bleak like that. Take a look: *"And he shall turn the heart of the fathers to the children, and the heart of the children to their fathers, lest I come and smite the earth with a curse"* (Malachi 4:6). God is going to reconcile the generations. He will restore the relationships between parents and offspring, fathers and children, so that in the end, we won't be cursed and punished. This is a pretty significant reference.

Sin is handed down from each of us like father to son and then in turn to the young rebel. The rebellion in our soul is a terrible sore spot with God. Marital dysfunction leaves irreparable damage with the kids. A good marriage that is faithful and enduring brings all generations together to reflect love, and it blesses the children most of all. We need this structure.

Parenting starts with marriage. As much as anything they might see, children want to know that Mom and Dad love each other. Marriage is the best model of God's love. Christians must demonstrate grace more successfully in order to impact growing children and even grown children. And for the same reason, God wants children to make their parents happy.

You think you're doing well until you do better. You do not know how bad you look until you grow. If you gain a bad name, it raises doubts, and others are less sympathetic. When we don't see ourselves realistically, we remain resistant and we do not anticipate the price we pay. When are we going to see what we're missing and feel the need to change? Let's be honest. We are in the dark until Jesus touches us with His Spirit.

The problem is that many Christians get all fired up in fellowship, but go home alone. If you take a log out of a fire and lay it aside, it will stop burning. What was white hot turns to glowing red and then to grey. It won't burn by itself. A single log can't catch on fire. I asked a fireman why that is. He told me that they need the heat from other logs. If you put a log back in the fire with the others, it starts burning again. A home needs a good church to be a part of life. "Exhort one another daily," and don't be hard-hearted (Hebrews 3:13).

I should never take my good marriage for granted, because it's a gift from God. How ungrateful I would be to forget my wife's love for me! How inconsiderate and unappreciative if I ever neglect my true love! I want to treat her like a precious flower. I hope, as a supportive husband, to assure my dear wife of my admiring love for her every day and of my thanks for her enduring acceptance and the much-needed undeserved help she gives.

Love Is for Giving

> *Let all bitterness, and wrath, and anger, and clamor, and evil speaking, be put away from you, with all malice: and be ye kind one to another, tenderhearted, forgiving one another, even as God for Christ's sake hath forgiven you.*
> Ephesians 4:31–32

Jesus took our place on Calvary. He lives to take first place in our heart. Our lives are no longer our own. We must stay giving and tolerant. Work to please Jesus. God has commanded us to forgive one another because this is basically His place.

Salvation comes in God's liberal forgiveness, we should forgive. My sin has left serious injury. I owe it now to help those who struggle.

It's not to my credit, but to God's credit. Who is able to pay God back? He deserves our service. You may question people in your life, but we owe Jesus our lives—not by complaining, but by serving with our complete attention. Set your time aside for Jesus. Who is deserving of it? Since I have sinned, I should hold nothing back. I want to give God as much as I can by *faith* with *love*.

When we are wronged, we take it too personally. We take things too seriously and get hurt. At times, the human language is disgusting. Each one of us takes our turn on the receiving end. I think of Ecclesiastes 7:22: *"oftentimes"* each of us has spoken poorly of others. We are all entitled to a bit of trouble from this world, and you should not think you're exempt when it comes to your turn. So don't jump and retaliate.

When we are "persecuted for righteousness' sake," the Bible tells us to *"rejoice, and be exceedingly glad"* (Matthew 5:10–12). God has His purposes, and we believers are now in His plan. That's not an invitation to have a persecution complex. There's no excuse for a pity party. It's your privilege to rejoice and be positive over and over again.

Friends can at times treat us unfairly. A good friend will help with a few diplomatic and timely words. Better are the wounds of a friend than flattery from enemies (Proverbs 27:6). When we learn to love our enemies as Jesus taught, we will be even better friends to those on our own side. No matter what, God does not want you to forget that He is the boss.

Let all bitterness be put away from you (Ephesians 4:31). Without a doubt, events run their course. When the end is known, God will be glorified and we will be justified. A person must be forgiving of life itself. Keep a sense of humor to get along. We will see future fulfillment in due time if we keep the faith (Galatians 6:9); don't lose heart and keep trying. Trust God who wants what's best. The Lord has started things in our lives, and He will renew our resolve.

"Count it all joy" when your faith is tested by trials because we should know that experience produces patience (James 1:2–3). The reason for tests in life is to measure progress. If we are patient, we will grow and mature. Love succeeds. The Bible also guarantees to us God's correction as we need it. The chastening never seems to be a very happy thing when He gives it, but afterward, it brings out the righteous fruit (Hebrews 12:11). We can praise God because both persecution and correction refine us.

Rejoice in the Lord always: and again I say, Rejoice.
Philippians 4:4

Praise our Savior and share His goodwill with everybody. In gladness of heart, rejoice and make a constant celebration. God, for Christ's sake, has forgiven you (Ephesians 4:32). Be thankful. *"But let patience have her perfect work, that you may be perfect and entire, wanting nothing"* (James 1:4). You want perfection; patience is the way. Yes, and to get perfect, you'd be content. This is your goal in life. Say your praises out loud. Stop the grumbling and teach your heart to be glad of what you have.

Our lives can be worn down by the friction of this world. It seems like you lose your feeling of being a live Christian, and we don't quite have the sense of a new born-again life anymore. Jesus is eternal hope. Do you break down like an old machine, how old cars deteriorate and give out and are junked and replaced? Never be afraid. Troubles won't rob you of your joy in Jesus, but they give you joy. Hope to the end. Face up to challenges.

Don't feel dejected. How many blows can you take? Does it seem like you can handle only one more before you drop? Don't tell yourself you can't take anymore; you can and probably will. Have patience. Find the strength until God's perfect work is finished.

Never be surprised that all kinds of ideas float around like the wind. Lifeless leaves fall to the ground. Jesus has forgiven you, and you are set free from sin. You are headed for Heaven. Don't act like this is old news: *Rejoice!* The resurrection is a New Testament promise, the best.

You just as easily get someone's anger in return for your cheer. Their hard attitude is revealing. They won't ask you why you're happy. If anyone asks, be ready to give an answer for your faith. You can't let your faith be eroded by strange doctrines as if dark clouds could cover your mind. Keep on thinking freely. Let someone sneer at your big smile. Don't be afraid to stay happy. It's not ever within us, but it is in God's reach from Heaven to liven up our days.

If you work cheerfully as unto the Lord, it is rewarding. It's hard to work alongside other employees who bruise easily, who tire quickly, and who make excuses rather than simply work. The whiners are often the ones who can't get things done. There are people you can count on to stay on the ball, who are not pretentious; they're very happy to do the job right. Concentrate and do everything without complaining. Satisfaction is a good feeling. There is no law against love.

You know you are close to the cooking when you feel the heat. That is the way it goes. Someone might not like you being too awfully positive. Unless you stay genuinely good around them, how are they going to realize how unhappy they are? Don't let them give you what they have. You don't want it. They actually want what you have, but don't rub it in. Make yourself welcome.

Let your zeal be known; the Lord is at hand. Does the imminent return of Jesus Christ excite you? Be rejuvenated. Your face will show it. Don't be anxious for anything, but pray about all things. Believe all things, everything that's true in Jesus and don't be talked out of what you know is true.

A lot of us have been treated severely by bitter Christians. People look at the faces of depressed, fuming Christians and see no special character. On the other hand, there are plenty of decent, pleasant people, not believing. The Bible teaches virtue, and we need to meditate on these verses, then our witness will be obvious. The demeanor of an honestly optimistic Christian has a major effect on friends, in your church, in your family, in your marriage, in a career, and with strangers.

Reclaiming Lost Love

> *Take heed to yourselves: If thy brother trespass against thee, rebuke him; and if he repent, forgive him.*
> Luke 17:3

Forgive. Jesus said, *"and if he repent, forgive him."* What is the secondary meaning inferred here? If he doesn't repent, don't forgive him. First of all, before that, Jesus said this, *"Take heed to yourselves."* Watch yourself so that you don't become tempted and sin again in some way. It's too normal to deny our faults and refuse to admit when we're in the wrong. While catching the mistakes of others, hold the line on your own sin.

If your marriage partner offends, tough love may regain respect. Correction might be called for, not your aggression or revenge; love must be the motive. Leave a door open. If we find a way to settle a gripe and show a readiness to forgive, there is a better chance for mutual cooperation. If your words are refused, find a third party. If you're seen as forgiving, you make peace. If possible, it lies in your power to do more. If a third person brought into the situation does not find a solution, what do you do? Take the matter out in the open. Jesus said, *"but if he neglect to hear the church, let him be unto thee as an heathen man and a publican"* (Matthew 18:17). At times, keep quiet, sometimes, speak out; otherwise, avoid situations.

People you talk to say God is forgiving and He will forgive and forget. When people don't repent, you still forgive and in your heart let it go, and you are no longer obligated. In Luke 17:3, Jesus said to rebuke the sinner, and "if he repent," forgive him. Everyone has to return to God to be forgiven (Luke 24:47). Jesus died for everyone's transgressions. Don't ignore the fact. Forgiveness comes by way of the cross. God has taught us from the beginning to repent. We can't do this for others. Say something and let them go.

To obey God yourself is one thing, but it is another thing to take God's instructions about your relationships with those who don't comply. Paul wrote that we should not keep company with a brother who sins (1 Corinthians 5:11). Paul listed some serious sins. It's harsh, but it's also merciful. Paul wrote specifically about our union with errant Christians. We can't avoid every sinner in the world and expect to reach the lost; however, we can properly separate ourselves from errant Christians. They should recover themselves or we need to obey God's word ourselves.

Paul told us that if a Christian won't work, *"neither should he eat…*

And if any man obey not our word by this epistle, note that man, and have no company with him, that he may be ashamed. Yet count him not as an enemy, but admonish him as a brother" 2 Thessalonians 3:10–15. That's strong. We're not used to hearing it.

Paul also wrote in this part of the Bible that a Christian man who won't provide for his family has *"denied the faith, and is worse than an infidel"* 1 Timothy 5:8. Average people, even ungodly people, faithfully care for their own families—so you sure don't want to see any kind of family neglect in your church.

You don't want doctrinal error in church either. These standards are taught in God's Word. The word of Paul says, *"A man that is an heretick after the first and second admonition reject"* (Titus 3:10–11), "being condemned of himself." Your conscience can say how far to take this doctrine of separation. Shun those who keep bad company. It's a matter of prayer, study, and wisdom.

> *And if he trespass against thee seven times in a day, and seven times in a day turn again to thee, saying, I repent; thou shalt forgive him.*
>
> Luke 17:4

Forgiveness will find solutions and redeem a person who errors. Does God want me to be right and forgiving too? Anyone can get into really bad trouble. Good marriages can get into deep difficulty. That's when love is on trial along with faith. Jesus has told us to solve conflicts, to rebuke, and to forgive.

Many times in life you are asked to forgive. How many times did Jesus suggest you forgive someone? He was not suggesting anything. Jesus was not asking. How many times will it take to forgive someone before you see a change in their behavior? A troubling type of person could get a change of heart sooner if you avoid them. What do you think? You've changed.

There are a lot of people around, and they need attention too. As it is, the latitude that Christians give may come more from our own individual personality traits or temperament, and sadly, not so often from sound biblical footing. God's unfailing love doesn't settle for less. It's not judgmental nor permissive, but love is able. This is true. We boldly embrace unconditional love with faith and forgiveness.

Love is applied by *faith*. This means faith in the cross. Jesus wants us to go the extra mile, time after time, seventy times seven, because He said. Jesus walked the extra mile for all of us; once, just one time, it was a steep walk up that hill.

If you are dealing with someone you really love rather than a casual acquaintance, your reaction will be different. For example, you would want to be gentler when training a child than when firing an employee for stealing. A child might require more positive attention, while another child might need sharper correction.

It was an old gag in the movies that someone would be treated wrong, only to find out that the mistreated person was a very important customer, the owner, or worse yet, the wife of the owner. The episode is familiar to all of us, so we laugh. What is the lesson in this classic routine? To be a Christian is to recognize that we all sin, and we should be fair, friendly, and kind to everyone we meet.

Grace miraculously overcomes sin. When someone crosses us, we blow up and hastily write them off. Wisdom with acumen understands there are times when it would be better to say nothing at all. Other times, we're afraid of confrontation, so we pass off problems and deny wrongs, sweeping them under the rug, and might call that forgiveness. We bear our own decisions.

God's guidance is needed because we carry our brother's life. Don't you say something when somebody's shoelace is untied? You may be the right person to advise someone about tough stuff. No one is an island. Sometimes, speaking the full truth takes courage and friendship. We can correct someone gently or sternly. A brother or sister or spouse may find an apology constructive, and the healing process can begin. If it doesn't seem to take immediate effect, give it the benefit of the doubt. Stay true to your principles.

Be genuine, and people will be receptive. This above all: to thine own self be true, and it must follow, as the night the day, thou canst not then be false to any man (William Shakespeare, from *Hamlet*). We want to be wise and point people in God's direction.

Jesus is the author and finisher of our faith. You can bank on it. When we go on condemning people out of hand and stand in the way of their change and growth, spotting faults, won't that be seen? Jesus forgives us and accepts us as we are, but He deals with what's wrong. Left alone, we would go round and round in circles like we're lost in the woods, chasing our tail, our own trail. I was lost, but now I am found.

God does not take us to Heaven with our unrighteousness. He is fixing it for us. We gain something in the process here on earth, and we take this to Heaven. Reconciliation, therefore, requires a good correction, an actual improvement—and it will be seen.

There must be accountability in marriage or one partner will misuse the other. We hurt others and assign blame; it becomes our failure. Our dumb temptations and weaknesses are mostly defeating to us. Honesty will change that. Hypocrisy doesn't fit in a loving marriage. More from our own character problems are we not unhinged, detached? Instead, we can be committed, loyal, and forgiving of one another, even with corrective criticism and tough talk. Love alone very easily proves that faith never fails.

Trust and Devotion

For I am come to set a man at variance against his father, and the daughter against her mother, and the daughter in law against her mother in law.
Matthew 10:35

Jesus said any step ahead for a believer would invite trouble. Too often to our dismay, as we grow in Christ, conflicts result. We surrender to Jesus specifically to leave sin behind and give our hearts to God in the hope that relationships with others might be better. Matthew 10 is all about the Great Commission, our new mission to the world in which we live. Jesus taught us to love the ones we know with a lot of devotion and good deeds that we automatically win them over. Building trust with people means everything. Jesus said, "Blessed are the peacemakers." Then why did Jesus say He was going to set family members against each other? Christians have Jesus; we have to persistently adjust to line it all up in daily life.

We cherish the gospel in our hearts. We live it for the peace it provides. How does the verse above relate here? Family solidarity is a priority. Jesus knew that evangelizing wouldn't be easy. We face opposition from those closest to us. Ask yourself if it is more important to you to please people, like your own parents, or to please God? We find ourselves at odds with the world and even at odds with family at home, siblings, and spouses sometimes.

You and I repented of our old ways in order to be forgiven and made perfect. Doesn't this help relationships? My outlook improves with the belief that Jesus prevails no matter how things look. We see a few Christians fall and think that Jesus has stopped moving in their lives. Consider how impossible that would be. When I see obstinate Christians and sense no life, I have to leapfrog over by faith to believe that God is working one way or another.

The words of Jesus are dynamic. He puts this new spin on life. Our unity and God's commitment to our life links us together. The work of the Church and our own personal walk, evangelism, and ministry start in the home. Healthy marriages create the atmosphere of approval and encouragement. On the other hand, Jesus is going to set some people against each other, and some others we know will fail us.

In time, our lives clash, even those of faith. Faith provokes people. Most people don't know Jesus. Conflicts happens. God has to get their attention first so they react, and from there, they come to believe or they turn away.

God's concept of marriage means a whole new view. First, we need to get more pared down when we are paired up. It's about leaving the old behind and pressing on to a higher level. As a man leaves home to marry (hopefully not to move in with her parents), so every new believer should check their old lives to serve the Lord. Don't think of merely maintaining. We are in the world, but we are no longer of the world. A newly married couple must give up some past allegiances to be allied in their life together. The excess baggage that we bring along can really hurt us. It's a load. Couples need to bring faith into their marriages. We can't be double-minded and expect blessings. You want a storybook marriage with a perfect place at home. God combines us as one to work well without the slightest misgiving. It helps to be settled in our minds if we expect truly anointed love. We need to feel secure and be sure.

The biblical definition of marriage has not changed, but in today's world, the tendency when the going gets rough is separation and divorce. This becomes a storm, and there comes a time when we must lighten the load to save the ship. Some husbands would be surprised how quickly their marriages would be healed if they gave in and gave up on what they think is important to them. Wives, likewise, have no idea the progress they could make if they would simply back off and slack off with their adamant demands. The imperative is the commitment husbands and wives have to their marriages, surely as important as devotion to the Savior. Let us not be weary...If we faint not...we will win. Love never fails.

Many marriage partners have left their first loves, the attraction, and counselors call it an impasse—incompatibility; the judge decrees the matter irreconcilable. The truth is that no two people are perfectly compatible. There are certain places in the Bible that say it is permissible to dissolve a marriage under certain circumstances. Today, there are far too many divorces, and we can attribute that to hard hearts. These days, many people don't get married. One has to balance the benefit with the risk and wisely judge that most things or most issues are not as important as the sacred marriage relationship. What surpasses the excitement of courtship romance is the experience of falling in love all over again with your mate.

Husbands, love your wives, and be not bitter against them.
Colossians 3:19

The Bible teaches us to avoid contention and to learn contentment. It means a commitment. There is a serious learning curve in marriage. Along with the hope of eternal security, we have the ever-present promise of Jesus doing the fine-tuning. It gets better and better. That is the challenge in our world. How satisfied am I with my wife? Boy, am I satisfied with her! Just like the verse above says, I love my wife. We hope to have plenty of time ahead to be together and to get to know each other. A bond of love thrives when a husband and wife and the Savior work together and when God comes first in a blessed marriage.

People nowadays often opt out of their marriages for another partner. Do we Bible-believing Christians mimic every worldly practice? Ministers are performing wedding ceremonies for divorcees, which in many cases are not advisable according to the Bible, and some pastors don't care. *"Art thou bound unto a wife? Seek not to be loosed. Art thou loosed from a wife? Seek not a wife"* 1 Corinthians 7:27. Christian congregations may look the other way because we are so compromised that we won't say anything. If confessing Christians minimize scriptural admonitions on remarriage and dare disregard the Bible, we invite God's correction. His people are sure going to get God's perfection.

Today's children are often raised in more than one home by two sets of parents, with brothers, sisters, half brothers, half sisters, stepbrothers, and stepsisters, and several churches at the same time too. Is that good? It is wrong. I know some people who don't want to hear about it because they want to be positive or passive.

A friend of mine was talking to me one time when he sort of mentioned his half cousin. I stopped him and asked, "Did you say half cousin?"

"Yeah," he said, "my half cousin."

"What is a half cousin?" I asked.

"My grandfather was married and had kids. When he got married a second time to a new wife, she gave birth to my dad. So my dad had half brothers. That's how I have half cousins."

You know kids get confused, but they assume a lot too.

Society is so twisted that people would rather allow adultery into a marriage because forgiveness isn't given that much room. Forgiveness prefers to restore lost love. The model of marriage is for life. It is the model marriage if we raise it up higher to embody the eternal relationship of the bride of Jesus Christ, the Church.

The salvation of love in Christian homes testifies of God's living presence. When family life lacks love, trust, and devotion inside the home, we cannot expect to adequately minister the gospel of Jesus outside. Simultaneously, mercy and compassion must be shown outside the home to bring such riches to our families. It is rewarding to reach out to those around us who are in need. Time is difficult to shuffle, but creating a good home for our children is essential, as well as the preservation of a safe and peaceful community.

Christians are hungry to see their spouses involved in important ministries. The place the Christian family involves itself is with a good fellowship in an organized church that is active in the local area. What others are doing is not for us to question. The Lord knows how to separate the believers from the pretenders. He knows the end from the beginning, and time is getting short.

Clear about what our mission should be, our task is to tackle the work with all our strength. It's like in the old movies when a man wins a million dollars and he runs home so excited that he even kisses his stern old mother-in-law. I think that deep down, we all want that. The plan of salvation signals God's love. We must love people so considerably that we get their attention and make a lasting impression, and they in turn tell others.

Any amount of love, gradual as it may seem, by faith, produces revival. This happens to a greater degree than anyone notices. Don't give up. Bitter marriages and bitter souls have powerfully corrupting influence, but let God be the judge. If you keep watch as long as it takes, you will see a wider ministry form. It may take decades. Lifelong hopes happen with endurance. Keep going and wait for God to come through.

Family is a significant part of our lives. Where there is constant fighting in the home with family members just trying to survive, it is a tragic existence. Love is hardest to believe in if you live in trouble. For millions of people the world over, it is a matter of being born in the wrong place, such as in war-torn areas and dictatorships. Families are ripped apart. There is a right and a wrong way to run a home; this is all the more reason to rely on our Father in Heaven. Everyone can pray to receive His salvation.

We can pause to assess life and stay aware of others around. The more we read the Bible as God intends, the more we see how contrary our thinking has been. God will lead us to success. He can stop counterproductive, destructive, and negative patterns.

Everyone naturally feels pressure. Let's be wise and live in healthy ways. When we understand what is right, we choose to do what we know. Aim to be happy. It is awesome to have a clear conscience with peace of mind. We all want love—everyone does.

Renewed by Forgiveness

> *And be renewed in the spirit of your mind.*
> Ephesians 4:23

Your attitude can be improved with some fresh thinking. This world is corrupt with sin. Every single person we know is a fallible human being. People don't meet our expectations; we get angry.

Why take it hard when we get friction? If plans don't go according to our specifications, we get irritated. Jesus taught His followers to endure and wait for His return (Mark 13:32–37).

When the return of Jesus seems too slow, we give up and ease up. People need you. We stumble too, but Christians have to bear up and urge one another on to the end.

Christians are renewed by a forgiving spirit; it becomes second nature. As it is, repentance should be our first nature. We would all wake up feeling better in the morning if we were working out our salvation (Philippians 2:12) with our bright enlightenment, not dwelling on others' faults. Faultfinding is a bad habit.

You begin to live and learn to appreciate everyone. In everybody's backgrounds and views, look for their better side. Think and speak well of them. Seek their good and see how to be of help. If we are humble, we surrender more to God. We will be more forgiving and much less demanding. God is aware of the situation here, and He is working it all out. Not everything works out for everyone: it's wrong to think so. God knows.

> *If it be possible, as much as lieth in you, live peaceably with all men.*
>
> Romans 12:18

We should find the right way to get along with our neighbors. Peace is not always possible. That is the catch. As much as it is possible within you—"as much as lieth in you"—to cope. We don't realize our potential, and we underestimate ourselves. We underestimate others. You might be surprised at how far you can go.

By praying and getting advice and support, you can hang in there longer than you thought. How much stress can I take? If we are in the conflict and stay patient, God will be able to do more and more with us. How much harm do I do? I could be glad I tried. How much good can we do together as Christians? You've said before that you've had enough. You have wanted to draw the line. Stay rational. We need to keep our heads and know our own limits. We could achieve a royal thing with a team of believers.

God is working with us all the time. We wouldn't ever find out what we are really made of until we've tested our endurance. Many times, we sell ourselves short. The verse doesn't say, "as much as is possible with the others," but "as much as lieth in you." Paul teaches us to live in peace. The onus is on us.

We think that it's useless to keep trying, and people tell us to quit. Pastors preach in church and talk about fighting sin and getting right with God, all without much mention of love. The stress is put on church structure, orthodoxy, or a hundred other things. Enduring relationships of love in Jesus is the Lord's top priority. God understands it all, and we need to go to Him. And if we're talking about marriage, it's about church too.

If we insist that someone should be more loving, we should look at ourselves. Loving our spouses the best can help the most. We have to believe it in order to do it. If we wait until love is reciprocated, we have lost it.

Be brave enough to put love first. Have faith that other people won't take advantage of us. We hope they do take advantage of what we offer, yes. They may not get a better deal. Trusting in God's love has no risk, ultimately, since He protects and provides for us. God gives victory over sin and restores our trust in things. It's hard to be positive with the anxiety that comes from life. We all need more positive reinforcement from loved ones. Real compliments help a lot too. Marriage simply cannot endure without the oil of forgiveness. For if ye love them that love you, what reward have ye? Matthew 5:46.

A friend once told me that he was worried about his marriage. I asked him if he had told his wife lately that he loved her.

"No," he said. "We're too busy fighting."

I asked, "Have you tried this? Just say 'I love you' to her. You have to say it once in a while. More than anything, she needs to hear that you love her."

"No, I haven't," he confessed. "She is always mad. We're tearing each other apart too much of the time."

"Well, the problem you have now is that if you start laying it on thick about loving her, she'll be suspicious that you got into some trouble and she'll think you're up to no good. If you just walk into the house and say you love her, it will look really odd to her. But you have to turn the marriage around to where you praise her more often. That is why she stays mad at you all the time—not because of all the negativity between you two, not for the wrong things you do, but because she needs more of those positives. Rehearse and practice. She wants to hear it. Let her know you care."

That was a few years ago, and they are no longer together.

Every one of us is lost until we repent and put our trust in our Maker. Marital problems have hurt each one of us—in our childhood, among friends, and on into our older adult lives. Praise God for all the love we have enjoyed and the wonderful memories over the years thanks to the institution of marriage. God is righteous. We can rest assured now through God's Word that He has secured our home in Heaven with Him. We were guilty, and just this quickly, He makes us fit for His kingdom.

Marriage is the most beautiful and best thing on earth. Through salvation, believers have God's divine blessing in marriage—a witness of Jesus and His eternal purpose in us, the Church. Marriage is a sacrament. Forgiveness is an element. Because of sin, we've been longing to be pardoned and absolved, and so we are. All our anger, attitudes, defense mechanisms, inferiority complexes, and the greed for more stuff increase the crazy need for acceptance, the fear of rejection, and our empty lives. Don't grab everything around you; get a hold of God.

Just as Christ forgives us and is patient with us, so a husband needs to be kind to his wife. The husband is the example of how Jesus loves the Church. In the same way, a wife demonstrates Christian devotion to Jesus when she sees good character in her husband and stays true to her feelings. The Apostle Paul said that this is a mystery, but it has been revealed.

> *Nevertheless, let everyone of you in particular so love his wife even as himself; and the wife, see that she reverence her husband.*
> Ephesians 5:33

One evening, I wanted to see the correct spelling of the word *utter*. I glanced down a page in the dictionary and my finger landed on a funny new word. There sat this word *uxorious*. It means, "excessively or foolishly fond of one's wife (< L,< *uxor* wife)," and in Latin, *uxor* means "wife." It doesn't pertain to the love a woman has for her husband. It has nothing to do with being luxurious, excessive, or immoderate. It's about a husband's love. *I am going to have to remember to use this*, I said to myself.

The very next evening I was sitting on the couch and was thinking in the back of my mind that Louise had agreed to marry me and had put on her engagement ring about a year before. I asked her, "Wasn't it about a year ago that we got engaged?"

"Tomorrow," she said.

Wow! I thought. *Tomorrow? That was close. I better do something special.* That's when I remembered that word from the previous evening: *uxorious*. My Louise is intrigued by language and vocabulary. She likes to learn new words. For example, she didn't believe me once when I said the word *feckless*, because she said I had made it up—until she looked it up. Now there I was, stuck at home with uxoriousness, so any surprise would have to come soon, as in right after work the next day.

A plan came into my head while I was at work. Louise would be home when I got there. Wasting no time, I would go up to the office-supply store on the first corner beyond the parking lot, where they had an assortment of cute cards, and then I would stop at the flower stand on the way home. I could write a little note in the card using my new word, which was perfect for the occasion. They had the perfect pretty card for romance. I got it and wrote a note inside: "I love you uxoriously." I signed the card and then got a beautiful bouquet of colorful flowers to take home. I was excited for Louise, praising and thanking God for the good tip on the timely word.

Louise was on the phone when I got home, so I set the flowers up with the card. From the other room, I heard her open the envelope.

Louise shrieked out loud, "What does this mean?" She came to me and asked, "What does *uxoriously* mean?"

"The word is *uxorious*. It means that a man is excessively or foolishly fond of his wife. It does not mean a love that a woman has for her husband. *Uxor* means 'wife.'"

During dinner, Louise asked where I had come up with this word. I said I had dreamed it up because there was no word to describe how I felt about her and how beautiful she was. I told her, "I invented the word and then put it in all of the dictionaries of the world."

She was so cute. She jumped up from the dinner table and ran for the dictionary to find the word. I really do love her. She was thrilled and tickled to see it there in print.

The next morning as I was getting ready for work, Louise just had to ask me about it again: "Did you get a word from the Lord?"

> *My purpose is that they may be encouraged in heart and united in love, so that they may have the full riches of complete understanding, in order that they may know the mystery of God, namely, Christ.*
>
> Colossians 2:2 NIV

Wisdom

Cast thy bread upon the waters: for thou shalt find it after many days. Give a portion to seven; and also to eight; for thou knowest not what evil shall be upon the earth. If the clouds be full of rain, they empty themselves upon the earth: and if the tree fall toward the south, or toward the north, in the place where the tree falleth, there it shall be. He that observeth the wind shall not sow; and he that regardeth the clouds shall not reap. As thou knowest not what is the way of the spirit, nor how the bones do grow in the womb of her that is with child: even so thou knowest not the works of God who maketh all. In the morning sow thy seed, and in the evening withhold not thine hand: for thou knowest not whether shall prosper, either this or that, or whether they both shall be alike good.

(Ecclesiastes 11:1–6)

CHAPTER 10

For all this I considered in my heart even to declare all this, that the righteous, and the wise, and their works, are in the hand of God: no man knoweth either love or hatred by all that is before them.

Ecclesiastes 9:1

In all that he had, Solomon saw *faith* and *love* as intangible. This wisdom is from the hand of God. Do you know from your experience what God is going to do? It may be one thing or another. It could be that life will go well—or maybe not. Start out with care. Keep both eyes open. Hope for the best. God will be there in the end. When you gain *love*, you'll have to take it by *faith*.

From the advantage of God's wisdom, Solomon examines our vulnerabilities and reveals our weaknesses. What can life be about? Later on in Ecclesiastes 12:13, Solomon sums up his writing and our whole duty: to learn how powerful God is and to live as He says. This is the Old Testament's version of judgment. It was a hard reality, the genuine article of faith, to believe.

> *For there is not a just man upon earth, that doeth good, and sinneth not.*
>
> Ecclesiastes 7:20

We are bound to go wrong, and we fail to recognize it. Even if we succeed in life, we feel unfulfilled; sin is in us. Is there no hope in any of our efforts? *"For the creation was subjected to frustration, not by its own choice, but by the will of the one who subjected it"* (Romans 8:20 NIV). Life can be lost in a split second. We want to triumph and win in the view of others. Why not try to yield all to God? God gives hope. We cannot count on ourselves or depend on people, but the Lord will finish what He has started. Accept God's strategy, and don't be resentful.

Our concern is not only security for a good life, but it's also about hope. Whether time is long or short, life deserves meaning here and a reward in Heaven. *"The fear of the Lord is the beginning of wisdom"* (Proverbs 9:10). Get God on board.

To know God, Solomon set faith against a backdrop of earthly life. The book of Ecclesiastes, in a way, is more like the New Testament than any other book in the Old. Without any of the specifics of the Old Law, it articulates the barrenness of sin and accentuates the sovereignty of God. What better way to illustrate our condition? Solomon's words are down to earth yet inspiring.

Obedience to God's Old Law was just one frustrating way to measure things. Israel was assured of failure and unsure of what else to do. They were sinners who had to trust God. How are we now? Jesus has given life back to us in the excellence of His Holy Spirit. We would be lost if not for Him.

To walk the course of love, Christians are guided by a trusting faith. Can we understand what the Bible teaches? It's not arrogant to be this confident. We can't know what course will be the most rewarding. God knows.

Faith is the mark of a mature Christian. The Holy Spirit of Jesus is present in our lives. Our old carnal nature obviously wants to get more control, contain God in a bottle or a box, as if we could measure out His Spirit whenever we choose.

God's ways are perplexing. His presence is not noticeable and His existence is not perceivable, especially to the sinner. On the other hand, lost souls can notice Him, as I did back before I received Him. You can expect to see Him work if you want. It's greater than anything. Be satisfied to call Him your Lord. Be less worried and more loving.

The love of Jesus in our hearts moves us in the right direction. We don't have to run away as if we fear Him. We are drawn to Him because Christians trust in what the Bible says to us. You can spend your time battling sin in your life, always on the defense and so tied down that you never get around to actually living and loving the way the Lord prescribes. Each of us has unlimited potential. Only by looking, praying, and gaining God's personal interest can we reach out and fulfill our purpose.

> *For whosoever will save his life shall lose it: and whosoever will lose his life for my sake shall find it.*
> Matthew 16:25

As devoted Christians, we find ourselves lost in God. After we know the truth and have it confirmed in us, it will be harder to stray away and even harder to stay away. But the longer we stay in sin, the harder it is to quit and go straight. Sin is addictive and habitual. The longer we live in victory, the stronger we will be, and the easier it will be to stay that way. When you have found how clean and free you really are in the true love of Jesus, you don't want to go back into bondage to anything.

Faith is like an airplane that is not going to get off the ground. If it doesn't race down the runway to gain speed, building pressure in a hurry to get lift; it's going to run out of time.

True faith brings spirituality and is not artificial or false. When we turn and receive God's Spirit, we gain confidence. Can anyone say they are loving if they selfishly take from others? Generous giving leads to more love. What gives Christians a direct link with God? The power of prayer brings His entire strength to combat the dullness that pervades our human heart. Love is true to real believers.

We don't obey God just because we are supposed to. There are a lot of unnoticed needs that don't automatically get met. Don't take it for granted that someone else will do what's needed. Assume they won't—and pray. There are some good reasons and some poor excuses as to why it's wrong to get involved. "Cast thy bread upon the waters," Solomon said (Ecclesiastes 11:1). Where do we cast ourselves? God places each of us where He sees fit.

God is already waiting for your faith so He can move. When you act on your faith in Christ, somehow, God's way is made clearer to you and it's likely seen by others. Trust yourself to the wisdom of God, and you will find true happiness. Attempting any other way is futile, a waste of time. Ecclesiastes 11:1–6 offers a very helpful definition of faith. Let's see how. Christians make the difference in their *love* through *faith* in Jesus Christ and His Holy Spirit.

Love and Found

> *Cast thy bread upon the waters: for thou shalt find it after many days.*
>
> Ecclesiastes 11:1

I was a young man once. Now I am getting older and my dreams are coming true. Don't hold back. Don't quit since you can't know what tomorrow will bring. Be generous. Jesus said, *"For I was hungry and you gave me meat"* (Matthew 25:35). When you give, you really give to Jesus. He is there when you visit the prison, the sick, the lonely, or the hungry. When you live to be old, Jesus will be there for you.

May we together pray for God's wisdom of love and faith. Jesus didn't qualify His second commandment with more exceptions and conditions. This commandment is like the first: love each other with all your heart, soul, and strength. It is not about who deserves love or how much they get it. This takes faith. You may be afraid you'll be taken for granted. The Bible has wisdom on the topic of gullibility. Don't we give help simply for God's sake? It is needed, but it is not typical for people to get capable help. I don't claim to be able, just available. If you worry too much, you never begin the doing, living, and loving.

There is much to dislike in others, so we get mixed up. Jesus did not equivocate in Matthew 25:35: *"I was a stranger, and ye took me in."* Are you doing anything to fulfill this verse? We have our suspicions about total strangers who need a place to stay. We think they must have done something wrong to be out in the cold, like they made some bad choices or crossed someone. Such explanations slow us down. What if we believe we can help a poor person or give to someone who won't repay? Be careful. It takes faith to give when there's probably no future in it for us.

When Jesus taught His disciples to visit prisoners in jail, He gave no indication as to why they had been arrested. He said, *"I was in prison, and ye came unto me"* (Matthew 25:36). Was He speaking of believers who get imprisoned for their Christian witness by tyrannical governments? We would be inclined to go visit them. (There probably couldn't be any visitors, though, if that were the case.) Jesus presupposes that His followers will go to prison for the purpose of visiting the criminal, the guilty, and the sinner despite the severity of their offenses. *"Judge not, that ye be not judged"* (Matthew 7:1). What if you think you're too good to visit criminals? Then Jesus warns of certain everlasting damnation: *"I was…in prison, and ye visited me not"* (Matthew 25:43). God corrects us to keep us out of trouble, poverty, and illness. He puts us to work. If not for His goading and prodding, I would have drifted away long ago.

Those who are at the end of their rope are more inclined to see. Christ gets through to them with mercy. It is not easy for people to fend off temptations, to challenge their pride, or to change philosophies. Nor is it simple for people to see what is right and wrong. We have God's message that saves lives, and the needy ones are more likely to accept your offer of help, friendship, and salvation.

We need credible faith with real love. Don't let anybody tell you they have it all figured out. We walk by faith. The future of this world is invisible. Where are you going in the long run? If you give yourself to God, He will take you, and He will take you far.

> *Pure religion and undefiled before God and the Father is this, To visit the fatherless and the widows in their affliction, and to keep oneself unspotted from the world.*
> James 1:27

The Lord Jesus' brother James wrote, "*visit the fatherless and the widows in their affliction,*" because they have problems. They can't help it. These children can be problem kids. Fatherless children miss a lot. Children of alcoholics have another set of issues. These situations aren't imaginary. Kids who have only one parent or no parents can often be overlooked. They live with complex emotions. Mentors who spend any length of time with them see and feel their difficulties. They need you, but it won't be easy.

Innumerable children are handicapped in their youth. The added harm comes when they don't find enough support from adults or peers. It's a blessed thing to see these children receive better attention, and it is touching when other children, friends and peers, show them care.

Face it, how many adults who suffered as kids are scarred by grief and, in turn, dump the resounding consequences on their own children? It would be nice if we all grew up unhurt, but if it happened, we shouldn't let the past haunt us now. Let's deal with it.

You don't have to be a Christian to notice. Orphans languish all around the world as a result of wars, disasters, and diseases. Children are abandoned, adopted, deserted, housed in orphanages, taken into slavery, and forced into combat.

Vast resources go to evangelize nations. Rescuing orphans to raise them in Christ in their country is a real savings. Seeing pictures of destitute kids or getting solicitations in the mail will trouble even the coldhearted. Those who have twisted minds recognize better what children in other places go through. So we don't really understand until it affects us personally. Many of us have the resources to help, but we live fashionably comfortable, orbiting too high above the clouds to feel another country's pain. Reentering earth's atmosphere causes way too much friction. Faith overcomes denial and touches tragedy with love.

Widows make wonderful saints, yet their later years are their hardest. Elderly people often get depressed, defensive, and flat-out rude, unfortunately. We've all heard, "Do not look a gift horse in the mouth," but this old adage may be forgotten by the aged. They can be cranky. Older folks are overtaken by anxiety and forget the little axiom, "Don't bite the hand that feeds you." More often than not, visiting them is a blessing, but doing so may complicate your life, because they beg for your time and your help or might become dependent on you. It can make you want to give up on them. Keep a respect for senior citizens. In their time, they shouldered their many responsibilities well. Admire them and the legacy they leave.

The global upward curve on aging doesn't look good. The birth rate has dropped dramatically nearly everywhere in the world, while there are increasing numbers of elderly—and folks are living longer than ever. You might wonder how we can afford retirement. How are you going to fare? It's in your own best interest to set the example of caring for others in the hope that someone will be there to care for you when your time comes. May it be someone who cares for you like God cares. Kindness for the fatherless and widows is in increasing demand.

Give and It Shall Be Given

> *Give a portion to seven, and also to eight; for thou knowest not what evil shall be upon the earth.*
> (Ecclesiastes 11:2)

When we give ourselves to God, we surrender all. Solomon's

point in this verse, to give seven portions, even eight, was that you wouldn't stop until you gave your all. Was he talking about donating, sacrificing, or fighting the world's evil? As we know from the Scriptures, Jesus calls us to be His representatives. Because He gave His life, completely surrendering Himself in the face of murderers for each one of us, you and I are to be just like Jesus. After giving ourselves to God, wholeheartedly, love proves our new nature.

Charity and sacrifice pretty well exemplify our truer Christian faith. Many of us get so involved in our own goals and successes, like using charity for tax deductions, that we lose sight of the purpose of charity. In fact, some people insist that it's good stewardship and honorable to give only to popular ministries. Is that necessarily God's way? Your charity to support becomes instead a pet hobby. The rich don't support; they sport tax shelters. Businesses donate to charities for their public relations and advertising. Why equate religion with a prosperous financial life? More than ever before, government and non-government organizations are doing wonderful things, but agencies don't do everything. Each of us needs to do more in the name of Jesus.

If you want to be restrained in giving, try rereading the Bible. Measured against our way of thinking, there are some seemingly impractical ideas in the pages, but it's practical advice. Can you live for yourself and expect blessings from God? He will provide so we can afford to give. We give because we are able to give, and we give when, at times, there are exceptional needs. We are to put the future in God's hands, where it belongs. We are unsure of what comes tomorrow. How much do you give? We have all the promises in Christ, and the victory has already been won. You want something done, then do it.

> *And I will very gladly spend and be spent for you; though the more abundantly I love you, the less I be loved.*
> 2 Corinthians 12:15

Like a father to his child, Paul told the church at Corinth that he would spend himself broke in his love for them. Even if they never returned the favor, and in fact, when they resented him for doing so, he was dedicated. What an accurate and telling picture of love! Paul "gladly" gave. Jesus gives us this extra special willingness.

If you were "spent," as Paul said here, you would have nothing more to give. When your money is spent, you are broke. When you "spend" yourself physically, you have no energy or strength left and can do no more. Would you expend yourself to the point of no return? You would rest and still get no energy back. When your body is spent, the doctor says that you will not spring back because you have broken your health. Most of us haven't yet loved that hard. Paul said that he would "be spent" for the Christians of Corinth. The more vulnerable souls need us to love them with all our hearts, all of our determination, and most of our strength. The greater faith comes as we labor in all our love for Jesus.

Following in the footsteps of Jesus begins with one step from you and me. We take the first step—faith. Does it stop with only this one extra step? People suspect that it won't stop with the first step. "Count the cost," Jesus said. With His grace, we can give until it hurts—and more. Christians give more whether or not they get reimbursed or reinforced.

Helping people is not always easy. A wonderful young lady named Diane was a dear friend of our family as I was growing up. When Diane was twelve years old, she was found to have tumors spreading throughout her spine. The doctors removed the tumors, along with her spinal cord. She went on to finish high school and university with top grades. She was a real inspiration.

Diane could tell you about coping. When I came back home in my mid-twenties, I told Diane about a couple of men I had met who had been injured and handicapped and who were tyrants. They were constantly belligerent, throwing verbal assaults at everyone around. Being dependent on others, they should've been humble, but they had everyone within reach frightened to death. This type of person is very needy and use bullying to get their way.

Diane told me that there are generally two kinds of disabled people: there are those who react exceptionally well, and there are those who don't do well at all; only a few people fall somewhere in the middle. Diane was a beautiful individual who was nice, lived peacefully, and was delighted to be a humongous booster to me.

You can't tell how you'd handle yourself if you had to adjust to a sudden lifelong challenge. Ask yourself how generous and open you are with disadvantaged people. This might give you a glimpse of yourself in any future tragedy.

I try to help where I'm wanted, oftentimes with those in big need. One person or another—counselors, caseworkers, or family members—have acted surprisingly hostile to me and acted defensive about my involvement. Who are they trying to protect, themselves?

In one particular mental ward that I used to visit at different times, I met a psych nurse; she was as cold as a Nazi Gestapo guard. She grated on me. At other times, in the same ward, a big friendly male nurse impressed me with a glorious command of his skills. My good friend, Mike, having a lot of experience as a mental patient, noted that there are two kinds of caregivers: there are those who are perfectly suited for the job and have found their place, and there are those who have no business in that position. He said there are fewer in between. If I volunteer, why would anyone feel threatened? I want to be of help to friends and be in turn an encouragement to the staff. There's nothing wrong with that.

God enables and equips us for what He leads us to do. He gives seed to the sower. Material giving is simply basic to Christianity. More is better. It does us good to give. People you help are likely to help others, and so the seeds are spread.

Susan, who prayed for salvation back in 1981, continued to falter for years. Christians I knew had given up on her too easily. After struggling in sin and confusion for a long time, she confessed to me recently that God was inescapable. I asked her about her faith. She had no doubt that Jesus came into her heart at the time we prayed together and that He had been her help through all these bumpy, dumpy years. I know she has lived an unbearably sad life and has suffered as a result. She has been free of cocaine for over thirty years.

Susan lives every day sweetly caring for neighbors in her public housing apartment building. Nearly all of her neighbors were homeless before moving into this twelve-story structure. She keeps in touch with her hurting friends. What's neat is that she herself is blooming fantastically in the fruit of the Spirit. She is blessed in her prayer life as never before. The lessons of her past are a help. When one member falls behind, we all suffer, but as she blooms, all of us are blessed with her.

There It Shall Be

> *If the clouds be full of rain, they empty themselves upon the earth: and if the tree fall toward the south, or toward the north, in the place where the tree falleth, there it shall be.*
> Ecclesiastes 11:3

When the vapor in a cloud meets a certain temperature in the air at the right atmospheric pressure, it condenses into rain and falls to the ground. But Solomon isn't talking about the dew point; it's the "do" point. Our heart gets to the conversion zone in ripe circumstances, and in an instant, we are hit by the moving of God's Spirit. We hardly see it coming. When the rain falls or the tree falls, there it shall be, and when our heart reaches the "do" point, there it shall be.

In a certain place when we give our lives to God in Jesus Christ, there we'll be. Solomon uses the simple illustration of a tree. If a tree falls toward the north one day, you won't come back later to find it has jumped up toward the south. When one of us is ready for salvation, Jesus will place us in this marvelous new life. If we commit our lives to God one day and the next day we sin, it creates doubt, but we're still growing.

Love lights the faith. Many come looking for Christianity wanting to know what to do. Does this hit the target for you? Some seek to know what it is, what they're missing, or how to get it back. They talk. Is our religion simply a list of instructions? People wander in and then go away, wondering what God says. They search inside themselves for the faith they think they lack. All the while, God's patient love is right in front of them. *Faith* ignites the *love*.

Good writers describe subjects with such vivid detail that we want to go along with them. We feel their words on the pages. The color and intrigue attract us. We are stirred to action. Their solutions are only too reasonable and right. We can't help but respond to their power of suggestion. They describe love. They define it. We see it. Am I satisfied? Can I be satisfied? People need the right version of Christianity in order to give themselves over to it.

Determination must be undeterred. Clear directions would sure help. The Bible has the answers. That's why God gives us teachers and writers to explain the explanation. What has happened? It is precisely that our faith has been activated.

We talk of love and pray for answers. We are aching for real solace. Am I comforted? We are lacking and wanting faith. Only God can console us, yet we share our lament with others. Compromising and maybe going only partway with God is not going to win love. Whatever God does is forever established. If you and I were convinced, then we'd move ahead. Great plans have come to life when the desires of the heart are free to be realized and that has to come through prayer—real actualities.

We move on from mediocrity and negative talk. With more reliance on God, we would be positive and brave. The angst and assurance of faith will break us from the grip of disturbing events. Are you cooking with the heat on? If we trust in God's forgiveness and His faithfulness and act with a reliable effort, then we can fulfill what He wants.

Every one of us needs hope, but sometimes, our focus is not on what's best for us. Agree with God. Good prayers go beyond what we ask or think. Why not ask for more? This will work for anyone. As we are drawn more toward God and occupied less in the distractions of the world, faith will bring His love to us and we'll put others first. Skip temptation, get direction.

But let him ask in faith, nothing wavering. For he that wavereth is like a wave of the sea driven with the wind and tossed.

James 1:6

Good things come to believers who trust. Our life is free, but we lose sight of God's will and use all the interferences as excuses. The driving forces hit us. To keep our faith from wavering, we can do something similar to what we might have learned in driver's education class. If you're in a car driving between two close objects, such as parked cars on a narrow street, pick a point farther ahead in the middle and aim for that. Keep your eyes off the objects on either side, or you might swerve away from one side and into the other. This is how you take daily life. Right in the same setting, believers can learn to avoid what pulls on us. With our eyes on Jesus, we slip through the close narrow places in the road to go where He wants us to go.

And every man that hath this hope in him purifieth himself, even as he is pure.

1 John 3:3

Hope itself is purifying. The Bible is now proving true. Theologians apply Bible prophecy to current times. God sees how much time is left. Think what the scale of destruction is going look like to the billions of people in these last days. Something like fifty-five or a hundred million people or more died in the few years of the Second World War. It depends on what you read. It's a much more explosive future ahead, maybe soon. It doesn't mean that we have no opportunities right now. Life is hard, but it's still fairly peaceful here.

Huge threats and terrible weapons at present keep nations cowed, but they have not quelled the discord and latent hatred underlying historic divisions. There won't be a prayer when the dam finally bursts. Suppose God's Holy Spirit continues to restrain the evils to the end of our days and doesn't let up until His work of grace is done.

In addition, we can look beyond the terrors of the future tribulation years to see God's ultimate plan to come. There will be peace on Earth someday. Be sober and rejoice in this heavenly hope.

We know the spirit of the Antichrist has long been at work in this world. The stage is being set, and one day, when the curtain is raised, bowls of God's judgment will be poured out. What we see in today's news are many insoluble strongholds: armed forces, economic empires, governments, motives, philosophies, religions, technologies, and bad moves. With a furious motion, these leagues will bind together, working one merciless rule. Satan, in his deadly self-destructive path, will attempt to sweep away civilization.

As the grip of the devil holds our friends and foes captive, they fail to hear our call. They are confused by so many clashing persuasions; evil darkens their minds. Many are already floundering with temptations and sinners' blindness. As these alarms sound in our time, this is all the more reason we must live out our lives in God's protective love. The New Testament says there is going to be absolute catastrophe, unexpected but final. We have to pray for a bolder faith to reach more hearts. With Christ, love is put into our lives. We believe all of this.

We win if in nothing else but love alone. You and I begin by focusing all our attention on what matters to God. What we want to do is to recognize that even with faith, we don't exactly identify everything clearly. Why always conceptualize in absolutes? Let's highlight love and enhance our awareness there; it's by faith. The Bible says all our old human attitudes are conquered without a doubt in Jesus. Put *faith* in *love* alone with Jesus, and there it shall be.

Love Succeeds

He that observes the wind shall not sow; and he that regardeth the clouds shall not reap.

Ecclesiastes 11:4

You can look at a barometer to see whether to grab a hat in the morning, but after you go out the door, there is no telling how the day will go. You can read God's Word to tell you what's true. What you do with it tells what's in your heart. Jesus teaches us the way to live. If you count on good weather to gauge life, you'll be like a wave of the sea, tossed to and fro. Naturally, people observe the wind and watch the clouds, so our love fluctuates. We are like mercury in a thermometer. Those who lose heart will not reap. Praise Jesus. He is perfect.

Somebody on his way to town gets a great parking spot the first time around the block, and that somehow means to her or to him it's going to be a wonderful day. It fosters a cheerful outlook. Unfortunately, the next morning, hunting for a parking place causes a big delay, and watch out—everyone better stay out of our way that morning.

Each of us has clouds and wind in our days, but we each take life differently. Some Christians seem unengaged with life. Where's their passion? They just poke along nonchalantly as if nothing ever happens. Challenge the apathy. If we don't rise above the storms, keeping our head above the clouds, doubt defeats us and steals our love. We need to pray constantly to overcome by faith.

If we start out apprehensive, we might get nothing accomplished. Think how we let these things hit us. It slows us down. Everybody experiences the antisocial behavior of a few thorny people, and after that, it becomes a little harder to make yourself friendly. On a day when I'm in a bad mood, I may begin to wonder if the courtesy I was trained in as a boy is getting me anywhere as an adult. I'm growing older and the traffic seems more aggravating. It has probably been like that all along. Solomon aptly said, "There's nothing new." Does the value of love hold up? You may have doubts. Life gets so hard that we stop and question everything. We choke. Things are important. You may not think so.

God's love grows in a good heart that with patience, bears fruit. Farmers plant their fields in early spring in order to do what needs doing, not knowing what the summer will bring. They will plow snow-covered ground before the winter ends. For them to wait would be too late. They take the risk. Crops have been lost before harvest. Farmers have been ruined in a bad season. There is only one way to get a crop, and that is to prepare the ground and plant.

Christians keep faith in order to change conditions instead of obsessing over situations. Stop reacting the way the world does. Love people as they are (they can be sour), or is your love like that of your old attitude (it could also be better)? Unreasonable and wicked people hassle us because they never seem to believe (2 Thessalonians 3:2). They notice the signs in the sky, but cannot read the signs of the times (Matthew 16:3). Love others first because that is God's approach.

Often, my kindnesses appear to have been wasted on those who don't appreciate it. Weak souls live in places all around us. Good deeds might go unnoticed. They might seem ineffective. I don't think it's worth it then. If we attempt to help people, give generously, and spend time on others only to be attacked, disappointed, or ignored, it doesn't necessarily mean we've failed. We all get our feelings hurt. It stings when our good advice is not taken. True faith operates on a higher level. We're not going to see love if we are watching and worrying about every knock we collect.

I would like to briefly mention Satan. He has had far too much publicity and gets blamed for things that he doesn't do. Some people are inclined to give him credit for everything bad that happens. Chances are that accidents happen. Our car breaks down, we get sick, or we lose a friend. Many things can hurt us. People upset us too. To say that Satan is always to blame is giving him too much credit. God gives us strength in these troubled times; give thanks.

Satan stands in the shadows and casts doubt to accuse us of all that goes wrong. He stands there pointing the finger at every sin we do or don't do. He relishes our sorrow. He wants us to grumble, complain, lower our standards, and works on us to become the broken people he can prey on. He wants to weaken our faith. You, however, ignore the temptation of things you see—the temporal—and look toward Heaven, which cannot be seen. Satan doesn't touch us. Hold on to the things that are everlasting. Resist the devil.

LOVE BELIEVES ALL THINGS

On one side of us, we have Satan pulling, and on the other side, we have God. We occupy a lot of room in the middle. More power is given to us in Jesus Christ—more than we realize. Today's conditions result from a long chain of events set in motion years and years ago. God teaches us how to choose to do the best we can in these worrisome times.

Some people get a flat tire, jump out of their car, and curse Satan. Flat tires are caused by nails and things that accidentally land in the road. We can praise the Lord because we have the common sense to carry a spare tire and a jack, so we can change the flat. With each and every hazard, turn and thank Jesus for our God-given ability to handle responsibility. Let us not give Satan any part of our thought. Send him away quickly with a word of praise for God, our Father.

Life's troubles are all the more reason for us to try to help others. Jesus is the One who asks you to be a servant, so lay it all at His feet. We have confessed our fallen nature, and from this point forward, we know there's no righteousness in our own strength. Could anything done in Jesus' name be in vain? When we fall short, it seems that our spent energies are for naught. Why not mark it down and chalk it up to call it practice? Be ready for when you finally get it together. In the thick of things, share the message with those around you. If we show a little kindness, we'll stand out in the darkness and win. Do good. Be an on-the-spot helper. This is how people are going to see the right way. Be a light in the night.

We look to the larger picture in Christ. Glorify your Father in Heaven. Be faithful. We ask Jesus to give us life, and He does. We don't seem to be satisfied, as if we need someone else's approval. Let go of that pessimism, be confident. Somebody else will take that place. The poor remain in this world, and it could be you or me. We have our trials. We are tempted to sin and we do sin. We experience guilt, both imaginary and real. Many Christians waste so much time battling goblins, whether fictitious or actual, when real happiness passes right on by. Jesus Christ gives us the best life. Some "shall not reap." True victory requires strong faith to see how His love is always our goal. And it is within reach.

Walk by Faith

> *As thou knowest not what is the way of the spirit, nor how the bones do grow in the womb of her who is with child: even so thou knowest not the works of God who maketh all.*
> Ecclesiastes 11:5

There's no sensation quite like the energetic kick of a baby in the womb. We look forward to the birth. We get sentimental. Deep down in our hearts, we dread the many pains each little kid is certain to face and the future as an adult, but we dream of the potential in life ahead. Who can imagine what opportunities are in store for an unborn baby? It's unhealthy to dwell in the past, and it is equally true that it's not good to be too anxious about tomorrow. We don't know the works of God. We should be happy to live by faith and count all the helpful things God does. *"Whatever thy hand findeth to do, do it with thy might"* Ecclesiastes 9:10. Let your heart be a calm haven from which to work. Rest with faith in Jesus. Solomon was not an unbeliever, never a doubter, but he was realistic.

We don't see where the wind goes. Keep in mind that it's not apparent what our work will produce. The aim of our lives is the great harvest at the resurrection. We don't know now how the seed we sow will grow. Who knows? God tends to the future. Don't let it slip from you; there is no reward in the lure of sin, and good is in the hand of God. Let's not think that God will repay our effort with disappointment.

We could bring lost souls to salvation if everything came by faith. We'd easily inspire the more timid, fainthearted Christians. How do we fail? Feed the starving and give comfort to hurting people, and never forget that your real objective is sharing eternity. We have the Spirit of God. We have the mind of Christ. Remember all the good times and wonderful people He has put in your life. Let's keep working together. Then read and teach the Bible as an activist, sharing the whole counsel of God's Word. You can be a friend to more people.

Let us go and reach out by faith and take hold of the work that endures. Our treasure will be in Heaven, where neither moth nor rust can corrupt (Matthew 6:20). Pray more. What we believe about our salvation determines how well we do.

For many of us, it is not just a question of how to be spiritual, but it's essentially a question of how to hang on to it. The wide variety of opinions by which Christians differ on doctrine is disturbing in itself. Disagreements about primary issues break down to secondary arguments, and the friction shakes up more than a few of us. We might begin to doubt our faith if surrounded and outnumbered by opposition. That's why it's good to fellowship with some reassuring friends. Obviously, we ought to be able to defend our faith—even when outgunned by skeptics. Their disbelief does not negate the faithfulness of God any more than their unrighteousness voids His righteousness. It's a rocky world. The support of other believers who understand our struggle and know what the grace of Jesus Christ means will help your love stay strong.

Many towns in America have a street named Broadway. Broad is the way to destruction. What a frightening thought! We see a lot of temptation in this world. The sin of so many sinners overwhelms the unguarded Christian heart. All the ungodliness is paralyzing because it is so shocking. Be glad you can say you are on the right road that leads to everlasting life, as narrow as it is. On this narrow road, you will find fewer who live to serve. You'll see this. It's disturbing. If a person never contributes, what is there to gain? Not as many people give out this new positively powerful *love* of *faith*.

If you are still trying to be a Christian, then you're probably not yet one. Are you seeking the approval of people more than that of God? It's natural to want that, yes. We definitely don't want to do something that will take people off track. We must move up and yet avoid the trap of promoting ourselves. You become spiritual when you lay your life at the cross of Christ. It's sanctification. Always work to glorify God. Whether we are interacting with people or sitting alone, the Holy Spirit is there.

Be alert to the direction of events. The history of Scripture points to the prophecies and the return of Christ for His kingdom. The doctrines tell of His character, His plan, and His lordship over us. We each should have a comprehensive outline in our mind of where love fits in. It is basic. Our religion isn't tempered by trends or traditions, but by His Word, the Bible. If anything, let your convictions affect the old stubborn world. Praise God, for He has promised us not only eternal life, but eternal love.

> *In the day of prosperity be joyful, but in the day of adversity consider: God also hath set the one over against the other, to the end that man should find nothing after him.*
> Ecclesiastes 7:14

When in life we feel like we are nothing, we should remember a little something. In the morning, before you stand on the scale to check your weight, you check to see that it reads zero. If the machine is set as near as possible to zero, then you will weigh yourself accurately. Have you thought that God sets our lives down to zero? When He sets us down flat first, then we can see what our true measure is as we step on.

Early in my Christian life, I got close to a nice Christian couple who became special to me. They later moved, and their marriage broke up. I heard that the wife left her husband and the kids and ran off to live in a very shameful way. The husband had all four young kids; the youngest was still a baby. When I moved to San Antonio, I looked him up and visited him.

He said to me, "Life has always been good to me, but maybe this is the time for my share of difficulty." Do you believe that? It was a hard lesson for me to accept how good people, important people to me, can fall apart. The good influence this couple had on my life stayed with me despite their divorce. I was really sorry about the breakup. It hurt so much. I, too, have been laid low and have still been a witness for God. God knows that we have trouble at times, so He gives us good days and tells us to enjoy them.

It's good to rejoice, especially when you have great days. Remember them, too, because you can never tell what's coming. God balances our lives with good days and bad. Do you believe this?

Some people will tell you they have no good days.

An old blues song has a line something like, "I don't look for no trouble; worries and troubles come around." Times get tough. Count your blessings. God gives everyone good days, but we don't need to get big heads when things go well. All we have to do is wait, and troubles do come around. God sends both the sunshine and the rain.

You can't say what's bad by looking at one day or by looking at yesterday. Jesus said, *"Every branch that beareth fruit, he purgeth it, that it may bring forth more fruit"* (John 15:2). It doesn't mean you are condemned; you are being commended by God for bringing fruit, and you are going to have much more in the near future. You can think things are hopeless, but God gives life to the dead; think what He will do with you.

Before a crop is planted, the ground gets cleared. God brings your life low, don't doubt. He has these plans to start something better in your life. If someone else prospers, it's not right for you to reject their success. God has plans for each one of us according to our course and our own special gifts and talents. His work accomplishes more with each new start. One plants and another waters, but it is God who gives life to the garden. You cannot predict everything that God is doing.

We know about the death, burial, and resurrection of Jesus. Do you think enough about the burial? Think about the second day. *"Verily, verily, I say unto you, Except a corn of wheat fall into the ground and die, it abideth alone: but if it die, it bringeth forth much fruit"* (John 12:24). Many are at rock bottom when they come to Jesus. Do you know where rock bottom is? It is under the water, at the bottom.

Stay a little while and think about things. Ponder for yourself the length of God's reach and forgiveness in Jesus Christ's atonement. *"Know ye not, that so many of us as were baptized into Jesus Christ were baptized into his death?"* (Romans 6:3). In the old English, way before Shakespeare, *atone* was "at one." Before you take another step, stop!

First, take time to be baptized. Remain a time buried in fellowship with Jesus.

You've met Jesus at the cross. Have you spent time in His death? He was buried in the tomb. *"Thou fool, that which thou sowest is not quickened, except it die"* (1 Corinthians 15:36). Paul wanted the resurrection power, so he surrendered, *"being made conformable unto his death"* (Philippians 3:10). We must rest with Him in His death.

A person who gets too afraid with failure or success could stop before even starting. Seeds in good soil bring forth *"some a hundredfold, some sixtyfold, some thirtyfold"* (Matthew 13:8). All we need is patience to wait, and Jesus will do the rest. Were you running from things when you got saved, or were you running after something? The Christian community asks converts to get up quickly and run a perfect race. Instead, teach them to stop and wait.

Solomon gathers disapproval for being covetous and extravagant. God blessed him to the loftiest height of Israel's history. He asked for wisdom, and God made him the wisest of all. He set out to do great things, and he did. He also got into lots of trouble. The first rule of wisdom, Solomon said, is to avoid the lure of women. Solomon is now dead, yet he still gets a lot of criticism. He accomplished the best things for Israel. Nothing is better, he said, than to enjoy life—as long as we learn to fear God. Solomon defined faith. Never shying away from a pursuit of everything, he lived his life as fully as a man can, with terrific joy and terrible grief.

Life is a mystery, really, so pray to God for His direction. We should be moving forward. Go without giving up, and reach farther. This is how we reassure ourselves. Jesus' Spirit is with us. See which way the wind is blowing, but don't be afraid of living. If you have given your life to God, then isn't that where you will find it? You can't know much about a baby in the womb before it's born, but we wait for the years ahead with eager optimism. Stay confident of a big future, and strive harder every day. The smile on your face will shine. Gain the victory by true *faith*, and you will have the genuine *love*.

Sow Thy Seed

> *In the morning sow thy seed, and in the evening withhold not thine hand: for thou knowest not whether shall prosper, either this or that, or whether they both shall be alike good.*
> Ecclesiastes 11:6

Cast your net into the water and wait to pull it up, then see what you catch. Hopefully, you see the purpose of this book. *Love Believes All Things*: it's a statement. Try love. Put faith into action. Second, expect to collect. Jesus will fulfill His promise. When I set out to study love, I had little idea how this important work would develop. It took several years to discover a basis for the premise of *faith* and *love* in the New Testament.

More than forty-five years of studying it, discussing, practicing, teaching, living, and writing it have led up to publishing. This included typing, editing, and much rewriting. Will it go far? Now there are two books. How much fruit will the effort bear? Few books endure, and most are forgotten.

Book sales and acceptance by readers won't necessarily make the effort valid. Well, for some people it would. Who do I think I am to come so boldly with two manuscripts, and am I qualified to comment on the great subject that we have here? I am a Christian. The important thing is to know that God blesses His followers.

Keep on praying in your life no matter what may come. Remember how rough it gets. How great to see someone trade in their sinful lusts to gain just one prayer: "Save me!" Pray with a powerful conviction to win the lost.

The work of this book is in the hand of Almighty God. The affirmation that the reader receives is totally from His hand by grace.

We don't know what prospers or fails. God gives us satisfaction in our hearts. Readers must understand the place this message has. I was a young man when this notion of *faith* and *love* hit me.

> *Rejoice, O young man, in thy youth; and let thy heart cheer thee in the days of thy youth, and walk in the ways of thine heart, and in the sight of thine eyes: but know thou, that for all these things God will bring thee into judgment.*
> Ecclesiastes 11:9

Solomon spoke with experience. "Rejoice," he said. Listen to your heart, but we should be aware that God will bring us into judgment. Inevitably, we will have our regrets in life. Don't let the fear of God or His commandments stop you from living right. Walk in the Spirit of Jesus. He would tell us to move on. He rules in our hearts with victory. Solomon, a prophet of the Lord, was a man who followed his heart with peace.

In my early days in Texas, my church was praying for a young lady named Barbara. She and I got to be friends, so we talked. I told her I could convince her of the truth of my beliefs if she just gave me enough time. She wouldn't let me say all of what I wanted to tell her, but she admitted that I had put a crack in her wall. She quickly stacked more bricks on top! Those were her words.

A few months went by and I was working in a program home with teens. I took a couple of the boys over to do yard work at the home of Jenny, our church secretary. While we were there, Barbara happened to come by to see Jenny. We were glad to see each other, and she asked me why I never came to visit her.

I said, "I've never been invited."

She replied, "Well, you're invited to come over to lunch tomorrow."

The next day, I went to her house for lunch. She was wearing a cross made from two nails welded together and strung on a necklace.

I asked her why she was wearing this cross. A little defensively, she asked, "Why does anyone wear a cross?"

I didn't say anything for a moment. Some people wear crosses simply as jewelry, and others wear crosses because they believe. I wondered if her thinking had changed.

"Well, I accepted Jesus as Savior three days ago, but I haven't told anyone yet."

LOVE BELIEVES ALL THINGS

The news was so exciting to me that it tickled my heart and I broke out laughing. She got mad. Indignant, she said, "Well, I did. I really did!"

And she really had. I assured her that I was not laughing at her and that I was thrilled to hear it. We'd all been praying and pulling for her, and I was very surprised that she had accepted Christ into her heart.

Barbara told me that she had gone to Jenny's to tell her that she had accepted Christ. Jenny was like an aunt to her. Barbara got there that afternoon but couldn't get it out. She had become a Christian and couldn't tell anybody. I was the first to know because I asked! Barbara continued to grow in the Lord, and the last I heard, she was living a devoted Christian life. Believe in God above all else and rejoice in His glory.

Life in Jesus for me isn't so much about the stars in my crown or rewards. I want to be doing something for our Savior. It's about doing something constructive, being helpful and fruitful. It is not out of fear of God as much as out of love.

I love to see fired-up Christians who are changing and charging ahead, believers who have no doubts. I'm staying out of the way of go-getters and getting behind them instead.

In other parts of the world, hundreds of thousands of converts don't have enough teachers to instruct them in the way. Many have no churches to go to and no Bibles to read. Across America, churches have plenty of class space, which is often empty now, and teachers who lack motivation and action. Attendance is stalled. That is why I love it all the more when a friend is set apart in dedication to serve Jesus.

Faith needs no proof. We don't need any further convincing when God has produced true life. Don't let anybody talk you out of what you know. Don't let troubles get you down. I still run into many of my old friends who've lived unselfishly for the Savior. I will hear indirectly about the lives of Christians I've known over the years who have been faithful, and their stories bless me tremendously. We shouldn't be so surprised. This hope of eternal life in Jesus Christ and life on Earth gives us love that is as enduring as our salvation.

Redeeming by Believing

For yet a little while, and he that shall come will come, and will not tarry.

Hebrews 10:37

Heaven is why we're here. People are unsure about death, but they are willing to go to the end undecided, staring in disbelief. Regrettably, their consciences are at ease; they don't give it a thought. Are we convincing enough with Christ's love to win their hearts over? Jesus has overcome. God's love must be our vocation and our preoccupation. Faith is our call.

I've been teaching at an assisted-living residence about twenty years. It's a resident-organized Tuesday evening Bible study here in Seattle. Usually seven to fifteen seniors attend. Several are over ninety. On special occasions, we've had thirty or more attend. For many people, this place might be their last address. It was started over thirty years ago by the residents.

I was asked to preach the funeral of one dear lady. She was one of the original ones who started this Bible study. She was also the most regular member. I brought this message about contentment from Psalm 23 to her extended family assembled at a funeral chapel. She was from the area but had no church or pastor.

One late Friday afternoon, I was called to the hospital by the brother-in-law of a man in our study group. Don was in assisted living because he had a mental impairment. Though he was bright and well-read, he was practically challenged to care for himself. When we first met Don a few years earlier, he had an ulcerated foot due to diabetes. He was wearing a plastic boot. At the age of fifty-seven, he was now dying.

Don had gone to the hospital with his foot so infected that he had lost his strength. Just three weeks earlier when he arrived, his blood sugar level measured 1,600—a record for this county hospital. He abruptly collapsed. The bacterial infection had entered his system.

That can happen to any of us. The doctors did everything to save Don's life, including amputation of his lower legs below the knees.

I was called to the hospital at the last of his life. They explained to me what had happened. A priest had been there to give Don his last rights. Don had been raised Polish Catholic, but had accepted Jesus while in the army. He was a serious believer. Thirteen family members were there for a bedside vigil. Since this man had no church or pastor, I was asked to come and lead. Don's family was quite aware of the value our Tuesday Bible study had in his life.

You can imagine how unprepared the family was for their loved one's death and how unprepared I was as I arrived at the hospital at 6:30 p.m. Don's three sisters, their husbands and children, and his mother were all gathered in a room outside the ward. A sister had prepared an order of service written with Bible verses, spoken words, and prayers; Romans 8:35–39 came near the end. As the Lord would have it, I had thought of this same passage on my way over in the car, but was undecided about what to say. We agreed that I would read this part and share a message with the Lord's guidance. As we left the room, I just left my heart open to share the passage. We rounded the hallway and met a nurse who had us put on protective gowns and gloves. God was with us in an unfamiliar but special way. It all felt unreal as the nurse led us into Don's room.

My friend was more alert than I expected. Though we had been warned that his feet were gone, it was nonetheless a shock to see him this way. His bandaged legs lay on top of the sheets. He was surrounded by medical equipment.

Since we were in a strange setting and a lot had happened to him, I reintroduced myself, thinking that he might have needed the benefit of noting exactly who I was. He was looking around the room, unable to speak, but able to recognize us. His face was a little puffy, but I recognized him and trusted that he knew who I was. Amazingly enough, his ninety-five-year-old mother took her place standing steady by his bedside to comfort him.

We began to follow the program. We read and said prayers. Then I stepped up to share familiar thoughts from the Bible. Putting my hand on his forearm while I read the passage from Romans, I addressed him and his family. He was always at our Bible study. I knew his heart and his faithfulness to the Word of God, and I spoke to this. I said, "Nothing is going to separate the love of God from this dear man. And over all the years, my friend hasn't let anything separate him from God."

I spoke of his deep and steady devotion. It was in my mind that Don's family members needed the Lord, and I knew my good friend would agree, I went on to express his faith in Christ, at the same time, hoping to reassure Don's own heart.

I reminded him of our yearlong Bible study on prayer as I told the others about it. "Jesus promised He would give whatsoever we ask in prayer, so we have been searching the Scriptures every week to see what we can do to get our prayers answered. It's a challenge. We must pray according to God's will; this is one of the qualifiers."

I said this as much for Don's benefit; we had his family's attention, but I hoped he'd remember he himself had raised this issue with his reference of 1 John 5:14. I thought the lessons from our Tuesday study would be of help at this time. Don's illness was incurable.

Don was a student of the Word. I described to the family what I knew of his salvation from when he was in the army in Texas. I myself also received Jesus into my life in Texas at nearly the same time and the same age. There was nothing else like getting saved with that great Texas hospitality—that big Texas Christianity. He and I had this in common. My friend couldn't speak about it now with the tracheotomy ventilator, but I did the talking for both of us.

I knew my friend loved reminiscing about those days. I tried to bring it all back with memories of the Texas home cooking, when local folks had us over for a feed and we felt welcome. They would make you eat more than you could take—and then some. Don and I had talked about how we were there about the same time in the early 1970s. He too enjoyed the hymn singing in church and the Southern gospel music on the radio. We loved it. We were both born in 1951, a couple of Seattle boys raised here and saved there. His family was learning a little more about it. Hopefully, my brave smile made the

LOVE BELIEVES ALL THINGS

room brighter as I told it. I prayed in my heart that Jesus would bless us all with His love.

My wife and I were there the next morning with the family. A doctor directed the nurse to reduce life support. Again, it was a wonderful thing to have thirteen family members there, especially his mother. Sadly, this is rare. Many die alone, having no hope. Each of us took a turn talking to him. We prayed and sang. Don was unable to say anything, but he was visibly comforted. The Lord's mercy was on him as a couple of hours passed. I opened my Bible to John 17 and read Jesus' entire great prayer. It was a familiar passage to Don.

It was wonderful to see my friend's eyes looking up at me.

I led us in four verses of "Amazing Grace." Louise read to the end of Psalms 148–150, "*Let every thing that hath breath praise the Lord. Praise ye the Lord.*" At that very moment, everyone's attention turned to the heart monitor over the bed. We looked up to see a big zero, and when I looked back down, Don was gone.

Later that month at our Tuesday evening Bible study, Don's whole family came for an awesome memorial. The room was packed with residents. My friend Dave from church played "The Caissons Keep Rolling Along" on his harmonica, and at the end of the meeting, he played "Taps" in honor of his service in the army. We remembered a kind man, his faith and devotion to Jesus. I opened my Bible and spoke. Don's loss was tragic, but we will be reunited soon.

The divine nature of our love for God sets Christianity apart from every other religion. From the beginning, God's plan included bringing Jesus into the world. Adam was the first person, a living soul with a natural body, and Jesus is "the firstborn among many brethren" (Romans 8:29). When Jesus was raised from the dead, He was the first of many—God's Son. We are being prepared for Him as His bride. Who can imagine how sacred marriage is? God made man in His own image (Genesis 1:27). God created us the best, even though we've sinned. He has fixed us up with His only Son in marriage to live forever in His kingdom.

It's a true wonder that we love God, since we've never yet seen Him. We live in a sad world. Don't you think God's divine love would prove more powerful? What's so hard about it is that we come from such a deficit, such a pit. Who tells us the larger truth? Millions of disingenuous voices spout half-truths and lies and point at us spitefully for believing in Christ. Amid all this resistance and dissonance, we are learning from the Bible to love God—and to love Him by faith. God has been good to me. I love my Savior. He saved my life. Everything in my life since then has been because of Him, and it's been a fantastic adventure.

> *Let us hear the conclusion of the whole matter: Fear God, and keep his commandments: for this is the whole duty of man.*
>
> Ecclesiastes 12:13

The book of Ecclesiastes shows the futility of empty human effort. It takes a hard look at our subjective world, a fit portrayal of miserable delusions. *"Fear God and keep his commandments"* is the Old Testament forerunner of the New Testament's *"faith and love."* The Old Law preceded but didn't prevent Jesus Christ's victory over sin, temptation, and condemnation.

Through the curse of sin, we have nothing to show for trying, but Solomon said he had a duty to live. His power with words and the worth he put into human faith, the value he saw in authenticity, speaks of our God-given instinct to live. We have God's permission to live, with his Holy Spirit.

The blood of Jesus is our right of salvation. The forgiveness of sin is our only hope. Are we supposed to balance the keeping of the Ten Commandments evenly with the grace of Jesus and make the needle rest in the middle? This being true, the push and pull of life, the angst, and worry, is the fulcrum to lever us into the will of God. So the answer is yes—and no! There is a struggle with the reason to live and the reason to love. Ecclesiastes isn't about the Ten Commandments but about the love of life.

Solomon's words give us permission to live, and in this sense, Jesus justifies our lives. We are here. *Our God is great.* Sow your seed.

Be aware of God's judgments. Life is riddled with tragedy. We need the faith and peace to believe, and we need to see how to live, even in our time. The service you do for God will, in fact, transform you.

You can't ever expect to see God's love without your faith. "*Lift up your eyes,*" Jesus said in John 4:35. "*Look on the fields; for they are white already for harvest.*" May the name of Jesus Christ be glorified, magnified, and set apart in our own generation. Here is wisdom: God demands our *faith*, and He commands our *love*.

Solomon found a God-given liberty in his life that allowed him to reach higher. He gained great understanding, he recognized that life shapes and smooths us, he welcomed the process. People are better for their trials. Solomon expected us to be civil with people because each of us ourselves can be rough on others.

Solomon built his kingdom to be open, active, and sophisticated. To be successful, he taught more dependence on God which made the difference.

The way he saw people, they had to get along to enjoy life like he did. It's not that they had no choice. Solomon gave a sense of well-being. He included in his time, pleasure like it was a treasure. Doing good came the same as morality. Solomon recorded his feelings to confirm his faith. He was blessed. In his mind, action was intensely important, more than thinking about things. You prove life by what you do.

If ye know these things, happy are ye if ye do them.
John 13:17

The Whole Picture

A new commandment I give unto you, That ye love one another; as I have loved you, that ye also love one another. By this shall all men know that ye are my disciples, if ye have love one to another.

John 13:34–35

CHAPTER 11

Love One Another

This is my commandment, That ye love one another, as I have loved you.

John 15:12

God transforms us so we receive His love the way He wants. Every Christian has God. We have our complaints about life, people, and things. You don't want to say too much or you'll end up getting angry. If you say it to someone's face, they get mad at you. We know this, and so it doesn't get said. It needs to be said, and said properly—yet people sure do talk about us.

People are afraid to ask for help. Sometimes, we need help, but often, the help we get makes things worse. The ones who need it most are the ones who most often won't ask. So we don't go there. Jesus came not only to sacrifice His life for our sins so we can go to Heaven, but also to give us better lives here now. With Jesus, we find His will, His wisdom, His love, and His Word that we love one another. This is His command.

We must pray for one another all the time as we live for Jesus. He rose from the grave to bring us together in His Holy Spirit. This is the reason we are Christians. We face many obstacles—a host of antagonists, innumerable problems, and irresistible temptations—yet God is going to win with us. Jesus came to give His love. God created us so we could love one another with distinction. Keep the faith.

When Christians tangle with each other, they get hurt and then lose their will to love. Nothing discourages me more than to see brother sin against brother. Nothing stands out about us in the mind of agnostic thinkers like the strife they see with believers. Won't we ever catch on? We are infamous for our differences. We think we honor and glorify our Maker, but we are trampling the life of another person whom God has made.

All Christians need added reassurance in their faith. Some of us are prone to feel downcast, and our confidence drops. We fight finances, fret over circumstances, and worry about the future. Patience flies out the window, hope wanes, and after all that, we also wrestle with the flesh. We get hammered by temptations. It's damaging. Do Christians have sufficient guidance about how to mature? We come up short in the area of much-needed fellowship with one another.

If I live a perfect life but have no love, I am nothing. If I bestow all I have to feed the poor, yet give no love, what good am I? Life's finer aspirations, such as education, success, travel—you name it—are to be pursued and attained, but some of the best people—the smartest, the richest, and the most famous—are unhappy.

People don't know what to look for in love. They get love, and then they lose it. Really, love is to abide in Jesus, obey Him, and love one another.

Jesus never fails, so neither should we. Hope is real. Are you and I as believers able to confidently and correctly explain love to others and, in fact, *be* this love for them? Christians grow from the true Vine, the source of life. We yield fruit. Jesus' love is His life. Surely Jesus knows exactly how to bring the fruit of His love in our lives.

I Am the True Vine

> *Every branch in me that beareth not fruit he taketh away: and every branch that beareth fruit, he purgeth it, that it may bring forth more fruit.*
>
> John 15:2

Be sure you are secure in your faith. Two questions suffice to shore up our souls. The first question is this: "Are you lost?" We all start out lost. We don't know at first what salvation is. Some of us are quicker than others to catch on. We learn of our blindness when someone is kind enough to tell us.

The second question is, "Are you a Christian?" Many people think they are Christians when in fact they are not. Some of my favorite Christians have doubts. The battle builds in their hearts, and they have a fear of missing Heaven. Is Jesus working in their lives or is He going to cut them off and drop them? We can be sure and confident in our salvation. Jesus sees doubts and speaks to these feelings with this command: *"Abide in me, and I in you"* (John 15:4). It makes a world of difference when God proves true in you.

Christians wonder why they have all the troubles they do. You might ask, "If I have all these trials, am I a Christian?" Yes. You have all these trials because you are a Christian. Don't let your mind wander too far. Ask yourself, "Have I borne fruit?" God knows it.

After repentance bears fruit, God prunes these branches. He cuts those that yield fruit in order to bring out more fruit. It's not as if Jesus is going to cast us off if we daydream a bit. That's not what He's trying to accomplish, not when He wants us to trust Him. In John 15, Jesus does not call us servants, but friends. He tells His approach: *"These things I command you, that ye love one another"* (John 15:17). Jesus instructs us about what to do and how we are to do it. He now wants to get us to work. *"Every branch that beareth fruit, he purgeth it, that it may bring forth more fruit."* The Bible says these experiences produce fruit in our lives.

Before I met Jesus, my life had gone from bad to worse. I had a rough childhood and a lot of good times, but in my late teen years just prior to my salvation, I suffered extremely devastating effects from a lot of illegal drug use. As bad as that year was before I got saved, the following year, 1972, was even tougher. It was my most painful year. Life for me became extremely troubled with Jesus Christ, and yet I was improving within myself. As my life got worse, I got better.

Things were different after I got saved. Up until then with everything I had experienced, I went downhill—but God brought so many people to help me, even if they couldn't see it, that for the first time in my life, I felt as if I was experiencing healing.

People start out on drugs because it feels good, but by the time the pain is too much, they are addicted and unable to quit. I didn't seek help until it hurt too much to go on. The ill will of the drug culture, the drain on my physical strength, and my declining mental health quickly reduced me to an immature level and childish conduct. Sadly, some people don't overcome their addiction until they die of it, directly or indirectly. Realistically, they would've lived longer if they had never started doing drugs in the first place. It was very frightening when I passed a certain point and found I couldn't escape. Jesus got me off drugs. I became more disturbed in recovery, yet I was becoming a stronger person.

I thank God that I had a safe, supportive environment in which God knit my life back together. I went through prolonged months of withdrawal from drugs with intense confusion inside and out. Physical and psychological healing is always uncomfortable. I was mixed up, and it showed. Work and money were not easy. I spent time in a trade school—the government's Manpower Training Act. Most of us dropped out.

Sleep was probably the main thing that restored my brain. I slept an average of fourteen hours a day at Omni House. It bothered them that I did little else. When I was awake, I read the Bible. It totally helped. Not much of it made sense to me, but as I gained understanding, my mind got healed and it was better than ever before. My new friends were patient and caring, yet very often, they were at a loss to know what to do about my bad attitude and poor habits. Christians were my salvation.

As indescribably difficult as those days were, I recovered. More than that, I matured. I hastily married the young woman on staff who had won me to Jesus, but then we quickly separated. It tore me up. I owed my life to her. After the divorce, I never saw her again. I was not to be defeated. Jesus tempered my faith with heartache to sober me up. I studied the Bible even more in order to figure it all out, and I saw myself grow. What convinced me for good was seeing my spiritual growth. I knew that I was a Christian, and I have not doubted it since.

God was shaping me as a potter shapes clay. Right away, I had to tell people about Jesus. Everybody ought to know. I was a bad example and so I was told, but I found ways to express my faith with zeal. People told me that I wasn't anyone who should be talking.

In those early years, I had bouts of doubts. That didn't stop me. I struck out with eager faith. Like three strikes and you're out, I struck out. I struck out a lot, and I stuck out. I also stuck it out and hung in there when I wanted to fall back. A potter works and pounds the air out of his clay before it goes to the throwing wheel, gets shaped, and then gets put into the fire. It all looks better now looking back.

We don't always get reinforcement from each other. We cut each other down when we should be building each other up. People are people. Christians are people. Jesus is working in our lives. The problem is that we don't recognize His part. If Christians ask for encouragement in such times, do they get it? We have a simplistic view. We look at someone else's problems, question their judgment, and knock their sincerity, but faith and leadership give others hope.

> *Now no chastening for the present seemeth to be joyous, but grievous: nevertheless afterward it yieldeth the peaceable fruit of righteousness unto them which are exercised thereby.*
> Hebrews 12:11

Jesus will trim every branch that bears fruit so that it will bear more fruit. A good pruning can cut a plant or tree way back. Have you seen growth taken down to the nubbins? As a teenager working in my grandmother's yard, a friend and I cut my grandmother's clematis vine completely off. I know now that these vines grow in a tangle, and it is not that straightforward to remove just a few stems at a time. We left nothing but the stalk. My grandmother came out and had a conniption fit. She thought we had killed it. We felt pretty bad.

Over fifty years later, the clematis is still growing outside the window of that house where I now live and where I sit to write. Ever since I inherited my grandmother's house years ago, I cut the nuisance vine most years; it grows beautifully. Its flower is quite fragrant. My cherry tree also gets pruned in the winter to stay healthy. You and I should care for one another in life's hard times; this is what fellowship is for.

In this world, we will have tribulation, but that does not mean we have entered the Great Tribulation. Bad times can get so severe that it really does seem like the end of the world. Our trials come only for our benefit. Count it all joy, knowing that the testing of our faith produces the fruit of patience so that we can always be corrected and perfected, thoroughly prepared for all good works (James 1:2–4). God loves us. No matter what happens, we must abide in Jesus.

> *Abide in me, and I in you. As the branch cannot bear fruit of itself, except it abide in the vine; no more can ye, except ye abide in me.*
>
> John 15:4

If we trust Jesus completely, we obey and love at all times. Difficulties should never be a part of your life, but they are not just part, they are the whole thing. They are what we are here for. We have conflicts; even Christians do. People get so horribly sick, they feel like they'll die just to feel better. Our gyroscope gets tweaked. Do we recover to grow more productive or not? God works in mysterious ways. When do we get around to the part where we love one another?

> *These things have I spoken unto you, that my joy might remain in you, and that your joy might be full.*
>
> John 15:11

We are supposed to love one another in bad times as well as in good times. We may think to ourselves how we'll love when everything and everyone around us improves or when we get our own act together. When do you think we're going to be ready? When friends have lows, that's when they need us most. When we experience dark times, we can shine the brightest.

We all have seen Christians who have their worries over the years. There can be strong fights. That may be exactly when God is most active in the situation. *"For whom the Lord loveth he chasteneth, and scourgeth every son whom he receiveth"* (Hebrews 12:6). God still loves you. Yes, we do have the good news for the lost, but we also have more good news for Christians. God loves you, and He is working with you right now.

God is at work. This is our problem. You may have to take the detour, but don't be deterred. Take faith in this thought. Abide in Jesus. He helps you.

Once in a while, a Christian will think that God is cutting them off. However, ask them if they think they have shown proof in their service to Jesus. We who grow fruit get pruned to bear more fruit. That is how we know God cares for us. When we abide in the Vine and bear more love, it follows that we will be shaped by God's hand. Bear the fruit of love, and you'll see you are one of God's own.

If my life goes through a slump, I don't want the bigger Christians to be picking on me. I want their friendship and kindness. I need to remember my own record of serving the Lord faithfully and fruitfully, and I deserve support from my fellowship.

Believers often just speak out without being careful. At other times when they should be critical, they aren't. Conflict and correction can get sticky. In murky times, we often miss the opportunities to help.

I'd rather learn from Scripture and be broken by God's Word than be taught in the school of hard knocks. Is our faith going to grow if we don't remain in His Word? If we endure and keep working against the odds, our faith grows stronger. Equally essential is the fellowship of the Christian body, keeping each other together and praying. We need to be good sports. Jesus tells us to love one another, and it's a privilege to be a part, not be apart.

Caught Nothing

> *And Simon answering said unto him, Master, we have toiled all the night, and have taken nothing: nevertheless at thy word I will let down the net.*
>
> Luke 5:5

The fishermen were washing their nets, and they were probably very tired, when Jesus came along the lake of Gennesaret. There was a crowd pressing in on Jesus. He looked at the two boats on the shore and saw that the fishermen were finished. Jesus got into Simon's boat and asked him to thrust out from the land. Then He taught the people from the boat.

When He stopped speaking, Jesus said to Simon, *"Launch out into the deep, and let down your nets for a draught"* Luke 5:4. Although they had caught nothing, the fishermen did what Jesus said, and so *"they enclosed a great multitude of fishes: and their net broke"* Luke 5:6. They had to call for help from the other boat. They filled both boats with such huge loads of fish that both boats began to sink.

I was teaching the Book of Nehemiah in Sunday school one time for a series and the lesson in Chapter Nine told the story of the way God blessed Israel even after they had sinned and were conquered. The people of Israel saw God's mercy and repented and turned toward God. After I had said this and elaborated on it, I had an exchange with a retired pastor who was there and he said that God brings us to repent only by His chastening, never by blessing. I pointed out to Pastor Oscar the story we had just read and also Romans 2:4 and

Titus 3:4–7. Here is another instance where Jesus blessed with a rich miracle in Luke and Peter repented.

> *When Simon Peter saw it, he fell down at Jesus' knees, saying, Depart from me; for I am a sinful man, O Lord.*
> Luke 5:8

Peter seems like the kind of person who stands out yet he sure sounds like us. We, too, would ask Jesus to leave us alone, even though we know He is righteous and right, because in His presence, we recognize that we are outright sinful. Why do you think Peter tried to retreat from Jesus? It could have been a reaction to what Jesus taught. What had He said? Maybe the proof of what He preached came through after Jesus told them, "Let down your nets." They were in shallow water. Jesus said to cast off into the deep. You and I don't want to get too deep.

Peter fell at Jesus' feet and begged, *"Depart from me; for I am a sinful man"* (Luke 5:8). What is the very next thing in Jesus' response? *"Fear not; from henceforth thou shalt catch men."* Simon Peter and his partners, James and John, decided right then to follow Jesus. *"And when they had brought their ships to land, they forsook all, and followed him"* (Luke 5:11).

These men had fished all night and caught nothing. They abruptly left it all behind to go with Jesus. Was it because they were giving up on fishing? Was it about the miracle Jesus performed or about the words He preached? Either way, the story speaks to our hearts and the empty lives we live and then leave when Jesus comes and calls. It's a full future with Him. The net broke, and both boats began to sink with the fish. What will Jesus do for you or for anyone you dare bring to believe? *"My cup runneth over"* (Psalm 23:5). Jesus fills our lives to overflowing so that we are able to share and love one another.

People the world over respond to this message because their lives are empty. Jesus said, *"Man, thy sins are forgiven thee"* (Luke 5:20). Does this sound like a fairy tale? Many people have their hearts filled to go preach the gospel.

When we come up with zilch, even after a long time, Jesus can come alongside. He fills our lives to overflowing. What have we been praying for? You and I are drawn to the potent question here in this classic story: "Am I committed?" We really do want this. What makes people full-fledged, and why are so many still fledgling Christians? There's a valid expectation that our faithfulness will lead to God's blessings.

All around the world, every month, hundreds of thousands of people are becoming Christians. *"And he shall bring forth thy righteousness as the light"* (Psalm 37:6). One person gets saved and leads others to Jesus Christ, and each new Christian will reach still more people. One young man in Kenya recently took a gospel tract, read it, got saved, and began to preach. He started thirty churches. I met him touring America.

Before I knew Jesus, there was no question that I was lost. But why do so many believers wonder if they are truly saved? This is intriguing to me. In order to ask Christ into our hearts, we should understand that we are all sinners and are desperately poor in spirit. Do you see how we who back off let others down? I was hoping to do better myself; there's nothing wrong with that. People are afraid of Christianity. Some of the claims Christians make are exaggerated, but then some of us think too small and we are scarred of unbelievers.

A few Christians are dissatisfied—angry at God and sour toward old friends. Believers' honest doubts come from unfulfilled expectations. Quite so, they give up trying. How do you prove faith? One numbing thought that trips us all up is the entertaining notion that Christians should be the best people around. That bothers us. I have wanted to study to show myself approved unto God (2 Timothy 2:15). Approved by God, this is a nice idea.

Tom, a friend of mine, and his identical twin brother were saved as teenagers at summer camp. They each made a heartfelt decision for Jesus. Tom told me that when they got home, their parents told them this was good but not to go overboard. That discouraged the boys. The parents themselves were raised in a Christian culture and had sent their two sons to camp, but they saw the fervor of their sons as being too much. Bible reading frightened the parents too. A few years later, both brothers got involved in a young adult group in a nearby church, and their remarkable recommitment followed.

Their mother received Jesus before she died, and soon after, the father got saved.

The two brothers and their wives have been serving for years in a couple of excellent missionary organizations, working to develop, teach, and train others in foreign countries. Most of the world is lacking scriptural literature and skilled leadership.

I have friends who say they believed and trusted their lives to Jesus early in their youth, but years went by before anything happened to convince them that they were genuinely growing in their faith. They had clearly understood their sinfulness and had felt their need. They were afraid of going to Hell, so they prayed to Jesus. They will tell you they are Christians today because of that summer camp commitment.

You can understand that there are many who compare themselves with others and feel unsure of their salvation. Remember, I didn't know much myself. I was eighteen when Christians began to witness to me. It took me a couple of years, but when I received Jesus, I saw the light in a flash. Many kids make an insincere profession of faith and never mature until later when an occasion presents itself for them to get saved. Many Christians do not have a straight answer when you ask for the reason they believe.

Many Christians have sworn that they got saved as kids, like a friend of mine who wandered in sin for years before firmly repenting. He didn't turn his life over to God 100 percent until he got infected with HIV. Then he lived thirteen more years; he served God wholeheartedly the rest of his life. He was legendary. The fact that he had a growing relationship with Jesus tells me that he probably did get saved when he was younger and that God was working in his life nonetheless. Established Christians see a conflict with dubious characters and spotty testimonies, but it is understandable; we all grow in different ways.

My neighbor came from a Christian community in India. She

was a descendant of converts of missionaries in the 1800s. When she and her husband moved to America, they thought they were Christians. After they got here, they were surprised by our culture. The husband was drawn to sin because in India, he had never seen pornography or heard of the permissiveness we have here. She lost him to his complete moral collapse. During that painful time, she came to Jesus—and His Holy Spirit helped her in a powerful way. She raised her three children by working hard in a professional career, sticking to it through very difficult times, maintaining a home, and strengthening her newfound faith.

As neighbors just a few houses apart, we became good friends. She's an unusually blessed woman. I'm impressed by her rich prayer life and am touched to see how God truly rewards her for her faithfulness. In India, if you had asked this couple if they were Christians, they would have said yes.

Another friend of mine also thought he was a Christian. He was a member of what he thought was a Christian church. He had a nice home and a wife and kids, but there were problems in their marriage. They went to their "unchristian" pastor in their non-Christian church. I say "unchristian" because the pastor gave "marriage counseling" to the wife in particular. After the divorce, that pastor married my friend's wife, moved into my friend's house, and took over raising my friend's children. Half of the investment accounts went with the divorce. Their pastor enjoyed that too. And their church let him keep his job.

You might have expected my friend to turn away from Christianity, but instead, he came to the church I belonged to and gave his heart to Jesus. He got saved in a beautiful way. He often wondered aloud why he had been able to join several churches and even become a deacon without knowing the Savior. He became an outstanding Christian with a clear appreciation of sound teaching. In addition, God blessed him with an attractive young wife who had taught in a missionary school in South America. She had never been married before, and she sang like an angel as a soloist in the choir. There was no doubt that God rewarded these two with each other because of their pure hearts. God cures sadness. He turns honest hearts to Him so He can bless. My friend really enjoyed coming to a biblical church, which is why he grew and then met this beautiful young lady. That's the way God ensures our faith.

If you know someone who has nothing going on, don't give up hope. When we have encouraged the discouraged and have taught the distraught, we are at our best in representing God. We have Christians who are unsure if they are saved, and we have non-Christians who think they are, "*Ye shall know them by their fruits*" (Matthew 7:16). They may not be saved yet, but they may be soon. If you know Christians with little to show, give them a hand. You don't know everything; that is why we *love* by *faith*.

There are times in the lives of faithful Christians when there isn't much fruit. Some may not show stability, but they can be growing stronger just the same. Churches also naturally pass into seasons of shortage, but it needn't raise questions, not always; we have to know when and how to say it. God may be pruning us as He promised. It isn't necessarily caused by a bad past, but may be for a good future. Instead of complaining, offer some vision and inspiration.

Everybody knows it's important to love others, but carrying this out is still a mystery to people and it's not simple a lot of the time. Getting along is a big part of life. It counts more than we think. I'm gaining more appreciation and respect from others. This is worth a fortune. "*Praising God, and having favor with all the people*" (Acts 2:47). My life was once very empty, but now in Jesus, I cannot contain the blessings. Handling more love takes grace.

Abide in the Vine

> *I am the vine, ye are the branches: He that abideth in me, and I in him, the same bringeth forth much fruit: for without me ye can do nothing.*
>
> John 15:5

We abide because we have the life of Jesus, and because of this, we are going to show growth. The process described here by Jesus progresses: we bear fruit, then more fruit, and then "much fruit." God loves His children, so He corrects and develops us. Isn't the fruit He talks about here really the fruit of the Spirit? Love is the first fruit. Our prayer life must be abiding and effective to do anything worthwhile. And if it gets tough, you're onto something. You are truly a Christian.

When God sees our actions, advancements, and the fruit of His Spirit, He prunes. As we take it patiently, our faith grows again. More experience brings better character and hope. Galatians 6:9 says, "*for in due season we shall reap, if we faint not.*" When we appreciate the promise of this hope, we are never ashamed.

The great love of God is expressed abundantly in our faith. Can anyone be so careless as to say that a certain Christian is not living in the personal care of Jesus Christ? If you're His, He corrects you. The verse above says that God gives us an increase as we grow: "*the same bringeth forth much fruit.*" Maybe you are losing something of yourself to gain more from God.

> *Hereby perceive we the love of God, because he laid down his life for us: and we ought to lay down our lives for the brethren.*
>
> 1 John 3:16

Life is sometimes harder than death! Some will die for Jesus, but we are called to live for Him. Christians have a new address (1 John 3:16). We have to love one another. This really isn't the same verse as the one we all know—the classic John 3:16. We know where that one is found. It's where we got saved. The lost, tired, and troublesome people are saved in John 3:16. "*God so loved the world*"—they who hear the truth—and "*should not perish.*" That's for the lost. We learn a new address in 1 John 3:16. When we know, not only do we not perish, but the love of God lives in our dedicated lives sacrificially (Romans 12:1), and it's obvious.

Jesus has raised the standard in the New Testament. Is it enough for us to simply stay out of trouble? Jesus taught the parable of the servant who hid his money in the ground while his lord was gone so he wouldn't lose it. Doesn't that sound like those religious people who struggle continually to live right? They don't want to be lost. Living sacrificially will hurt. So many more safe pious people, in fact, are static, but the joy of the sanctified life is ecstatic.

We raise the bar higher. When I was in high school, I went out to watch my friends compete in the spring track meets. I especially enjoyed the sense of heart that the high jumpers brought to the game. Their event required them to run up to the bar bare-handed and throw themselves up and over it in order to clear the bar without touching it or knocking it off its pegs. At the starting line, the runner would pause, one foot in front of the other. He would stand in that position for a long time with intense concentration fixed on the bar. When he was ready, he would run as fast as he could, plant his feet, and push his legs before sailing straight up, arcing in a stately curve above his goal. Even his landing in the sawdust was graceful. Then he would set the bar a little higher, go back, and try for a higher jump. There is true devotion in the sport of track. Jesus has now raised the bar higher for us. God raises us up.

Our New Testament is called "New," and Jews call their Bible "The Law and the Prophets." World War I was not called World War I at first. For twenty years, it was called the Great War, the war to end all wars—until World War II came and went.

God has set the Old Law in the past. Israel was punished for not keeping the commandments. Do you think Christians teach often enough the difference between the old and new covenants? It would be nice if we explained it plainly. This would also help to parse the four gospels better. The new is far above the old covenant. Let's celebrate grace by which we grow.

We talk too frequently about all the things we've done wrong. Our faith in Christ is never directed to obey the Ten Commandments, nor be penalized for disobeying them, nor, for example, to be stoned to death. We are called by Jesus to bear the fruit of the Spirit, to think better, and to speak better things. We conduct our lives in a way that glorifies Jesus. Why were we born here, because of His eternal purpose and for God's promise of Heaven's reward.

This larger principle cannot be overemphasized: *faith* and *love* work together. Christians need to strive together with this goal (1 Timothy 1:5). If there's a way to unite us, this should be the one reason. Tragically, people all over the world are being taught lesser messages, so Christianity is splintered into factions. Many people are let down and are hurting. The New Testament condemns both sin and self-righteousness in new terms. The human heart of Christianity has misplaced God's love.

You can pray to extend your sphere of influence. Reach beyond your limitations. Move God in prayer on behalf of millions of people whom you have never met. Through prayer and intercession, you can do more than your physical abilities could ever do. You must not underestimate your power in God. You shouldn't fall short of the distances He sets.

I must let God have His way in my heart if I expect to see Him in my prayers. Prayer doesn't just happen because we bow our heads. It isn't effective because we bend our knees. Kicking a habit is good, and repenting is healing, but if you have a real serious need, surrender your heart. Prayer can feel like groping in the dark to find an entrance with God. It's important to please His heart. You and I know Jesus, and that relationship opens the door; we love each other with a lasting relationship—one on one.

New Christians think their life is safe now until they fall. The peaks and valleys will come and go. Will the new Christian grow? God has promised to correct those who follow Him. Troubles come. Those times don't seem good. The better times are great, but we should rejoice in our tribulations. It's really distressing. They will bail out on God at the first bump. Some Christians will bail out on you just for disappointing them once. After a few times of trial and error and going up and down, a novice Christian might begin to learn that God is working at all times. *"A friend loveth at all times, and a brother is born for adversity"* (Proverbs 17:17). We mature by bearing each other up and staying loving.

Remember, God is perfecting our faith. None of us is perfect (Romans 3:23). That means we are not quite there yet. We have no way of knowing if we are abiding in Jesus since we walk by faith. When things are tough, spiritual clarity is everything. Unless God acts in our lives, we walk alone. If we work as a team, our faith and love can bring crowds to salvation. Let's show everyone that God cares. Bringing Christians to see this new way of thinking will prove that love only works with faith.

Justified by Faith

> *Therefore being justified by faith, we have peace with God through our Lord Jesus Christ.*
> Romans 5:1

You have heard people ask, "Is he justified to say that?" Somebody makes a critical statement and someone else asks, "Was that justified?" Or suppose a man takes a swing at another man or shoots him, and you hear it said that he was justified. Police officers and homeowners can shoot people if it's justified. You can kill someone in self-defense. What does it mean when you and I are justified in Christ? Look at what we are justified to do.

The Apostle Paul is not suggesting that we can do anything we want. We are justified to live in the Holy Spirit, to take His leading and walk by faith. Having said this, you and I are justified in Christ in the broadest sense of the word. A person who is a Christian has a right to think so. We are able to go to God, and our lives are fully covered by His favor and grace. We are cleared to have peace through Jesus every day. We have a right to be happy.

All our life would be fruitless if it weren't for God's special purpose for us. When I keep my focus on the one powerful thought that "Jesus has justified me," it solves everything. It means righteousness. The absolution from sin that has been given to millions has become ours. We believe in the God who raised Jesus our Lord from the dead. Jesus was sacrificed for our sins and then raised victoriously for our justification. Everything we go through brings praise and glory to God through Jesus. We rejoice forever in this.

After we become Christians, we are still defensive. We feel guilty and we struggle with the old sin life. As soon as we get saved, we see ourselves wrestling with our faith as well as with our flesh. It will take a long, long time if we're going to ever have our hearts free from sin. We try to believe God, but we need to be taught by Him again. Are we at peace in our faith? Since we are justified, we can be happy, satisfied, and sanctified. His grace is not settled enough in our minds, and our *love*, in effect, suffers for lack of *faith*.

> *By whom also we have access by faith into this grace wherein we stand, and rejoice in hope of the glory of God.*
> Romans 5:2

If we held to what we've believed, we would be relieved. Through faith, we have full access to this grace, and we excel. Even when we forget, even if we neglect it, we stand in salvation. Have we not already entered into the kingdom of God? We pray. We possess all of His great love. It's not of us, but it is of God. The Bible repeatedly assures us that from here on out, Christians will never again be separated from eternal life. We have peace with God. We ought to be so excited that we never have a day without this joy.

We see the hope of God in the many verses we have covered. Why do so many who subscribe to the Scriptures see mostly the "threat" of God? We have the Lord's help at every turn. We live and work all our days. Have you found yourself resisting the Savior? We defy Him when we need Him. An inescapable sense of failure grips us, but the Bible says we are going to overcome. Our joy withers as we face various trials; instead, we need to rejoice continually and be glad in the hope of victory and the promise of salvation.

There are Christians I have met over the years who are ripe for ministry, and I know them because I've been there like them. In turn, you and I are going to be the ones to help because we recognize those ones who falter. We know who will accept help.

I was in the foyer after the worship service one Sunday when one of the young men asked me if there was a Bible he could give to his friend standing there with him. We went into a classroom to a shelf where there were used Bibles to choose from. With some quick conversation, we got acquainted. It was an opportunity for me to share a little, swap stories, and pray with both of them. The new guy said he had "received God in his heart" fifteen years before in a brief encounter in a church, but he had never joined a fellowship. He said they had quickly run an explanation by him, but he didn't get the complete picture. He had only prayed with the pastor for salvation. He expressed regret for his wasted years. I encouraged him to live more for the Lord. I hope he never loses his new clarity, because he is just now gaining his first love.

This is a Christian who, until recently, walked in the ways of the flesh. In his late thirties, he had been living a broken, desperately unhappy life. This friend just lately had broken up with a woman he had been living with. He's had an incurable drinking problem too. This is another reason you'd imagine he hasn't grown spiritually. Depression has got the best of him, and he needs long-term help.

Since first coming to our Sunday service, our eager friend has begun to walk in his faith. He came again, and we had another great visit together. He's a capable person, thoughtful and courteous. He and I went hiking together in the mountains. He's wide open, so we talked enthusiastically. I quoted Scripture. Back home for dinner, I was blessed to spend a time interacting with him on a range of subjects.

I love being a part of a person's life-changing course. I don't know how well he will do. Someone might think that one individual coming into the assembly doesn't make a revival. It does if it's a revival for him. The value may not be in big numbers. True worth may be in the benefit to that one person's life. We expect things to happen fast—instantly. All businesses run on one sale at a time and each individual is a customer.

> *And not only so, but we glory in tribulations also: knowing that tribulation worketh patience.*
>
> Romans 5:3

Be grateful for troubles because victories make faces shine. Your Creator has made you this way. He not only designed us to grow stronger under fire, but the Lord has also made us capable victors so we come out on top.

When we first start our walk as Christians, we don't know what's coming next. Challenges to our faith are inevitable. Novice Christians hit that dip in the road and disappear. It seems like there's no way to get back up. If you have never been there, how will you know how to respond? When I first became a Christian, I thought all my troubles were over; sunny days were sure to shine. Grudgingly, I had to learn this is the way life goes.

When someone is bothered, the common thing to do is to bother others. Don't take it out on others. I get that. Don't think problems rob you of your patience. I've been told that I don't handle difficulties well. Hard times teach us patience. Maturity tells us we can learn from problems. I find that with my new, improved attitude, impatient people grate on me and I complain about all their grumbling. What deference or tolerance do we show? We don't have to draw the line on every quarrel we get into. It's all right. Let people be wrong.

Bad times will hit. That's when Christians might doubt their confidence. Inappropriate reactions might make it look as if faith is false, and worse yet, people might feel as if God isn't even there. Your reaction to a new convert in trouble may push them further off balance. Friends and family, as helpful as they can be, find faults in new believers—and then panic sets in. You can take the advantage and the opportunity to step in with grace. The good Lord is waiting to prove Himself again—and to prove Himself through you.

God starts us out with a few small things, so He can build up to more important business (Luke 16:10, 19:17). Life is a growing process. What happens is that we take two steps forward and then three steps back. So what? That isn't necessarily a bad thing. It could be costly, but the lessons learned can be invaluable. Do failures come because God is silent in opposition? This is when a mature Christian friend lends a hand and helps others to understand.

> *And patience, experience; and experience, hope.*
> Romans 5:4

We start out as sinners. God has to build our character until we grow. Our heavenly Father corrects us, and it isn't joyous. It grieves us, but afterward, it yields the fruit of righteousness. He allows greater trials in our lives to give us bigger victories so we're able to yield much more fruit for Him. We have new and improved lives in Jesus Christ because we are justified first of all, and then we have love, joy, patience, and peace that surpass all understanding. This is faith. Through struggles and troubles, we have gained a better experience than otherwise. To our character, God adds brotherly kindness, and to brotherly kindness, love. We aren't going to be disappointed in the future with such great hopes.

> *And hope maketh not ashamed; because the love of God is shed abroad in our hearts by the Holy Ghost which is given unto us.*
> Romans 5:5

Rejoice in the grace of the Lord Jesus Christ regardless of the complexity. "*God has poured out his love into our hearts*" Romans 5:5 NIV. No matter what grade of sin, grace is greater. God's Holy Spirit is very willing to pour His love into your heart.

Our progress is noted when we bear fruit. God comes along and prunes us, but we are not ashamed. He is not cutting us off from Himself. There is not a chance of that because we abide in Him. We live in Him, and He in us. There are times when I am disappointed, discouraged, tired, and useless. When we fish all night and catch absolutely nothing, Jesus comes alongside and blesses us with the smallest correction, as if we should try one more time. He can bless us with more of a catch than we can handle. Surprisingly, we do handle it.

I have been fouled up, immature, and even crossed up with fellow human beings. Admittedly, the damage was done, but did that ruin me? Along the way, the kinder human beings let me by with only a few words. Someone has let you off the hook before.

These softhearted souls aren't always Christians either. All that work and pain can cause us to grow. With God's governance, experience helps. With support from one another, we can let the past go and trust and obey God, and this is exactly how love comes to fruition.

By considering our own faults, we try to be better to each other. It doesn't take a genius to see how people exploit the faults and victimize those in distress. The troublemakers see our vulnerabilities, and they wound us. Sinners dare their mortality to excuse their deadly immorality. Christians face hardships. Take the many injustices in stride. It's easier to live with the passing of time if we hold to our hope and faith with a clean conscience, not sinning against God or against our brothers and sisters. We love them. We will endure cheerfully to love others even more permanently.

I Love God

> *If a man say, I love God, and hateth his brother, he is a liar: for he that loveth not his brother whom he hath seen, how can he love God whom he hath not seen?*
>
> 1 John 4:20

The one who puts God first loves others the most. What if some people say they love God, yet you know that they hate people? We have to get it straight in our own thinking, get it in the right order, and get it all in line with the direction of the Bible. People don't often love Jesus enough because they might not be inclined to love others. It's about the way we see each other. We see one another all right. People don't always look good every day. We need to see by faith. *"We walk by faith, not by sight"* 2 Corinthians 5:7. The state of the world doesn't have to stress us out. God is invisible; we have to picture Him better. Christians who abide in Jesus thrive. I love God, so I am able to love my brother also.

> *And this commandment have we from him, That he who loveth God love his brother also.*
> 1 John 4:21

It makes sense that those who love God will love their neighbors in the same way. I had a dear Christian friend who insisted that those verses that tell us to love your brother mean, "Love the Christian brethren, because the unbelievers and heathen of the world are not brothers and sisters, but they're sinners, enemies; you don't love them." He saw the world as the enemy. Could a man like that be a Christian and say things like that? I spoke to him about his objections. It wasn't easy for him to get grace in his head, and it was even harder for him to retain any new outlook. He told me that he had been unhappy all his life. He said that he stayed that way, a wounded, troubled, angry soul, because he feared God.

Christians can fight this commandment to love. Varying ideas, modus operandi, and wrongheadedness continue to reside in the minds of all true believers. The Word of God cuts two ways: the truth will judge the unbelievers of the world, but it will also cut us who believe. If we are going to Heaven, Jesus will prune us back for our benefit so we can continue to grow in good ways, and He helps us love one another too.

Down deep, I know why I pray for everyone (1 Timothy 2:1). You may have heard, as I have, that Christians shouldn't pray for the sins, habits, and misfortunes of the unsaved, but they should only pray for their salvation. This is one of many bad ideas within our circle, pray they meet their fate. God wants us to pray about the situations unbelievers face. Ask God to solve their difficulties especially so that they will come to see and believe.

It is our duty to help everyone, not just Christians. The world around us has seen our hard attitudes. Unbelievers are quick to pick up on our faults, but they're not quick to forget. Let's pray to make a better impression. Isn't God working with everyone? *"As we have therefore opportunity, let us do good unto all men, especially unto them who are of the household of faith"* Galatians 6:10. Christians should want to bless everybody in the household of faith, but not to the exclusion of everyone else.

Over the years, I've heard semi-believers say our Bible is not a trustworthy translation. The rumor is that centuries have taken a toll on the original writing. Experts have a great amount of research to authenticate the early manuscripts. I think the problems are in our reading today.

The world sees many examples of our impoverished spirituality. Those who look down on us have a habit of being critical, if not bigoted. It's difficult for us to get next to them with the true story. It's more difficult for me to keep on loving my Christian family since they unwittingly hurt my ministry in Jesus Christ and have tripped me up personally. It's tough to forget the times. Their rudeness undercuts my efforts. Without a doubt, God tells us to love our neighbors. Support fellow Christians to keep them fired up and ready for every good opportunity. God wants to give spirit and strength to each of us to love one another.

God understands us, and at the same time, He loves us. It's amazing. God keeps up with the human condition. Jesus became one with us, so He encourages us to hang on. The sympathies God has don't bring Him down to our level, although you might say it does; rather, His love elevates Him and lifts up His glory. In someone's eyes, God might look ordinary, but His familiarity with everybody speaks of His goodness.

God was cast temporarily in a bad light in order to provoke Moses to intercede for his fellow Israelites. Consider Exodus 32. Moses is reminding the Israelites of the first time he went up the mountain to receive the tables of the covenant. There he waited forty days and forty nights until God gave him the two handwritten stone tablets (written by God Himself!). God let Moses play the good role.

God then told Moses to go because of trouble in the camp, "*for thy people, whom thou broughtest out of the land of Egypt, have corrupted themselves*" Exodus 32:7. Doesn't this sound like a spouse's indignant accusation? "Your son did this" or "Your daughter did that." Moses realized that God wouldn't destroy the Israelites, because that would break His promise. So he asked God, "*Lord, why doth thy wrath wax hot against thy people?*" Exodus 32:11. (In this case, there really was just one parent!) Whose people are they, really? God is the Creator of all. That sure takes the responsibility off us. When we love the Creator, we love His creation and take responsibility.

Another biblical example of God's gracious compassion is the manner of Christ's birth (not just Christ's incarnation, which of course is the ultimate example). Jesus' parents weren't married. How scandalous to the righteous, but how appealing to the sorry sinner. The imperfect soul can dare to approach this holy God.

When Jesus was young, He behaved like a typical teenager. We read how Jesus felt at the temple, caught between parental norms and an expanding awareness of His calling. What an example to any struggling youth who reads this! The Holy Spirit, God Himself, allows Jesus' perfect humanity (Hebrews 10:5, 10) to spread through us with humility. We've never seen God's flawlessness with our eyes, yet we love others with their imperfections through our imperfect eyes, and we do it in *love* by *faith* in Jesus Christ.

We have a special message for Christians: we are to love God. You and I end up loving God with all we have which is less than enough, but we can love Him more for all we know. Love increases and the blessings follow.

Second, tell them that God loves them. Faith grows to see how great His love is. God loves you right now. This changes you. Third, tell them to love one another. This is where we are. This is why we come to Jesus—to live for others. We have traded in our addiction to sin for the goal of eternal life, yet for some reason, we are still scared to die. The moment people receive Jesus, they begin to grow and see love for one another, and we live for God, to see Him.

Come and Dine

> *And he said unto them, Cast the net on the right side of the ship, and ye shall find. They cast therefore, and now they were not able to draw it for the multitude of fishes.*
> John 21:6

They caught nothing, they were on the wrong side of the boat. Jesus told them to go to the right side of the boat so they could find the fish. Do you believe this? Then you must believe the Bible. What if I told you that a friend and I were fishing and caught nothing, but a stranger on shore hollered to us to hang our line on the other side of the boat, and we started pulling in so many fish that we began to sink? This is literally a fish story.

Peter went fishing after he saw the resurrection. The others all went with him. They fished all night, yet oddly enough, they caught nothing. Their nets were empty. Then a stranger on shore yelled out, *"Cast the net on the right side of the ship."* John recognized that the man on the shore was Jesus, and he told Peter.

It was as if the crowds hung on every single word that Jesus spoke, yet they caught nothing of what He had said—and that goes for the twelve disciples as well. Nobody can understand how much Jesus had come to give. We should know better.

When we do as Jesus says, we learn to obey; we learn His wisdom and we gain insight. We see love come to us more abundantly in the resurrection power of Christ. Peter drew the net up. This time, it did not break, and the boats stayed afloat. We need to point this out to our friends. This passage puts Jesus on the edge of the shore where most of the twelve had gone to fish. This is why you and I need to stay close.

Lots of believers languish with all their hope waiting to be renewed. Many Christians haven't succeeded. Jesus has to do it. We brood about the believers who wander and fall into temptation. We've heard the horror stories of servants of the Lord who abandon the fellowship and have fallen into sin.

There might be more stray believers than the faithful few we see in church. Many friends have confessed Jesus; where are they today in relation to the Holy Spirit? You wonder if the faithful who sit in judgment are any better. We shouldn't fret about those who aren't with us. To start with, we pray. What about the ones who fail to grow? They could be cut off or pruned to grow. We want to see love, more love, and much more love.

Jesus has set a higher goal for us. If we're not there yet, that doesn't mean we aren't getting there. It doesn't mean we don't deserve it. Some say right out loud that the evidence is inconclusive. Have faith. Believe. Jesus gives New Testament love the likes of which has never before been seen on earth or even in Heaven. God promises—and He delivers.

Suffice it to say that someone came to each of us with the gospel. Remember that God loved us long before we loved Him. This is why people are trying to obey. Jesus tells us to love one another. Who first asked, "Am I my brother's keeper?" That was Cain (Genesis 4:9). Yes, we certainly are our brother's keeper. It garners new meaning, though, if we consider it a privileged responsibility to disciple others and to care for each other, all by faith.

> *Simon Peter went up, and drew the net to land full of great fishes, an hundred and fifty and three: and for all there were so many, yet was not the net broken.*
> John 21:11

The net did not break, so they didn't lose any fish. They counted every one of them. Pray to God for answers, especially in times when we have nothing to show. Some of us will do well, while others of us will fall (Ecclesiastes 9:12). Does that mean one person matters more than another? Like the huge catch Peter hauled in, great evangelistic revivals are famous, but the saved come one person at a time.

Compare this story with the one in Luke 5, when Jesus met Peter the first time. Both times, they had been fishing all night and had caught nothing. Jesus told them to cast their nets once more, and they caught so many fish that they couldn't pull the nets in. The first time, Peter's net broke from being so full. After the resurrection, even though it was full, the net didn't break. I like to believe that ideally, not only will we Christians fill empty nets, but we will also hold and keep everything God points us to.

We have to be careful not to draw doctrine solely from stories in the four gospels or to guess without the support of more Scripture. This is about love that's full and doesn't break.

When the sad disciples went back to fishing, Jesus went to them. They seemed unaware of the great salvation He had accomplished a few days earlier. As we go to win more souls for Jesus, try to keep track of them. They profess faith in Christ, and we need to further their faith and nurture their hearts. I worry about Christians who place their lives in Jesus' hand, as simple as it sounds, but have yet to glimpse the magnificence of what has actually happened. Certainly, Jesus will keep coming after you the rest of your life.

American Christians in the past often grew up in churched families, attended church activities, received Jesus early in life, and benefitted from a secure home. They took life for granted with loving and wise parents. These advantages paid off, but they didn't nearly feel the forgiveness they received for their sins. They feel a deficit in their spiritual understanding of grace compared to others who come out of the world.

A few of these lifelong Christians tell me they've lacked the experience of a sinner's conversion. They envy other Christians who have a worldly, sinful background. Those who are young when they first believe approach life with a limited view of salvation. In other words, they are Christians who remain inexperienced with the outside world. They might not even remember being saved, or if they do, they do not remember it well.

A Christian can honestly lack motivation. They fail to retrieve deeper instruction from the Bible. I suspect their love has less of an effect. You don't want to be average.

The angels of Heaven rejoice when a soul is saved (Luke 15:10). The church family sometimes pays less attention. (Maybe we have been disappointed too many times by false starts from those coming forward for Jesus.) On the other hand, it is our fault if we don't see to it that beginning believers grow. The weight is on us. New brothers and sisters saved outside of organized ministries miss a personal follow-up. They aren't going to bear fruit if we don't go to where they are and give help. Jesus would have us come alongside them. To follow up on them is to follow Jesus.

The Savior walked beside the water watching those disciples as they fished. We do matter to God, so we should also matter to one another. We need to know what's going on around us, find out we can do, and do our best.

The Apostles witnessed the death, burial, and resurrection of Jesus. They saw firsthand the brilliance of God in the birth of grace. There is significance in the wording with this passage. It says their net didn't break, as it had done in previous occasions. In the first "full-filling" fish story (Luke 5), the net broke; in this same chapter, the brief parables of the cloth and the one about wineskins are written. Jesus told these parables: *"No one tears a patch from a new garment and sews it on an old one. If he does, he will have torn the new garment, and the patch from the new will not match the old. And no one pours new wine into old wineskins. If he does, the new wine will burst the skins, the wine will run out and the wineskins will be ruined. No, new wine must be poured into new wineskins"* (Luke 5:36–38 NIV). Anyone who has received a new life understands this.

These two parables are in this chapter where Jesus calls the disciples to new life. Peter, James, and John were fishing and caught nothing. Jesus not only promised to fill their lives, but He planned to give them new lives so they could contain the whole of it all. Their nets broke, and their boats began to sink. From then on, they followed Jesus. Filled with the Holy Spirit and full of grace, these three fishermen would become great Apostles, with signs and miracles to confirm their ministry. The remainder of their lives was spent preaching the truth in the preponderant power of Jesus Christ. They are the foundation of the Church, permanent and prominent throughout eternity.

God knows how each Christian comes to be saved. Regrettably, among each other, too often, we are left on our own. Huge numbers of people are finding Jesus all over the world without sufficient guidance for their spiritual growth. Is this the individual's fault? God knew the desire of my heart to be saved. He brought me to a special place thousands of miles away where I got the best care. Isn't it the duty of our leadership? If we work with others with little result, you might say it is their fault. You and I can always do more. The key to evangelism is in educating born-again believers, integrating them into fellowship, and helping them find their way and a ministry. The world knows we are Christians by our love for one another.

Judgment starts at the house of God (1 Peter 4:17). We have a big job ahead of us here in our own backyard. It's a job that has great potential. It's the discipleship of countless Christians, and it should be easier with believers than convincing some who oppose us. What exactly is so hard about convincing those who agree with us—or is it just plain difficult to convince ourselves of any improvement or any involvement? Love will change another person's heart. If we know to do what's good and don't do it, it is a real shame.

Atheists say that the Bible spins like a fairy tale or a myth. They say that in ancient times, people were primitive and they liked fables and stories. Television didn't exist back then, so things had to be appealing to the mind's eye. They claim that heroic Bible characters were fabricated to control the masses.

In recent literature, superheroes like Superman can fly, see through walls, bend steel, and go faster than a bullet. Can we show salvation to these blinded minds? Cynics look at us and think Christianity was concocted only to dazzle us into following the crowd. They don't think it is believable when we say that we will live with God forever in endless splendor. They claim that religion was made up to swindle money and power. We have the greatest story, but we can't prove it. No, words alone can't define faith or reveal Jesus to the world; we have to show them love in action.

Jesus told the disciples to try one more time. They could have said it was no use trying, that they had fished all night and had caught nothing. Modern man studies to conquer every area of life, but will it solve real life? If you fail for so long, you want to give up. This is when encouragement from just one person might turn us around. We might need a little nudge.

> *Jesus saith unto them, Come and dine. And none of the disciples durst ask him, Who art thou? knowing that it was the Lord.*
>
> John 21:12

Jesus was gloriously changed in appearance, visibly alive for sure. He is human yet divine. What do you say? Jesus has great work for us to do with our own two hands, and He invites us to share in His divine nature: "Come and dine."

Jesus got the disciples to net a catch, then invited them to a ready meal. We are slow to take in the quality and quantity of God's love. Do you believe you can hold all He gives? Somehow, it didn't occur to Peter that it was Jesus on shore telling them where to fish. Peter should have known from experience that only one man could've known where to find fish. John had to tell Peter that it was the Lord, and only then did he realize it. Peter dove in the water and swam to shore. If we mentor others in the knowledge of Jesus, as John did for Peter, Christians won't have to miss any of these blessings.

You may feel that you've been at it so long with nothing to show for your labors. You might have failure. This doesn't have to materialize. God gives us authority in prayer, and He assures us we'll have victorious lives. Christians must help each other bear spiritual fruit. We should pray for each other nonstop and expect more. Watch and pray for God to make something to happen—an undeniable blessing of His, one that's truly irrefutable. This is our claim. The Bible teaches victories for all believers. Ask Jesus to help your unbelief.

It isn't our white-knuckle effort that succeeds; it's by God's grace. God may have us go back and give it another white-knuckle effort. Our failures don't need to forbid our success or disqualify us. God's correction can teach us to abide in Jesus Christ, to stick it out and see Him work, to stay with Him and work it out. The curse of sin was removed at the cross. God's power causes us to triumph.

You might not be able to hold on to all the blessings by yourself, but you do have a place here. You may feel like quitting like Peter. He fished all night without a catch. You might feel that your net breaks every time or that your boat always sinks. How much are we missing? We need each other. Who would dispute the facts? We must say so and stay together. Organized religion and programs are a big part of life. Community serves a purpose—people.

Jesus gave the disciples the miracle of full gospel fishing, and their net broke—before the crucifixion. The next time, with a full catch of big fish, the net held. The moral of the story is that you must be saved in Jesus and have faith to see the love.

John was the only alert disciple; he showed Peter that it was Jesus on the shore. He also saw to it that Peter was let in at the door when Jesus was on trial. You and I must show the way again and again by patiently instructing others. John seemed to get it—to understand. There is much involved in producing a fruitful garden, including our time.

Jesus laid down His life voluntarily to secure our place with Him. There is no greater love. In conclusion, the inclusion of people in God's eternal plan requires our love, service, and sacrifice. God is always there. Do you hunger for righteousness even more after losing? Maybe you do. We are zeros without Jesus. Others become pluses with us.

Growing in Faith

And to godliness, brotherly kindness; and to brotherly kindness, love. For if you possess these qualities in increasing measure, they will keep you from being ineffective and unproductive in your knowledge of our Lord Jesus Christ.
2 Peter 1:7–8 NIV

Peter wrote later on that we should add to our faith so that we can add love or else we will be *"ineffective and unproductive in [our] knowledge of our Lord Jesus Christ."* What happens when we stop growing? We plateau—or maybe there is no leveling off. You either rise or decline. If we stop increasing, we start shrinking back from the love of Jesus. Love is the first element to fall off. We lose our first love.

As a sinner, I met Jesus. I couldn't let my faith plateau for fear of returning to sin. I certainly prayed to grow. *"For if these things be in you, and abound, they make you that ye shall neither be barren nor unfruitful in the knowledge of our Lord Jesus Christ"* 2 Peter 1:8. The first thing we should add to our faith is virtue or purity. Add knowledge to virtue and then have self-control. Add patience to these, and to patience, godliness. To godliness, add brotherly kindness. Add all this up: you have love. Christians never want to lack love. Christians don't forget it; can't be blind or unable to see ahead and still be a Christian. Peter addressed this exact situation, saying that he who lacked these things was blind, *"and hath forgotten that he was purged from his old sins"* 2 Peter 1:9. It's like a person who is saved by faith alone and then forgets. The power is not in the one who believes, but in the one who retrieves.

Too often, the message we get in church is to just try harder. Christians grow, not by believing in ourselves or by trying to make it happen, but only through the true Vine when we abide in Him. What a mistake to try working by yourself. We need to drop our self-reliance and work with others to spread the good news.

You and I might be satisfied to think we are godly, but we are not self-righteous. Peter said we should add brotherly kindness to our godliness (2 Peter 1:7). People basically were the same back then as they are today. We need to love one another; we should get along with each other. There are good Christians who don't get along well with others. I don't always get along with people. Some Christians live a very clean life, and they don't feel any need to reach out in brotherly kindness. True repentance and godly remorse have a great effect. Peter's painful story was that of his sudden new process in progress; it literally lasted to the end of his life.

I grew up in a family where we fought with each other a lot. My father belittled us and there was a lot of griping. It was hard to be happy. As a teen, I went headlong into illegal drug abuse. Getting high in the hippie days was fun at first, and it promoted peace and love. That was what attracted me. Being "loaded" was a social thing, but when we all lost our minds and got paranoid, things got prickly and pretty ugly between us. It got terribly frightening.

I found my new Christian friends to be generous, trustworthy, and supportive. They went all out and treated me like a million bucks, so I got saved. I had never seen or felt so much care. I am writing nearly fifty years later to say that God continues to bless me with fellowship, and honestly, everyone should know how grateful I am. You want to do something extra.

> *Wherefore the rather, brethren, give diligence to make your calling and election sure: for if ye do these things, ye shall never fall.*
>
> 2 Peter 1:10

You shall never fall if you do these things. All things will work together for you. You are called. We are "the called" for the purpose of God. We should give all diligence to secure our assurance of salvation. We can know. *"Being confident of this very thing, that he which hath begun a good work in you will perform it until the day of Jesus Christ"* Philippians 1:6. This is why we love God. There is no maybe about it in Jesus. *"For all the promises of God in him are yea, and in him*

Amen, unto the glory of God by us" 2 Corinthians 1:20. God pours His love into our hearts for all who will see.

Those who don't have the Holy Spirit of Jesus Christ have no part. How can you be certain, and when do you find out if you're in? When you are in, you stay in. We are sealed by *"the Spirit in our hearts"* 2 Corinthians 1:22. If it is by faith we stand, and if faith is not visible, how would you know for sure? A Christian really can be confident. God has granted us these unbounded promises in the New Testament: "love believes all things" 1 Corinthians 13:7; "love never fails" 1 Corinthians 13:8. We can't lose when you and I are totally forgiven.

> *For so an entrance shall be ministered unto you abundantly into the everlasting kingdom of our Lord and Savior Jesus Christ.*
>
> 2 Peter 1:11

Peter's words reflect the perspective of his later life. *"Abundantly"* describes it well. These were not just his thoughts about Heaven, but it was his personal experience as a man of God. He bridged the glory of the everlasting kingdom to the world he lived in. He gave these perspectives to more believers.

Ministry happens when a door is opened to the wonders of Heaven. Learning to get along with others takes a life of dedication. If there is anything that has haunted me through my years of sweet fellowship in faith, it would be the sour taste and critical clashes I've had to endure with other believers. We disappoint each other. Love is not seen in bitter frustration, and it doesn't get mad or out of control with wild fighting. God takes us beyond the limits of family and far beyond our social clubs or cliques. It is a lot more than "If you scratch my back, I'll scratch yours" or "Me first!" Healthy families have positive feelings for each other. Jesus is our model. Love is, first of all, gentle, but it is helpful as well. We are strong. Love sees what is right, and this is what unifies us.

We all have trying times. Some of us won't put up with trouble.

It gets too disheartening. Some children grow up in a bad church family, and those memories make them more reluctant to follow Jesus as adults. They keep a safe distance from others and avoid the personal conflicts that hurt, but they miss the intimacy. You could suppose that Christians who are withdrawn have little to show or are slow to grow. We want to look for these people; they're not necessarily coming to us.

John Chapter 5 tells us that Jesus healed a man at the pool of Bethesda and moved on in the crowd. This man was healed, but didn't learn enough to get saved. Jesus later found the man again and told him, *"Sin no more, lest a worse thing come unto thee"* (John 5:14).

In John Chapter 9, Jesus put mud on the eyes of one who was blind and told him to go wash. This man couldn't see Jesus to know who had healed him. Jesus returned to him and asked, *"Dost thou believe on the Son of God?"* (John 9:35).

In John 21, Jesus went after the resurrection and found His disciples fishing. These three stories tell us to go again and again and again to those who need to be followed.

> *Greater love hath no man than this, that a man lay down his life for his friends.*
>
> John 15:13

Too often, Christianity has been perceived as exclusive. Have we considered the lives of our fellow human beings as important as our own? We gain nothing of value when we live only for ourselves. Remember Luke 9:24. Jesus said, *"Whosoever will lose his life for my sake, the same shall save it."* Christianity has often been perceived as intrusive, when instead, it should be effusive, inspiring. Inquiring people with penetrating minds want to know how to get through to people. To love is to lay down our lives for other people. Anything short of this is amiss. God requires more.

We love one another; one follows the other. People do need you and you need others. It just kind of works this way. Not everyone sees it like this. It's our job to turn it around. You can see it's a stretch. There's resistance. Persuading others of love is a big deal.

> *Beloved, I wish above all things that thou mayest prosper and be in health, even as thy soul prospereth.*
> 3 John 2

The Apostle John in his later life prayed for believers to be prosperous. He had big hopes for their well-being, as much as he was already confident of the glory in their soul. We may often have everything we want, but first, we must be settled in our hearts. Our inner spirit does well when we abide in prayer. When Christians pray, put God first, and allow Him to renew their minds; it is amazing. Let's number our priorities. Many more souls are to be won over before Jesus comes back.

Prayer works by love, and love works by prayer. Prayer only works through Jesus Christ. When you feel drained, you can ask to be filled. When we fish all night and catch absolutely nothing, Jesus comes along and blesses us with some caring correction, like telling us to try fishing from the other side of the boat. He blesses us with a bigger catch than we think we can handle. Surprisingly, we handle it all. One of the neatest things in life is when another believer refreshes you along the way.

> *And the Lord make you to increase and abound in love one toward another, and toward all men, even as we do toward you: To the end he may stablish your hearts unblameable in holiness before God, even our Father, at the coming of our Lord Jesus Christ with all his saints.*
> 1 Thessalonians 3:12–13

CHAPTER 12

Love Everyone

> *By this shall all men know that ye are my disciples, if ye have love one to another.*
>
> John 13:35

Jesus told His disciples their love would impress the world. He said *all men*, everybody, will see. They can tell who the true believers are by the way we love each other. From the start, God intended to get the message of salvation through to all of the world by our genuine concern. That's a tall order. I am working just to win one soul.

We are a minority. Think in terms of saving the entire planet, not just on one given day, but over the course of all the years. Multiply that out. Jesus didn't ask us to win everyone. We have a long way to go just to tell them. God's Great Commission, our Great Commitment to reach out to all the world and save some.

> *For though I be free from all men, yet have I made myself servant unto all, that I might gain the more…I am made all things to all men, that I might by all means save some.*
>
> 1 Corinthians 9:19, 22

These are what I call 100 percent verses, because they say it all. A lot of verses have words like *whole, complete, everything,* or *full.* Look for these words when you read the Bible. We need to see the larger picture. We cannot assume that we honor the words of the Lord without taking Him seriously. Note those words, phrases, and verses that show 100 percent. Christians have a penchant for laying the foundation over and over again without building on it. In reality, reaching the world for Jesus is an unapproachable end. Do you feel like me—hungry to be fed with protein? To a large extent, Christians don't have this total vision.

> *Look not every man on his own things, but every man also on the things of others.*
> Philippians 2:4

If I expect to reach the world, I make sacrifices for the sake of others. Love can do more than we expect. Every Christian, or "*every man,*" should be dedicated to evangelism. This call is accepted orthodoxy; it's traditional. Christians must be more concerned for others than for themselves. We can do it with grace. God doesn't ask us to do the impossible. It is impossible to us, but it's possible with God. We can give of ourselves to save others. You can believe that Christianity isn't always practical in a worldly sense, but it's right.

God works it out. We take care of ourselves so that we can take care of others. When you bless people, you get something back. Jesus sees what you do. Maybe you are worried about what God sees in you since it's not all good. If you're busy with sin and hiding from God, you will not be doing what He tells you. When we get headed in the right direction, our sinful thoughts and actions drop away. It comes down to this: rather than fulfilling old nagging temptations, let's act on faith and move in God's direction.

Communism, with its collectivism, captures the minds of millions who willingly subject themselves to it. It does require such a larger portion of the population to simultaneously comply. Communism is willful. It is exercised by force using the ideology that individuals live for the state and for the welfare of all. The Western philosophy of free democracy advances the premise that the state and the government exist to serve its individual citizens. These two opposing ideas are afraid of each other. They perform much differently. Patriotism, whether of totalitarianism or of freedom, involves great sacrifice. Sadly, it can be someone else who is to sacrifice. The ideals of communism drive people mad with passion, often with more zeal than most seem to have. All hearts fall short in God's eyes; it's not easy for average Christians to be selfless.

Christians have a tall mountain to climb to give this love. We can start by getting on our knees and praying. Converts awake from the darkness of sin empowered and say, "I must tell the world!" How long will it take for this wonderful "first love" to wear off? It would be exciting, but not sensible, for instance, to sell everything we have and give all the money away in one week, even for evangelism. Instead, use it wisely and, in the years ahead, give it out in shares. Don't give up in the face of the world's resistance and skepticism. Love is patient and long-suffering; you don't push it, let it fly.

The population is growing faster than we can keep up with. Winning one person at a time will take too long. There is a whole world waiting to hear. Admit it—we aren't going to make it happen. One person gets saved and says, "I must tell someone!" There must be at least one person who'll hear and be converted. What's wrong with telling everybody? We can't fill those shoes with the testimony of one new born-again believer. We pray. We work. We wait.

> *I exhort, therefore, that, first of all, supplications, prayers, intercessions, and giving of thanks, be made for all men,*
> 1 Timothy 2:1

The beauty of Christianity is that we love everyone and pray for "*all men*," as in every last person, both young and old. Just before Jesus died, He left it to us to love so that "all men" would see. We must pray to the point that everybody repents. Can the world pick up on Jesus' love? Our all-knowing God gives us a special open prayer line. Jesus came for everyone—not for the righteous, but for every sinner. God gave His Son for the whole world. Go to Him and reason with Him, so He will show the way of salvation to all, *"Who will have all men to be saved, and to come unto the knowledge of the truth"* 1 Timothy 2:4. If God tells us this, He absolutely wants you and me to love everybody and pray for them too.

The scope of the plan God has and His ultimate goal of the whole world should change us completely. To try hard but fall short of His all-encompassing will would be wrong. If someone professes Christ and sees no need to announce it to everyone, do they understand what they've believed? It's a sin not to share what Jesus has done for us. The job of sharing our faith raises fear for some of us Christians. A believer who finds love difficult may not've really received Christ. Has this kind of person professed the truth only superficially? Jesus told the disciples to love everyone. Teach to reach as far as you can (Galatians 4:19) until Christ is fully formed in us.

The Savior of All

> *For therefore we both labor and suffer reproach, because we trust in the living God, who is the Savior of all men, specially of those that believe.*
> 1 Timothy 4:10

This is very urgent. We have not yet fulfilled the Great Commission. When is Jesus coming? If it weren't for faith, the breakdowns, difficult circumstances, and disappointments would kill the efforts. Paul told Timothy to command, teach, and remind the brethren.

God is love. Do we know Him? Do we really love one another? If not, then we're not getting through to the world either. We fail and we still call ourselves faithful. It's God who works, accomplishing this work everywhere. The care of the Father, the Holy Spirit, and Jesus works in us so we can walk faithfully in righteousness.

Serving others in the name of Jesus lifts up *faith* and *love*. Everybody loves, but we cannot say that every person is a Christian. We involve ourselves more because our sacred Scriptures say to be fervent in spirit. We all need development in spiritual life.

> *Meditate upon these things; give thyself wholly to them; that thy profiting may appear to all.*
> 1 Timothy 4:15

Maybe our testimony does reach further than we suppose. The hard attitude we see toward Christianity is definitely a sign that the potency of our message is recognized. Courageous believers are carrying the news to distance places. There are numerous global ministries increasing and supporting each other in every way, helping and interrelating together in the great harvest of souls. We work and pool our resources, carefully yet generously, often giving the credit to others. Praise the Lord! Heaven awaits us, but for now, God has crucial business here on earth to touch everyone.

> *Recompense to no man evil for evil. Provide things honest in the sight of all men.*
> Romans 12:17

The world expects a higher standard of character in our religion. Many of those who have heard of Christianity, all of them, want more from us. They know that much. Here is what I call a 200 percent verse: *"Recompense to no man evil for evil"* (Romans 12:17); we are not to return evil for evil to 100 percent of all people, and we have to be honest, *"in the sight of all men."* This makes it a 200 percent Bible verse—double the emphasis.

A big part of our job as ambassadors is to remain humble and honest in order to bring others to know our Savior. It makes a strong impression. We succeed at love to show the great hope in Jesus Christ. We already have victory—if we don't blow it. *"For the grace of God that bringeth salvation hath appeared to all men"* (Titus 2:11). Everybody ought to know. Our love alone makes the difference—to the degree we appreciate and apply the truth. This is what we've learned. It's what Jesus meant when He told us to *"love one another,"* lift each other up in faith, and stick together.

We're not all cut out to handle the more complex issues in the mission field; leave that for those who are called, schooled, and experienced. To pay, pray, and stay, our part at home is equally essential. *"As we have therefore opportunity, let us do good unto all men, especially unto them who are of the household of faith"* (Galatians 6:10). This says a lot about the necessity for a local church, our bond to one another, and the effectiveness of a good fellowship. Having faith, we go out. Our stability bears fruit many times over.

> *Whom we preach, warning every man, and teaching every man in all wisdom; that we may present every man perfect in Christ Jesus.*
> Colossians 1:28

Our goal is to present every man, woman, and child perfect here. How is our faith going to change everyone? It works with our faithfulness. Our objective is more than perfecting only those who are with us. We preach, teach, and warn the wayward. We are committed to getting it done. It falls on us to stay in church and to be true and work to love one another. Our money goes to one who buys seed for someone else who plants. Others water, and God gives the increase. Unified Christianity speaks volumes to the world.

Let us not tire of doing God's work. We sow to the Spirit and reap eternal life, *"for in due season we shall reap, if we faint not"* (Galatians 6:9). Let's continue. Our long-term efforts inside our little circle of home churches give credibility to missionaries on the frontier.

> *Every man's work shall be made manifest: for the day shall declare it, because it shall be revealed by fire; and the fire shall try every man's work of what sort it is.*
> 1 Corinthians 3:13

God has an intimate concern for every person worldwide. He cares as much about people in Timbuktu as He cares about you and me. The presence of God in our world is not a fable or a fairy tale. In the end, God will test all things. Those efforts we make now to bear up will prove to be everlasting. The Holy Spirit is right now leading, cleansing, and revealing.

Let's prove a point by using a little scientific experiment—and there really is little science involved in this project. Get a sheet of thin plywood, six feet by three. Stand it on end and cut out a small peephole where a student can look through. Have two students in the class come up front. While one student stands behind the blind, have the other stand eight or ten feet away. The one behind the blind is hardly seen by the other; he sees the other person in front from head to toe. Then have them switch places and complete the test by reversing roles. What have we confirmed? Just because you can see everything about another person does not mean that the other person has seen you.

Christians who spend their time looking out at the world from a high tower are little noticed for their watch over things. We will be lost in history if all we have done is rattle off words. Nobody will have seen us.

It's too easy to criticize and hide. Am I able to be open and vulnerable in relationships? God is bigger and more real than Santa Claus. He really knows when we've been good or bad. What we should be thinking about is blessing others.

Turn the tables, place yourself out in plain view, and the other person in back of the blind looking out. You can be a big witness for Jesus, bold as broad daylight, but can you see behind the blind or see the lives of those who are hidden from you? You may not know it, but they see you. You should hope that they like you.

Paul said, *"Every man's work shall be made manifest."* God will show it for what it is. Was the Apostle saying that the sins of the world will be revealed or the sins of Christians will be revealed—or was he saying that it will be the good deeds of believers and their rewards? When he said, *"Every man's work,"* Paul was plainly saying *every man*, everyone and everywhere, will be judged by God.

Jesus said, *"By this shall all men know that ye are my disciples, if ye have love one to another"* (John 13:35). Picture yourself in the presence of Jesus. Instead of reading that verse, pray to hear your Lord saying this directly to you. It's unmistakable. There's no complication in the translation. The plainness of meaning could not be misconstrued. Obviously, the hardness is in our heart and especially in the unbeliever's soul. God loves. This is His will. He is speaking to all of us right now, today, if we would only stop, listen, and obey. Let the whole world judge us. We see the lives people have, but we must maintain this famous unconditional love. Hope that they see you in plain view so they can believe and be saved.

They May Be Saved

> *Even as I please all men in all things, not seeking mine own profit, but the profit of many, that they may be saved.*
> 1 Corinthians 10:33

Paul had the best attitude; he wanted to win over the whole world. He was not seeking anything for himself. There was no profit in it for him. He was looking for the profit of others. Paul sought the lost to bring tribute to God the Father by winning them to His Son, Jesus Christ. Paul held on and tried in every way within his limits and did everything he could for people so that some of them might be saved.

When we are at a standstill, trying to fill our own needs, we don't give enough. Too many of us are poor and weak. That's just it! There is the answer. How often do we consider that others are in urgent need? *"By this shall all men know that ye are my disciples."* Paul knew the words of Jesus, how He had said, *"if ye have love one to another."* Paul was bound to tell the world of the favor he found in God. He had Jesus in him, and he had learned to give. Jesus put everything He had into Paul in order to get all He could out of him.

Let no man seek his own, but every man another's wealth.
1 Corinthians 10:24

This verse defines the word *love*. Like a proverb, it's easy. It's like the Golden Rule. "*Let no man seek his own, but every man another's wealth.*" See the double emphasis. Paul wrote that we can make better choices by placing others ahead of ourselves, taking our place at the end of the line. It starts by putting Jesus first. We all might know this, but do we practice what we read? Jesus squeezes me to get all He can out of me. He takes all the bad stuff out, and the good business comes out of me too. When we do the right things consistently, the world sees we are, without a doubt, disciples of Jesus Christ.

As Christians, we should work together. The one who wholeheartedly accepts Jesus may immediately announce, "I am going to win the whole world!" It will not be very long before you see that person worn down and returning home with his head down and his tail between his legs. It's not realistic to expect that everybody is going to believe you and come automatically.

On the other hand, some people who receive Jesus say, "Now I am going to find someone to save." This person is going to last longer. How are we going to get the attention of people? Jesus said, "*if ye have love one to another.*" We are not going to love the crowd if we cannot love each face we see.

Use a bit of kindness when you tell others what they need to hear. What do they do to be saved? They simply have to believe in Jesus and repent of their sins. Not everybody around us has had the truth explained plainly enough so they can really understand it. Our generosity with a little smoothness will gain their confidence and build rapport. Then we can sit down and spell it out to them. They recognize a pattern they can repeat.

Zeal makes faith stand up and walk to show that it goes with love. Let's help others see that faith alone is not enough. Without Jesus, faith fails. We place the genuine gospel in the hearts of those we speak to, and we reach them by conveying compassion. Passion in action rings true. Does God have victory in your personal story?

If God is not in it, then there is no value in anything—especially love. You can't do it alone for long. We abide in Jesus Christ, trust in Him, and depend on Him to do everything well. And doing wrong sure ruins it.

> *And to make all men see what is the fellowship of the mystery, which from the beginning of the world hath been hid in God, who created all things by Jesus Christ.*
> Ephesians 3:9

You may not see what results from your attempts to reach the world. I hope never to forget the number of Christians, and even other good folks, who helped me and shaped me into what I have become. Most of them may never be aware of it.

It was early 1971 in the Siskiyou Mountain Pass of Southern Oregon. It was cold, dark midnight, and rainy when my last ride let me out on an exit ramp. It was near the town of Grants Pass. Hitchhiking from Sacramento to Seattle, I tried for a while to thumb another ride going north, but decided it was too late, especially since there was no traffic. I walked down to an all-night gas station. I asked the attendant if there was a hostel or someplace like that in town where I could stay the night. The man said he didn't know of any place. I told him I'd walk back to the highway and sleep under the overpass.

An act of kindness by a very special Christian played a big part in opening my eyes to Jesus. The owner of an old Volkswagen bus stopped to buy gas. I knew hippies and communes had flocked to that area; I figured I might ask for a place to stay. The driver, a young, attractive woman about my age, was just starting her engine. I asked her if she knew of anywhere I could stay the night. She said she didn't, so I told her I'd walk back to the highway and sleep under the overpass.

I was walking away from the gas station and up the road, when she pulled her Volkswagen bus up alongside the shoulder. She told me to throw my gear in back and jump in front. She told me that she lived with her parents, but I could sleep in the bus and we wouldn't tell them. In the morning, she would be going to work at 8:00, and on her way, she would take me back to the freeway. She was real pretty, too, with long brown hair and Hollywood looks.

She said she was from Seattle. She had graduated from Queen Anne High the same year I got out of West Seattle. Our conversation was progressing quite nicely, and I was trying to say everything right to strike up a friendship. I told her about the 1960 VW bus I had owned. Mine was rare with twenty-one windows and a sunroof. I should've kept it, but it was always breaking down. Her response was that yes, VW buses have good vibes. That rattled my cage. That is when I rallied and told her that I should thank her for picking me up. She said, "Don't thank me, thank the Lord." It went in one ear, you know, and out my other, but that really did surprise me.

We pulled up to her house too soon. She told me to stretch out my sleeping bag in the back and be real quiet, so her folks wouldn't discover I was there. Then she went into the house for the night.

I was trying to think how to keep myself from getting dropped off at the freeway the next day without having a chance at romance. I wanted to get to know her, but at nineteen, with long hair and a beard and being spaced out on drugs, I didn't have much to offer. The next thing I knew, she came out of the house, opened the front door of the bus, and threw in a pillow. That startled me. As soon as she did that, her mom stuck her head out of the front door of the house and yelled, "Mary, what are you doing?"

"Oh, nothing, Mother," she said, and she went back into the house. I was thinking about how sweet she was, like an angel, and right then, she came out again. That was all right with me. She jumped back in behind the steering wheel this time, started the engine, and yelled, "My mother knows you're here, so I'm going to take you to a motel and get you a room."

"I don't have any money," I said. "Take me back to the freeway."

She said she was paying for my room. I didn't know what to say. I wasn't used to that kind of generosity. This thing about her buying me a room was most unusual to me. Maybe it was because I didn't stay in motels. I was young, and people in Seattle seldom helped each other like that. The hippie culture was about helping one another, but this struck me as different. She took me to a one-level motel and gave me money to go into the office and get a room while she waited. I came back out, and she told me she wanted to see my room. I was all right with that. She drove me down the parking lot to the unit number, pulled up, and shut off her engine.

When I got my gear out of the bus, she followed me into the room. Sure, I was all right with that, too. We stood in the room for a moment looking at each other. Then she threw her arms around me with a hug. I thought she was coming for a kiss, but she turned her head, so I kissed her on the cheek. She backed up and looked right at me. She was the star of the show. Wow! She came in for another hug, so I kissed her again on the cheek. Poof! She was gone out the door. I went out after her and was racking my brain to think of what I could say to keep her from leaving. She had started the bus up and was backing out of the spot. The situation looked pitifully hopeless for love. That's when I blurted out, "I haven't even thanked you yet!"

She said out her window, "Don't thank me, thank the Lord," and she drove away.

There was nothing I could do. I slept there that night and headed back to Seattle in the morning. I saved up for a month and got the $8 to pay her back. I got a ride with a friend who was driving to California. I got a room in Grants Pass at the same motel. I walked all over that town expecting to see her house. I could picture the driveway in front where she had parked and the steps to the front door where her mother had leaned out. I walked all over that little town, but didn't find the house.

I spent a sad night in the motel. The next day, I hitchhiked back to Seattle. Nearly everyone who picked me up on the trip home was a Christian who told me about Jesus. I remember a husband, wife, and their two kids who dropped me off on this side of the Columbia River. After talking to me on the way, the man asked if he could pray for me before he let me out. I got back to Seattle thinking all about Mary and the people who had talked to me, and I tried to quit dope and drugs. I didn't just want Mary, but I wanted what she had. Mary is one good reason why I was saved and why I serve the Lord like I do.

Later that same year, I hitchhiked to Texas, where I would receive Jesus. As I rode south again on the interstate through Grants Pass looking out the window, I saw a big part of this little town I hadn't noticed before. I told myself I would have to go back again to look for Mary's place. We didn't stop nor did I tell the driver my story. I stayed with my ride and kept it to myself as we cruised by at 70 mph. A week later I arrived at the halfway house in Texas, where a few days after that, I would receive Christ into my heart. I even passed by Grants Pass again in 1973 and wanted to tell this angel how my life had been saved. Mary will never know this side of Heaven what a big measure her kindness to me had played in my salvation.

> *And the Lord make you to increase and abound in love one toward another, and toward all men, even as we do toward you: to the end he may stablish your hearts unblameable in holiness before God, even our Father, at the coming of our Lord Jesus Christ with all his saints.*
> 1 Thessalonians 3:12–13

Not only does the Lord help us live right, but He also increases our love toward all people. To this end, Paul wrote that Jesus will establish our hearts blameless, clean, and clear in holiness before the face of God, our heavenly Father. Let this be increasingly true as we draw near the end of this age. What kind of Christians ought we to be with His soon return? We want Him to find us living for Him, but do we win anyone here now? We are told to love fervently—not only to love one another, but to love all others if we truly love the Lord our God. Take life in a more serious way. What is missing is a glorious vision of eternity. Think of what a blast it will be like when Jesus takes us home!

We might offer a better explanation to people who refuse to believe. They are alienated from God. We are being neutralized by them—by the very ones we are trying to rescue. They are estranged, but they have marginalized us. The world rejects us, and the Church feels repulsion for the world. That's good if we want to keep separate. Shouldn't we welcome them in our churches, or should we treat them as strangers? How long until newcomers feel right? We want to reach the world. How do we know what to do? Without God's direction and help, we could never begin a new approach.

I want to speak for the lost souls, having been one myself. That was many years ago. I have to think about what it's like for lost souls now. There was such a long way for me to go when I started out. I began wondering about Jesus. He was looking for me—an unbeliever. This goes without saying, so unfortunately, it's left unsaid.

We must place ourselves in another's shoes. I don't know what you've gone through, and you wouldn't know what I've gone through. We can only guess what goes on in another person's life. The friction and infighting in our churches sure hurt the outreach. Jesus wants us to give it all we have in order to touch everyone around us in a powerful way.

While you and I are struggling to keep control of our lives, those on the outside are going out of control. We should agree that we have relatively little control of our lives in these unpredictable times. Any half-hearted outreach will likely fail. That's when we overstress. The setbacks are critical. We can choose to learn to relax, give it over to God, and receive His peace. We might do better.

We have to be smart enough to take care of ourselves and avoid a fall. Pray to God for health and protection. If all you tell everyone around what bums they are, how are they going to hear the bigger news that God loves them? He will help people. It's probably not beyond anyone's imagination to gain a better perspective and to finally put all their stock and trust in God. People simply have to call out for salvation.

People may be picking too high a goal and setting tough standards and set a pace that results in sore disappointments. Compared to this troubled world, we must see the hope of Jesus. It positively resonates with many of the lost. Don't be too surprised, though, because anyone is capable of faith and you never know who might accept the truth. We are not getting our message out to the world yet because we have a long way to go ourselves.

For All Saints

> *Praying always with all prayer and supplication in the Spirit, and watching thereunto with all perseverance and supplication for all saints.*
> Ephesians 6:18

God wants each of our lives to improve. Paul told the Ephesians to pray ceaselessly for *"all saints."* Where there is no prayer, there is no answer and no change. We can be sure of that. All I have to do when I am disappointed with life is to look back and see how far God has brought me. It's all for the better.

With desperate sin, hooked on drugs, and bound for Hell, I had lost hope. When I'm angry these days, I know that anger comes from my forgetful mind, neglectful faith, and ungrateful heart. It's embarrassing when it gets to me. Not everything happens all at once. Let's trust our Lord, keep the expectation of salvation, adjust our outlook, and love God with all our hearts. He helps us a whole lot. The Scriptures apply to all who believe, but the Scriptures also are addressed to anyone and everyone.

> *If ye continue in the faith grounded and settled, and be not moved away from the hope of the gospel, which ye have heard, and which was preached to every creature which is under heaven; whereof I Paul am made a minister.*
> Colossians 1:23

Many people come to Christ with joy, and then later somehow slip away from the gospel. Two thousand years ago, the Apostle Paul admonished Christians to hold true to the faith *"and be not moved away from the hope."* He urged us to preach it to the end of our lives.

This is how we came to believe, at one time someone cared enough to tell you. We learned the truth, and we accepted Christ. We should be thankful and tell others. We received the charitable kindness of Christians, so we carry on in their footsteps. Everyone in our time deserves to hear God's offer of salvation, new life, and they need to have the message explained and brought home to them by a good example.

The Holy Spirit, the fortification of our soul, lights our path. After this, there should be no occasional stumbling along the way. Do you believe everything about this? You might expect it. Jesus said people will know we're Christians by our love (John 13:35). In the end, God is going to judge sinners, and already now, He is revealing every thought a person thinks, by His Holy Spirit or perhaps through us in our witness. When the impact of salvation hit our soul, we surrendered attitudes, ambitions, habits, inhibitions, idleness, and lusts—and we began to live to see Jesus' name lifted up. We don't live by ourselves.

God never fails. We should not fail at love. Tell God all the wonderful ways you love Him, recount His blessings, and sit alone with Him for a while. Think of Him. He will not fail to bless. Study the Scriptures and meditate on them. God gives us life in order to increase and abound. Does at least a part of the answer depend on us? There is no excuse to slip. If we were more blessed by God in love alone, then everyone else should certainly see it.

> *I am debtor both to the Greeks, and to the barbarians;*
> *both to the wise, and to the unwise.*
> Romans 1:14

All who are set free by God's mercy remain beholden to all those still bound in sin and headed for Hell. Paul considered himself a debtor to the lost, a slave to the uncircumcised, and a fool to the unwise because he was truly grateful for the free gift of eternal life in Jesus Christ, every category and type of person.

If you see that a business is hiring for good pay, you owe it to your unemployed neighbor to share the good news. Does it matter if you like your neighbor or not? Even if you hardly know your neighbor, you should go over and tell him where they are hiring. Why keep it a secret? Certainly if you cross paths with your neighbor, you'll be saying something.

Unless we are unkind, we should pray to be outgoing. The unlovable can be transformed by Jesus and become lovable, more irresistible than you would like to admit. We owe it to those closest to us, and we need to reach the outside world too; it's a world we very much live in.

> *For though I be free from all men, yet have I made myself servant unto all, that I might gain the more.*
> 1 Corinthians 9:19

Christians are justified to love. For this God works all things together for our good. He works in our lives. God directs us into the greater purpose of reaching the whole world for Jesus. Love produces everything God wills. We can feel this new freedom of effort in His grace as we see evidence of God's ways demonstrated through us. This is a new definition for love, and it is different from others. We owe it to tell everyone, but people find it difficult to believe; they resist perhaps because even we find it hard to understand.

The first thing we admit when we meet Jesus is that we are lost, and everyone is lost. Love is the first commandment. We Christians are not getting it. We don't love. We don't talk about it enough, don't teach it enough, and fail at it. Let's be honest. God has to be our love. Therefore, we fail for not allowing this thought that love has to be by faith in Jesus.

Christians should befriend sinners. We must honestly respect them. What exactly are we afraid of? It sounds contradictory to some when we give credit to unbelievers who actually may have something good to offer. You can invite strangers into your life. There are creative ways to reach our neighborhood. It takes time to get acquainted with non-Christians, to discover their stories, and to allow their preferences and show deference; we should overlook their differences. We need to get them to like us and to be like us. Do you have a problem with this?

For All Jews

> *And unto the Jews I became as a Jew, that I might gain the Jews; to them that are under the law, as under the law, that I might gain them that are under the law, not being myself under the law, that I might by all means save some.*
> 1 Corinthians 9:20

Here is a passage I would say few have explored in depth. When did Paul become a Jew? He was born a Jew. He said so in another few places. Here he wrote, *"I became as a Jew,"* as he no longer saw himself as Jewish. As a Christian, Paul longed to see his country saved.

Paul counted himself no longer a Jew. He then *"became as a Jew"* in order to win over the Jews (see 1 Corinthians 10:32). He acted like he was under the Old Law in order to gain those who saw themselves as under the law, though he was no longer under the Old Law, and neither were the Jews. That law was removed by God at the cross.

Paul was not under the Law (see 1 Corinthians 9:20 KJV). The New Scofield of 1967 footnote). This really feeds into my heartache for Christians who pay little attention or ignore the change of covenants in Jesus' life and the Law of the Spirit. This is the biggest difference with immature Christians. They don't see it. When the King James Bible was taken from the earlier manuscripts, they left out this whole line, *"not being myself under the law,"* and modern Bibles have it back in there again. The old translators must've thought they couldn't believe their eyes, like we are all under the Law. This is amazing; the updated versions have put it back in and the Old Law is totally out. It proves my point once more; many try to reinsert the Old Law not only in Paul's day but still today in church. They've run that gag by us millions of times.

What Jesus taught was already seen in Judaism. Do you see what Paul saw? Jesus spoke the language of the Old Testament far better than any Pharisee ever dreamed. Now He is the New Testament. He preached what should have been their message. One Old Testament prophet's riposte was "*for man looketh on the outward appearance, but the Lord looketh on the heart*" 1 Samuel 16:7. Jesus did not bring a new morality. It was more than that. This new change came at the cross by the power of His blood. Forgiven, we become more willing to obey. It's for love.

Jesus asserted His position over the leaders much in the same way as they talked tough to people. He pressed them hard and took things further. "*Ye have heard that it was said by them of old time, Thou shalt not commit adultery: But I say unto you, That whosoever looketh on a woman to lust after her hath committed adultery with her already in his heart*" (Matthew 5:27–28). Jesus put no new specific meaning to it that was not already there. The seventh commandment condemned adultery, and the tenth commandment condemned even coveting a neighbor's wife. See the tenth commandment: "*Thou shalt not covet thy neighbor's house, thou shalt not covet thy neighbor's wife*" (Exodus 20:17). Many reading the Bible might have a difficult time, even modern educated Christians, distinguishing between Old and New Testaments. Besides that, we need to hold to the New over the Old Testament.

> *To them that are without law, as without law (being not without law to God, but under the law to Christ) that I might gain them that are without law.*
>
> 1 Corinthians 9:21

Paul is speaking to the Gentiles. The world is guilty and lawless, and Paul is a debtor to the Law of Christ, saved. Paul said he is no longer a Jew in the Old Law, but a Christian now.

He was schooled in the Old Testament Law, Jewish, and was at one time subject to those commandments with no leniency. Didn't God love him for his zeal? Didn't Paul retain his colossal uncompromising disposition after he was saved? At first, Paul was taught severity for any rebellious people who broke God's Word, whether they were of Israel or of another nation. *"But anyone who sins defiantly, whether native-born or alien, blasphemes the Lord, and that person must be cut off from his people"* (Numbers 15:30 NIV). Paul was set free in Christ to travel far outside of Israel, searching for Gentiles to save. He was free in his soul to serve.

Paul would not allow himself to duck this great responsibility: *"Yea, woe is unto me, if I preach not the gospel!"* 1 Corinthians 9:16. In his former self, he was strapped to the Old Law and separated from the world, but that burden was lifted off him on his way to Damascus. What this means is that Paul, you and I, all became bound to the New Law of love.

> *To the weak became I as weak, that I might gain the weak: I am made all things to all men, that I might by all means save some.*
>
> 1 Corinthians 9:22

We want to get the whole world on board, and there are people getting on board. Paul, who knew the Old Law, said that we had better not deprive the weak, and we should not overpower the strong. When he spoke to those in high authority, he showed respect. He showed respect to the powerless. He related to them and took no advantage of his credentials. Paul attended to the needs of others laboring with his own hands.

You've prayed to receive Christ into your heart; expect that He has come in. You know He hears prayers. What if I said God never answers any of my prayers? You would doubt my salvation. I'd quit. What if I told you God answered every prayer of mine, but He always said no? Who wants that? He said yes at least once; I asked Him in. God tells Christians—all of us—to pray for our own benefit. This stands true for everybody. Pray for the benefit of others.

Patient toward All

> *Now we exhort you, brethren, warn them that are unruly, comfort the feebleminded, support the weak, be patient toward all men.*
>
> 1 Thessalonians 5:14

Paul urges Christians to help all the difficult souls out there. He tells us in this verse to be patient with everyone, starting with the unruly, *"all men."* What is true today must have been just as true in that day—people resist instruction. If kids are not taught to follow instructions as they grow up, they have a harder time following through in life. Paul warns them because there are consequences to every action. He asks us to tell them because their every move is important.

Teach the brethren, reach the lost, and redirect the sinners. Perhaps we are not taking advice ourselves from verses like this. It takes patience to counsel those many unique individuals with their various quirks.

We must work our way toward the spiritual mind of Christ. Be fervent yet patient. When we open ourselves to new experiences, people, and places, our own character improves.

Love does not demand its own way. Our love belongs to Jesus and it's generous. We too frequently use our own reasoning, which is good because God wants thinking people but too much is more than enough. Try to be bold when you will and stretch yourself. If you limit yourself to just a few special people, the quality of your life will suffer. Spiritual life needs to be humble but glad to be alive. Love requires us to be involved and patient with all.

> *See that none render evil for evil unto any man; but ever follow that which is good, both among yourselves, and to all men.*
>
> 1 Thessalonians 5:15

LOVE BELIEVES ALL THINGS

The Bible uses our common sense, experiences, and God's leading. He is in all places and among our friends. Do we *"ever follow that which is good,"* really? We tend to *"render evil for evil"*—that's bad. I've wondered, for instance, why we're prone to be vindictive. The comfort we receive from God can comfort others. Advice and sympathy are more than words. Do your convictions help you practice to show it? How often do you volunteer your time to lend a hand? Love takes time to be there and arrive with what it takes to meet someone's needs.

In the 1990s, I got acquainted with a lonely spinster named Lucile. The elderly gentleman who used to take her to church was hospitalized, so I volunteered and became her regular driver. After I picked her up once for the Wednesday evening meeting at church, she rode with me many times and there were others to pick up too. Sometimes, after dropping others off at home, I would take her for a ride. Almost ninety, dear Lucile had a complex personality. She was in decline, as were her house and her social life.

Lucile loved the fun we had picking up friends on the way to church. She surprised me, and we became fast friends. I learned that she had been in our church since she was nine years old. She was an exceptional Christian, a very diligent, lifelong servant of Jesus. Lucile had lived in the same house since she was five. She had cared for both her mom and dad until they died at home. She had been a full-time nurse for over fifty years, had taught countless kids in Sunday school, and was devoted to our church.

On the way home, I would stop at the store for her. I lined up helpers to do her chores, arranged for carpenters to work on her house, and found others to care for her health. Lucile encouraged me and actively helped me in my goals.

I grew to love Lucile. She had a very special place in the hearts of quite a few people. At our church's huge hundred-year anniversary banquet, this faithful saint was recognized for her nearly eighty faithful years there. Everyone admired Lucile and her big role throughout the many decades! During the next several years, Lucile and I spent a lot of good time with each other. One Saturday morning during a phone call, I was told that she was gone. My first thought was *How awesome!* She would now have what she had always wanted, which was to see Jesus. There is no doubt that Jesus wanted to see Lucile.

Those of us still here have more work to do. A good friend at church suggested that with Lucile gone, I would again have more time to myself. I said that God would soon find someone else to fill my time. Some people suggest that I am too busy doing things all the time. Do you know what I say? We all are doing something all the time.

I told you my story about Lucile, so I could tell you this next story. A week and a half later, the new assignment came. At work one day, I answered the phone and talked with Duane, a longtime customer from another town. I asked him how he was doing. Duane said he had just come back from visiting his wife's sister in Alabama. For some reason, he mentioned that the sister had a grandson in his twenties who was staying in Seattle at the Union Gospel Mission. I told Duane I had worked there at times. I knew that if he stayed any length of time at the mission, he would likely join their recovery program. I told Duane that I would go there and look him up.

Duane went on to explain that his wife, Elaine, had a twin sister, Eileen, who had basically raised her grandson, Matt. His mother, Eileen's daughter, was a troubled woman. Matt's father was no good, and his stepfather was worse. Eventually, Matt went in and out of the navy, in and out of jail, and landed in Seattle. My friend Duane said he would find out more information and call me.

In the same conversation, Duane told me that his daughter, Missy, was in the state mental hospital. I said that I had visited patients there, even though it was over an hour away. He was glad to hear that I would visit his daughter as well as his nephew.

That following Saturday morning, I called the Union Gospel Mission front desk. I asked for Matt and got transferred to someone on the fifth floor. I knew then that he had been brought into the recovery program. I prayed. Somebody on the fifth floor went and got Matt. When Matt got to the phone, I introduced myself. I explained how his uncle Duane had told me about him being there, and I told him that if he would like, when he had some free time, I would be happy to take him out for a cheeseburger.

In a slow, deep drawl, he growled, "I don't have any uncle named Duane, and I sure don't know who you are."

"Well," I said, "Duane knew who you were and where I could find you."

That gave me enough credibility with him, especially after I explained the part about his Alabama grandmother and her sister's husband, Duane, here in Washington.

He paused and answered, "You will have to excuse me; I have been living on the streets and have to be careful."

Matt agreed to meet later in the afternoon when his duties were over. I pulled up to the front door and was surprised to find him to be tall, good-looking, and very well dressed. The first thing he told me was that he had called his grandmother and she told him that I was a friend, and she explained to him about Duane and Elaine.

Matt said, "I didn't know I had family up here, and that makes you family too." He told me he had landed in the mission recently and had given his heart to Jesus.

We went to the best burger joint I knew, and while we ate, I told him about his cousin. He was not aware of her. I told him that she was institutionalized and that I hoped to visit her. He wanted to go, too, and I had hoped for that.

Getting in to see Missy turned out to be more difficult than I'd expected. We were turned away. She was locked in the mental hospital with a ten-year criminal sentence, too disturbed to go to prison. Matt and I had to go through security clearance, which took a couple weeks. We did get in eventually, and I was extremely happy to see those two meet. They were pretty excited too.

Missy, in her early twenties, explained that she was adopted by her grandparents when she was a young child because her mother had gone to prison. Her biological mother is the daughter of Duane and Elaine. Missy started out as their baby granddaughter, but her grandparents adopted her and became her mom and dad. After the adoption, her mother became her older sister, which made her aunts and uncles her sisters and brothers.

Matt's grandmother, Eileen, was the twin sister of Elaine. So Matt is actually Missy's biological second cousin. They each spoke of the same great-grandmother whom they remembered from an early age. They were tickled to have the same memories of her. Praise the Lord that He leads me into the lives of people like this! There must have been something running through the generations of the family. I believe that the connectedness and the love renewed on this occasion meant more than anyone could have guessed.

Missy was locked up in Western State Hospital, an antiquated building with dangerously insane criminals. Men and women of every age roamed the hallway, and she was more worried about the staff. How could she find help there? I told her that even if it takes years and decades to achieve her goals, she has the time. God grants blessings along the way, and the best part of life can still happen, even when she gets to be forty or fifty. Missy's real mother, a Christian now in her forties, had become a rehabilitation counselor.

I asked Missy if anyone visited her or wrote to her. She said no. Missy still had a church bulletin in her Bible. She said it was from the last time she had gone to church, when she was in the youth group. She knew her pastor was still there, so I suggested that she write to him. He didn't write back, but he did ask a church member to write. That first letter came with instructions about what would and wouldn't be involved in their correspondence. That didn't last long.

> *To speak evil of no man, to be no brawlers, but gentle, shewing all meekness unto all men.*
>
> Titus 3:2

It is too bad that so many fine Christians fail to see the rich blessings of an outreach of faith in a challenging ministry. With regular visits, I earned Missy's confidence and was able to bring my wife in to fellowship, as well as some other friends. Missy is a believer and has recovered her life. She became a dear friend. She fought it there in the state mental hospital for nine extremely hard years before returning home. She found a good church, got a part-time job, and started college. Missy came to Seattle on her vacation and stayed with us. She came to Bible study, visited our church camp, saw a live band on stage at a park, and went to a pro baseball game with Louise. That was extremely rewarding.

I worry about Christians who shy away from risky people, playing it safe instead of walking into new situations by faith. If we become convinced of the rewards and potential of helping others, our hearts will be compelled to win more of the world to Jesus Christ. Now that we have trusted in Jesus and have been forgiven, what is our repentance about? We have turned from sin and come to righteousness. We should look on the bright side, the right side, and learn obedience to love, to heal, and to help.

Every Man

Let your speech be always with grace, seasoned with salt, that ye may know how ye ought to answer every man.
Colossians 4:6

Christians beam with joy and love as they look toward the prospect of eternal riches. It brings us together in a real sense of belonging. This uncommon hope of life hereafter is the common belief of every Christian. If one accepts the reality of the gospel, it then follows that one's view of life, including one's goals and values, will change. Persuaded, we become totally changed. The level of commitment we have toward each other directly reflects the dedication, or the lack thereof, that we have to the Lord.

God gives this conscientiousness by His Spirit—a will to act and influence. The hostilities from the world build stronger faith in us so we can awaken our friends. Our approach to life is one aspect. God grants an amazing measure of courage to motivate His church in love. His Holy Spirit lives right inside our hearts to work through our lives. A greater part of the victorious life is won because God is firmly in command with love.

> *He is the propitiation for our sins: and not for ours only, but also for the sins of the whole world.*
>
> 1 John 2:2

Either you believe it or you don't. God changed His mind about you. You have turned from wrong to right. At one time, we walked in the ways of this world, fulfilling the lusts of the flesh and the desires of the mind, and we were destined to wrath. Unbelievers are darkened in their mind. We could have been condemned with the world. There is more than that, though. We have fled from our doubts to believe in God and have turned away from despair to find happiness.

Instead of anger, we have hope. What about the rest of the world? Jesus died for all of them too. They live without a purpose. They lack reason, and they're cynical about goodness. People have many sins to be repented of and much good to turn to.

How painful it is to see God's love denied, our love rejected, and hope ignored. Does our message simply sound like we obey and get righteous? What's the difference between behavior modification that some teach and obedience as we've heard it in church? The Christian who only wants to convict the world of sin has yet to recognize that sinners see no wrong in what they do. Though sinners point out others' faults, they might not see sin in themselves.

There is no use explaining what is right or reasonable with people who are opinionated or irrational. If they won't listen, they can't hear, just as sure as they have no feelings or don't feel the same way when you tell them how you feel.

Some look at life as a cause-and-effect process, and as you're trying to get them to improve, they see you as just another part of the problem. In their mind, there is no God, so they see no God in you. Disapproval of any kind from us or from God won't register with them because they haven't even given us permission; as far as they're concerned, God doesn't exist. They are impoverished and impervious. How do we counter? Our decency isn't lost on them. Believe in God. We reflect the panorama of God's eternal kingdom, and somehow, it shows on our faces.

> *For the Father himself loveth you, because ye have loved me, and have believed that I came out from God.*
>
> John 16:27

Our Father in Heaven especially loves you and me since we love Jesus and believe in Him. Wow, this is amazing! He gives us credit, a lot of credit, for the fact that we've sorted through the confusion in our world to see the truth. God loves us for it, and oh—if we could only see how much! Jesus came from Heaven to Earth to save us. He has been up in Glory for all these years, preparing a fabulous home for us. He won this as soon as He laid down His life here at Calvary.

Think how glorious Jesus was when He rose from the grave. Imagine His love then and how His love grows since He rose and how big this will be by the time we get there! Can we draw on this hope right now? He wants full blessings for us. Jesus knows all about what's wrong. While He is long delayed in returning, the world goes on in sin and suffering. Sinners keep sinning like the passengers on the *Titanic* who kept dancing and drinking until it hit. We can hold to our great hope by keeping faith in order to see God's generous love. I believe there's a lot going on nowadays in our lives that moves God, that affects Him, and that reflects again and again forever in all eternity, to His glory.

> *If any of you lack wisdom, let him ask of God, that giveth to all men liberally, and upbraideth not; and it shall be given him.*
>
> James 1:5

God is very determined to give opportunity to everyone, to "*all men*," by Jesus Christ. Ask God for the wisdom it takes to follow Him and win souls all your life. God won't get angry if we ask, but He gives us the secrets of His mystery, and we explain them to others. By His Holy Spirit, God definitely directs us to those who want to know. He will give us amazing grace to walk by faith to answer anybody who asks us the reason for our love. With patience, we can make it clear—even to those who oppose us.

We see it better with experience; reason alone is not good enough to explain it. No sign in the sky is going to impress people who don't already see. Our conduct will not begin to communicate to those who don't give respect. We pray for civility. Perhaps in their despair, a little of our joy will affect them for the hope of Heaven.

After they have stuffed their emptiness tight with pleasures, crammed in treasures for this life, and taken their losses, maybe the perfect love of Jesus will taste good to them. It would be new to them. Just as we came to know Jesus by His love and were saved by faith alone, so we can only hope to share our faith by faith and so we can win them by our love.

> *For the love of Christ constraineth us; because we thus judge, that if one died for all, then were all dead; and that he died for all, that they which live should not henceforth live unto themselves, but unto him which died for them, and rose again.*
>
> 2 Corinthians 5:14–15

Christian, we must decide to do all we can to find the lost. Those who claim to know Christ should live for others. The world today has yet to see our full dedication. Can't we see the extent of God's passion for people? It's spelled out in the Scriptures. It isn't our place to change the Scriptures to fit our thinking. We need to think in the way God intends, and we ought to apply ourselves to His purpose. We're supposed to believe everything in the entire Bible.

Gentle unto All

And the servant of the Lord must not strive; but be gentle unto all men, apt to teach, patient.

2 Timothy 2:24

Every Christian is a servant of the Lord. Having been saved, are we committed enough to be patient? To be a Christian, a person must repent. We all would agree on that. In repentance, we flee from our past ways, whatever they may be, to come to Jesus Christ. The other half of the problem, understanding our sin for what it is, requires us to take hold of the righteousness God calls us to. Repentance is not only turning away from sin by faith, but it is turning toward righteousness to love.

God has a plan for Christians. We try to be like Jesus. We have not understood God's will as well as He has revealed it. A big part of growing is learning and knowing our place with Jesus. This means knowing our individual aims and our shared goals.

The servant of the Lord must not strive with others. We are at odds with the world, but not with people. Many of us feel insecure in our beliefs. If you've noticed, we say some pretty weird things. Do most Christians understand their calling? Friends may not have identified their spiritual gifts, their ministry, or their talents, or they may not have yet shaped a style. Unprepared, Christians get touchy with others of different persuasions and don't spend adequate time with them. Paul said, *"but be gentle unto all men."* Are we too demanding? Christian ministry just doesn't work that way. Patience helps.

I don't know that any of us have the personality to be Christian. We need to live as examples of Jesus sufficiently enough to teach the world. If we suffer for Him, we will be rewarded, but if we deny the Lord, He will deny us. We are going to live with Him on high because we are given to Jesus. Christians need to start living devoted lives so we can persuade others, and it also helps imposters to see themselves for who they are. This encourages people to become more genuine, and it reinforces their testimony. We have to cut through the distractions and connect with more people. Start by reminding friends of the lessons they've learned, and don't ever forget what you know to be right. It's easy to slip.

> *And whosoever shall compel thee to go a mile, go with him twain.*
>
> Matthew 5:41

Christians should take an extra step for any "whosoever" Jesus sends them. It could be for anybody who asks us for our reasons. We must be willing to discuss our beliefs. We are afraid to sound foolish, because sometimes we are. We tend to be too cautious. Without a doubt, the New Testament teaches us to be bold for Jesus.

Our great God in Heaven will prepare the way for us. Why aren't we afraid of what we're missing spiritually? Certainly, there are more blessings not spoken for than those that are. If someone pushes us into something that we find difficult, it's an opening for a ministry we may not otherwise have had. Willingly walking the extra mile is the avenue into another person's sphere. We gain a place there because we're willing. It could be an open door for the Savior that Jesus has not yet had. Pray that it is their time of salvation.

Jesus does more than we realize, and people are more open than anyone knows. Do you wonder why many Christians feel left out of the work of worldwide evangelism? Assume everyone prays, even if they don't say it; you and I can help their understanding.

> *For the promise is unto you, and to your children, and to all that are afar off, even as many as the Lord our God shall call.*
>
> Acts 2:39

This promise was to Israel and then to everyone else, everywhere. We are told by God to stir the hearts of all the lost near and far and to prove Jesus Christ has this plan. Let me say it again: since we have taken the responsibility to accept Jesus into our hearts, we assume the mission of spreading the news. We're not ashamed of influencing, persuading, and convincing people. They cannot see it. Do you know Christians who are afraid to love everybody? Whatever your likes or dislikes are, God calls us to love all others, even the tough ones who have their own ideas. Could it be wrong to try and tell them? Show them your unconditional love. They may not have ever seen it before, and they may not ever see it again.

When we suffer and endure for Jesus just the same as He did for us, we offer the very love of Jesus in a direct way. We are most effective if we meet resistance patiently but firmly. The world views Christians as agitators. Believers can shape a greater place for love as they give people more credit.

Most people look for their own way to Heaven, but we are only accepted when we repent by faith in the cross, the atonement. Once you see and believe, what does it take on your part to cultivate faith in others? First of all, because Jesus loved me before I loved Him, I need to believe that God is working just as much in everyone else. The good Lord was there long before we ever began to catch on. Love is the lost talent. God wants the hearts of people to open. Simply see that this is true and Jesus will help your efforts.

> *And the times of this ignorance God winked at; but now commandeth all men everywhere to repent.*
> Acts 17:30

No matter what people may think, God is busy working in the details of everyone's life. Who is out of reach? People see that this planet is out of control, but God is watching everybody and everything. He is sovereign. You and I come along in time. What can we do with it? The thing we must do is give our hearts to Jesus; this is closely followed by a most marvelous thing—leading others to accept Jesus into their hearts.

People may compare their lives with others, trying to see who they know or who has more things or better experiences. God makes sure we each get our fair share one way or another. We have good times and bad. *"I will therefore that men pray everywhere, lifting up holy hands, without wrath and doubting"* (1 Timothy 2:8). Without anger or doubt, do we gripe about people, or do we get a good grip on God's love? We won't be judged by what's happened to us; it's not about what we've done, but it is about who we are in Jesus.

> *And I, if I be lifted up from the earth, will draw all men unto me.*
>
> John 12:32

Many take it for granted that everyone, *"all men,"* will go to Heaven. To them, that's love. They may or may not think of Jesus as the only way. Perhaps they believe there are different ways to fit different people in, as if you get your own individual way. *"Enter ye in at the strait gate: for wide is the gate, and broad is the way, that leadeth to destruction, and many there be which go in that way"* Matthew 7:13. Who disputes Jesus? How do we reconcile these two seemingly opposing ideas that *"I will draw all men unto me"* and *"broad is the way, that leadeth to destruction"*? That's a challenge. Christians must not think poorly of the many souls who are going to the grave without hope, but we should see the significance of this proclamation that Jesus is drawing everyone to Himself. Jesus has been lifted up. He is totally willing to save anyone who calls to Him. I believe this puts some weight on us.

May we who follow Jesus be willing to call everyone to come! Let God be the judge. Who are we? Our sins have been forgiven. We're not worthy in the least. How can we think that we are better than anyone else? We're not better than God.

Life will go much better for the ones who will love all others in the name of Jesus. This is the way God has planned it from the beginning. It is no use to struggle with God on this. *"It is hard for thee to kick against the pricks"* Acts 26:14. Life flows in this direction.

It's true that it depends on our perspective whether we view it as positive or negative and whether we are optimistic or pessimistic.

Christians walk by faith, believing that God will bless and guide us along. We do get it right once in a while. A clock that has stopped will tell the right time exactly twice a day.

There is a movement in this world for Jesus. Does anybody Christian today think that the fields are no longer ripe for harvest? It's not for us to wish the end on anyone. Jesus has placed before us, "*an open door, and no man can shut it*" (Revelation 3:8). Soon, the time will come when that door will close—and no man can open it.

I would be seeing life in a dim light if I thought God only calls some people. It's urgent to reach everyone we can. The time is near for His coming, yet He is patient, "*not willing that any should perish, but that all should come to repentance*" 2 Peter 3:9. Simply put, they could not receive the love we give if Jesus had not been born for everyone.

How poor indeed we would all be if Jesus had not died on that tree! He surely has taken our sin on that cross, the one that was lifted up on the hill of Golgotha, and He gave His life for all of us. Our love is what counts now. All we have to do is believe it. As far as we can see and know, it is our destiny to fulfill the everlasting love of our dear Savior.

The New Testament message of faith and love has scarcely touched the lives of many Christians in this deeper way of loving one another. The world has lived too long without this hope. God's children have the power now to accomplish all of His will on Earth. Ask for the wisdom of faith in the love of God. Let's stick together in our Lord Jesus Christ until He comes.

Love Believes All Things

All things that the Father hath are mine: therefore said I, that he shall take of mine, and shall shew it unto you.
                                                            John 16:15

AFTERTHOUGHT

Let him that stole steal no more: but rather let him labor, working with his hands the thing which is good, that he may have to give to him that needeth.

Ephesians 4:28

As stated earlier, let God be the judge. Who are we? Our sins have been forgiven. We're not in the least bit worthy. Do we think we're better than anyone else? We're not better than God. What have you allowed Him to do with you? If there's any decree of God's standard for life, it's His command to love. God loves, and He expects us to love others.

All along the path of our Christian walk, we have been taught that God wants us to love everyone, but then we hear harsh talk of the damnation and destruction of the "enemy," as if we relish the idea. Because of this split-minded attitude, Christians find drudgery in what our days consists of. Jesus is drawing everybody to Himself. Jesus told us that we must love one another in the way we should love Him, and so we must love everyone.

People today live like there's no tomorrow and like there'll be no future. A hundred years ago, people planned ahead. They were building a future. They literally paved the way for us, building roads, houses, and schools. Previous generations didn't live in the moment; they searched for opportunities beyond their time.

Some people think that if the end of the world is near and if Jesus is about to come back, then there's nothing to live for here. This might explain the apathy that is keeping people from getting involved. Many Christians are frozen out, along with much of the world, as if we should just get all we can for ourselves as soon as possible. Whatever age you may be and whatever age you are living in, there are plenty of constructive things you can do with your time. This is all the more reason to search the Scriptures and pray to God. The fire must start in our hearts, and it begins with God in His Holy Spirit. People say they don't know where to begin. These days, I am scratching my head trying to figure out where to finish. Loving God and loving others never ends.

A long time ago, we had a regular customer at the gas station where I worked who drove a beautiful car, dressed real nice, and was a good-looking man. He told us one day that he had a wife and kids, and if it wasn't for them, he wouldn't be in business, but would instead have a simple job like us and would be taking it easy. I got the picture. I think that's all he said. He was a classy guy. I don't know if he was just being a friend who could relate to us or if he was trying to motivate us. I think he was saying that it helps everything to have somebody, someone special you believe in and are loving them.

There are a lot of things I can't do for people. Most often, they can take care of their own affairs, even if they find it difficult to do. They might need courage. I try to be an encouragement. I praise God because He encourages me.

Let no corrupt communication proceed out of your mouth, but that which is good to the use of edifying, that it may minister grace unto the hearers. Ephesians 4:29

APPENDIX

Scripture Passages

(KJV)
(Emphasis added)

Love Everyone

John 3:16 For *God so loved the world*, that he gave his only begotten Son, that *whosoever believeth in him* should not perish, but *have everlasting life*.

John 12:32 And *I*, if *I* be lifted up from the earth, will draw *all men* unto *me*.

John 13:35 By this shall *all men* know that ye are my disciples, if ye have *love one to another*.

Acts 2:39 For the *promise* is unto you, and to your children, and *to all* that are afar off, even as many as the Lord our God shall call.

Acts 17:30 And the times of this ignorance God winked at; but *now commandeth all men everywhere* to repent.

Romans 1:14 I am a debtor both to the Greeks, and to the Barbarians; both to the wise, and to the unwise.

Romans 12:17 Recompense to *no man* evil for evil. Provide things honest in the sight of *all men*.

Romans 16:19 For your obedience is come abroad unto *all men*. I am glad therefore on your behalf: but yet I would have you wise unto that which is good, and simple concerning evil.

1 Corinthians 3:5 Who then is Paul, and who is Apollos, but ministers by whom ye believed, even as the Lord gave to *every man*?

1 Corinthians 3:13 *Every man's* work shall be made manifest: for the day shall declare it, because it shall be revealed by fire; and the fire shall try *every man's* work of what sort it is.

1 Corinthians 3:18 Let *no man* deceive himself. If *any man* among you seemeth to be wise in this world, let him become a fool, that he may be wise.

1 Corinthians 4:5 Therefore judge nothing before the time, until the Lord come, who both will bring to light the hidden things of darkness, and will make manifest the counsels of the hearts: and then shall *every man* have praise of God.

1 Corinthians 8:3 But if *any man* love God, the same is known of him.

1 Corinthians 9:19, 22 For though I be free from *all men*, yet have I made myself servant unto *all*, that I might gain the more…To the weak became I as weak, that I might gain the weak: I am made *all* things to *all men*, that I might by *all* means save some.

1 Corinthians 10:24 Let *no man* seek his own, but *every man* another's wealth.

1 Corinthians 10:33 Even as I please all men in all things, not seeking mine own profit, but the profit of many, that they may be saved.

1 Corinthians 5:14–16 For the love of Christ constraineth us; because we thus judge, that if one died for all, then were all dead: and that he died for *all*, that they which live should not henceforth live unto themselves, but unto him which died for them, and rose again. Wherefore henceforth know we *no man* after the flesh.

Galatians 6:10 As we have therefore opportunity, let us do good unto *all men*, especially unto them who are of the household of faith.

Ephesians 3:9 And to make *all men* see what is the fellowship of the mystery, which from the beginning of the world hath been hid in God, who created all things by Jesus Christ.

Ephesians 6:18 *Praying always* with all prayer and supplication in the Spirit, and watching thereunto with all perseverance and supplication for *all saints*.

Philippians 2:4 Look not *every man* on his own things, but *every man* also on the things of others.

Colossians 1:23 If ye continue in the faith grounded and settled, and be not moved away from the hope of the gospel, which ye have heard, and which was preached to *every creature* which is under heaven; whereof I Paul am made a minister.

Colossians 1:28 Whom we preach, warning *every man*, and teaching *every man* in all wisdom, that we may present *every man* perfect in Christ Jesus.

Colossians 4:6 Let your speech be always with grace, seasoned with salt, that ye may know how ye ought to answer *every man*.

1 Thessalonians 3:12 And the Lord make you to increase and abound in love one toward another, and toward *all men*, even as we do toward you.

1 Thessalonians 5:14–15 Now we exhort you, brethren, warn them that are unruly, comfort the feebleminded, support the weak, be patient toward *all men*. See that none render evil for evil unto *any man*; but ever follow that which is good, both among yourselves, and to *all men*.

1 Timothy 2:1 I exhort therefore, that, first of all, supplications, prayers, intercessions, and giving of thanks, be made for *all men*.

1 Timothy 2:4 [He] will have *all men* to be saved, and to come unto the knowledge of the truth.

1 Timothy 2:8 I will therefore that *men pray everywhere*, lifting up holy hands, without wrath and doubting.

1 Timothy 4:10 For therefore we both labor and suffer reproach, because we trust in the living God, who is the Savior of *all men*, specially of those that believe.

1 Timothy 4:15 Meditate upon these things; give thyself wholly to them; that thy profiting may appear *to all*.

1 Timothy 2:24 The servant of the Lord must not strive; but be gentle unto *all men*, apt to teach, patient.

Titus 2:11 For the grace of God that bringeth salvation hath appeared to *all men*.

James 1:5 If any of you lack wisdom, let him ask of God, that giveth to *all men* liberally, and upbraideth not; and it shall be given him.

2 Peter 3:9 The Lord is…not willing that *any* should perish, but that *all* should come to repentance.

1 John 2:2 He is the propitiation for our sins: and not for ours only, but also for the sins of the whole world.

1 John 2:5 But *whoso* keepeth his word, in him verily is the love of God perfected: hereby know we that we are in him.

Believes All Things

Matthew 3:2 Repent ye: for the kingdom of heaven is at hand.

Matthew 4:17 From that time Jesus began to preach, and to say, Repent: for the kingdom of heaven is at hand.

Matthew 4:19–20 He saith unto them, Follow me, and I will make you fishers of men. And they straightway left their nets, and followed him.

Matthew 6:33 But seek ye first the kingdom of God, and his righteousness; and all these things shall be added unto you.

Matthew 7:24 Therefore whosoever heareth these sayings of mine, and doeth them, I will liken him unto a wise man, which built his house upon a rock.

Matthew 9:37–38 Then saith he unto his disciples, The harvest truly is plenteous, but the laborers are few; pray ye therefore the Lord of the harvest, that he will send forth laborers into his harvest.

Matthew 11:6 Blessed is he, whosoever shall not be offended in me.

Matthew 11:28 Come unto me, all ye that labor and are heavy laden, and I will give you rest.

Matthew 13:24 Another parable put he forth unto them, saying, The kingdom of heaven is likened unto a man which sowed good seed in his field.

Matthew 16:17 Jesus answered and said unto him, Blessed art thou, Simon Barjona: for flesh and blood hath not revealed it unto thee, but my Father which is in heaven.

Matthew 16:24–25 Then said Jesus unto his disciples, If any man will come after me, let him deny himself, and take up his cross, and follow me. For whosoever will save his life shall lose it: and whosoever will lose his life for my sake shall find it.

Matthew 20:16 So the last shall be first, and the first last: for many be called, but few chosen.

Matthew 21:42–44 Jesus saith unto them, Did ye never read in the scriptures, The stone which the builders rejected, the same is become the head of the corner: this is the Lord's doing, and it is marvelous in our eyes? Therefore say I unto you, The kingdom of God shall be taken from you, and given to a nation bringing forth the fruits thereof. And whosoever shall fall on this stone shall be broken: but on whomsoever it shall fall, it will grind him to powder.

Mark 1:15–17 And saying, The time is fulfilled, and the kingdom of God is at hand: repent ye, and believe the gospel. Now as he walked by the sea of Galilee, he saw Simon and Andrew his brother casting a net into the sea: for they were fishers. And Jesus said unto them, Come ye after me, and I will make you to become fishers of men.

Luke 1:16 And many of the children of Israel shall he turn to the Lord their God.

Luke 9:23–25 And he said to them all, If any man will come after me, let him deny himself, and take up his cross daily, and follow me. For whosoever will save his life shall lose it: but whosoever will lose his life for my sake, the same shall save it. For what is a man advantaged, if he gain the whole world, and lose himself, or be cast away?

Luke 11:9 I say unto you, Ask, and it shall be given you; seek, and ye shall find; knock, and it shall be opened unto you.

Luke 12:6 Are not five sparrows sold for two farthings, and not one of them is forgotten before God?

Luke 13:3 I tell you, Nay: but, except ye repent, ye shall all likewise perish.

Luke 14:27 And whosoever doth not bear his cross, and come after me, cannot be my disciple.

John 1:12 But as many as received him, to them gave he power to become the sons of God, even to them that believe on his name.

John 3:15–17 That whosoever believeth in him should not perish, but have eternal life. For God so loved the world, that he gave his only begotten Son, that whosoever believeth in him should not perish, but have everlasting life. For God sent not his Son into the world to condemn the world; but that the world through him might be saved.

John 4:10 Jesus answered and said unto her, If thou knewest the gift of God, and who it is that saith to thee, Give me to drink; thou wouldest have asked of him, and he would have given thee living water.

John 5:24 Verily, verily, I say unto you, He that heareth my word, and believeth on him that sent me, hath everlasting life, and shall not come into condemnation; but is passed from death unto life.

John 6:47 Verily, verily, I say unto you, He that believeth on me hath everlasting life.

John 7:38 He that believeth on me, as the scripture hath said, out of his belly shall flow rivers of living water.

John 11:25–26 Jesus said unto her, I am the resurrection, and the life: he that believeth in me, though he were dead, yet shall he live: and whosoever liveth and believeth in me shall never die. Believest thou this?

John 12:26 If any man serve me, let him follow me; and where I am, there shall also my servant be: if any man serve me, him will my Father honor.

John 15:7 If ye abide in me, and my words abide in you, ye shall ask what ye will, and it shall be done unto you.

John 20:29 Jesus saith unto him, Thomas, because thou hast seen me, thou hast believed: blessed are they that have not seen, and yet have believed.

Acts 2:32 This Jesus hath God raised up, whereof we all are witnesses.

Acts 2:38 Then Peter said unto them, Repent, and be baptized every one of you in the name of Jesus Christ for the remission of sins, and ye shall receive the gift of the Holy Ghost.

Acts 3:19 Repent ye therefore, and be converted, that your sins may be blotted out, when the times of refreshing shall come from the presence of the Lord.

Acts 4:12 Neither is there salvation in any other: for there is none other name under heaven given among men, whereby we must be saved.

Acts 5:32 And we are his witnesses of these things; and so is also the Holy Ghost, whom God hath given to them that obey him.

Acts 8:17 Then laid they their hands on them, and they received the Holy Ghost.

Acts 16:30–31 Sirs, what must I do to be saved? And they said, Believe on the Lord Jesus Christ, and thou shalt be saved, and thy house.

Acts 26:20 But shewed first unto them of Damascus, and at Jerusalem, and throughout all the coasts of Judaea, and then to the Gentiles, that they should repent and turn to God, and do works meet for repentance.

Romans 3:28 Therefore we conclude that a man is justified by faith without the deeds of the law.

Romans 5:1 Therefore being justified by faith, we have peace with God through our Lord Jesus Christ.

Romans 5:8 But God commendeth his love toward us, in that, while we were yet sinners, Christ died for us.

Romans 6:23 For the wages of sin is death; but the gift of God is eternal life through Jesus Christ our Lord.

Romans 9:33 As it is written, Behold, I lay in Zion a stumbling stone and rock of offence: and whosoever believeth on him shall not be ashamed.

Romans 10:8–13 But what saith it? The word is nigh thee, even in thy mouth, and in thy heart: that is, the word of faith, which we preach; that if thou shalt confess with thy mouth the Lord Jesus, and shalt believe in thine heart that God hath raised him from the dead, thou shalt be saved. For with the heart man believeth unto righteousness; and with the mouth confession is made unto salvation. For the scripture saith, Whosoever believeth on him shall not be ashamed. For there is no difference between the Jew and the Greek: for the same Lord over all is rich unto all that call upon him. For whosoever shall call upon the name of the Lord shall be saved.

Romans 10:17 So then faith cometh by hearing, and hearing by the word of God.

Romans 11:6 And if by grace, then is it no more of works: otherwise grace is no more grace. But if it be of works, then it is no more grace: otherwise work is no more work.

Romans 12:2 And be not conformed to this world: but be ye transformed by the renewing of your mind, that ye may prove what is that good, and acceptable, and perfect, will of God.

Romans 12:3 For I say, through the grace given unto me, to every man that is among you, not to think of himself more highly than he ought to think; but to think soberly, according as God hath dealt to every man the measure of faith.

Romans 14:18 For he that in these things serveth Christ is acceptable to God, and approved of men.

Romans 15:13 Now the God of hope fill you with all joy and peace in believing, that ye may abound in hope, through the power of the Holy Ghost.

1 Corinthians 1:18 For the preaching of the cross is to them that perish foolishness; but unto us which are saved it is the power of God.

1 Corinthians 8:3 But if any man love God, the same is known of him.

1 Corinthians 13:7 Beareth all things, believeth all things, hopeth all things, endureth all things.

1 Corinthians 15:1 Moreover, brethren, I declare unto you the gospel which I preached unto you, which also ye have received, and wherein ye stand.

2 Corinthians 1:20 For all the promises of God in him are yea, and in him Amen, unto the glory of God by us.

2 Corinthians 1:24 Not for that we have dominion over your faith, but are helpers of your joy: for by faith ye stand.

2 Corinthians 2:16–17 To the one we are the savor of death unto death; and to the other the savor of life unto life. And who is sufficient for these things? For we are not as many, which corrupt the word of God: but as of sincerity, but as of God, in the sight of God speak we in Christ.

2 Corinthians 9:8 God is able to make all grace abound toward you; that ye, always having all sufficiency in all things, may abound to every good work.

Galatians 3:22 But the scripture hath concluded all under sin, that the promise by faith of Jesus Christ might be given to them that believe.

Ephesians 1:3 Blessed be the God and Father of our Lord Jesus Christ, who hath blessed us with all spiritual blessings in heavenly places in Christ.

Ephesians 1:13 In whom ye also trusted, after that ye heard the word of truth, the gospel of your salvation: in whom also after that ye believed, ye were sealed with that holy Spirit of promise.

Ephesians 2:4–7 But God, who is rich in mercy, for his great love wherewith he loved us, even when we were dead in sins, hath quickened us together with Christ, (by grace ye are saved) and hath raised us up together, and made us sit together in heavenly places in Christ Jesus: that in ages to come he might shew the exceeding riches of his grace in his kindness toward us through Christ Jesus.

Ephesians 3:20 Now unto him that is able to do exceeding abundantly above all that we ask or think, according to the power that worketh in us.

Ephesians 6:18–20 Praying always with all prayer and supplication in the Spirit, and watching thereunto with all perseverance and supplication for all saints; and for me, that utterance may be given unto me, that I may open my mouth boldly, to make known the mystery of the gospel, for which I am an ambassador in bonds: that therein I may speak boldly, as I ought to speak.

Philippians 1:6 Being confident of this very thing, that he which hath begun a good work in you will perform it until the day of Jesus Christ.

Philippians 2:15–16 That ye may be blameless and harmless, the sons of God, without rebuke, in the midst of a crooked and perverse nation, among whom ye shine as lights in the world; holding forth the word of life; that I may rejoice in the day of Christ, that I have not run in vain, neither labored in vain.

Hebrews 11:6 But without faith it is impossible to please him: for he that cometh to God must believe that he is, and that he is a rewarder of them that diligently seek him.

1 John 1:9 If we confess our sins, he is faithful and just to forgive us our sins, and to cleanse us from all unrighteousness.

1 JOHN Chapters 3 and 4

From 1 JOHN 3
v.16 - This is how we know love.
v.17 - Jesus Christ laid down his life for us. And we ought to lay down our lives for our brothers and sisters.
v.17 - If anyone has material possessions and sees a brother or sister in need but has no pity on them, how can the love of God be in that person?

LOVE BELIEVES ALL THINGS

v.18 - Dear children, let us not love with words or speech but actions in truth.
v.19 - This is how we know that we belong to the truth and how we set our hearts at rest in his presence.
v.20 - If our hearts condemn us, we know that God is greater than our hearts, and he knows everything.
v.21 - Dear friends, if our hearts do not condemn us, we have confidence before God .
v.22 - ..and receive from him anything we ask, because we keep his commands and do what pleases him.
v.23 - And this is his command: to believe in the name of his Son, Jesus Christ, and to love one another as he commanded us.
v.24 - The one who keeps God's commands to love lives in him, and he in them. This is how we know that he lives in us: We know it by the Spirit he gave us.

-- 1 John 3: 16 - Love in a nutshell - Then a note about the antichrist - suddenly, 1 John 4:1-5, and then back to the love of Jesus in the rest of Chapter 4.

From 1 JOHN 4
v.7 - Dear friends, let us love one another, for love comes from God. Everyone who loves has been born of God and knows God.
v.8 - Whoever does not love does not know God, because God is love.
v.9 - This is how God showed his love among us: He sent his one and only Son into the world that we might live through him.
v.10 - This is love: not that we loved God, but that he loved us and sent his Son as an atoning sacrifice for our sins.
v.11 - Dear friends, since God so loved us, we also ought to love one another.
v.12 - No one has ever seen God; but if we love one another, God lives in us and his love is made complete in us.
v.13 - This is how we know that we live in him and he in us: He has given us of his Spirit.
v.14 - And we have seen and testify that the Father has sent his Son to be the Savior of the world.

v.15 - If anyone acknowledges that Jesus is the Son of God, God lives in them and they in God.

v.16 - And so we know and rely on the love God has for us. God is love. Whoever lives in love lives in God, and God in them.

v.17 - This is how love is made complete among us so that we will have confidence on the day of judgment: In this world we are like Jesus.

v.18 - There is no fear in love. But perfect love drives out fear, because fear has to do with punishment. The one who fears is not made perfect in love.

v.19 - We love because he first loved us.

v.20 - Whoever claims to love God yet hates a brother or sister is a liar. For whoever does not love their brother and sister, whom they have seen, cannot love God, whom they have not seen.

v.21 - And he has given us this command: Anyone who loves God must also love their brother and sister.

Read in full chapter, did the Apostle John change subjects back and forth here, we can see this as one thought. Read 1 John as one identifying the anti-christ - VS - THE One True CHRIST. Ask yourself the feeling, PLEASE, to expect the second coming, my second book with this whole revelation, INCLUDING ALL OF 1 John Chapters 3 and 4 to the end to identify who the real anti-christ will be, those who simply will not have faith nor love.

What we mean to each other is every bit as important as all in Christianity. We are neighbors, sisters and brothers. Each part belongs to one another. If we believe in God, believe in all. In conclusion, we believe the inclusion of all those who belong. We are one in the Spirit, inseparable, and victorious.

LOVE BELIEVES ALL THINGS

Who wants to love if they are supposed to give? No / This is why my two books are neglected; So then, "Love Believes All Things" requires our devotion to sacrifice this is our Cross carry. We fall short if we won't try faith to see and believe it all. Generousity is part and paecel inbedded in the big ministry of the Gospel of Jesus Christ,-

This publishing proccess is taking a couple yeaars. So here comes another important thought. Kyle

www.ingramcontent.com/pod-product-compliance
Lightning Source LLC
Chambersburg PA
CBHW020452030426
42337CB00011B/88